The Pacific World
Volume 9

American Empire
in the Pacific

THE PACIFIC WORLD
Lands, Peoples and History of the Pacific, 1500–1900

General Editors: Dennis O. Flynn and Arturo Giráldez

Note: These series details are necessarily provisional; titles may change prior to publication.

The Pacific World

Lands, Peoples and History of the Pacific, 1500–1900

Volume 9

American Empire
in the Pacific

From Trade to Strategic Balance, 1700–1922

edited by
Arthur Power Dudden

ASHGATE
VARIORUM

Published in **The Pacific World Series** by

Ashgate Publishing Limited
Gower House
Croft Road
Aldershot
Hants GU11 3HR
England

Ashgate Publishing Company
Suite 420
101 Cherry Street
Burlington, VT 05401–4405
USA

ISBN 0–7546–3049–8

Ashgate website: http://www.ashgate.com

British Library CIP data
American empire in the Pacific : from trade to strategic
    balance, 1700–1922. – (The Pacific world : lands, peoples,
    and history of the Pacific, 1500–1900)
    1. Imperialism 2. United States – Foreign relations – Pacific
    Area 3. United States – Foreign relations – 18th century
    4. United States – Foreign relations – 19th century
    5. Pacific Area – Foreign relations – United States
    6. Pacific Area – Foreign relations – 18th century 7. Pacific
    Area – Foreign relations – 19th century
    I. Dudden, Arthur Power, 1921–
    327.7'3'05

US Library of Congress Cataloging-in-Publication Data
American empire in the Pacific : from trade to strategic balance, 1700–1922 / edited by
    Arthur Power Dudden
        p. cm. – (The Pacific world)
    Includes bibliographical references.
    ISBN 0-7546-3049-8 (alk. paper)
        1. Pacific Area – Foreign relations – United States. 2. United States – Foreign
    relations – Pacific Area. 3. Imperialism. 4. Pacific Area – History. 5. United
    States – History – Philosophy. I. Dudden, Arthur Power, 1921– II. Series.

DU30.A44 2003
330.48'27305–dc21

2003052111

This book is printed on acid free paper.

Printed in Great Britain by The Cromwell Press, Trowbridge, Wiltshire.

Contents

Acknowledgements

The chapters in this volume are taken from the sources listed below, for which the editor and publishers wish to thank their authors, original publishers or other copyright holders for permission to use their materials as follows:

Chapter 1: Felix Gilbert, 'The English Background of American Isolationism in the Eighteenth Century', *William and Mary Quarterly*, 1 (Williamsburg, VA, 1944), pp. 138–160.

Chapter 2: Julia B. Curtis, 'Chinese Export Porcelain in Eighteenth-Century Tidewater Virginia', in John Yolton and Leslie Ellen Brown (eds), *Studies in Eighteenth Century Culture*, 17 (East Lansing, MI, 1987), pp. 119–144. Copyright © 1987 ASECS.

Plate 9: Bowl, Courtesy of Association for the Preservation of Virginia Antiquities.

Plate 25: Dinner Service from 'Geldermalen' (Williamsburg, 1986) Colonial Williamsburg Foundation.

Chapter 3: Gunther Barth, 'Strategies for Finding the Northwest Passage: The Roles of Alexander Mackenzie and Meriwether Lewis', in Edward C. Carter, II (ed.), *Surveying the Record: North American Scientific Exploration to 1930* (Philadelphia, PA, 1999), pp. 253–266. Copyright © 1999 American Philosophical Society.

Chapter 4: Jacques M. Downs, 'The Legacy of Old Canton', in *The Golden Ghetto: The American Commercial Community at Canton and the Shaping of American China Policy, 1784–1844* (Cranbury, NJ, 1997), pp. 320–341 & 453–457. Copyright © 1997 Associated University Press, Inc.

Figures: Russell & Company, Shanghai, c. 1875. Watercolor on paper by unidentified artist. Note the colonnaded verandas, the extensive gardens, and the general 'compradoric' architectural style. Courtesy of the Peabody & Essex Museum, Photo by Mark Sexton.

The American Consul's Four-in-Hand, from stereoscope photography. Notice the unusual construction of the sedan chair. The bearers carry in Indian file, not abreast. While this arrangement undoubtedly facilitated getting through narrow streets and crowds, it must have been difficult to turn sharp corners. Courtesy of the Peabody & Essex Museum.

Chapter 14: Noriko Kawamura, 'Wilsonian Idealism and Japanese Claims at the Paris Peace Conference', *Pacific Historical Review*, 66 (Berkeley, CA, 1997), pp. 503–526. Copyright © 1997 Pacific Coast Branch, American Historical Association.

Chapter 15: John W. Long, 'American Intervention in Russia: The North Russian Expedition, 1918–1919', *Diplomatic History*, 6 (Oxford, 1982), pp. 45–67. Copyright © 1982 Society for Historians of American Foreign Relations.

Chapter 16: Malcolm H. Murfett, 'Look Back in Anger: The Western Powers and the Washington Conference of 1921–1922', in B.J.C. McKercher (ed.), *Arms Limitation and Disarmament: Restraints on War, 1899-1939* (Westport, CT, 1992), pp. 83–103. Copyright © 1992 Praeger.

General Editors' Preface

The Pacific Ocean comprises over one-third of the surface area of the earth, so perhaps it is not surprising that observers have traditionally conceptualized this vast body of water as a colossal barrier to interchange until recent times. Current discussions about the 'Pacific Rim', the 'Pacific Century', and 'Asian economic miracles' (including suddenly rising 'Asian tigers/dragons') reflect this background view that meaningful and lasting trans-oceanic Pacific activity is recent and unprecedented. Indeed, the late twentieth century did witness huge surges in activity across and within the Pacific. This series, however, *The Pacific World: Lands, Peoples, and History of the Pacific, 1500–1900*, aims to call attention to important, but often ignored, trans- and intra-Pacific interactions that have been developing since the sixteenth century. Few people have fully realized the significance of the Pacific World legacy between the sixteenth and early twentieth centuries. Each volume in this series offers a selection of previously published articles, with individual editors providing fresh introductory essays that summarize and evaluate individual literatures on which each possesses expertise. Particular volumes may need to look back before the fifteenth century or forward into the twentieth, but the focus of the series is this period from 1500 to 1900.

The Pacific World is modeled after Variorum's successful series, *An Expanding World: The European Impact on World History, 1450–1800* (A.J.R. Russell-Wood, General Editor). Both series highlight broad themes and large-scale geographic interconnections that transcend traditional nation-state and regional conceptions of history. *The Pacific World* volumes focus on subjects that cannot be properly confined to any isolated nation or to a particular continent. Both series emphasize large-scale historical connections over several centuries.

The Atlantic Ocean, like the Pacific Ocean, clearly served as an effective barrier to human interaction for thousands of years, helping to explain many of the unique social and environmental characteristics of the Americas *vis-à-vis* the rest of the world. The late-fifteenth-century arrival of Europeans in the 'New World' without doubt fundamentally altered the trajectory of world history. *An Expanding World*, as well as other literatures that incorporate Alfred Crosby's seminal work on the 'Colombian Exchange', amply document reverberations emanating from the post-1492 diffusions of humans, flora, and fauna between the Americas and the rest of the world. Overviews of Atlantic history today are constructed against a backdrop of multi-century interconnections among continents, whether the discussion turns to precious metals, plantations, slavery, competing empires, or any number of other topics.

It seems odd to us that the Pacific Ocean is rarely portrayed as a coherent unit of analysis, as are the Atlantic Ocean, the Indian Ocean, Braudel's Mediterranean Sea, or other important commercial waterways. Treatment of the Pacific Ocean as exceptional does indeed make sense up to the seventh decade of the sixteenth century, since significant bi-directional trade proved impossible until the 1560s. The first European to sail westward across the Pacific was Magellan in 1521, indeed, but countervailing trade winds and ocean currents thwarted repeated attempts to return eastward to the Americas until Andres Urdaneta discovered the correct northern route in 1565. Soon thereafter, in 1571, Spain founded the city of Manila which finally opened the world's greatest ocean to voluminous trans-oceanic traffic.

The community of world history scholars largely ignores trans-Pacific trade prior to the twentieth century. Where acknowledgement is made, it tends to focus upon the thousands of tons of American silver destined for China during these centuries, as well as the Chinese products returning via Acapulco. But what may seem to some to be unimportant and tenuous direct links between Asia and the Americas, turn out on closer inspection to involve global trends of tremendous significance. We refer here to what John R. McNeill calls the 'Magellan Exchange'. It seems that the silver-laden Acapulco-Manila-China galleons also served as an important vector for introduction of American foodstuffs such as the sweet potato, peanut, and maize. Cultivation of these new products wrought tremendous demographic transformations on the Asian mainland and archipelagos in the western Pacific. Asian population growth, in turn, reverberated back through world trade networks, including Pacific ones. It turns out that trade history is intimately intertwined with epidemiological, ecological, demographic, and cultural histories. None can be properly understood without consideration of the others.

The Pacific World series is also a development of the 'Pacific Centuries' conferences we have helped organize since 1994. An unplanned but common theme emerging from Pacific Centuries conference volumes is that demand-side forces within China played a key role, whether one considers American silver, California's New Almaden mercury mines, Pacific island environmental history, forests in the American Pacific Northwest and Siberia, or any number of other topics.[1]

In 1999 the San Francisco Maritime Museum presented a Gold-Rush-era exhibit featuring a Yankee Clipper ship named the *Frolic*. Responding to a lively demand for products in California, the *Frolic* transported Chinese goods across the Pacific to San Francisco. The problem was that San Francisco contained no buildings in which to sell goods in great demand. The solution was to ship prefabricated two-room buildings (disassembled and laid flat in the hold) from Canton, assemble them in San Francisco, sell the merchandise, then sell the buildings (disassembled again) for transportation by cart elsewhere in California. The museum exhibit showed several pictures of such Chinese buildings standing a century later. It is worth noting that the nearby Sierra

---

[1] S.M. Miller, A.J.H. Latham, and D.O. Flynn (eds), *Studies in the Economic History of the Pacific Rim*, London: Routledge, 1998; D.O. Flynn, L. Frost, and A.J.H. Latham (eds), *Pacific Centuries: Pacific and Pacific Rim History Since the Sixteenth Century*, London: Routledge, 1999; Dennis O. Flynn, Arturo Giráldez, and James Sobredo (eds), *Studies in Pacific History: Economics, Politics and Migration*, Aldershot: Ashgate, 2002.

Nevada mountains contain abundant forests. Why ship buildings from Canton when virtually endless supplies of lumber exist near San Francisco? The answer is that it was cheaper to transport pre-fabricated structures from Canton than to construct them with Northern Californian timber. In other words, it was cheaper to transport a house 7,000 miles via sea than to move its main material 130 miles by land and river. It is also worth noting that Chinese represented the largest ethnic group of miners during the California Gold Rush. The point is that by the mid-nineteenth century the Pacific Ocean had long ceased to be a barrier; rather, it was a freeway.

Landmasses contain the most formidable barriers to trade and social intercourse, mountains above all. Water transportation has long been much cheaper. Indeed, this is the reason that even today most people live on or near navigable water. A half-century ago Fernand Braudel taught us that land-based histories are fraught with conceptual danger. The lesson has yet to be fully absorbed. Water connects cheaply and yet water geography remains an under-appreciated facet of history. Since Pacific water connects with that of other oceans and seas, as well as with landbased transportation systems, we consider the subject matter of this series to be a subset of world history. Nonetheless, a premise of *The Pacific World* series is that the Pacific represents as coherent a unit of analysis as the Atlantic Ocean, the Indian Ocean, and many seas throughout the world.

The conception of the Pacific in this series is deliberately broad and inclusive. Our Pacific World encompasses all lands and archipelagos in and around the Pacific Ocean, from the Arctic to Antarctica, and from the Americas to the Indian Ocean. Everywhere touched by Pacific waters is included, since areas within the Pacific region have become progressively integrated over the centuries. It is obvious that this brief series cannot address all aspects of Pacific history. Its more modest aim is instead to provide outlines of fundamental trends involved in the creation and development of the Pacific World. We know that popular characterizations are false when they portray the Pacific World suddenly shooting to prominence in the mid-twentieth century, out of nowhere. The goal of this series is to encourage more thoughtful consideration of the multi-century evolution of connections within and across the world's greatest ocean. The 'Pacific Century' and other similar concepts lack depth without an integrated, multi-century historical context for perspective. True global thinking demands complete global coverage, including oceanic components. Scholars need to redress past neglect of the Pacific Ocean, important in its own right and an increasingly crucial connector of landmasses.

Dennis O. Flynn and Arturo Giráldez
Pacific World History Institute &
University of the Pacific

1 October 2000

Thus this mysterious, divine Pacific zones
the world's whole bulk about;
makes all coasts one bay to it;
seems the tide-beating heart of earth.
HERMAN MELVILLE, Moby Dick (1851)

Introduction

Arthur Power Dudden

The American Empire in the Pacific grew up from England's colonies settled during the seventeenth and early eighteenth centuries along North America's Atlantic seaboard from Massachusetts Bay, Maine, and New Hampshire to Georgia, which had become linked over time into an imperial British continuum. Eventually, these 13 British colonies declared their independence to form the United States of America.

In 1689 hostilities between England and France erupted as a result of rivalries over the balance of power in Europe, and tensions between their empires in America and Asia. Their wars inevitably involved the colonial populations of both nations. In King William's War, as colonists called the first of these conflicts, Yankee seamen hailing from New England sailed aboard English privateers to hunt down French ships and cargoes, buccaneering sometimes beyond their license into the Pacific Ocean via Panama and the Isthmus of Darien to prey upon Spanish vessels. Oriental gold, pearls, gemstones, and wonderfully woven fabrics began to turn up in British America, though such treasures mostly arrived through Mediterranean channels.

Spain, following the epochal discoveries by Columbus and Balboa, had laid claim to the rest of South America – except for Brazil which was grabbed by Portugal – starting with Peru of the golden Incas. Spanish *conquistadores* seized Aztec Mexico and also took over the principal islands of the West Indies plus the Gulf of Mexico's littoral westward from the Floridas. Spanish control next surged far beyond Texas to California. Missionary friars won over the Native American Indians to Madrid's Roman Catholic authority and the Spanish tongue. In 1521 across the Pacific Ocean, Magellan claimed the Philippines archipelago for Spain. Thereafter, for two centuries, the fabled Manila–Acapulco galleons conveyed cargoes of Mexican silver westward to pay for exotic imports from China. From the Philippines on eastward passages, they carried the coveted Chinese wares to Acapulco for overland transit to Vera Cruz and transshipments to European or colonial markets.

In 1699 John Higginson of Salem, Massachusetts, wrote about East Asia's prospects to his brother Nathaniel, an East India Company official in Madras:

> What you propose of living in Boston and managing a wholesale trade of East India goods, I approve, as best for you . . . All sorts of calicoes, aligers, remwalls, muslins, silks for clothing and linings, all sorts of drugs prosper for the apothecaries, and all sorts of spice, are vendible with us . . .
>
> Some of the China ware, toys and lacquer ware will sell well, but no great quantity . . . For musk, bezoar, pearl, and diamond. I believe some of them may sell well, but I understand not their value.[1]

---

[1] 'Higginson Letters', in *Massachusetts Historical Society Collections*, 3rd Series, VII (Boston, 1838), p. 209.

Tea, surprisingly, found no place on Higginson's list. This commodity, carried by the East India Company's merchantmen, began to reach England's colonists around 1700, with Chinese porcelains showing up soon afterward. By the mid-eighteenth century teas and other goods from the Far East were pouring into Britain's 13 colonies. But Boston's famous Tea Party of 1773 protesting against the East India Company's newly strengthened monopoly led the Crown and parliament to retaliate the following year with punitive legislation against Massachusetts, sparking resistance and protests throughout the colonies.

Bloody clashes at Lexington and Concord in 1775 opened the lengthy conflict that climaxed with American independence in 1783. The war escalated from a localized outbreak of revolutionary violence within the British Empire to the reactivation of the centuries-old dynastic and territorial struggle among Europe's powers. Holland, France, and Spain joined the fray, viewing London's colonial problem as a providential opportunity to avenge themselves. Any prospect of Americans directly trading with Asians now became stymied by the spread of maritime warfare, until the Treaty of Peace in 1783 ended the fighting and recognized their republic's independence. American merchants and underwriters immediately prepared to participate in the rich traffic controlled by the East India Company.

Sailing thousands of leagues, ships from New York, Philadelphia, and Boston were soon flaunting the 'Stars and Stripes' at Canton, the only port in China open to foreigners. Yankee sailors, Quaker supercargoes, and missionaries began to mingle with Europeans motivated, like themselves, to promote trade with China and Christian redemption. Within a few decades, adventurers of all descriptions were projecting across the Pacific Ocean their homegrown version of a seemingly limitless American destiny. Russian Alaska, the Kingdom of Hawaii, Japan, Korea, Samoa, and Spain's Philippine Islands would grow in importance in popular reflections about the Pacific Ocean. U.S. gunboats forcibly opened Japan in 1854, while China's apparent opportunities for trade and Christian conversion led to the purchase of Alaska (1867) followed by annexations (1898) of the Hawaiian and Philippine Islands. To help its citizens realize their individual quests for trade and conversion, over the coming decades the United States government launched a steam-powered, screw-propelled, and armor-plated modern navy, proclaimed the Open Door policy toward China, and proceeded to build the Panama Canal. At the same time, racial hatreds swelled against Asia's yellow peoples and Japan's own imperial dreams. The American Pacific was developing typically into an American Empire.

An American empire in the Pacific – however unlikely it might once have seemed – had initially rested on Britain's colonists gaining their independence, and next on their attaining the goals set out by their leaders for self-governance and national development. By 1850 the United States of America was managing itself well enough, even if boisterously, as a federal republic, while expanding its territory at a great rate. Congress was admitting new states into the Union one after another, usually in pairs consisting of a slave state and a free state to protect the institution of slavery against the rising clamor of its opponents. Beyond its original frontiers, America's republic sprawled from the Atlantic Ocean and Caribbean Sea to the Gulf of Mexico, and the Pacific Ocean, to overcome rival claims of France, Spain, Mexico, and Great Britain. With California's entry, the original 13 states grew to 31. As Henry Adams famously observed, 'American society might be both sober and sad, but except for Negro slavery it was sound and healthy in every part'. It would take no less than the Civil War (1861–65) to end the institution of slavery.[2] But the war's terrible violence would overshadow the dream of manifest destiny and temporarily stall the progress of imperial growth.

Two incentives, Felix Gilbert believed, had inspired the planting and growth of England's colonies in North America: the promise of financial rewards and the necessity of constructing a more perfect social order.[3] The economic motive required close ties with Europe for export and trade; the utopian motive favored separation from Old World affairs. Not all the northern colonies were religious foundations, nor were all southern colonies commercial enterprises. Nowhere could one find a universal American viewpoint about England or Europe; each colony felt itself to be autonomous and independent, even uniquely so. Yet, from the outset, the government in London regarded its American plantations as an entirety, and dealt with them using a common set of ideas and as much of an overall policy as possible.

This was particularly the case following the Stuart Restoration of 1660, when, under a subcommittee of the Privy Council, the Lords of Trade and Plantations (redesigned as the Board of Trade after 1696) continued to implement royal authority. In 1721 the Board of Trade described the vast region from Nova Scotia to South Carolina as the 'Empire in America'. Whatever problems arose originated largely from immigrants slipping into the backcountry, causing charter-based conflicts between colonies with sea-to-sea grants, such as Virginia, and those with predetermined limits, such as Rhode Island and Pennsylvania. In fact, fractious encounters with the common enemy, France, in the Great Lakes and Ohio Valley led, in 1754, to a remarkable colonial congress at Albany and a proposed Plan of Union within the British Empire. However, the French menace ended in 1764 with France's catastrophic defeats and the loss of her once great empire in Canada and India. No substantial progress in creating a unified colonial attitude toward foreign affairs occurred until after 1776.

To become a power only to behave like the other powers held little appeal in neither the rebellious colonies nor in the youthfully independent United States of America. Striving to create a new social order themselves, 'a more perfect Union' within the Constitution of 1787, Americans hoped to sponsor a new purpose for international relations, to reform the fundamental reasons for the tenets of a nation's

---

[2] *The United States in 1800* (Ithaca, NY: Cornell University Press, 1955), p. 114. This book consists of the first six chapters of Volume 2 of Henry Adams' *History of the United States during the First Administration of Thomas Jefferson* (New York: Charles Scribner's Sons, 1889).

[3] Gilbert, chapter 1 below.

foreign policy instead of forever maintaining them as essential and proper. Nearing the close of his two four-year terms as the country's first president under the new Constitution, George Washington delivered his 'Farewell Address', a political testament to guide the American people into the future. Washington's counsels to the citizenry comprise the first comprehensive and authoritative statement of American foreign policy.

The most important tasks of Washington's first four years had been given to establishing the new federal administration, choosing a location for the capital of the United States, and determining the course to follow in financial and economic policies. In contrast, throughout his second term foreign policy issues, which prior to 1792 had surfaced only intermittently, came to the forefront and dominated political life. In February 1793 war came to America's doorstep when Great Britain, Holland, and Spain joined the German powers in their reaction against the French Revolution. This had serious implications for the United States in that any attacks against France's West Indies might possibly provoke Paris into demanding assistance in accordance with the Franco-American Alliance of 1778. On the other hand, American intervention could pose great dangers to the young republic, if only because British Canada and Spain's colonies in North America surrounded its frontiers, while George III's navy ruled the Atlantic waves.

On 22 April 1793, President Washington issued a Proclamation of Neutrality. However, the French Republic's minister, Edmond Genêt, was already at hand, directly appealing over the government's head to pro-French Americans to draw the United States into the conflict, and further violating America's neutrality by outfitting privateers in local seaports. Meanwhile, Britain's scornful disregard for the rights of neutrals, as demonstrated by its navy's rough behavior on the high seas, reawakened old enmities. Amid fresh fears that the British government was preparing to start a war, Washington sent John Jay as his special envoy to London in a desperate effort to reduce the tensions aggravating Anglo-American relations. However, apart from agreeing to vacate its frontier outposts, Britain conceded almost nothing, even refusing to stop interfering with neutral shipping in wartime.

In Congress, in the spring of 1796, the Senate ratified Jay's Treaty but only barely, while the House of Representatives balked at providing funds to implement the treaty's terms before it grudgingly acceded. Washington saw the House's attempt to influence foreign policy as a partisan-inspired violation of the Constitution, inasmuch as treaty-making power had been entrusted to the president and the Senate and incorporated no role for the House. Although the debates revealed the power of partisan divisions over foreign policy, the outcome represented a national approval of the government's conduct of it. As Gilbert has asserted elsewhere, 'Washington could rightly consider that if his first administration had established the foundations for the internal organization of the republic his second administration had laid out the course for the management of foreign affairs. Washington felt himself free at last to cast his final address.'[4]

---

[4] Felix Gilbert, *To the Farewell Address: Ideas of Early American Foreign Policy* (Princeton, NJ: Princeton University Press, 1961), Chapter 5, pp. 115–136.

Washington saw himself as standing above parties. His message to his countrymen was a body of counsels from 'an old and affectionate friend', daring to hope that now and then they might 'recur to moderate the fury of party spirit, to warn against the mischiefs of foreign intrigue, to guard against the impostures of pretended patriotism'. 'The great rule of conduct for us, in regard to foreign nations', he proclaimed, 'is in extending our commercial relations to have with them as little political connection as possible. So far as we have already formed engagements let them be fulfilled, with perfect good faith. Here let us stop.'[5] Washington's 'great rule' guided American foreign policy for over a century, wielding its powerful political influence over generations to come. However, two precarious decades would follow its delivery, as Washington himself had feared.

Wars sparked by the French Revolution and Napoleon's conquests raged from 1793 to 1815. Great Britain's blockades obstructed American trade. French resentment at Jay's Treaty provoked attacks on American shipping by French privateers, which touched off a retaliatory 'undeclared' naval war between the United States and France. In 1805 their disastrous defeat at Trafalgar exposed the profound defects of the French and Spanish naval commands, and turned Napoleon thereafter toward campaigning on dry land. Nonetheless, American merchant ships and crews regularly became ensnarled into French and British warring. At the same time, land-hungry frontiersmen were demanding war against England in order to facilitate the conquest of Canada. War was declared on England (on 18 June 1812) for this reason and others, including press-ganging seamen, paper blockades, and repeated violations of the three-mile limit. In naval battles, both at sea and on inland lakes, the Americans were, for some time, surprisingly successful. The Treaty of Ghent – a document strangely silent on those maritime questions that had been the chief cause of the controversy – brought the war to a close in 1814. Napoleon's exile to St Helena after his defeat at Waterloo put George Washington's 20-year cautionary period to rest. Americans were freed at last to pursue their destiny by adventuring across North America, along the route charted by Lewis and Clark (1804–1806), as Gunther Barth relates it for us,[6] to the Pacific Ocean and eventually beyond, even to Asia's mainland.

That destiny centered itself initially on reviving the once rich East India Company traffic in teas and other luxury goods imported from China, as our intimately related essays by Julia B. Curtis and Jacques M. Downs illustrate.[7] Curtis uses archeological evidence from the James River basin of south-eastern Virginia – shards of broken Chinese export porcelain wares in fact – to portray the growing affluence and gentility of eighteenth-century colonial society before the War of American Independence. Downs' book, *The Golden Ghetto*, from which our selection originates, lays out the

---

[5] 'Washington's Final Manuscript of the Farewell Address, Dated September 19, 1796', *Ibid.*, p. 145.

[6] Barth, see chapter 3 below.

[7] Curtis, chapter 2 below, and Downs, chapter 4 below.

first 60 years of American trading with China and the shaping of the nation's China policy, 1784–1844.

Downs' account of the lives of American tea merchants in Canton shows how they gradually became dependent on carrying opium illegally into China to pay for imports of teas and costly porcelains, silks, carpets, lacquer wares, and beautifully carved ivories or jades. By 1820 opium had replaced the gold or silver specie required to settle the payments owed. Whatever moral standpoint we choose to adopt towards this matter for ourselves, it would be a grievous oversimplification to regard it as just an earlier chapter of the sordid chronicle of worldwide narcotics distribution. The China trade encompassed much more than the opium business. American and other foreign merchants in the trading factories at Canton worked long hours during the tea-packing and tea-shipping seasons, customarily over stretches of six to 12 years. Canton [Guangzhou] was the sole port open for such 'barbarians from afar'. Although isolated by law and custom from Chinese society, American merchants and clerks, like all foreign traders, lived in almost sybaritic luxury extravagantly maintained by their Chinese servants. Many traders amassed the fortunes they sought. Known as their 'competency', their fortunes, huge in early nineteenth-century terms, were used to underwrite numerous industrial or commercial ventures at home, to endow their New England, New York, and Philadelphia families with a 'made in China' aura for generations to come. Each firm projected its own specific image. Russell & Co. was still the dominant house at the end of this era, even if internally torn apart by rivalries for control among the Russell, Sturgis, Forbes, and Delano families. (Warren Delano was Franklin Delano Roosevelt's maternal grandfather.) Russell & Co. did not close its doors until 1891, long after its rivals had withdrawn from the trading sector.

To the proud Chinese, smuggled opium became an unqualified evil. Around 1838, the official attack upon it grew steadily more effective. Lin Tse-hsu, an imperial commissioner, arrived in Canton bearing extraordinary orders to terminate the traffic. In retaliation, Great Britain sparked the first Opium War (1839–1842), and ravaged several coastal cities, overwhelming Peking's feeble resistance. The Treaty of Nanking (1842) ended the war on the victor's terms. China opened five seaports, including Canton, to British trade and residence, and ceded Hong Kong outright. China also accepted a treaty-bound schedule of tariffs and the humiliating principle of extraterritoriality as upheld through consular courts. Though themselves disturbed by Britain's brutality, American merchants and missionaries demanded identical privileges for themselves. Their clamors brought Massachusetts Congressman Caleb Cushing to the mouth of the Pearl River below Canton, sent there by President John Tyler and Secretary of State Daniel Webster to obtain commercial equality for American merchants with the British and other foreigners trading with the Chinese.

Cushing's Treaty of Wangshia on 3 July 1844 opened diplomatic relations between the United States and China. Its provisions upheld the right of the Chinese to regulate their own trade and maintain, inviolate, their sovereign territory. Special articles allowed Americans in China to engage Chinese teachers and to purchase books as recommended by Cushing's missionary advisers and interpreters. Most important, the treaty's most-favored-nation clause and Britain's policy of free trade opened the door to Americans for the choicest fruits of gunboat diplomacy without firing a shot: extraterritoriality and a bearable schedule for tariffs. 'It has long been clear that America did not cut her China policy out of whole cloth,' Downs tells us, 'but received it pretty nearly complete from her nationals resident in China.'[8] Trading illegally in opium, not tea or silk, was nevertheless the China policy's economic foundation.

The commerce at Canton lured increasing numbers of other Americans and Europeans into Pacific oceanic enterprises. For a while the fur trade was considered to be the legitimate key to the China market, whilst whaling, though carrying more American seafarers into the Pacific than any other industry, was important for extracting oil, tallow, and whalebone for domestic consumption. The route to China favored by exporters lay south-eastward across the Atlantic Ocean around the Cape of Good Hope at Africa's southernmost point into the Indian Ocean, then far beyond India and the spice islands of the East Indies, into the Pacific Ocean from the west and, finally, northward to Canton.

The fur hunters' route entailed greater risks and more hazardous adventures. From Boston, New York, Philadelphia, and several small havens in between, they had to navigate round South America's tempestuous tip, either by tacking through the fog-bound Strait of Magellan or sailing around Cape Horn itself, to enter the Pacific from the east. The fur seal quickly became a victim of the China trade. The chase spread into the high southern latitudes to the rookeries of the Juan Fernandez Islands off the coast of Chile and the wild, uninhabited islands south of New Zealand and Australia. Sailors were put ashore on these bleak, rocky isles for weeks and months at a stretch to club down the defenseless mammals as their ships sailed away to hunt elsewhere. Once an island's herd was extinguished or frightened away, interest in that spot ceased. Ruthlessly, Americans outdid themselves tracking down fur seals. They caused violent furors in and around New Zealand and Australia, inspiring the British to make claims to all of Australasia. By 1805, 1–3 million seals had reportedly been taken from Mas Afuera in the Juan Fernandez Islands alone, exhausting the natural supply. Then, the frenzied hunt raced away to more northerly regions of the Pacific along California's coasts and its offshore islands to Vancouver Island's Nootka Sound, where the search for sealskins was combined with the hunt for the more highly prized sea otters and many other kinds of mammal.

Farther north, the Russians had linked a chain of fur trading stations from Siberia across the Bering Sea stepping along the Aleutian Islands and down Alaska's shores beyond the apex of British and American activity to a point below the mouth of the Columbia River. Certain shadowy Americans carried Russian or British furs to Canton, circumventing Chinese restrictions against Russian seaborne imports as well as the East India Company's monopoly. Others conveyed supplies to the outposts of the

---

[8] Downs, chapter 4 below, p. 339.

Russian-American Company, posing problems for its agents by trading rum and firearms for sealskins directly with Aleut natives.

In 1821 Congress bestirred itself. The House of Representatives formed a special committee under John Floyd of Virginia to uphold American fur trading interests and territorial claims in the north-west. John Jacob Astor and William Clark added their pressure behind the scenes as Missouri's Senator Thomas Hart Benton laid out an imperial vision for the Pacific Basin and the Orient beyond:

> Upon the people of Eastern Asia the establishment of a civilized power on the opposite coast of America could not fail to produce great and wonderful benefits. Science, liberal principles in government, and the true religion might cast their lights across the intervening sea. The valley of the Columbia might become the granary of China and Japan, and an outlet to their imprisoned and exuberant population. The inhabitants of the oldest and the newest, the most despotic and the freest governments, would become the neighbors and the friends of each other. To my mind the proposition is clear, that Eastern Asia and the Americas, as they become neighbors should become friends; and I for one had as lief see American ministers going to the emperors of China and Japan, to the King of Persia, and even to the Grand Turk, as to see them dancing attendance upon those European legitimates who hold everything American in contempt and detestation.[9]

Ironically, the maritime fur trade had begun to decline at the very moment Benton was declaiming his grandiose ambitions.

The whaling industry had now superceded hunting and trading furs. Alexander Starbuck's history of the American whale fishery lists 46 whaling expeditions to the Pacific before 1800.[10] Early whalers concentrated their efforts in the 'onshore fishery' off Chile and Peru, though some ventured far westward into the 'middle ground' of the Tasman Sea between New Zealand and Australia. British controls curtailed such activity during the War of 1812 and again in the 1840s. In 1820 Honolulu hailed its first Yankee whalers, and they were soon heading out from the Hawaiian Islands across the north central Pacific Ocean to the newly discovered fisheries off Japan's eastern coast. By 1835 other fisheries had opened up near Alaska and the Aleutian Islands, in the Sea of Ohkotsk in 1847, and in the Bering Sea and Arctic Ocean before 1850. The northern Pacific afforded the principal hunting ground for American whalers, with off-season havens in Hawaiian anchorages. The American whaling industry peaked between 1835 and 1855, with an annual average of more than 400 whale ships arriving at Honolulu. No fewer than 722 of the world's 900 whalers were American flagged vessels, the great majority of which fished in the Pacific Ocean. Whaling voyages soon lengthened from an average of three to four or even five years, as hunters drove

---

[9] Thomas Hart Benton, *Thirty Years View; or a History of the Working of the American Government for Thirty Years, from 1820 to 1850* (New York: D. Appleton and Company, 1856), vol. 1, pp. 13–14.

[10] A. Starbuck, *History of the American Whale Fishery from its Earliest Inception to the Year 1876* (Waltham, MA, 1878); reprinted in 2 vols (New York: Angary-Antiquarian, 1964).

the great creatures ever farther northward, and the importance of safe harbors for supplies and repairs rose correspondingly. Yet the hermit kingdoms of Japan and Korea refused to permit Westerners to moor in their waters, even denying rescue or succor to the tempest-tossed or shipwrecked, while China's facilities failed to meet the whalers' everyday needs long after the treaty ports were opened.

The whaling industry's collapse was abrupt and final. In 1861 the Civil War interrupted and diverted American shipping. Clipper ships and whalers alike found themselves either scuttled to block Confederate seaports or overcome by rebel sea raiders. Petroleum products for lighting and lubricating replaced whale oil; steel substituted for whalebone. Grass grew in the streets of New Bedford and Nantucket.

Inevitably, demands arose for naval protection when Americans entered the Pacific Ocean. Shipowners and their captains backed proposals for exploratory expeditions to reduce the hazards of navigating unknown or uncharted waters. In the 1820s United States naval patrols from the newly formed Pacific Squadron undertook the duties of a constabulary and made more or less regular forays westward beyond New Zealand and Australia to South-east Asia. Their presence was capped by the East India (later Asiatic) naval station established in 1835, and guaranteed by the acquisitions of Oregon and California.

Foreign policy-making was being imposed upon the United States, in truth, by the swelling population of its citizenry active in the central and southern Pacific together with the increasing value of their properties there. Official United States policy toward the Pacific Islands to the middle of the nineteenth century was simply that of proclaiming (and occasionally maintaining) liberty and equality of opportunity for its citizens in trading goods, hunting mammals, and saving souls. On 7 February 1821 Captain John Davis of New Haven became the first person known to have set foot on Antarctica, the southernmost continent, but it took the virtually simultaneous extermination of fur seals in that region to quell the clamor over rival claims that his exploit had sparked. Only for the Hawaiian Islands, where missionaries backed the merchants and both parties claimed influential connections on the mainland, was, in Donald D. Johnson's apt appraisal, 'a form of international caveat enunciated'.[11] In 1842 President John Tyler applied the Monroe Doctrine there, warning Great Britain and France not to attempt an annexation of that insular kingdom. Holding to George Washington's advice, American foreign relations functioned from an isolationist shelter.

Nevertheless, as Charles Vevier makes clear in his essay,[12] praised by Walter LaFeber as 'a small classic',[13] the term 'continentalism' best expresses the prevailing

---

[11] Donald D. Johnson, with Gary Dean Best, *The United States in the Pacific: Private Interests and Public Policies, 1784–1899* (Westport, CT: Praeger, 1995), p. 60.

[12] Vevier, chapter 5 below.

[13] W. LaFeber, *The American Age: United States Foreign Policy at Home and Abroad since 1750* (New York: W.W. Norton & Company, 1989), p. 119.

ideology of American values from 1845 to 1910. The United States of America, opinion-makers held, possessed identical national and imperial boundaries inside a physical framework of continental extent. Safeguarded behind its isolationist postulates, America was viewed as the geographical stage where a manifest destiny drove its people to build a unique society upon solid foundations of freedom and democracy. Throughout these years also, observes Vevier, numerous strong-minded men and women sought to deepen commercial and evangelistic contacts with Asia 'that added a maritime dimension to the era of territorial expansion that preceded the Civil War'.[14]

Martin Borden's inclusion of James K. Polk among 'America's Ten Greatest Presidents' from Washington to Franklin Roosevelt,[15] according to our essayist Norman A. Graebner,[16] rested more on Polk's territorial gains than the success of his domestic program. At his inaugural, Polk confided his four key objectives to the historian George Bancroft, his choice for secretary of the navy, as: tariff reduction; an independent treasury rather than another central bank; settlement of the Oregon boundary; and acquiring California. Of the two expansionist issues – Texas and Oregon – raised by the elections campaign of 1844, Texas posed no challenge for Polk. Texas had won independence from Mexico in 1836, and now accepted Congress's invitation to join the United States. It became a state in the Union in December 1845, provoking Mexico into breaking off diplomatic relations and leading to the Mexican War of 1846–48.

Oregon posed the more serious difficulty. The long-standing American offer to extend the north-western boundary along the 49th parallel to the Pacific Ocean had seemed reasonable and practicable. However, during his campaign for the presidency, Polk won support from western Democrats by demanding all of the Oregon territory (jointly ruled with Great Britain from 1818 to 1846) to the tip of the Alaska panhandle, and joining the belligerent outcry for 'Fifty-four forty or fight!'. Once in the White House, however, Polk stalled.

The British government, weary of the squabble, offered to accept the 49th parallel as the boundary while retaining all of Vancouver Island. Polk, true enough, sold out his rabid supporters, but his settlement of this thorny question quickly proved so satisfactory that even the western extremists allowed the matter to rest. Nevertheless, Polk did supply another clear example of the power that domestic politics held then and since over United States foreign relations.

At this time Polk had also been busily negotiating with Mexico City to purchase California. But his callous eagerness, on top of Mexico's fury over Texas's defection, only provoked hostilities along the Rio Grande. As a result, Congress declared war against Mexico in May 1846. Once the war started, Polk became determined to prolong it, hoping to coerce the Mexicans into surrendering California. Again, Polk succeeded.

---

[14] Charles Vevier, chapter 5 below, pp. 324–327.

[15] Norman Graebner, 'James Polk', *America's Ten Greatest Presidents*, in Morton Borden (ed.) (Chicago, IL: Rand McNally & Company, 1961, 1962), pp. 123–128, 134–135.

[16] Graebner, chapter 6 below.

The Treaty of Guadeloupe-Hidalgo delivered California and New Mexico into United States sovereignty. With Oregon and California's rich lands and spacious harbors, it became virtually certain that the United States would prove itself a powerhouse in the North Pacific Ocean region, perhaps even in East Asia.

Two decades earlier, in fact, President John Quincy Adams had called for scientific exploration expeditions – comparable to those launched by Britain, France, and Russia – to improve the nation's commerce by acquiring a sophisticated knowledge of the globe. Following the precedent set between 1831 and 1836 by the memorable voyage of HMS *Beagle* with Charles Darwin aboard as its volunteer naturalist, from 1838 to 1842, the Great United States Exploring Expedition cruised almost 90,000 nautical miles around the world, accumulating vast collections and charting many hundreds of islands, reefs, straits, harbors, and coastlines including the north-west coast of North America. The expedition's officers and crewmen produced a stupendous array of charts for Antarctica and the Pacific Ocean, created the basic structures of modern anthropology, and made a significant contribution to the organization of science within the United States government.[17]

In 1853 President Millard Fillmore dispatched another great scientific investigation, the North Pacific Expedition. Its orders were to chart the coasts and explore the waters of Japan, the China Sea, and the North Pacific Ocean to render these vast regions safer for whalers and merchantmen. The expedition lasted more than two years. After surveying the Yellow Sea and the Sea of Okhotsk, mapping the foggy Aleutian Islands chain, and sailing north through the Bering Strait to the icepacks of the Beaufort Sea, navigators mapped the mouth of the Amur River in Siberia, ending up with a rich harvest of scientific and hydrographic returns. One important official who never forgot the North Pacific Expedition was its sponsor in Congress, Senator William H. Seward of New York, who, later in 1867 as secretary of state, would contrive to purchase Alaska for the United States from Russia with the aim of protecting American commerce with the Far East.

In fact, leaders of both major political parties were hoping that, as a result of trading and whaling, the North Pacific Ocean might become, in William H. Goetzmann's words, 'a vast American lake', the bridge to the wealth of East Asia.[18] American entrepreneurs looked longingly to the Empire of Japan. The handful of Americans already there, however, were systematically rebuffed, if not wholly excluded, by both the Japanese and the Dutch at their trading monopoly on the sealed-off islet of Deshima inside Nagasaki's harbor. Many Americans felt certain that either the British or the Russians would pry open Japan before long, and consequently block their chances. The expansionistic American Geographical and Statistical Society of New York, backed

---

[17] See further William Stanton, *The Great United States Exploring Expedition of 1838–1842* (Berkeley and Los Angeles: University of California Press, 1975).

[18] W.H. Goetzmann, *New Lands, New Men: America and the Second Great Age of Discovery* (New York: Viking Penguin Inc., 1986), p. 332.

by New England's whaling interests, urged the United States authorities to deploy greater naval strength in the western Pacific to back up Americans' bargaining powers, and, as our essayist John H. Schroeder relates,[19] Commodore Matthew Calbraith Perry's expedition of 1853–54 would be the first step.

The United States' next step, in 1867 immediately after the Civil War, was to purchase Russian Alaska. Seward's dream was realized in a monetary transaction. But why on earth, after 126 years of Russian sovereignty, did Tsar Alexander II offer to sell Alaska to the United States? In his essay[20] N.N. Bolkhovitinov has accounted for the sale of Alaska within the context of Russian–American relations in the nineteenth century, from a Soviet scholar's perspective. Nonetheless, Russia chose to withdraw voluntarily from its Pacific imperial adventure in North America just when the United States was embarking on its own aggrandizement.

However, before reaching any climax or conclusion prematurely in this history of American empire in the Pacific, a popular myth needs to be recognized for what it is, then banished as a misconception that many Americans have shared, and continue to hold.

It is, or was, something of a commonplace to believe that there has never been such an entity as an American Empire, nor any widespread support for American imperialism. Of course, it is true that the United States authorities have not yet ruled a Roman-style empire, nor any conglomeration of territories and populations as inclusive as the once great Spanish, Portuguese, French, or British empires at their peaks. Likewise, before the Mexican War (1846–48), it holds true that national expansion beyond the original 13 states never turned into a blatant aggrandizement beyond recognized boundaries. The westward movement to the Mississippi River and thence to the purchases of Louisiana and Florida was understood only as a natural solution to the problem of population growth and a justifiable response to available economic opportunity. Its romantic expression came in the late 1840s in celebrations of a divinely inspired manifest destiny. Manifest destiny's darker side nevertheless lay concealed beneath its triumphant progression to the Pacific Ocean atop the sufferings of untold thousands of Native Americans and other indigenous peoples. Most western tribesmen had already been overwhelmed by competing empires of Europeans or by their incurable diseases.

For the hundreds of thousands of square miles it would grow to encompass land beyond Oregon and California, the American Empire in the Pacific owed its birth to a number of grandiose dreams coming true. Backed by President Andrew Johnson, Senator Charles Sumner of Massachusetts adroitly managed to persuade his fellow senators to fulfil their patriotic obligation and ratify the treaty to purchase Alaska on 9 April 1867 with a three-hour, fact-filled speech full of manifest destiny sentiments. Sumner's dream come true was his vision of expanded republican forms of government

---

[19] Schroeder, chapter 7 below.

[20] Bolkhovitinov, chapter 8 below.

in the United States, free from Europe's control and extending to the farthest tip of the continent. However, the commercial empire envisaged by Secretary of State William Henry Seward may very well have been inspired by Senator Benton's imperial prospect of 1821. Alaska's role cannot be subject to the second clause. An isthmian canal would eventually become essential to defend the southern corridor. Seward's oceanic route for trading with China and Japan was to extend directly between Alaska and the future canal, from San Francisco to Honolulu and beyond. In 1867 Seward himself arranged for the United States to take possession of Midway Island. The acquisition of the Hawaiian Islands would then, some day, constitute his final move, although that feat could not be accomplished as quickly as he hoped. Even so, after 1887 the naval forces necessary to advance Seward's strategy for an Asian Pacific Empire came to be based at Pearl Harbor.

It was also in 1867 that 15-year old Mutsuhito became the Mikado, the highest authority in Japan, taking the name of Meiji. In Emperor Meiji's name, Japan modernized the country within a generation, attempting to overtake the West and make up for the country's lengthy isolation. At breathtaking speed, Japan's leaders transformed their feudal society into an industrialized, militarized, and nationalistic civilization. Its diplomats labored to overturn the one-sided treaties imposed on Tokyo by the United States and other powers, which patronizingly implied the racial inferiority of the Japanese people. The treaties confined Japan's economy behind inequitable tariff schedules and compromised its sovereignty, yielding extraterritorial rights to foreigners. When Great Britain relinquished its own rights of extraterritoriality in Japan in 1894, the United States followed suit, but Washington reserved the right to restrict Japanese immigration.

China was a different matter. Mandarins maintained their traditional disdain for merchants and industrialists. Scholars directed the imperial court's foot-dragging against modernization, spurning Western philosophy, culture, and the arts as barbarian. Inside the United States, racist agitation and acts of brutality spread from coast to coast against the population of more than 100,000 Chinese workers. Pressure rose to exclude any new immigrants – a stand supported by both major political parties in their platforms of 1880. In 1882 Congress suspended immigration from China for a period of ten years, the initial step toward the eventual policy, in 1904, of permanent exclusion. A scramble for concessions by the great powers, much like Africa's partitioning, threatened to slice China up into three colonies – British, French, and German. In addition, the United States became a great power in East Asia in its own right, annexing the Hawaiian Islands (1898), the Philippine Islands (1898–1902) after the Spanish-American-Cuban-Filipino War, and the six eastern Samoan Islands (1899) in order to gain Pago Pago's splendid naval harbor. Incredibly, China's Ch'ing (Qing) dynasty (1644–1912) was visibly expiring, threatening, by its impending demise, to extinguish the oldest empire on earth.

The next five of this book's essayists address these developments directly, as well as the conditions or actions they spawned in the half-century or so following

1870. Jeffrey M. Dorwart reveals the cameo part played by John M.B. Sill, America's frontline diplomat there, in opposing the Japanese penetration of Korea.[21] Sill's forthright pronouncements served up a foretaste of John Hay's Open Door policy first proposed in 1899. And, for almost the identical point of time, George F. Pearce examines the reasons why the United States abruptly overturned its traditional anti-colonial policy to favor outright the takeovers of insular territories and alien peoples.[22] Pearce's dissection of public opinion over the annexation of the Hawaiian Islands, which he mined from editorials and commentaries in the nation's press, further serves to introduce the opening salvos of the debate among historians over the same question. Significantly, Hawaii's annexation inaugurated a foreign policy for the United States that would reap an even more extended empire in less than year. The actual existence of an American Pacific Empire now moved public zealousness to the front burner, favoring an isthmian canal to join the Atlantic and Pacific Oceans together.

In 1888 Captain Alfred Thayer Mahan, USN, 46 years old and ten years short of retirement, had delivered as ordered a series of lectures before a handful of officers at the newly opened Naval War College, which, four years later, he caused to be published in book form titled *The Influence of Sea Power upon History, 1660–1783*.[23] In this book Mahan presented a persuasive explanation for England's ascendancy during the seventeenth and eighteenth centuries, claiming that it overcame the rivalry of Holland, France, and Spain on account of its naval power. He demonstrated how the rise and fall of sea power, and therefore of nations, was linked to the commercial and military control of the sea. His book supported the faith of the British people that greatness lay in their far-flung empire constructed and sustained, as indeed it was, on the strength of their navy. Mahan's thesis galvanized Germany, France, Japan, Russia, and the newly imperialistic United States, together with Great Britain itself, into a race toward naval modernization and costly warship construction programs. Mahan combines the subject of the Panama Canal for our readers with the vital necessity of sea power in protecting the American Empire's new colonies and its commercial sea lanes.

China's Boxer Rising during the summer of 1900 had provoked a dramatic retaliation from the foreign powers against the murderous rampaging of the clandestine organization, the Fists of Righteous Harmony, and its siege of the diplomatic legations in Peking. President William McKinley had ordered 2,500 American troops from the Philippines to join the relief expedition being assembled by eight nations. Secretary of State John Hay, in his definitive second Open Door Note of 3 July 1900, laid down United States policy for: (1) the protection of American lives and property; (2) the protection for open and impartial trading; (3) the integrity of China's territory and sovereignty. Though fragile and insubstantial against empire-builders, the United States

---

[21] Dorwart, chapter 9 below.

[22] Pearce, chapter 10 below.

[23] A.T. Mahan, *The Influence of Sea Power upon History 1600–1783* (New York: Sagamore Press, 1957).

Open Door policy began, in time, to carry considerable weight. In sum, Hay conveyed the United States' determination to keep China intact in the face of foreign threats and the trading door open. The Open Door policy could not invariably succeed of course, but, like the Monroe Doctrine, it would lodge itself in the public mind at home as the morally righteous and patriotic course for American foreign relations to take in East Asia.

The international expedition crushed the Boxers by force, and rescued the trapped diplomats and their families. Foreign troops thereafter remained in China to guard their legations, stationing themselves between Peking and the seaports. A single American infantry battalion moved into barracks at Tientsin shortly after the revolution of 1911, followed by another in 1914 to safeguard access routes to Peking. The navy's Asiatic Squadron grew to 48 vessels, and was standing by, Washington proclaimed, to deliver, if called upon, 'severe and lasting punishment' to any threat to the safety of Americans anywhere in East Asia. President Theodore Roosevelt explained that 'our future history will be more determined by our position on the Pacific facing China than by our position on the Atlantic facing Europe'.[24] This sounded feasible enough at the time, but the tangled record of the Boxer indemnity, laid out by Michael H. Hunt,[25] illustrates the problems caused by American authorities acting on assumptions that were never seriously questioned and making decisions which took no serious account of Chinese viewpoints. China would resent Washington's indifference, and often feel frustrated by American policies.

At the same time, Japan and the United States, as though deliberately to complicate matters, were competing openly for influence over China, while America's exclusionist immigration statutes, together with local and state discriminatory practices, rubbed sensitive Japanese feelings raw. Japan and the United States were, in truth, converging slowly but inexorably on a collision course.

Expansionism was motivating both nations. Following the purchase of Alaska and acquisition of Midway Island, the United States pushed its Pacific Empire west and south from California. It annexed the Hawaiian and the Philippine Islands, Guam and Wake Islands, and the six eastern Samoan Islands. It then immediately started to develop naval bases at Dutch Harbor, Pearl Harbor, Subic Bay, and Pago Pago. Construction also began on the Panama Canal. For Japan's part, Tokyo annexed the Lew Chew Islands renaming them the Ryukus, and calling the largest Okinawa. In addition, by trouncing China in the Sino-Japanese War (1894–95), Japan seized both Taiwan, which it renamed Formosa, and the Pescadores Islands off Taiwan's coast. Japan's triumphs earned applause from some Americans as signs of progress in their Asian protégé. However, when Japan decisively defeated Russia (1904–05) and annexed Korea between 1905 and 1910, renaming that ancient kingdom Chosen, many

---

[24] As cited in O. Edmund Chubb, *20th Century China*, 3rd edition (New York: Columbia University Press, 1978).

[25] Hunt, chapter 11 below.

Americans viewed Japan not so much with respect for its prowess but with alarm at these latest manifestations of the 'Yellow Peril'. With American forces virtually at Tokyo's doorstep and China's empire dissolving, East Asia's balance of power would henceforth be at stake.

In 1908, in a show of strength, President Roosevelt ordered the navy's entire complement of 16 battleships to embark on a goodwill cruise across the Pacific Ocean and around the world. At Yokohama, crowds greeted the 'Great White Fleet'. A rousing reception for the crews featured rows upon rows of schoolchildren waving American flags and attempting to sing 'The Star-Spangled Banner'. The two governments promised to respect each other's possessions, maintain the status quo in the Pacific region, and also to uphold the Open Door principle of equal opportunity for the commerce and industry of all nations. Roosevelt emphasized the peaceful intent of America's relations with Japan, and the emperor's emissaries insisted that Japan had never even contemplated making war against the United States. The tenor of these exchanges pleased President Roosevelt, who left office just after the 'Great White Fleet' returned home. Relations with Japan nonetheless, in Charles Neu's apt labeling, would continue to exemplify a 'troubled encounter'.[26] At this juncture Kenton J. Clymer's essay examines the trials and tribulations of American missionaries colonizing the Philippine Islands, and weighs the burdens of the American Pacific Empire on an imperial balance.[27]

During Woodrow Wilson's presidency, many assumptions that Americans held about world affairs in general, and East Asia in particular, came to grief. Wilson wholeheartedly believed in the Monroe Doctrine and the Open Door for China. He compassionately responded to Asia's revolutionary nationalism. He favored granting independence to the Philippines. He wanted to protect China against the ambitions of Japan and Russia. Wilson's Presbyterian faith and his connections with its missionaries convinced him that Christianity could serve fittingly as the instrument for China's rebirth. He was poorly equipped for any crisis to arise with Japan, let alone a succession of them. In short order, Japan and the United States quarreled over: (1) renewed anti-Japanese tensions in California; (2) Japan's wartime seizures of Germany's holdings in China; (3) the Twenty-one Demands made by Japan on China; (4) America's military interventions, following the Russian Revolution of 1917, in Archangel and Murmansk in northern Russia and Vladivostok in Siberia, which John W. Long analyzes for us;[28] and (5) the Treaty of Versailles. Japan tried unsuccessfully to force a racial equality treaty into the treaty's covenant for the League of Nations, which Wilson rebuffed. Instead, to persuade the Japanese to join his beloved League, he capitulated to Japan on keeping China's Shantung province. 'The problem', as our essayist

---

[26] C.E. Neu, *The Troubled Encounter: The United States and Japan* (New York: John Wiley & Sons, 1975).

[27] Clymer, chapter 13 below.

[28] Long, chapter 15 below.

Noriko Kawamura explains concerning the League of Nations, 'was that Japan was apprehensive about, indeed repelled by, an international body dominated by Western powers.'[29]

At home, the struggle over the treaty's ratification between President Wilson and the Republican majority leaders of the Senate turned into what William L. Langer later described as one of the most disheartening chapters of American history.[30] To build public support, Wilson took to the road, criss-crossing the country and telling his audiences that his ideal of a world without wars, for which their soldiers had fought, was being sabotaged by narrow-minded partisan jingoists. In Colorado a paralyzing stroke felled him. Broken in body by this cruel fate and shielded by his wife and physician from public contacts, the nation virtually lacked a head of state for 17 months. With Wilson in seclusion, the Senate twice rejected the Treaty of Versailles, and the United States never did join the League of Nations.

His successor, President Warren G. Harding and Secretary of State Charles Evans Hughes brought a soothing respite from Wilson's self-certain obduracy. Even so, they still had the problem of how to reverse Japan's wartime gains and revive the Open Door policy, while coping with rival revolutionary movements in China, and appeasing the Japanese. The prospect of a naval armaments race had already alarmed the American people almost as much as it did among the war-drained nations of Europe. Under Hughes' leadership and Harding's prodding, relates Malcolm H. Murfett,[31] the Washington Conference of 1921–22 produced an entirely new naval limitations treaty system for Asia and the Pacific. The prospect of a naval arms race evaporated. And, through the Kellogg-Briand Pact of 1928, 62 nations would renounce war as an instrument of national policy. Peace was now a reality – or so it seemed.

The history of the American Empire in the Pacific did not end at these post-1918 signs of progress, as we all know. The future shock was at hand. In hindsight, all this was nothing more than a brief breathing space. Japan's surprise attack on Pearl Harbor on 7 December 1941 wrote the headlines proclaiming the American Pacific Empire's next war.

Select Bibliography

Adams, Henry, *The United States in 1800* (Ithaca, NY: Cornell University Press, 1955).

Anderson, Fred, *Crucible of War: The Seven Years War and the Fate of Empire in British North America* (New York: Alfred A. Knopf, 2000).

Andrade, Ernest jr, 'The United States Navy and the Washington Conference', *The Historian* 31, no. 3 (May 1969), pp. 345–363.

---

[29] Kawamura, chapter 14 below, p. 319.

[30] William L. Langer, 'Peace and the New World Order', in Arthur Power Dudden *Woodrow Wilson and the World of Today* (Philadelphia, PA: University of Pennsylvania Press, 1957), p. 90.

[31] Murfett, chapter 16 below.

Bak, Richard, 'The Polar Bears', *Michigan History* 72, no. 3 (1988), pp. 40–45.

Bancroft, Hubert Howe, *The New Pacific*, 3rd rev. edn (New York: The Bancroft Company, 1915).

Barratt, Glynn, *Russia in Pacific Waters, 1715–1825* (Vancouver, BC: University of British Columbia Press, 1981).

Beale, Howard K., *Theodore Roosevelt and the Rise of America to World Power* (Baltimore, MD: The Johns Hopkins University Press, 1956).

Beasley, W.G., *The Rise of Modern Japan: Political, Economic and Social Change since 1850* (New York: St Martin's Press, 1995).

Beisner, Robert L., *Twelve against Empire: the Anti-Imperialists. 1898–1900* (New York: McGraw-Hill Book Company, 1968).

Benton, Thomas Hart, *Thirty Years View; or a History of the Working of the American Government for Thirty Years, from 1820 to 1850*, 2 vols (New York: D. Appleton Company, 1856).

Blum, John Morton, *The Republican Roosevelt* (Cambridge, MA: Harvard University Press, 1954).

Boyle, John Hunter, *Modern Japan: the American Nexus* (Orlando, FL: Harcourt, Brace, Jovanovich, 1993).

Bradford, James C., ed., *Command under Sail: Makers of the American Naval Tradition, 1775–1850* (Annapolis, MD: United States Naval Institute Press, 1985).

Bradford, James C., ed., *Captains of the Old Steam Navy: Makers of the American Naval Tradition, 1840–1880* (Annapolis, MD: United States Naval Institute Press, 1986).

Brandes, Joseph, *Herbert Hoover and Economic Diplomacy: Department of Commerce Policy, 1921–1928* (Pittsburgh, PA: University of Pittsburgh Press, 1968).

Brookes, Jean I., *International Rivalry in the Pacific Islands* (New York: Russell and Russell Company, 1941).

Buckley, Thomas H., *The Washington Conference, 1921–1922* (Knoxville, TN: University of Tennessee Press, 1970).

Caruthers, J. Wade, *American Pacific Ocean Trade: Its Impact on Foreign Policy and Continental Expansion, 1784–1860* (New York: Exposition Press, 1973).

Chubb, O. Edmund, *20th Century China*, 3rd edn (New York: Columbia University Press, 1978).

Clemens, Samuel Langhorne [Mark Twain], 'To the Person Sitting in Darkness', *North American Review* 172 (February 1901), pp. 161–176; reprinted by Anti-Imperialist League, n.d.

Clyde, Paul H., *United States Policy toward China: Diplomatic and Public Documents, 1839–1939* (Durham, NC: Duke University Press, 1940).

Coffman, Edward M., 'The Intervention in Russia, 1918–1921', *Military Review* 68, no. 9 (September 1988), pp. 60–71.

Cohen, Paul A., *History in Three Keys: the Boxers as Event, Experience, and Myth* (New York: Columbia University Press, 1997).

Cohen, Warren I., *America's Response to China: A History of Sino-American Relations*, 3rd edn (New York: Columbia University Press, 1989).

Collin, Richard H., *Theodore Roosevelt, Culture, Diplomacy and Expansion: a New View of American Imperialism* (Baton Rouge, LA: Louisiana State University Press, 1985).

Cruz, Romeo V., *America's Colonial Desk and the Philippines, 1898–1934* (Quezon City, PI: University of the Philippines Press, 1974).

Cumings, Bruce, *Korea's Place in the Sun: A History* (New York: W.W. Norton & Company, 1997).

Dana, Richard Henry jr, *Two Years Before the Mast: A Personal Narrative of Life at Sea* (New York: Thomas Y. Crowell Company Publishers, 1907).

Daws, Gavan, *Shoal of Time: A History of the Hawaiian Islands* (Honolulu, HI: University of Hawaii Press, 1968).

Dennett, Tyler, *Americans in Eastern Asia: A Critical Study of the Policy of the United States with Reference to China, Japan, and Korea in the 19th Century* (New York: The Macmillan Company, 1922).

Dingman, Roger, *Power in the Pacific: The Origins of Naval Arms Limitations, 1914–1922* (Chicago, IL: University of Chicago Press, 1976).

Dobson, John, *Reticent Expansionism: The Foreign Policy of William McKinley* (Pittsburgh: Duquesne University Press, 1968).

Downs, Jacques M., *The Golden Ghetto: The American Commercial Community at Canton and the Shaping of American China Policy, 1784–1844* (Bethlehem, PA: Lehigh University Press, 1997).

Dudden, Arthur Power, ed., *Woodrow Wilson and the World of Today: Essays by Eric F. Goldman, William L. Langer, and Arthur S. Link* (Philadelphia, PA: University of Pennsylvania Press, 1957).

Dudden, Arthur Power, *The American Pacific from the Old China Trade to the Present* (New York and Oxford: Oxford University Press, 1992).

Dudden, Arthur Power, 'The American Pacific Where the West Was Also Won', in Sally M. Miller, A.J.H. Latham, and Dennis O. Flynn, eds, *Studies in the Economic History of the Pacific Rim, Studies in the Growth Economies of Asia* (London and New York: Routledge, 1998), pp. 94–104.

Dudden, Arthur Power, 'Japan', *Encyclopedia of U.S. Foreign Relations*, Vol. 2 (1997), pp. 446–458.

Dudden, Arthur Power, 'The Philippine Annexation: An Experiment of Profound Interest', in Dennis O'Flynn, Arturo Giráldez, and James Sobredo, eds, *Studies in Pacific History, Economics, Politics, and Migration* (Aldershot, Hants and Burlington, VT: Ashgate Publishing Ltd, 2002), pp. 212–222.

Duus, Peter, *The Japanese Discovery of America: A Brief History with Documents* (Boston, MA: Bedford Books of St Martin's Press, 1997).

Embree, Ainslee T. and Gluck, Carol, eds, *Asia in Western and World History: A Guide for Teaching* (Armonk, NY: M.E. Sharpe, 1997).

Encyclopedia of U.S. Foreign Relations, Jentleson, Bruce W. and Paterson, Thomas G., senior eds, prepared under the auspices of the Council on Foreign Relations (New York and Oxford: Oxford University Press, 1997).

Fairbank, John King, *The United States and China*, 4th enlarged edn (Cambridge, MA: Harvard University Press, 1983).

Fairbank, John King, *The Great Chinese Revolution, 1800–1985* (New York: Harper & Row, 1986).

Fairbank, John King, Coolidge, Martha Henderson and Smyth, Richard J., *H.B. Morse: Customs Commissioner and Historian of China* (Lexington: University Press of Kentucky, 1995).

Farnsworth, Beatrice, *William C. Bullitt and the Soviet Union* (Bloomington: Indiana University Press, 1967).

Friedel, Frank, *The Splendid Little War* (Boston, MA: Little, Brown and Company, 1958).

Fuchs, Lawrence H., *Hawaii Pono: A Social History* (New York: Harcourt, Brace, Jovanovich Publishers, 1961).

Gallichio, Marc, *The African American Encounter with Japan and China: Black Internationalism in Asia, 1895–1945* (Chapel Hill, NC: University of North Carolina Press, 2000).

Gardella, Robert, *Harvesting Mountains: Fujian and the China Tea Trade, 1757–1937* (Berkeley, CA: University of California Press, 1994).

Gardner, Lloyd C., *Safe for Democracy: Anglo-American Responses to Revolution, 1913–1923* (New York and Oxford: Oxford University Press, 1984).

Gardner, Lloyd C., *et al.*, *Creation of the American Empire*, 2 vols (Chicago, IL: Rand NcNally Publishing Company, 1976).

Gianakos, Perry E., ed., *George Ade's 'Stories of Benevolent Assimilation'* (Quezon City, PI: New Day Publishers, 1985).

Gibson, James R., *Otter Skins, Boston Ships, and China Goods: The Maritime Fur Trade of the Northwest Coast, 1785–1841* (Seattle, WA: University of Washington Press, 1992).

Gilbert, Felix, *To the Farewell Address: Ideas of Early American Foreign Policy* (Princeton, NJ: Princeton University Press, 1961).

Gleeck, Lewis E. jr, *The American Governors-General and High Commissioners in the Philippines: Proconsuls, Nation-Builders and Politicians* (Quezon City, PI: New Day Publishers, 1986).

Goetzmann, William H., *New Lands, New Men: America and the Second Great Age of Discovery* (New York: Viking Penguin, Inc., 1986).

Goldman, Emily O., *Sunken Treaties: Naval Arms Control Between the Wars* (University Park, PA: Pennsylvania State University Press, 1944).

Goldstein, Jonathan, *Philadelphia and the China Trade, 1682–1846: Commercial, Cultural, and Attitudinal Effects* (University Park, PA: Pennsylvania State University Press, 1978).

Gould, Eliga, *The Persistence of Empire: British Political Culture in the Age of the American Revolution* (Chapel Hill, NC: University of North Carolina Press, 2000).

Graebner, Norman, 'James Polk', in Morten Borden, ed., *America's Ten Greatest Presidents* (Chicago, IL: Rand McNally & Company, 1961, 1962), pp. 113–138.

Griswold, A. Whitney, *The Far Eastern Policy of the United States* (New York: Harcourt, Brace Publishers, 1938).

Harris, Townsend, *The Complete Journal of Townsend Harris: First American Consul General and Minister to Japan.* Introduction and Notes by Mario Emilio Cosenza (New York: published for the Japan Society by Doubleday, Doran & Company, 1930).

Hayden, Joseph Ralston, *The Philippines: A Study in National Development* (New York: The Macmillan Company, 1942).

Henning, Joseph M., *Outposts of Civilization: Race, Religion, and the Formative Years of American–Japanese Relations* (New York. New York University Press, 2000).

Hibbert, Christopher, *The Dragon Wakes: China and the West, 1793–1911* (London: Penguin Books, 1984, 1988); first published by Longmans, 1970.

Hing, Bill Ong, *Making and Remaking Asian America through Immigration Policy, 1850–1900* (Stanford, CA: Stanford University Press, 1993).

Hoover, Herbert, *The Memoirs of Herbert Hoover, Years of Adventure, 1874–1920*, Vol. 1 (New York: The Macmillan Company, 1951).

Hsü, Immanuel C.Y., *The Rise of Modern China*, 5th edn (New York and Oxford: Oxford University Press, 1995).

Hunt, Michael H., *Frontier Defense and the Open Door: Manchuria in Chinese–American Relations, 1895–1911* (New Haven, CT: Yale University Press, 1973).

Hunt, Michael H., *The Making of a Special Relationship: the United States and China to 1914* (New York: Columbia University Press, 1983).

Iriye, Akira, *Across the Pacific: An Inner History of American–East Asian Relations* (New York: Harcourt, Brace, & World Publishers, 1967).

Iriye, Akira, *Pacific Estrangement: Japanese and American Expansion, 1897–1911* (Cambridge, MA: Harvard University Press, 1972).

Jenista, Frank Lawrence, *The White APOs: American Governors on the Cordillera Central* (Quezon City, PI: New Day Publishers, 1987).

Jensen, Ronald J., *The Alaska Purchase and Russian–American Relations* (Seattle: University of Washington Press, 1975).

Johnson, Donald D. with Best, Gary Dean, *The United States in the Pacific: Private Interests and Public Policies, 1784–1899* (Westport, CT: Praeger, 1995).

Johnson, William S., 'Naval Diplomacy and the Failure of Balanced Security in the Far East, 1921–1935', *Naval War College Review* 24, no. 6 (1972), pp. 67–88.

Karnow, Stanley, *In Our Image: America's Empire in the Philippines* (New York: Random House, 1989).

Keeton, G.W., *The Development of Extraterritoriality in China*, 2 vols (New York: Howard Fertig, Inc., 1969; by arrangement with Longman's Green & Co., Ltd); first published in 1928.

Kennan, George F., *Soviet–American Relations, 1917–1920*, 2 vols (Princeton, NJ: Princeton University Press, 1956–58).

Kennan, George F., *American Diplomacy*, expanded edn (Chicago IL: University of Chicago Press, 1984).

Kennedy, Paul M., *The Samoan Tangle: A Study in Anglo-German Relations* (New York: Barnes & Noble for Harper & Row Publishers, 1974).

Kushner, Howard I., *Conflict on the Northwest Coast: American–Russian Rivalry in the Pacific Northwest, 1790–1867* (Westport, CT: Greenwood Press, 1975).

Kuykendall, Ralph S., *The Hawaiian Kingdom*, 3 vols (Honolulu, HI: University of Hawaii Press, 1938–67).

LaFeber, Walter, *The American Age: United States Foreign Policy at Home and Abroad since 1750* (New York: W.W. Norton & Company, 1989).

LaFeber, Walter, *The Clash: A History of U.S.–Japan Relations* (New York: W.W. Norton & Company, 1997).

Langer, William L., 'Peace and the New World Order', in Arthur Power Dudden, ed., *Woodrow Wilson and the World of Today* (Philadelphia, PA: University of Pennsylvania Press, 1957).

Latourette, Kenneth Scott, *A History of Christian Missions in China* (London: Society for Promoting Christian Knowledge, 1929).

Lee, Jean Gordon, *Philadelphia and the China Trade, 1784–1844* (Philadelphia, PA: Museum of Art, distributed by University of Pennsylvania Press, 1984).

Link, Arthur S., *Wilson*, 5 vols (Princeton, NJ: Princeton University Press, 1947–65).

Lower, J. Arthur, *Ocean of Destiny: A Concise History of the North Pacific, 1500–1978* (Vancouver, BC: University of British Columbia Press, 1978).

Mahan, Alfred Thayer, *The Influence of Sea Power upon History, 1660–1783* (New York: Sagamore Press, 1957).

May, Ernest R., *Imperial Democracy* (New York: Harcourt, Brace & World, 1961; Harper & Row Publishers, 1973).

May, Ernest R. and Thomson, James C. jr, eds, *American–East Asian Relations: A Survey* (Cambridge, MA: Harvard University Press, 1972).

May, Ernest R. and Fairbank, John King, eds, *America's China Trade in Historical Perspective: The Chinese and American Performance*, Harvard Studies in American–East Asian Relations 11 (Cambridge, MA: Harvard University Press, 1986).

McClain, James L., *Japan: A Modern History* (New York: W.W. Norton & Company, 2002).

McCormick, Thomas J., *China Market: America's Quest for Informal Empire, 1893–1901* (Chicago, IL: Quadrangle Books, 1967).

McCoy, Alfred and Roces, Alfredo, *Philippine Cartoons: Political Caricature of the American Era, 1900–1941* (New Manila Quezon City, PI: Vera-Reyes, Inc., 1985).

McCullough, David, *The Path Between the Seas: The Creation of the Panama Canal, 1870–1914* (New York: Simon & Schuster, 1977).

McEvedy, Colin, *The Penguin Historical Atlas of the Pacific* (New York: Penguin Putnam, Inc., 1998).

Miller, Stuart Creighton, *'Benevolent Assimilation': the American Conquest of the Philippines, 1899–1903* (New Haven, CT: Yale University Press, 1982).

Miyoshi, Masao and Harootunian, H.D., eds, *Japan in the World* (Durham, NC: Duke University Press, 1993).

Moore, John Bassett, *Four Phases of American Development: Federalism, Democracy, Imperialism, Expansion* (Baltimore MD: The Johns Hopkins University Press, 1912).

Morton, W. Scott, *Japan: Its History and Culture*, 3rd edn (New York: McGraw-Hill Book Company, 1994).

Motteler, Lee S., *Pacific Island Names: A Map and Name Guide to the New Pacific*, Bishop Museum Miscellaneous Publications, 34 (Honolulu, HI: Bishop Museum Press, 1986).

Mowry, George E., *The Era of Theodore Roosevelt, 1900–1912* (New York: Harper & Bros. Publishers, 1958).

Naske, Claus-M. and Rowinski, Ludwig J., *Alaska: A History of the 49th State*, 2nd edn (Norman, OK: University of Oklahoma Press, 1987).

Neu, Charles E., *The Troubled Encounter: The United States and Japan* (New York: John Wiley & Sons, 1975).

Nordlander, David J., *For God and Tsar: A Brief History of Russian America, 1741–1867* (Anchorage, AK: Natural History Association, 1998).

Osboure, Thomas J., 'Trade or War? America's Annexation of Hawaii Reconsidered', *Pacific Historical Review* 50 (1981), pp. 285–307.

Paolino, Ernest N., *The Foundations of the American Empire: William H. Seward and U.S. Foreign Policy* (Ithaca, NY: Cornell University Press, 1978).

Parrini, Carl F., *Heir to Empire: United States Economic Diplomacy, 1916–1923* (Pittsburgh, PA: University of Pittsburgh Press, 1969).

Peterson, Barbara Bennett, ed., *Notable Women of Hawaii* (Honolulu, HI: University of Hawaii Press, 1984).

Pido, Antonio J.A., *The Pilipinos in America: Macro/Micro Dimensions of Immigration and Integration* (New York: Center for Migration Studies, 1986).

Pierce, Richard A., *Builders of Alaska: The Russian Governors, 1818–1867* (Kingston, Ontario: The Limestone Press, 1986).

Preston, Diana, *The Boxer Rebellion: The Dramatic Story of China's War on Foreigners that Shook the World in the Summer of 1900* (New York: Berkley Books, 1999, 2000).

Pringle, Henry, *The Life and Times of William Howard Taft*, 2 vols (New York: Farrar and Rinehart Publishers, 1939).

Pusey, Merlo John, *Charles Evans Hughes*, 2 vols (New York: The Macmillan Company, 1951).

Reischauer, Edwin O., *Japan: The Story of a Nation*, rev. edn (New York: Alfred A. Knopf, Inc., 1974).

Roberts, Priscilla, ed., *Sino-American Relations since 1900*, Centre of Asian Studies Occasional Papers and Monographs, No. 93 (Hong Kong: University of Hong Kong Press, 1991).

Salamanca, Bonifacio S., *The Filipino Reaction to American Rule, 1901–1913* (Quezon City, PI: New Day Publishers, 1984).

Salman, Michael, *The Embarrassment of Slavery: Controversies over Bondage and Nationalism in the American Colonial Philippines* (Berkeley and Los Angeles: University of California Press, 2001).

San Juan, E. jr, *From Exile to Diaspora: Versions of the Filipino Experience in the United States* (Boulder, CO: Westview Press, 1998).

Schaller, Michael, *The U.S. and China into the 21st Century*, 3rd edn (New York and Oxford: Oxford University Press, 2002).

Scheiner, Irwin, *Modern Japan: An Interpretative Anthology* (New York: The Macmillan Company, 1974).

Scholes, Walter and Scholes, Marie V., *The Foreign Policies of the Taft Administration* (Columbia, MO: University of Missouri Press, 1970).

Schulzinger, Robert D., *American Diplomacy in the Twentieth Century*, 3rd edn (New York and Oxford: Oxford University Press, 1994).

Schurman, Jacob Gould, *Philippine Affairs: A Retrospect and Outlook* (New York: Charles Scribner's Sons, 1902).

Segal, Gerald, *Rethinking the Pacific* (London: Oxford University Press, 1990).

Sewall, John S., *The Logbook of the Captain's Clerk: Adventures in the China Seas* (Bangor, ME: printed for the author by Chas. H. Glass & Co., 1905); republished in *The Lakeside Classics*, No. 93, ed. Arthur Power Dudden (Chicago, IL: The Lakeside Press, R.R. Donnelley & Sons Company, 1995).

Shannon, Timothy J., *Indians and Colonists at the Crossroads of Empire: The Albany Congress of 1754* (Ithaca, NY: Cornell University Press, 2000).

Shiels, Archie W., *The Purchase of Alaska* (College, AK: University of Alaska Press, 1967).

Smith, Barbara S. and Barnett, Redmond J., eds, *Russian America: The Forgotten Frontier* (Tacoma, WA: Washington State Historical Society, 1990).

Sondheim, Stephen and Weidman, John, *Pacific Overtures: A Musical* (New York: RCA Records, 1976).

Spence, Jonathan D., *The Search for Modern China* (W.W. Norton & Company, 1990).

Stanley, Peter W., ed., *Reappraising an Empire: New Perspectives on Philippine–American History*, Harvard Studies in American–East Asian Relations 10 (Cambridge, MA: Harvard University Press, 1984).

Stanton, William, *The Great United States Exploring Expedition of 1838–1842* (Berkeley and Los Angeles: University of California Press, 1975).

Starbuck, Alexander, *History of the American Whale Fishery from Its Earliest Inception to the Year 1876* (Waltham, MA: the author, 1878); reprinted in two volumes (New York: Argosy-Antiquarian, 1964).

Starr, S. Frederick, ed., *Russia's American Colony* (Durham, NC: Duke University Press, 1987).

Statler, Oliver, *Shimoda Story* (Rutland, VT and Tokyo: Charles S. Tuttle, 1969).

Stevens, Sylvester K., *American Expansion in Hawaii, 1842–1898* (Harrisburg, PA: Archives Publishing, 1945).

Stevenson, Robert Louis, *A Footnote to History: Eight Years of Trouble in Samoa* (New York: Charles S. Scribner's Sons, 1892).

Tansill, Charles Callan, *The Foreign Policy of Thomas F. Bayard, 1885–1897* (New York: Fordham University Press, 1940).

Thompson, Arthur W. and Hart, Robert A., *The Uncertain Crusade: America and the Russian Revolution of 1905* (Amherst, MA: University of Massachusetts Press, 1970).

Thomson, James C. jr, Stanley, Peter W. and Perry, John Curtis, *Sentimental Imperialists: The American Experience in East Asia* (New York: Harper & Row, 1981).

Tin-Yuke, Char, comp. and ed., *The Sandalwood Mountains: Readings and Stories of the Early Chinese in Hawaii* (Honolulu, HI: University Press of Hawaii, 1975).

Unterberger, Betty Miller, *America's Siberian Expedition, 1918–1920: A Study of National Policy* (Durham, NC: Duke University Press, 1956).

Van Meter, Robert H. jr, 'The Washington Conference of 1921–1922: A New Look', *Pacific Historical Review* 46 (1977), pp. 603–624.

Varg, Paul A., *Missionaries, Chinese, and Diplomats: The American Protestant Missionary Movement in China, 1890–1952* (Princeton, NJ: Princeton University Press, 1958).

Varley, H. Paul, *Japanese Culture: A Short History*, expanded edn (New York: Praeger Publishers, 1973).

Walworth, Arthur J., *Black Ships Off Japan: The Story of Commodore Perry's Expedition* (New York: Alfred A. Knopf, Inc., 1946).

Walworth, Arthur J., *Wilson and His Peacemakers: American Diplomacy at the Paris Peace Conference, 1919* (New York: W.W. Norton & Company, 1986).

Webb, Melody, *The Last Frontier* (Albuquerque, NM: University of New Mexico Press, 1985).

Wei, Betty Peh-T'i, *Shanghai: Crucible of Modern China* (Hong Kong: Oxford University Press, 1987).

Wei, Deborah and Kamel, Rachel, eds, *Resistance in Paradise: Rethinking 100 years of U.S. Involvement in the Caribbean and the Pacific* (Philadelphia, PA: American Friends Service Committee and Office of Curriculum Support, School District of Philadelphia, 1998).

White, John Albert, *The Siberian Intervention* (New York: Greenwood Press, 1969); first published by Princeton University Press, 1950.

Williams, William Appleman, *Tragedy of American Diplomacy*, new edn (New York: W.W. Norton & Company, 1988).

Wilson, Rob, *Reimagining the American Pacific: From South Pacific to Bamboo Ridge and Beyond* (Durham, NC: Duke University Press, 2000).

Young, Marilyn Blatt, *The Rhetoric of Empire: American China Policy, 1895–1901* (Cambridge, MA: Harvard University Press, 1968).

Zabriskie, Edward H., *American–Russian Rivalry in the Far East, 1895–1914: A Study in Diplomacy and Power Politics* (Philadelphia, PA: University of Pennsylvania Press, 1946).

1

The English Background of American Isolationism in the Eighteenth Century

Felix Gilbert

When the colonists began their opposition to the en-
croachments of the British government, the legal justification
of their resistance was their conception of the rights of Englishmen. Before the War of Independence Americans had
lived in the intellectual and cultural atmosphere of England;
they were the proud heirs of the great English tradition of
freedom, handed on in an unbroken succession from the days
of Magna Carta; they had taken from English political experience the principle of "no taxation without representation".
When drafting their new Constitution, they intended merely
to improve the old English version by divesting it of those
features which had made possible the lapse of the British
government into despotism.

This English tradition formed no contrast to the spirit of
Enlightenment philosophy which dominated all Europe and
also the minds of the colonists in the eighteenth century.
Europe's enlightened "philosophes" took Montesquieu and
Blackstone as their teachers and thereby accepted the British
constitution as the ideal constitution per se or they admitted
at least that it contained the basic principles of an ideal political organization. The English tradition could easily be fused,
therefore, with those general ideas about the nature of man
and about the "Rights of Man" which eighteenth century philosophy had developed. Beneath the philosophical and gener-
alizing language of the Enlightenment in which the constitutions of the new world were couched the English tradition
remained clearly perceptible.

Similarly, the roots of the guiding principles of early
American foreign policy exhibit the English influence. A pub-
lic discussion of foreign affairs formed an intrinsic element of
English political life in the eighteenth century. Certainly
England was not ruled by the will of the people or by public
opinion in the eighteenth century; political power rested sol-

---

*This essay is an adaptation of part of an extended study by Dr. Gilbert
on the European background of American foreign policy, which will be published in the near future.

Dr. Gilbert has been a member of the Institute for Advanced Study,
Princeton, New Jersey, since 1939. He is a Ph.D. of the University of
Berlin, and was formerly assistant to the editors of the German diplomatic
documents on the origins of the war of 1914. A student of political ideas
and international affairs, he was co-editor with E. M. Earle and Gordon
Craig of *Makers of Modern Strategy,* (Princeton, 1943).

idly in the hands of a small clique of Whig aristocrats. But whereas on the European continent absolutism stifled public political discussion, and foreign affairs especially were considered as an arcanum—managed and understood by the monarch and a few nobles alone; in England the Whigs, as the heirs and beneficiaries of the "Glorious Revolution" and bound to its traditions, had an interest in airing political issues in Parliament and in gaining the support of public opinion. Debates in Parliament were secret then; but speeches of parliamentary leaders were frequently published anonymously, and all political problems of significance were extensively discussed in numerous pamphlets. Thus throughout the years from the Peace of Utrecht to the American Revolution a steady trickle of pamphlets concerned with the issues of British foreign policy appeared and developed into a spate in times of war and political crisis.

Thus English political life certainly could provide patterns of thought from which the colonists could draw their lessons in forming their system of foreign policy. It is difficult, however, to determine the precise nature of the influence exerted by this English discussion on the ideas of the colonists concerning foreign affairs. The English discussion on foreign affairs showed no consensus of opinion; on the contrary, divergent and contradictory counsels were given for the conduct of British diplomacy. This lack of clarity may be explained by the fact that the period between the Peace of Utrecht and the Seven Years War was one of profound change: England left the steady course which she had pursued previous to the eighteenth century, and embarked on new waters. The practical tasks which confronted British diplomacy in the eighteenth century must be clearly grasped in order to understand the issues which stimulated the English public debate on foreign affairs and the lessons which it could teach the colonists.

During the eighteenth century, the European state system underwent a complete transformation in accordance with which England's role in European power politics changed decisively.[1] Since the beginning of the sixteenth century, when the contest for the possession of Italy had covered Europe with a network of antagonisms and alliances, European di-

---

[1] Recent works of fundamental importance, covering the English history of the period, are Basil Williams, *The Whig Supremacy 1714-1760* (Oxford 1939) and W. L. Dorn, *Competition for Empire 1740-1763* (New York 1940); Dorn's and Williams' work contain extensive bibliographical guides; A. M. Wilson, *French Foreign Policy . . . of Cardinal Fleury 1726-43* (Cambridge 1936) also has an excellent bibliography.

plomacy had been dominated by the rivalry of two great dynasties, the houses Bourbon and Hapsburg. The center of action had been mainly in central and southern Europe. England had been more a spectator than a participant in this conflict; she was interested only in the prevention of the danger which the continental supremacy of one power and the establishment of a universal monarchy might present to her security and independence. The war of the Spanish succession was the last great struggle between the houses of Bourbon and Hapsburg. Then Louis XIV's bid for European hegemony had been checked by the Great Coalition, led by Austria and England. After this war a new situation arose. The statesmen, influenced by the doctrines of mercantilism, which stressed the importance of economic centralization and foreign trade, became increasingly aware of the connection between economic and political power. Economic advantages became the openly acknowledged motive of political struggles between nations. The influence of commercial and colonial interests made itself increasingly felt in diplomatic decisions. International conflicts no longer grew out of struggles for territorial expansion and continental hegemony but out of the desire for trading privileges and colonial possessions. Consequently the political center of gravity shifted from southern and central Europe to the Atlantic seaboard, and the importance of England in the European state system was enhanced. The significance of the Franco-Austrian hostility paled in comparison with the importance of the Anglo-French "competition for empire". The leadership in the fight against France devolved upon England.

Other events accentuated the emergence of a new political constellation. Austria, excluded from direct access to the ocean and to the new sources of wealth, tried to replace this relative loss of strength by embarking on a new policy; she turned to the southeast, building an empire in the Danube valley and in the Balkans, and was drawn into the new orbit of Eastern European politics. It is the century of the appearance of Russia in the politics of Europe and of the rise of Prussia which, by its territorial expansion, bridged the formerly separated eastern and western half of Europe. Europe began to be formed into a connected whole; the foundations were laid of a concert of European power, extending from Petersburg to London and Madrid.

The gradual disappearance of the continental conflicts between France and Austria, the vehemence of the Anglo-French colonial rivalry, and the incorporation of Russia and Prussia into the European system were events that made the eighteenth century a landmark in the history of European diplomacy. It was the great achievement of the elder Pitt that he perceived this rise of a new political constellation in Europe and firmly adapted England's foreign policy to the new situation. He saw that the old Anglo-French rivalry had changed its objects. In planning the course of English foreign policy, he placed commercial and colonial aims above all others. Oceans and colonies needed to be the main scene of action. England's relations to the European continent became of secondary importance and had to be subordinated to these new aims. The main task of British continental diplomacy was to restrict France to the Continent and to keep her from employing her forces overseas. With Austria gradually losing interest in western Europe, Prussia was to take Austria's place as England's ally in checking France.

Thus, at the beginning of the Seven Years War, Pitt reorganized English foreign policy in accordance with the new economic interests and political alginments. Yet before this decisive and lasting turn in British history was reached, statesmen and public alike, dimly aware of the changing conditions, groped in search of a popular foreign policy. One indication of the prevailing uncertainty is to be found in the frequent shifting of alliances and sudden diplomatic revolutions. Zigzag diplomacy was characteristic of the first three decades of the eighteenth century. England entered this period in alliance with Austria; in 1717 she moved over to the side of France, but in 1730 she returned to the Austrian entente after she had gone through a series of negotiations, treaties, and alliances with nearly all the European powers.

Significantly, the attitude towards foreign policy of the two parties contesting for power in England also underwent a revolution. In the seventeenth century, the Whigs and Tories had been the representatives of opposite systems not only in regard to domestic affairs but also in regard to foreign policy. As King George I once said[2], the "old Tory notion" which had developed during the seventeenth century was "that England can subsist by itself, whatever becomes of the rest of Europe"; and he added that this notion had been "justly exploded by the Whigs ever since the revolution". The Whigs represented the opposite point of view, claiming that England's safety was dependent on the maintenance of a balance of power on the European continent. England, therefore, should take an active interest in the diplomatic movements of the continent.

---

[2] Townshend Manuscripts, *Historical Manuscripts Commission Eleventh Report*, Appendix, pt. IV (London 1887), p. 103.

Yet just when, after the accession of the Hanoverian dynasty, the Whigs had come to power, the foundations of European diplomacy began to shift, and the Whigs themselves became doubtful of the wisdom of rigid adherence to their old principles. They split into various groups, recommending various courses of action. The differences of opinion which once had formed the dividing line between Whigs and Tories now became sources of discord within the Whig party itself. It was said of Robert Walpole, the first Whig Prime Minister, that he adopted the foreign policy of the Tories for the Whig party. He proclaimed: "My politics are to keep free from all engagements as long as we possibly can,"[3] and once he emphasized in the House of Commons: "This nation is a trading nation and the prosperity of the trade is what ought to be principally in the eyes of every gentleman of the House".[4] His main goal, therefore, was the preservation of peace, because peace was the presupposition of a flourishing trade. Walpole always used England's influence on the continent to remove possible causes of friction and to compose conflicts. He saw the foremost interest of British foreign policy "not in the maintenance of the balance of power, but in the tranquility of Europe,"[5] and thereby he clearly deviated from the traditional "meddling" policy of the Whigs. In contrast to Walpole, his successor, Carteret, who guided English foreign policy in the war of the Pragmatic Sanction, returned to the "old system"[6] of the Whigs. He considered it his task to "jumble" the heads of princes, to depose kings and establish emperors. Under the pretense of the maintenance of the "balance of power," he gave free rein to his inclination to pile up alliances and accumulate treaties. It was the great realist Pitt who ended this wavering between divergent lines of policy and placed English foreign policy on a new basis. He united the opposing systems, taking from each what seemed useful. He acknowledged England's interest in the affairs of the continent, but he subordinated it to the strengthening of England as a maritime and trading power.

This fluid diplomatic situation formed the background for the arguments of the pamphleteers who were discussing the issues of foreign policy.[7] The battle of the pamphlets started along the

---

[3] Walpole to Townshend 1723, quoted in Coxe, *Memoirs of the Life and Administration of Sir Robert Walpole* (edition of 1816), II, 408.

[4] House of Commons, Debate of March 8, 1739.

[5] Bathurst in House of Lords, February 13, 1741.

[6] Cf. R. Lodge, "English neutrality in the War of Polish succession," *Transactions of the Royal Historical Society*, Fourth Series, XIV (1931), 143.

[7] As far as I can see, the pamphlet literature of the period has never been systematically analyzed. W. T. Laprade's *Public Opinion and Politics*

ENGLISH BACKGROUND OF AMERICAN ISOLATIONISM   143

traditional lines of the seventeenth century struggle between Whigs and Tories. There were those who stood for England's interest in the preservation of the balance of power, and there were others who emphasized the advantages of England's insular position, characterizing the attitude of their opponents as "Quixotism" and an attempt to "revive the Ages of Knight Errantry."[8]

In the course of the eighteenth century, however, the fundamental controversy—"interest in maintenance of balance of power on the continent" versus the advantages of insular position—was enriched through the introduction of economic and constitutional considerations. It was said by those who stressed England's indifference to the affairs of the continent that trade was England's main interest and that trade flourished best in peace. "A trading nation should avoid war if possible."[9] Constitutional considerations were brought into the discussion as a result of the accession of the Hanoverian dynasty to the English throne. Was the participation in the strifes of Europe really beneficial to the English people or did it serve merely the interest of the Hanoverian dynasty and enhance the glory of its continental dominion? The Act of Settlement had explicitly established the provision that "in case the Crown and Imperial dignity of the Realm shall thereafter come to any person not being a native of this Kingdom of England, this nation shall not be obliged to engage in any war for the defense of any dominions or territories, which do not belong to the crown of England, without the consent of Parliament." The desire to demonstrate to the crown the limits of its influence and to prevent any undue extension of its power stimulated the discussion of this question.

Nearly all contributions to the public discussion on foreign affairs can be reduced to one of these arguments or to a combina-

---

in Eighteenth Century England deals only with the first quarter of the century and is merely a factual reproduction of the content of newspapers and magazines. A. M. Wilson's book on Foreign Policy . . . of Cardinal Fleury discusses a few single pamphlets of special importance. B. Williams's (on p. 67) and B. Turnstall's (on p. 282) Pitt biographies refer to the effect of Mauduit's "Considerations"; R. Pares's article, "American versus Continental Warfare 1739-63", English Historical Review, LI (1936), 429-465 is of fundamental importance. It covers the military aspects of the public controversy comprehensively and brilliantly.

My analysis of the battle of the pamphlets is based on a collection of English pamphlets in the Cornell University Library; this collection was brought together by an Englishman, James Hustler of Acklam, at the beginning of the last century and was bought for Cornell when his library was dissolved. In addition, I used pamphlets of the New York Public Library and of the Huntington Library in San Marino.

[8] Considerations offered upon the approaching peace . . . . , London 1720.

[9] The Treaty of Seville, and the measures that have been taken for the last four years, impartially considered, 1730.

tion of them. Bolingbroke's "Patriot King,"[10] a comprehensive political program which contained a systemtic survey of the guiding principles of English foreign policy, neatly balanced and summarized all these arguments: "Great Britain is an island, and, while nations on the continent are at immense charge in maintaining their barriers, and perpetually on their guard, and frequently embroiled, to extend or strengthen them, Great Britain may, if her governors please, accumulate wealth in maintaining hers; make herself secure from invasions, and be ready to invade others where her own immediate interest, or the general interest of Europe requires it . . . I said the general interest of Europe; because it seems to me that this, alone, should call our commerce off from an almost entire application to their domestic and proper business . . . as we cannot be easily nor suddenly attacked, and as we ought not to aim at any acquisition of territory on the continent, it may be our interest to watch the secret workings of the several councils abroad; to advise and warn; to abet and oppose; but it never can be our true interest easily and officiously to enter into action, much less into engagements that imply action and expense. Other nations, like the *velites* or light-armed troops, stand foremost in the field, and skirmish perpetually. When a great war begins, we ought to look on the powers of the continent, to whom we incline, like the two first lines, the *principes* and *hastati* of the Roman army; and on ourselves like the *triarii*, that are not to charge with these legions on every occasion, but to be ready for the conflict whenever the fortune of the day, be it sooner or later, calls us to it, and the sum of things, or the general interest, makes it necessary. This is the post of advantage and honour, which our singular situation among the powers of Europe determines us, or should determine us to take, in all disputes that happen on the continent . . . by a continual attention to improve her natural, that is her maritime strength, by collecting all her forces within herself, and reserving them to be laid out on great occasions, such as regard her immediate interests and her honour, or such as are truly important to the general system of power in Europe; she may be the arbitrater of differences, the guardian of liberty, and the preserver of that balance, which has been so much talked of, and is so little understood . . . ."

Although the debate of the pamphleteers on English foreign policy revolved around a few identical fundamental arguments, it developed in different stages, clearly distinguishable from each other. In the first half of the century the discussion is entirely dominated by the Hanoverian argument. The popular preoccupa-

___

[10] Bolingbroke, *Works*, IV, 310-312.

tion with this question, whether or not the Hanoverian continental commitments deflected English foreign policy from the proper course, may be deduced from the outspoken titles of some of the pamphlets which asked: Was "the interest of Great Britain steadily pursued," or was "the interest of Hanover steadily pursued"?[11] This controversy became particularly heated when, after Walpole's fall, Carteret imposed on England an extremely active role in the war of the Pragmatic Sanction. Pitt, then still a young man, and lacking the balanced judgment on foreign affairs which he achieved in later years, spoke bitter words in the House of Commons:[12] "This great, this powerful, this formidable king dom, is considered only as a province to a despicable electorate," words that were echoed frequently in the pamphlets of the period. The most trenchant formulation can be found in a pamphlet ascribed to Chesterfield:[13] "The whole strength of the British empire was to be steer'd by the Hanover rudder." Chesterfield, who had had a rich diplomatic experience, was convinced that Carteret, with his numerous treaties of subsidies and alliances, had exceeded the limits of a sound British foreign policy; yet he did not take the extreme stand that England had no interest in the continent at all or that the balance of power was a mere chimera. He tried to devise a definitive rule for England's relation with the continent. "We might lay it down as an invariable Maxim, never to enter into a Land-War, never, but when the Dutch Barrier was in Danger."

A few strategically minded pamphleteers looked upon the problem from a more comprehensive point of view. They asked:[14] "Whether it might be more conducive to the true interest of this nation to rely wholly upon that situation which disjoins it from the rest of the world, to encrease its naval force, and to give its great application to the marine without concerning itself with the intrigues of the neighbouring states; or once more to cover Flanders with our troops, to negotiate, to fight, and to expend our treasure, in restraining the overgrown power of France, and in preserving the balance of Europe?"

On the whole, however, the public preferred to look at the alternatives of British diplomacy from a simple but more in-

---

[11] *The Interest of Great Britain steadily pursued, in answer to a pamphlet entitled The Case of the Hanover Forces*, London 1743. H. Walpole is considered to be the author of this pamphlet. It was answered by a pamphlet ascribed to Chesterfield: *The Interest of Hanover Steadily Pursued*, London, 1743.

[12] December 10, 1742.

[13] *The case of the Hanover forces in the pay of Great Britain impartially and freely examined* . . . . London 1743.

[14] *The Interest of Hanover steadily pursued* . . . . London 1743.

triguing angle—the question whether their foreign policy
served the British people or the Hanoverian dynasty.

The basis of the discussion shifted when, in the fifties,
England became again a participant in a great European war.
It was an entirely changed situation, in which the debate on
foreign affairs was then renewed. One pamphleteer states
frankly[15] that he has been "no friend to Continental Measures
in general" and that he was especially opposed to "such continental measures as engaged us during the three last Wars,
as Principals," but the continental measures now adopted are
"necessary both with regard to our Honour and Our Interest."

Now no one dared to charge Pitt, who steered England
through the Seven Years War, with un-English and Hanoverian sympathies. Factions and constitutional bickering had
disappeared from the debate, and the discussion centered much
more objectively around the true alternatives of British foreign policy. A pamphleteer,[16] at the beginning of the war
point by point enumerated the arguments which could be
made in favour of the alternative propositions. He explained
first the reasons why England should keep aloof from the continent: "(1) Great Britain, being an Island, is secure from an
Invasion, and having no designs of making conquests, and no
interests of her own to pursue on the continent, has no need of
foreign Assistance. (2) The strength of Great Britain lies in
her Fleets: these should be her principal, her only care. And
if we carry on the War wholly by Sea, and have nothing to do
with the Continent, we shall have everything to hope and
nothing to fear." Similarly, he listed the arguments in favour
of England's intervention in the affairs of the continent.

This pamphlet showed the widened scope of the controversy. The purposes as well as the means of English foreign
policy were scrutinized. Did England's interest lie mainly on
the continent or mainly in colonial expansion; was it possible
to limit military efforts to naval warfare, or was it necessary
to enter the continental battlefields with a standing army?

As long as the French were contesting the English expansion over the American continent, Pitt, without much obstruction by the clamorous, yet unconvincing and inefficient
opposition, could pursue his dual policy of colonial aggrandizement on the one hand and of the Prussian alliance on the
other. Yet the opposition had a much better case when, after

---

[15] *The Important Question discussed, or a serious and impartial Enquiry into the Interest of England with regard to the Continent.*
[16] *The Important Question concerning Invasions, a Sea War, Raising
the Militia and paying Subsidies for foreign Troops,* London 1755.

the defeat of the French in Canada, Pitt stuck to the Prussian alliance and a continuation of the war.[17] At this moment the most famous of all English pamphlets of the eighteenth century appeared: Mauduit's "Considerations on the present German War." It has been said of this pamphlet that it caused Pitt's downfall. Its amazing success was due no less to the brilliancy of its reasoning than to its timeliness.

Mauduit did more than marshal the outworn arguments; he tried to discover the reality behind the concepts used in the controversy; his pamphlet culminated in an analysis of the term "continental connections." He showed that this term had a different meaning when applied to the war of the Spanish Succession than when used to describe England's policy towards the continent in his own time. In the war of the Spanish Succession, the whole continent had been united against France. England had been only one member of a large coalition; in his time, England was allied only to a few secondary powers like Prussia, Hanover, and Brunswick.

.   The present alliances served much more limited objectives than the participation in the Great Coalition. No longer did issues like the freedom of Protestantism or the prevention of a Universal Monarchy necessitate England's interference in continental politics. Even subsidies were no longer necessary; on the contrary they were even detrimental to the English interests, for they kept alive disunity among the German states. Without British interference one power would get the upper hand in Germany and establish unity. A united Germany would form then a perfect counterweight against France. Thus, if England stayed out of the continent, she could ultimately benefit by the creation of a balance of power, the perennial panacea of British diplomacy. There was a mixture of falsehood and truth in Mauduit's reasoning. In his time, a united Germany was an Utopia; he also failed to see that even a disunited Germany neutralized an important part of the French forces. But he judged correctly when assuming that the aims of the British and their allies in the War of the Spanish Succession were fundamentally different from those which Pitt pursued when he allied England with Prussia in the Seven Years War. None had shown more convincingly than Mauduit that continental connections did not always have a beneficial effect on the strength of the English position.

This battle of the pamphleteers about the English continental interests and the advantages of an insular position was, in a sense, a continuation of the old Whig and Tory strife

---

[17] *A Letter addressed to two great men* . . . . London 1760.

over foreign policy, despite the many new elements which entered the discussion in the course of the eighteenth century. Yet the discussion of the eighteenth century made the English public for the first time fully aware of the implications of the old Tory position, which recommended seclusion from continental quarrels, and thus this whole idea seemed quite new to them. As one of the pamphlets[18] said, the idea of keeping away from continental wars "never entered into any Man's Heart till of late years." What, asked the Dutch diplomat, Count Bentinck, with astonishment, in 1745,[19] would the English statesmen of the last century, should they be alive, think, "if they had heard an English nobleman say that it signify as little who is Emperor, as who is Lord Mayor of London?"

In his letters to the Netherlands, Bentinck also mentions that he had heard in London drawing rooms a new term used to characterize this policy of keeping away from the continent: "des principes isolés." The great popularity of this view in eighteenth century England was well known also on the continent. A French handbook on European politics explicitly referred to the new English trend "a rompre ce qu'elle appelle Continental connections, ou liaisons avec le continent."[20] As we have seen, in this controversy over the issue of "continental connections" the alternatives had been a colonial and maritime expansion or a European policy with continental wars. Yet there was even a third group; they were thorough pacifists who declared that the insular position of England made a complete abandonment of all power politics entirely possible. Their motto could be found in a pamphlet[21] ascribed to Lord Hervey: "From a warlike Genius, and an Enterprizing Minister, Good Lord deliver us." England was in no need of bellicose statesmanship; for[22] "Nature has separated us from the continent . . . and as no man ought to endeavour to separate whom God Almighty has joined, so no man ought to endeavour to join what God Almighty has separated." This group claimed that its view served the trading interests better than any other. Some of these pamphleteers willingly ad-

[18] *The Important Questions concerning Invasions,* London 1755.

[19] *Briefwisseling en Aantee Keningen von William Bentinck, Heer von Rhoon* . . . . uitgegeren door C. Gerretson en F. Geyl: Deel I (Utrecht 1934); Letters to the Countess of Portland, August 10 and September 7, 1745, p. 131 and 139.

[20] Peysonnel, *Situation Politique de la France et ses Rapports Actuels avec toutes les Puissances de l'Europe,* (Neuchatel 1789) p. 71.

[21] *Miscellaneous Thoughts on the present Posture of our foreign and domestic Affairs,* London 1742.

[22] The Earl of Pomfret in the House of Lords, December 10, 1755.

mitted that England had a strong interest in intercourse with other powers because of her commerce:[23] "Treaties of commerce are Bonds that we ought to contract with our neighbours," yet as to the nature of such bonds the same author stated that "a trading nation ought not to concern itself with particular nations, or Schemes of Government in distant countries ... her interest requires that she should live if possible in constant Harmony with all Nations, that she may better enjoy the Effects of their friendship in the benefits resulting from their Commerce." Another writer[24] assumed that Britain could be sure of being left in peace because of other nations' interest in continuing trade with Britain. Still another pamphleteer[25] stated that all treaties of Great Britain with the various powers of Europe "have not produced any advantage to us." Therefore he drew up a general rule: "A Prince or State ought to avoid all Treaties, except such as tend towards promoting Commerce or Manufactures . . . All other Alliances may be looked upon as Encumbrances." The pamphlets of this pacifist group represented the most radical position in the discussion on the aims and means of English foreign policy during the eighteenth century.

Although it may lie somewhat outside the range of this study, it seems impossible to leave the discussion of the "battle of pamphlets" without touching upon the question as to their practical impact and influence on the conduct of English foreign policy. Probably the mighty Whig families were not swayed one way or another by the arguments of the scribblers. Reared on their country estates and drawing their strength from their ruling position in their counties, with the self-assurance of a class traditionally accustomed to wield power, they relied more on their instinct than on technical knowledge, more on an imperturbable confidence in their ability to handle emergencies as they arose than on any capacity to prevent them by foresight. Yet they had come to power as the protagonists of Parliament and people against the crown, and, even under the Hanoverian dynasty which they themselves had established, the contest between crown and parliament was a living issue. Thus they needed to keep contact with public opinion and to make sure of its continued support. The special emphasis on the dangers of the Hanoverian influence in

---

[23] *A modest Enquiry into the Present State of Foreign Affairs,* London 1742.

[24] *A detection of the Views of those who would, in the present crisis, engage an incumber'd Trading Nation, as Principals, in a ruinous expensive Land-War,* London 1746.

[25] *Political Maxims,* by Phil. Anglus. London 1744.

English foreign policy might be partly explained by the particular effectiveness of this argument in arousing the distrust of the public against the court. The stress on the trading interests of England may be linked with the special position of the merchants in English political life. They were a small, yet an independent and influential group, which could make its voice heard and, if necessary, turn the scales of a decision at a critical moment. Thus all the concrete issues of eighteenth century England's domestic and foreign policy are involved in this debate on the corollaries of England's peculiar geographical situation, her special interests in trade, and the question whether it was possible to keep England free from "continental connections."

Bostonians subscribing to the austere *News Letter* or the equally bleak *Evening Post,* the more fortunate Philadelphians enjoying the lighter and more entertaining fare of Franklin's *Pennsylvania Gazette,* the Virginians with their *Virginia Gazette* of Williamsburg, or Charlestonians imbibing the refinements of Southern civilization by reading the highly literary *South Carolina Gazette*—all found foreign news predominating in their newspapers.[26] The newspapers reported not so much the events of their own town or region or news from other colonies, as the "latest intelligences" from distant Europe. When the dispatches from Europe were late, publication of the papers was sometimes deferred until the arrival of the next boat. European news not only dealt with events in the mother country, with parliament and court, but also with affairs from Warsaw and Madrid, from Paris and Vienna. Editors kept a continuous record of European events, sometimes even withholding more recent news from publication in favor of older dispatches that had been delayed. In short, the colonists did not lack factual knowledge of the political situation in Europe.

However, the information that a reader could glean from his newspaper was limited. Newspapers were licensed by the government and were in constant danger of suppression in case of undue criticism; editorial comment was hardly known. Were the colonists able to penetrate beyond factual statements? Were they informed about the preceding deliberations and discussions? More specifically, was the debate then taking place in England on foreign policy, and its issues known to the colonists?

One way of learning about the English trends of thought was a sojourn in England. During the critical period of the Seven

---

[26] Cf. F. L. Mott, *American Journalism* (New York 1941), particularly pp. 48-49.

Years War, Franklin stayed in England and participated in the debate on the question of continuing the war after the French defeat in Canada.   In two pamphlets he revealed himself as a follower of Pitt.   His main purpose was to call attention to the great value of Canada in order to prevent the exchange of Canada for Guadeloupe.[27]   At the same time, however, he attacked those pamphleteers who demanded immediate peace.   Notes which he jotted down some years later[28] show that he had become well acquainted with the arguments of the debate.   He spoke disparagingly of the "whims about the balance of power," of the "English European quarrels" and of the "continual connexions in which [the colonies] are separately unconcerned."   Franklin was, of course, an unusually acute observer and no other American had a better opportunity to gain intimate knowledge of the English political scene than he; but lesser men with lesser opportunities often brought home considerable knowledge of the questions that were agitating Parliament and the coffee houses.   Indeed, the number of those who had been educated in the mother country or who had visited it and therefore had some contact with English politics should not be underestimated.

Certainly the intellectual life of the colonies was not cut off from English thought.   Important intellectual developments and productions of England had their repercussions in the colonies. John Adams's *Autobiography* reveals the impression which the reading of Bolingbroke made on him.[29]   From this source we learn —not without amusement in view of Adams's future revolutionary career—the great satisfaction he felt with George III's first speech to Parliament which proved him worthy of the title of a "Patriot King."[30]   Bolingbroke's views on English foreign policy, therefore, were known to Adams.

The fame of Israel Mauduit's "Considerations on the present German War" had also spread across the ocean.   Jasper Mauduit, the brother of Israel, seems to have owed his election as Agent of Massachusetts to the fact that he was mistaken for this famous kinsman.   Even more important in informing the colonies of the main issues of the English debate on foreign affairs was the *Political Disquisitions,* by James Burgh.   This book was regarded

---

[27] *The Interest of Great Britain Considered with Regard to her Colonies and the Acquisitions of Canada and Guadeloupe;* also *Of the Means of Disposing the Enemie to Peace,* cf. C. vanDoren, *Benjamin Franklin* (New York 1941), pp. 288 *et seq.*

[28] B. Franklin, *Works,* ed. Bigelow, IV, 308 *et seq.*

[29] J. Adams to James Burgh, December 28, 1774, *Works,* IX, 351.

[30] J. Adams, *Works,* II, 141.

as the "bible" of the Whigs.[31] Burgh emphasized that the people were the "fountain of all authority and government." He demanded a more adequate representation of the people in Parliament and attacked the influence of the court and the parliamentary corruption; he also denounced a standing army and spoke in favor of a militia. In short, all tenets of British eighteenth century progressivism were set forth in the book, including a program of foreign policy. Burgh was a pacifist who considered war "the peculiar disgrace of human nature,"[32] and who thought it wiser "to keep clear of quarrels among other states."[33] Since the times of Queen Anne, England unfortunately had "attached herself to continental schemes."[34] There was no reason "to intangle ourselves with the disputes between the powers of the continent",[35] "continental connections" had only "ruinous effects."[36]

Small wonder that Burgh's ideas found an enthusiastic reception in the colonies, for his radical Whiggism was the political credo of the American revolutionaries. Moreover, Burgh was a great champion of the American cause; he devoted a special chapter to proving that Parliament had no right to tax the colonies. He was eager to befriend the leaders of the colonies, taking great pride in his intimacy with Franklin[37] and sending his work to John Adams "as a small token of respect for his Patriotic Virtue."[38] Adams reciprocated by promising "to make the Disquisitions more Known and attended to in several parts of America."[39] Adams seems to have been successful. Burgh's book was frequently quoted in newspapers; the list of subscribers to its first American edition in 1775 contained many leading names of the colonists such as Washington, Jefferson, Bowdoin, Hancock, and others. Moreover, there is ample evidence that the *Disquisitions* was carefully read in its entirety by many Americans and achieved for a time at least the position of a minor classic in this country. More than a decade after publication, the authors of Publius's essays on the new Constitution considered Burgh's book one of the few worthy of direct quotation in *The Federalist*.[40] Jefferson, in 1814, included it in a reading list for a friend as one of the half-dozen

---

[31] Cf. the article on Burgh in *The English Dictionary of National Biography*.

[32] Burgh, *Political Disquisitions*, Philadelphia 1775, II, 341.

[33] Burgh, *Ibid.*, III, 288.

[34] Burgh, *Ibid.*, II, 388.

[35] Burgh, *Ibid.*, I, xxii.

[36] Burgh, *Ibid.*, I, xxii.

[37] Burgh, *Ibid.*, II, 276.

[38] Inscription in the dedication copy of Burgh's work in the Adams Library in Boston.

[39] J. Adams to James Burgh, December 28, 1774, *Works*, IX, 351.

[40] *Federalist* 58.

books essential to an understanding of "Modern Politics" and rated it as comparable to Locke, Sidney, Montesquieu, Priestley and *The Federalist*.[41] The popularity of Burgh's book in the colonies is an indication that at least the fundamental outlines of the debate on the advantages and disadvantages of "continental connections" were known in America at the time of the first Continental Congress.

It is unnecessary to scrutinize still further the exact channels through which the colonists became acquainted with the British controversy over foreign policy. For by one stroke the English controversy on foreign policy and continental connections was transferred to the colonies, on the eve of independence, by Thomas Paine in his famous pamphlet *Common Sense*.

At first glance, it may seem surprising to connect Paine's words with the political controversy which had developed in England, for they seem the hurried product of an emergency situation, peculiar to the colonies, written to press a few timely political demands like that of declaring independence. A closer study, however, will show that these practical political recommendations form only a part of a very skillfully organized whole. The pamphlet contains two parts. In the first section, a few general considerations on the difference between society and government and on the purposes of government led Paine to a thesis which in the age of Montesquieu and Blackstone must have sounded extremely revolutionary. He maintained that the English constitution was not perfect, that on the contrary, it was a most unsatisfactory instrument of government. In justification of this unusual statement he argued that a "simple thing" is better than a "complex thing"[42]; the mixed nature of the English constitution with its monarchial, aristocratic and republican elements, and its complicated system of checks and balances was proof of its imperfection. He implemented this criticism by a detailed discussion of the faults of any monarchial constitution and the first section ended with the statement that monarchy can never be an ideal system of government. This first part was mainly critical in character, yet through this negative attitude it reveals what Paine considered the ideal form of government to be—a republic, in which all power emanates from the people.

In the second part, Paine plunged rather suddenly into the discussion of the "state of American affairs"[43] and advised a constructive program for a policy of the new world. Yet there is a

---

[41] H. S. Randall, *Life of Thomas Jefferson*, (New York, 1858), I, 55.
[42] *The Life and Works of Thomas Paine*, Patriots' Edition, (New York 1925), II, 102.
[43] "Thoughts on the Present State of American Affairs", Paine, *Ibid.*, p. 122.

significant connection between the first and the second sections: the constructive program of the second part is the logical sequence of Paine's criticism of the European monarchies in the first part. Because the English constitution was faulty, and because Europe was unable to achieve a perfect constitution, it was the duty of America to break with Europe, to make use of her unique opportunities, and to realize the ideal republic. Paine proclaimed that now the propitious moment for the separation from the old world had come, that America had all the means necessary to achieve independence. Just because Europe had failed it was America's responsibility to fulfill her own political tasks. This grandiose plea culminated in the brief outline of the future constitution of America.

If we analyze the various threads out of which the fabric of *Common Sense* is woven, the fibre of American political and social conditions seems to predominate. Unquestionably, Paine tried to enliven his work with local coloring. He illustrated the danger of being tied to England's "rotten constitution" by a reference to the severe moral customs of New England according to which "a man who is attached to a prostitute is unfitted to choose or judge a wife."[44] The familiar theme in eighteenth century political literature of the emergence of society and government from the state of nature reads like a new story as told by Paine in the light of American frontier conditions. When, in describing the origins of government, he wrote about the "convenient tree under the branches of which the whole colony may assemble to deliberate on public matters"[45] and which will serve as the first state house, we are reminded of the first representative assembly in America convening on wooded Jamestown Island, and of the Pilgrims taking their first steps towards an organization of social life in their new home.

Still more strongly *Common Sense* bears the imprint of the extremely critical situation in Philadelphia during the last months of the year 1775, when Paine was writing his pamphlet.[46] Galloway, Duane, Dickinson, the early leaders of the opposition movement, were beginning to cede their place to the Adamses and the Lees, the radicals from Massachusetts and Virginia. Discord among the leaders of the opposition had been long concealed. Each faction had pursued its own line of action while avoiding all funda-

---

[44] Paine, *Works*, II, 107.

[45] Paine, *Ibid.*, p. 100.

[46] A few remarks on the connection between the program of action of the radicals and Paine's pamphlet can be found in P. Davidson, *Propaganda and the American Revolution 1763-1783* (Chapel Hill, 1941). Otherwise, this question has hardly been discussed.

mental issues such as that of independence which would of necessity have led to a rupture between them. At the end of the summer of 1775, however, circumstances had become such that a continuation of this policy of evasion was no longer possible. The position of the moderates became weakened by the English government's unfavorable reception of the colonists' attempts at reconciliation. The commercial situation made it impossible to postpone any longer definite decisions. After the non-exportation agreement became effective in September 1775, it was clear that this complete suspension of exports could not last beyond the winter. Either the whole measure would have to be abandoned and such a step clearly would have meant the beginning of a capitulation to England—or American ports had to be opened to the ships of other powers, a measure that would have meant a definite break with England, since the claim of the mother country to exclusive trade with its colonies was the cornerstone of the whole colonial-mercantile system of the eighteenth century. In the fall session of the Continental Congress, a most important debate was concerned with the problem of the "opening of the ports." No decision was reached. The moderates did not want to alienate England permanently, and some of the radicals believed that America should try to continue to live on her own resources. Similarly, the issues of naval armament and of confederation remained undecided. In other important respects, however, the radicals gained the upper hand. The Congress vigorously applied itself to the organization of the army. It recommended the adoption of constitutions to the various colonies and established a committee of secret correspondence for the purpose of exploring the attitude of foreign powers. Still, in spite of these measures, the radicals were not satisfied. The letters of John Adams show their disappointment in the failure of their program to find complete acceptance.

This was the state of affairs when Paine composed *Common Sense*. The practical demands of this pamphlet suggest that he knew well what happened behind the closed doors of the Continental Congress. All the arguments of the radicals in the fall and winter of 1775 were summarized in Paine's pamphlet. He spoke disparagingly of continuing petitions to the king, advocated the building of an American navy,[47] urged the immediate formation of a confederation,[48] stressed the importance of foreign assistance and advised opening the ports. The culmination of Paine's treatise, the first public call for independence, was only the logical

---

[47] Paine, *Works,* II, 154 *et seq.*
[48] Paine, *Ibid.,* pp. 144 *et seq.*

corollary of these postulates. It was as though Paine had been asked by the radicals to set their program before the public.

So much for the American background of *Common Sense*. As we have seen, Paine's pamphlet argued that the foundation of an independent America was necessary not only for reasons of political expediency but as the fulfillment of a duty to mankind. The demands for an independent America were embedded in a general social philosophy which can clearly be traced to trends of political thought, which were current in England whence Paine had come to the colonies only twelve months before.[49]

When discoursing on the defects of the monarchies, Paine re-tells a well known biblical story; Samuel announced to the Jews that they had provoked the ire of God by begging for a king, and he forewarned them of the sufferings they would have to bear under a monarchy. This chapter of the Bible is famous in the history of political thought.[50] A stumbling block to the political theorists of the Middle Ages who believed in the monarchy as the ideal form of government, it was popular with all thinkers of republican convictions. Milton used it extensively in his *Defensio pro populo Anglicano;* so too, did Algernon Sidney in his *Discourses on Government*.[51] By alluding to the same story, Paine reveals himself a true follower of the great republican tradition in English political thought.

At the same time, Paine's ideas were intimately related to contemporary English political thought. He seems to have been an attentive reader of Hume's political essays. What Paine states about the origin of government and particularly about the different ways of acquiring monarchies corresponds exactly to Hume's explanations in the essays "Of the original contract" and "Of the origin of government." Furthermore, Paine's distinguishing between republican and monarchial elements in the English constitution and his evaluation of their relative importance are an obvious elaboration of a question which Hume had raised in his essay "Whether the British Government inclines more to absolute monarchy, or to a Republic?"

[49] Despite the many biographies written on Paine, no study on the development of his "mind" has been made, although it is easy to reconstruct the evolving pattern of his ideas.

[50] P. Kirn, "Saul in der Staatslehre," in *Staat und Personlichkeit*, E. Branderburg zum 60. Geburtstag dargebracht (Leipsig 1928), pp. 28-47.

[51] Algernon Sidney, *Discourses on Government*, Vol. II, Chapter III, Section III; "Samuel did not describe to the Israelites the glory of a free Monarchy; but the evils the people should suffer, that he might divert them from desiring a king."

But of all the works which influenced Paine, Priestley's *Essay on the First Principles of Government* was the most important. Their fundamental political ideas were identical; both claimed that the people should enjoy as much liberty as possible and should have complete political power. Priestley had not openly attacked the monarchial system of government, yet he had expressed some doubts about the wisdom of the principle of heredity by saying that "in its original principles" every government was an "equal republic."[52] He had broached the idea on which Paine's criticism of the English constitution was based—that a "simple thing" is better than a "complex thing."[53] This notion was by no means familiar to the eighteenth century. Usually, the eighteenth century conceived life in terms of an artificial mechanism, thus the more complicated machine appeared as the more perfect one. Consequently, involved mechanical concepts such as "balance of power" and "mixed government" were favorite principles of political thought. Yet the greatest similarity between Paine and Priestley is to be found in their descriptions of the emergence of a representative government.[54] Paine's passages are nothing but a paraphrase of Priestley's words; whoever reads the respective sections of the two books side by side will be inclined to assume that Paine wrote *Common Sense* with Priestley's pamphlet on his desk.

The prevalence of the English element in Paine's ideas on constitutional questions makes it seem natural that he also followed English trends of thought in his ideas on foreign policy. The group of Utilitarian philosophers, to which Priestley belonged, whose philosophical and political outlook,[55] Paine shared, had very definite ideas on foreign affairs; they were pacifists and therefore bitter enemies of England's involvement in continental quarrels. An analysis of Paine's

[52] J. Priestley, *An Essay on the First Principles of Government and on the nature of political, civil, and religious liberty.* (London 1771), p. 40.

[53] Priestley, *Ibid.*, p. 19: "The more complex any machine is, and the more nicely it is fitted to answer the purpose, the more liable it is to disorder."

[54] Cf. Priestley, *Ibid.*, pp. 6-7 and Paine, *Life and Works*, pp. 98-101.

[55] The development of radical Whiggism into utilitarianism, in which Paine takes part, needs further elucidation; for instance, there is no satisfactory study on Priestley. The fundamental work remains E. Halévy, *The growth of philosophic Radicalism*, translated by M. Morris (London 1934); L. Whitney, *Primitivism and the Idea of Progress* (Baltimore 1934) is very suggestive, and H. V. S. Ogden's article, "The decline of Lockian Political Theory", *American Historical Review*, XLVI (1940), 21-44 is good in describing the negative side of this development, namely the loss of prestige of the theory of natural rights.

ideas on foreign policy will show that, also in his views on foreign policy, he followed their pattern of thought, and had evidently been much impressed with the arguments directed against England's involvement in continental quarrels.

Since the main purpose of Paine's pamphlets was to point out the advantages of an immediate declaration of independence, it was from this angle that he viewed the question of foreign affairs. He held the opinion that a declaration of independence would procure the immediate assistance of France and Spain, while as long as the bonds between England and the colonies were not formally severed, France and Spain would never dare to help the colonies; they would fear a possible betrayal by a compromise between mother country and colonies, not to mention that their help would be a striking violation of international law. Paine claimed, however, that independence would have advantages lasting far beyond the present emergency.[56] It would secure peace for America: "France and Spain never were, nor perhaps ever will be, our enemies as Americans, but as our being subjects of Great Britain." There is not "a single advantage that this continent can reap by being connected with Great Britain." On the contrary, America's "Plan is commerce, and that, well attended to, will secure us the peace and friendship of all Europe; because it is the interest of all Europe to have America a free port." These arguments were summarized in the famous sentence: "Any submission to or dependence on Great Britain tends directly to involve this continent in European wars and quarrels . . . As Europe is our market for trade, we ought to form no partial connexion with any part of it. It is the true interest of America to steer clear of European contentions."

Thus Paine's program of foreign policy is obvious: he advocated not only separation from England, but renunciation of all political alliances; America should become a free port to serve the commercial interests of all nations. The arguments on which this program was based are America's peculiar geographical position and her trading interest which protected her from attacks, because all states were interested in maintaining trade with America. The similarity of this program to the ideas of the English radicals who had attacked England's "continental connections" and had emphasized the peculiarity of the English geographical situation and her special interests as a trading nation is striking. Paine himself mentions in *Common Sense* the "miseries of Hanover"[57] there-

---

[56] Paine, *Works*, II, 129-131; also p. 126.
[57] Paine, *Ibid.*, p. 126.

by showing that the English parallel was uppermost in his mind. There can be no doubt then that Paine in his program on foreign policy merely applied to America the ideas and concepts of the English controversy on the merits of "continental connections."

It is well known that the success of *Common Sense* was sensational. The propaganda of the radicals quickly made it known all over the country[58]; more than 120,000 copies were reputedly sold in less than three months. Now the movement for independence became a powerful political force. Before the publication of *Common Sense*, hardly anyone had dared to voice "this dreadful, this daring sound"[59] of the word independence; after the success of *Common Sense*, it was continuously discussed in homes and in meetings, in letters and newspapers.

Paine's indubitable merit consisted in that, through him, the thoughts of others came to life; by the brilliancy of his style, they were transformed into a political weapon. Moreover, the most unique and effective feature of *Common Sense* is the fact that it combines the practical with the ideal, political advantage with moral duty. Thus he represented independence "not merely as a striking practical gesture but as the fulfillment of America's moral obligation to the world."[60] The same must be said about Paine's program of foreign policy in general. If Paine's proposals were adopted, foreign trade would flourish, foreign aid would be secured, but more than that: these measures would lead to a better and more peaceful world.

However, the strongest reason for the lasting influence which Paine's ideas on foreign policy exerted was that they filled an absolute gap. Faced by the necessity of a declaration of independence, it became essential to lay out the system of foreign policy which the new republic should follow; but the position of America in the constellation of the political powers of the world had as yet not attracted the attention of the colonists.[61] Thus they turned eagerly to the ideas which just at the moment of need were developed in *Common Sense*, and from now on every utterance on foreign policy seems to start from Paine's words and to echo his thoughts. It is in the brilliant synthesis of *Common Sense* that one must look for the

---

[58] Cf. P. Davidson, *Propaganda and the American Revolution*, p. 215.

[59] Force, *American Archives*, 4th series, III, 1013, "To the people of Pennsylvania, Oct. 11, 1775."

[60] Crane Brinton in his article on Paine in *D. A. B.*, XIV, 159-166.

[61] The approach of the colonists to foreign policy is discussed in the first chapter of my book.

immediate background of both the Federalist Foreign Policy crystallized in Washington's *Farewell Address* and the "republican tack" upon which Jefferson set the ship of state in 1801. And back of Paine's ideas and principles, adapted though they were to the American situation, lay more than fifty years of hot, confused debate as to the correct foreign relations for England to follow in a world in which suddenly the horizons of power policy had shifted and widened.

2
Chinese Export Porcelain in Eighteenth-Century Tidewater Virginia

Julia B. Curtis

Chinese export porcelain constitutes one of the largest groups of artifacts recovered from archeological sites in Southeastern Virginia and is present on nearly all colonial sites so far dug in the James River basin. The artifact, the Chinese exportware shard, or whole vessel with a history of Virginia ownership, is a physical manifestation of numerous facets of eighteenth-century society. Its presence in Virginia is eloquent testimony to a pattern of world trade as intricate as the complex intellectual network of the Enlightenment. The presence of eighteenth-century Chinese porcelain shards at colonial sites in Virginia bespeaks the growing gentility of colonial society, a gentility evinced in the decoration of the colonials' houses and the growing popularity of such social ceremonies as tea and coffee drinking. The increasing use of Chinese porcelain, reflected in contemporary inventories and in Virginia's archeological collections, attests to the growing affluence of Virginians in the eighteenth-century.

The quality of Chinese exportware that came to Virginia is a manifestation of Virginia's status as a British colony and the status of even its wealthiest citizens as provincials. Conversely, however, the types of wares found on Virginia's colonial sites were common to other international markets, such as those of Holland and Sweden. The survival of eighteenth-century inventories, the existence of hundreds of collections of eighteenth-century exportware in Europe and America, and the discovery of Dutch and Swedish wrecks carrying Chinese export porcelain make it possible to analyze the thousands of exportware shards in Eastern Virginia's archeological collections from a socio-economic as well as an art-historical perspective.

The presence of such large quantities of Chinese porcelain in Virginia has amazed both Chinese ceramicists and students of American social history. Its transmigration to colonial Virginia is directly related to the growth of trade between China and Europe and to the craze for oriental trade goods, or "china-mania," which the China trade generated in Europe. The craze specifically for Chinese porcelain arose first in Holland, then, in the late seventeenth century, in England. The Virginians, as provincial citizens of the British Empire, adopted the enthusiasm only after it was firmly established in London.

A number of excellent works describe the origins of the China trade which ignited the European craze for Chinese porcelain,[1] but the specific cause of the "china-mania" that affected colonial Virginia lies in the foundation of the Dutch and English East India companies in the seventeenth century. In 1600, Queen Elizabeth I granted a group of English merchants a charter to trade with the East, and in 1602, the Dutch monarch chartered a similar company. Both companies were founded to supply Holland and England respectively with spices at a profit to the company stockholders. The two companies were often competitors in the same Far Eastern markets and on numerous occasions fought each other for territory. In 1623, for example, the Dutch massacred all the natives and Englishmen at the British factory, or warehouse, at Amboyna in the Moluccas, or Spice Islands. While the principal goods in which the two East India companies traded remained the same for two hundred years, their importance to the trade changed markedly over those two centuries. Until the mid-seventeenth century, spices were the most valuable homebound cargo, but by 1700, Chinese and Indian textiles had displaced spices as the most valuable trade commodities. Although the Dutch began buying teas in bulk from the Chinese in 1637, according to T. Volker, tea and coffee became the most significant areas of growth in the eighteenth-century, by which time spices had become a relatively minor commodity of trade. From 1600 to 1800, porcelain remained a relatively minor commodity when rated by value, although not necessarily by bulk. But whereas the Dutch brought porcelain to Holland in generally ever-increasing quantities throughout the seventeenth century, the British, until the 1680s confined the bulk of their porcelain trade to the area east of the Persian Gulf.[2]

During much of the seventeenth century, England was an economic and cultural backwater, with a relatively small market for any kind of luxury items, including Chinese porcelain. Holland, on the other hand, was enormously rich and had a large middle and upper class living extremely well off the proceeds of the country's world-wide empire of trade. The Dutch were enthralled by Chinese exportware. In 1602, Dutch seamen captured the Portugese carrack, the *San Jago*, with a sizable cargo of porcelain, which was sold at auction in Middleburg. In 1603, the *Santa Catherina*, another Portugese merchantman, was captured and its contents sold in Amsterdam. Never had so much Chinese porcelain reached Northern Europe, and it created an enormous stir, particularly amongst the French and the Dutch. During the first half of the seventeenth century, the Dutch imported Chinese porcelain literally by the ton.[3] Chinese porcelain figured prominently in seventeenth century Dutch still-lifes and inventories.[4] Dutch inventories and current excavations in Amsterdam reveal that the Dutch used Chinese porcelain for eating and drinking as well as for decoration. The Dutch also appear to have brought Chinese export-ware to Virginia in the first half of the seventeenth century.

I have argued elsewhere[5] the circumstantial case for Dutch transportation of the early seventeenth-century Chinese porcelain found at Virginia sites, so I shall allude only briefly to my arguments. First, the records at the India Office Library indicate clearly that the British East India Company was not bringing any appreciable amount of porcelain to London, from whence it was later transshipped to America, until the 1680s. Even then they had some trouble selling the wares. The Dutch, on the other hand, were bringing tens of thousands of pieces to Holland from about 1610 on. Furthermore, most of the types of Chinese exportware found on early seventeenth-century Virginia sites are identical to wares excavated from two Dutch East Indiamen, the *Witte Leeuw*, sunk in 1612, and the *Banda*, sunk in 1615.[6] Finally, Dutch traders were a significant presence in the Chesapeake Bay from the 1620s on. In 1619, a Dutch ship brought the first Blacks to Virginia, and in the 1620s and 1630s, Dutch boats plied the Chesapeake in search of tobacco. Between the 1640s and 1660, when they were excluded from trade in Virginia by the Navigation Acts, Dutch merchants established permanent factories in Norfolk and elsewhere in the Chesapeake in order to facilitate their trade in tobacco.[7] These traders probably supplied the Virginia colonists with their earliest Chinese porcelain, apparently sporadically and in small quantities.

Virginians enjoyed a modest amount of Chinese porcelain in the seventeenth century, mostly in the form of bowls of various sizes. After about 1715, however, the amount of Chinese porcelain began to increase markedly, as a rising standard of living gentrified tidewater Virginians and encouraged the drinking of tea, coffee and chocolate. The Chinese porcelain that came to tidewater Virginia in the eighteenth century undoubtedly came from London.

English enthusiasm for things Chinese apparently took a great leap forward with the arrival of Charles II's Portuguese bride, Catherine of Braganza, who appeared in England in 1662 with an equipage of oriental objects, including lacquered furniture and tea, which caused amazement amongst the upper classes. But according to Hugh Honour, tea had probably entered England through Holland in the 1650s; in 1658, Thomas Rugge wrote that the "excellent and by all Physicians, approved, China drink, called by Chineans Tcha, by other nations Tay, alias Tee, is sold at the Sultaness Head Coffee House, . . . by the Royal Exchange, London."[8] So by the restoration of Charles II in 1660, two drinks which would generate an enormous demand for Chinese porcelain were being imbibed in London, and "china-mania" had taken root among the upper classes in England.

Although the East India Company records mention little Chinese porcelain imported to England before the 1680s, there is evidence of interest in the porcelain earlier in the seventeenth century among the very affluent. Charles I had sixty-five pieces of "purselaine" at Somerset House. An early example of interest specifically in Chinese ceramics is illustrated in a 1644 inventory at Tart Hall, cited by Peter Thornton, which contained glass, basketwork and brassware in addition to Chinese porcelain, in a manner similar to the cabinets of curiosities at Dresden and elsewhere on the continent. By 1678, the Dutchess of Cleveland must have amassed a "large" collection of Oriental porcelain, because in that year she sent it to Paris to be sold.[9] A recently published catalogue of Chinese and Japanese ceramics at Burghley House, near Stamford, based on an inventory of 1688 and a will of 1691, indicates that at least one major English country house had assembled a collection something like Queen Mary II's before Mary moved from Holland to England.[10]

Daniel Defoe credited Queen Mary II with bringing "in the Custom or Humour . . . of furnishing houses with China-ware, which increased to a strange degree afterwards, piling their China upon the tops of Cabinets, Scrutores, and every Chimney-Piece. . . ."[11] Mary's interest in Chinese porcelain was evident while she was still in Holland. Nicodemus Tessin described her audience chamber at Honelaarskijk as being "richly decorated with Chinese work and pictures. . . . The chimney was full of precious porcelain, part standing half inside it, and so fitted together that one piece supported another." Celia Fiennes, the aristocratic late seventeenth-century traveler, found Queen Mary's Water Gallery at Hampton Court "decked with China," but Mary's collection at Kensington Palace particularly impressed the English aristocracy.[12] It is in part to Mary's enthusiasm for Chinese ceramics, which originated in Holland, that the English owed their China-mania. The beginning of Mary's reign coincided with a marked increase in the importation into England of tea and coffee. By the 1690s, these two trends combined to create a vastly increased demand for the products of the Chinese potter in both table and ornamental wares, and the British East India Company attempted to meet this demand.

The records of the Honorable East India Company are voluminous but the sales records are very spotty and exist only from 1694 to 1722. Nevertheless, when combined with records of Company orders issued to its supercargoes, or purchasing agents on the ships, an excellent overview of the types of Chinese exportwares brought to the West can be ascertained. As K. N. Chaudhuri, historian of the Honorable East India Company, has observed, the importation of Chinese exportware to London was directly related to the growing custom of drinking tea, coffee, and to a lesser extent, chocolate, in England and the colonies.[13] Nevertheless, during the years for which records of auctions exist, a trend is discernible away from a variety of wares, particularly decorative "rollwagens" (tall, slender vases), large covered jars, and figures, to the plainer wares for table and tea and coffee drinking. Thus, by 1720, when Virginians began to increase their importation of Chinese porcelain in which to consume the new beverages, the Honorable East India Company had switched to a policy of bringing in enormous quantities of "ordinary wares" to meet the growing demand in England, Ireland and the colonies.

In 1704, for example, the East India Company offered a wide variety of objects for sale, wider than it offered a decade later. At a sale of the *Union's* cargo in 1704, merchants could buy a lot of seventy Dutchmen sitting, twelve Men on Sea Monsters, "21 ditto broke," sixty-five pulpitts with Paderies, three images with golden bellies and black faces, three Devils, and ten "fine hubble-bubble (houkas) at 61 shillings. At the same sales, utilitarian wares predominated, but even those staples of the trade, tea, coffee and chocolate cups, were scalloped, ribbed, octagonal, square and came in all sorts of color combinations, such as rouge de fer and gold, cream and red, and black with gold rims.[14]

By 1712, the *Dispatch Books* of the East India Company reveal that the standardization which characterized the Company's porcelain purchases in the eighteenth century had begun. The Company's order for that year consisted chiefly of two sorts of wares: dinner services and beverage sets. These included 40,000 chocolate cups with handles, 110,000 tea cups with saucers, 6,000 tea pots, 10,000 milk jugs, and 2,000 sets of small sugar bowls, two to a set. The Company charged the supercargoes, its emissaries to China, not to buy "large pieces such as Jars, Beakers or great dishes or bowls . . ."; by 1712 they were no longer fashionable.[15]

The trend towards standardization continued. A surviving sales catalogue of 1721 offered blue and white coffee cups in groups of 10,000 divided into five lots, 77,336 blue and white tea cups and saucers divided into twenty-seven lots.[16] The pulpits with or without paderies, small boys on toads, the large ladies with odd hands, and other figures listed in the 1704 sales are missing from the lists in 1721. This standardization occurred at the very moment when tidewater Virginia began importing Chinese exportware in bulk. Given the nature of the East India Company's imports, it is small wonder that the earlier eighteenth-century wares found in Virginia are more various and variously decorated than the later eighteenth-century wares. Furthermore, it is not surprising that, at most of the colony's eighteenth-century sites, a monotonous array of utilitarian forms decorated with underglaze blue, and later, polychrome glazes, confronts the student of Virginia's artifacts.

Further research is necessary before the entire network of eighteenth-century trade between China, London and Virginia can be spelled out. By mid-century, however, it is clear that dinner wares and tea services were available in Norfolk at stores run by merchants who also imported English and possibly Dutch wares. In the *Virginia Gazette* of July 25, 1766, the Norfolk merchants Balfour and Barraud advertized "china bowls of all sorts, plates, dishes, chocolate cups and saucers, coffee and tea cups and saucers, tea and milk pots, mugs etc.," as well as earthenware, delft, Dutch tiles and "English China [porcelain] of all types. . . ." Chinese porcelain has been found at plantations on both sides of the James such as Shirley, Flowerdew Hundred and Mt. Pleasant. Surviving letter and account books may indicate whether their owners could also have purchased Chinese porcelain in the stores that sprang up at Cabin Point and other tobacco inspection stations on the James after the establishment of these stations in the 1730s.[18]

Historians have graphically depicted the rigors of life in seventeenth-century Virginia, with its high mortality rate, the prevalence of earth-bound, or post, buildings, as opposed to buildings with a stone or brick foundation, and the planters' susceptibility to the vicissitudes of tobacco prices.[19] Despite a depression in tobacco prices which began in the late seventeenth century and lasted into the 1740s, Virginians' standard of living began to improve within the first three decades of the eighteenth-century.[20] The 1730s saw the beginning of a building boomlet that was responsible for so many of the well-built houses on the banks of the James and York Rivers and in the town of Williamsburg. These houses are a symbol of the gentrification of colonial Virginia about which Richard Bushman writes so eloquently.

Bushman makes a most articulate case for studying the American colonial in the context of Anglo-American culture. He points out that American colonial centers responded to cultural innovation at about the same rate as did provincial English cities. "Dancing masters, theatre companies, and wig makers showed up in Williamsburg and Philadelphia about the same time as they did in Bristol and Lincoln."[21] The Governor's Palace in Williamsburg, built between 1709 and 1714, was a major landmark in Williamsburg's establishment as the new capitol of the colony, but the Palace also evokes the hundreds of small manor houses built between about 1690 and 1740 that still inhabit the English countryside and country towns.[22] Houses such as these, which we in Virginia think are very grand until compared with large English country houses, became the seats of the fabled Virginia gentry, and because of the nature of the plantation system, these houses became the center of the planters' cultural lives. In these houses, as in their English counterparts, the Virginia upper and middle classes gathered their neighbors and extended family to take part in a growing number of social ceremonies which displayed the social graces, wit and learning of the participants. Chinese porcelain provided the Virginia gentry with the implements to carry out these social ceremonies.

Before discussing the material evidence of these eighteenth-century social ceremonies in diaries and inventories, it is necessary to allude to what the archeologists call "food ways." A look at contemporary diaries and inventories very quickly persuades the reader that eating and drinking were no longer something done to sustain life but had become highly involved and also routine social events. The taking of a large meal some time between noon and dark, and the drinking of wine, tea, coffee and chocolate were all occasions which encouraged the attendance of guests outside the immediate family. Furthermore, these social events took up a great deal of time. An hour's immersion in the London diary of William Byrd II,[23] owner of Westover, will convince you that after Byrd read his Greek and Hebrew and did his exercises, his day was filled with a progress from a meal to a coffee house, where he often took chocolate, to a tea, and to a punch party at night. Even at his plantation in Virginia and in Williamsburg, he was constantly entertaining or being entertained at dinner and afterwards at tea or coffee and still later at supper, with wine and/or punch, and once in a while, coffee following.

A study of Byrd's three extant diaries — dating from 1709 to 1712, 1717 to 1721, and 1739 to 1741 — tells us much about the uses to which Chinese porcelain could have been put in eighteenth-century Virginia.[24] In the earliest diary, dated 1709 to 1712, exportware was probably little used for drinking tea; the references to tea are generally medicinal. When Byrd's neighbor, Col. Benjamin Harrison, of Berkeley plantation, was dying, Byrd sent him some tea, which "he drank a great deal of. . . ." The following day, Byrd gave him "tea with ten drops of spirits of saffron," but despite this treatment, Harrison died.[25] In the years covered by the first two diaries, Byrd generally had boiled milk for breakfast, although by 1717, he would sometimes drink chocolate.[26] By 1739, when the last diary commences, Byrd almost always drank tea, or less frequently, coffee, every morning.[27] In London, tea was also drunk, especially with ladies, after dinner, which was eaten some time after noon.[28] But upon returning from London in 1720, Byrd usually served coffee, not tea, to guests after dinner at Westover. It was not until 1739, the period of his last diary entry, that we know Byrd routinely served tea to visitors who came in the afternoon and coffee to guests after dinner.[29] By the 1720s, we have seen from London sales records, tea and coffee services were being sent to the West from China, and tea and coffee cups and saucers constitute probably the biggest single source of shards at archeological digs in the James River basin.

Finally, another noticeable change in Byrd's drinking and entertaining habits is the increasing frequency with which he drank punch after the 1720s. One can find numerous references to drinking punch in the middle years, 1717 to 1721, particularly in August, 1720, and Byrd even gave it to his slaves on occasion.[30] In the later years, he apparently drank punch chiefly in Williamsburg. On May 2, 1740, for example, Byrd dined at three o'clock at Wetherburn's Tavern and, as he put it, "entertained the Governor. I ate boiled tongue. After dinner we drank arrack punch till 6 and then walked."[31] The several punch bowls listed in the inventories of the period attest to the popularity of punch in mid-eighteenth-century Virginia. Arthur Allen III, of Bacon's Castle, Surry Co., died possessed of two glass punch bowls in 1728.[32] Colonel John Allen, of Claremont Manor, in Surry County, had a silver punch ladle and probably five Chinese export and three earthenware punch bowls when he died in 1742.[33] The sixteen "china bowls" listed in the Raleigh Tavern inventory of 1771 are probably punch bowls too; directly following their listing is a listing of two silver punch ladles and two silver punch strainers.[34]

The survey of inventories from various counties written from 1728 to 1775 indicates that the trends discernible in Byrd's diary are also seen in other households and taverns. Tea equipages and coffee and chocolate pots and cups figure prominently in colonial Virginia households, attesting to the Virginians' improving standard of living and increasing gentrification.

Eighteenth-century inventories from Surry and York Counties illustrate the complexity of tea, coffee, chocolate, and punch consumption as a socioeconomic phenomenon. Drinking punch was relatively simple. The inventories list punch bowls which, when small, could be drunk from directly. Otherwise, punch required glasses, which most of the affluent households surveyed would have contained, and a punch ladle and perhaps a strainer.[35] Only the bowl might have been of Chinese porcelain. But tea, coffee and chocolate drinking required numerous objects to do it properly, many of which were of export porcelain.

Tea was the most complicated of the three beverages to consume and has left us the largest group of shards. Several inventories abbreviate the tea equipage by referring to "1 set of China and board," as in Peyton Randolph's inventory of 1775, or to a "tea table and furniture," such as was found in the hall and the room above the chamber at Bacon's Castle, in Surry County, in 1728.[36] But such brief references give a simplistic idea of the implements necessary to the eighteenth-century tea ceremony in colonial Virginia. Affluent households often contained tea tables; Arthur Allen III, of Surry County, possessed two Dutch tea tables at his death in 1728. Inventories listed tea boards, usually mahogany, but occasionally japanned, as at the Peyton Randolph house in Williamsburg in 1775.[37]

The tea was often kept in cannisters, as in two japanned tea chests and cannisters found in the little middle room at the Governor's Palace in 1770. Tea kettles were often listed in the kitchen, sometimes with trivets. They were often copper but Governor Botetourt owned one Dutch lead boiler with tea kettle and four Dutch lead coffee pots and lamps. Henry Wetherburn died in 1760 owning both a silver tea kettle and tea pot. Tea pots came in all sorts of materials and are occasionally listed as having a tea pot stand. The majority of tea pots listed were not of Chinese export porcelain; they were often of metal.[38]

The inventories list tea bowls and saucers, in those days without handles, but the inventories imply that sometimes tea and coffee cups shared the same saucer. The Raleigh Tavern inventory of 1771 lists "44 china saucers, 17 cups, 11 china coffee cups." A few of the armorial services still extant illustrate this practice.[39] Tea services almost always had a "slop basin," or waste bowl, and generally a sugar dish, a milk pot, and, at Wetherburn's Tavern in 1760, "a spoon and tong stand." One plate was occasionally listed with the rest of the vessels mentioned.[40] However, there was no mention of anything being served with tea in Byrd's diary.[41] In eighteenth-century Virginia, the tea itself appears to have been the focus of the ceremony. Tea spoons are mentioned in inventories of more affluent households and sugar tongs as well.[42]

Coffee and chocolate were less complicated beverages to administer than tea but required coffee and chocolate mills for grinding. Governor Botetourt had on hand 21 1/2 pounds of "India coffee" at his death in 1770. Coffee and chocolate pots also came in metal as well as almost every kind of ceramic; Raleigh Tavern had two tin coffee pots in 1771, and Governor Botetourt had eleven Staffordshire coffee pots as well as other ceramic and metal pots.[43] The ceramics listed in the inventories are often reflected in the shards.

The present state of our knowledge makes it difficult to generalize about the degree to which the possession of tea, coffee and chocolate sets filtered down the economic ladder. In her study of Yorktown inventories between 1730 and 1750, Mary Beaudry points out that the value of estates listing some semblance of a tea equipage ranged from £23 to over £2000. Of the thirty-four estates listed in Beaudry's appendix, nine were valued between £100 and £300, and ten between £300 and £600. The fact that rudimentary tea services were found in three York County estates valued at under £90 would seem to indicate that, as Beaudry puts it, "the social significance of tea-drinking caused those other than the very wealthy to strive" to obtain the equipment for this genteel ceremony. Beaudry further hypothesizes that the fact "that there is no [economic] cut-off point at which the amount of total estate value may be correlated with ownership of so-called status goods . . . is indicative of a community in which there existed no firm distinctions between social strata."[44] If Virginians had the money to buy goods associated with an affluent lifestyle, they simply bought them and used them.

Beaudry's conclusions are borne out in large part by the archeological remains in Yorktown, Williamsburg and Jamestown. Tea and coffee wares and Chinese porcelain are found on widely distributed sites. It could be argued, however, that the three towns were largely inhabited by wealthy planters in season and by merchants the year round. Furthermore, most of the rural sites dug in tidewater Virginia had been the plantations of the gentry, so their archeological remains are hardly typical of the poor farmers who made up the bulk of Virginia's population. Scholars must do much more work on the inventories of this group and archeologists dig more sites associated with men of modest means before we can hypothesize about the implications of the inventories and the shards for the poorer classes of eighteenth-century tidewater Virginia.

One point the inventories make clear: the possession of Chinese export porcelain was widely diffused among affluent Virginians. Of the thirty-four households listed in Beaudry's appendix, twenty-two owned some Chinese export porcelain.[45] In 1728, Arthur Allen III had eight china cups and one china plate with his tea table and furniture in the hall at Bacon's Castle in Surry County. By 1742, his relative John Allen died possessed of nine china plates, seventeen china dishes, as well as six chocolate cups, nine tea cups and a "set of china" not enumerated.[46] The 1760 inventory of Wetherburn's Tavern indicates that a Chinese export porcelain tea service and five china bowls were in use at the tavern. At neighboring Raleigh Tavern, the biggest single listing in the 1771 inventory is for 122 china plates, but the tavern also boasted large numbers of china tea and coffee cups and other sundry pieces of chinese porcelain. In 1775, Peyton Randolph's house in Williamsburg contained eight dozen "red and white china plates" and "22 ditto"(i.e., red and white dishes,) as well as "a Sett of Ornamental China" and sundry other pieces of exportware.[47] Thus the Virginia inventories reflect the trend revealed by the sales records of the East India Company, that utilitarian table wares formed the bulk of the British porcelain trade by the 1720s. The shards found in Virginia also reflect this pattern of importation and use.

A study of the eighteenth-century Chinese export porcelain shards and whole vessels found in the James River basin indicates that, in general, the tablewares of the Virginia gentry were markedly inferior to the dinner and tea services of the English and continental upper classes. The difference in quality reflects the Virginians' status as provincials. Furthermore, the provincial quality of Virginians' porcelain is borne out by the fact that it resembles closely the types of wares common to, for example, the Swedish and Dutch markets of the mid-eighteenth-century. The dating of these eighteenth-century tablewares was greatly advanced in 1974 with David S. Howard's publication of *Chinese Armorial Porcelain*, in which he illustrates pieces from over 3000 armorial services that he groups by borders and dates by studying the coats of arms on the exportware services illustrated. Howard's almost infallible method enables us to date with some precision the eighteenth-century shards in the James River basin.[48]

The sales records of the India Office indicate that the Chinese exportware produced in the early eighteenth century was more variously decorated than the later wares; this fact is reflected in the decoration of the shards found on Virginia's eighteenth century sites. Furthermore, the general level of quality of the porcelain was quite high through the 1720s, the paste, or body, quite free of impurities and a bluish-white, and the glaze very glassy and relatively thin, so that it bonded very well with the body of the vessel. The cobalt used was generally quite pure and produced a bright, deep blue, in marked contrast to the later blue and white wares, on which the blue can be quite ink-like or, conversely, very faded. The painters sometimes took the trouble to modulate the tone of the blue, creating shadings, as they have on these shards from saucers depicting two male Chinese figures found at Flowerdew Hundred, near Hopwell. (Illus. 1) The man on the left is probably an attendant; he lacks the formal garb, including waistband, of the man on the right. Early wares were sometimes molded, like a small saucer decorated with flowers and tendrils found by Noel-Hume in Williamsburg in a 1705 context,[49] or ribbed, like the bowl shard decorated with a vigorously painted lotus scroll and vine pattern from Flowerdew. (Illus. 2) The earlier wares sometimes had a decorative design called *an hua*, or secret design, carved on them. A tea bowl and saucer from Flowerdew Hundred with blue and white border has a small abstract floral design, (Illus. 3) whereas a milk jug or bottle from Governor's Land, west of Jamestown, with diaper borders, has a larger lotus-like design decorating its rounded sides. Blue and white wares sometimes had a brown, or cafe au lait glaze on the outside, but could also have a soft celadon green glaze, as does the tea bowl with a landscape in underglaze blue on the bottom of the bowl. (Illus. 4)

By about 1690, imari ware, decorated with underglaze blue and overglaze iron red and gold, had become popular in Europe, and is frequently found on sites in this area. A plate rim from Jamestown, painted in an asymetrical design with vigorous rococo swirls, is very similar to those found at King Carter's Corotomen, which burned in 1725. (Illus. 5) Finally, a unique piece in the James River basin dates from this period. The famille verte shards found at Jamestown probably made up a cache-pot, or round-sided flowerpot, and are incised with a very well-carved lotus flower and spear petal pattern. Some of the decoration is in underglaze blue, and the blue bands contain a border of iron-red flowers, green leaves and black dots characteristic of the famille verte, or green family, palette prevalent around the turn of the century. The combination of underglaze blue and famille verte died out shortly after 1700.

With the advent of the 1730s, the amount of exportware dispatched to Europe began to increase markedly and the quality to vary considerably. By the beginning of the eighteenth century, the body even of exportwares was relatively free of imperfections and the potting is almost uniformly excellent, unlike seventeenth century wares. Until about 1760, the great difference in contemporary wares relates to the quality of the painting, not the potting. Shards resembling a complete teabowl decorated with large petals containing a peony spray and a landscape with a lake, a pagoda and a mountain in the distance, are found on numerous local sites; hundreds, if not thousands, must have been used in tidewater Virginia. The suggestive brushwork and the use of a very few strokes to depict the flowers and landscape bespeak the speed with which it was painted. (Illus. 6) A punch bowl, probably made c. 1735, and found at Newtown, near Norfolk, now known as Pleasant Point, is an extreme example of speedy painting. (Illus. 7) The figures are depicted with four lines and a blob for the man's torso and arm, the mountains by a long stroke and a blob, and the pine trees by a few horizontal brushstrokes crossed by vertical strokes. A blue and white saucer from Jamestown, decorated with graceful storks amid flowers and trees carefully outlined and without any wash, is an example of pencil drawing from the 1740s. A small teapot of blue and white decoration found at the Drummond site on Kingsmill Plantation, east of Jamestown, is a superb example of the potter's art. (Illus. 8)[50] The tea pot is made of a soft paste porcelain, a slightly different clay from the normal exportwares, which absorbs the cobalt blue differently and thus allows for very precise brushwork. It is very similar to tea wares made for A. J. Sichterman, an officer of the Dutch East India Company from Groningen, the Netherlands, about 1745.[51]

By the mid–1720s, a new range of colors became available to the Chinese potters, called famille rose, or the pink family. It almost certainly derived from a European technique of enameling on metal; the glaze, a translucent pink, is composed of gold and tin oxide. It is painted onto the body of the piece which has already been glazed at 1300 degrees centigrade, like the blue and white porcelain; it is thus on the overglaze and the piece must be fired a second time at a lower temperature. As Margaret Medley has observed, "the stability of the [rose family's] enamel pastes permitted delicate shading of tones in a wide variety of colour combinations. Minute details could be picked out in different colours without fear of these running [during firing,] so that the birds and flowers, for instance, could be painted with a marvelous attention to detail rivaling that of the European miniaturist."[52] Extremely little famille rose of that quality found its way to Virginia.

Nevertheless, the famille rose porcelain found on tidewater Virginia sites is not without interest. A famille rose bowl, made about 1735 and decorated with deep red and yellow flowers and a deep pink diaper border interrupted by floral cartouches, is now the property of the Association for the Preservation of Virginia Antiquities, but has a history of descent in the family of the minister who baptized Pocahontas. (Illus. 9) Large shards from a nine-inch plate found at the College of William and Mary are painted with an undulating iron-red border of cloud collars and a central landscape containing cherry-trees picked out in heavy pink overglaze. On these and similar wares, the use of the famille rose enamels is quite carefully confined but heavily applied. Another later, c. 1745 example, perhaps more typical of famille rose, is a punchbowl decorated with heavily enameled peonies and large green leaves on brown branches from Jamestown. (Illus. 10)

A variation of the famille rose palette, composed of black outline filled in with faint grey wash and modulated pink or orange overglaze, sometimes with bits of gold added, was made particularly successfully between about 1730 and 1750 and occasionally appears on eastern Virginia sites. The shards from a saucer from Jamestown provide an example of the intricacy of detail possible using this glaze; the saucer, decorated in gold and faint touches of iron-red, is not of the first quality but nonetheless attractive and well-painted. (Illus. 11) Imari remained a popular ware in this period. Numerous pieces were found during the excavations of Wetherburn's Tavern. A partial dinner plate from Kingsmill Plantation is a particularly well-preserved example of the ware and conveys a sense of why it was popular in Europe and in Virginia. (Illus. 12)

Blue and white exportware continued to be popular in the middle decades of the eighteenth century. A coffee cup from Jamestown is decorated with the ubiquitous giant peony, a carefully executed latticework fence and bamboo. (Illus. 13) This motif is used continuously through the 1770s with varying quality of painting. A blue and white teabowl from Kingsmill with cafe au lait exterior is painted very hastily, with single blobs of blue depicting the leaves and a few brushstrokes shading the petals of the peony. (Illus. 14) The shards of the coffee cup and saucer from Jamestown dating about 1765 are decorated with a landscape style frequently encountered on shards from eastern Virginia sites, with willow trees, plum blossoms depicted by circles, large houses and tiny sailboats, all drawn with few and heavy brushstrokes typical of the later cruder blue and white wares. (Illus. 15) Finally, the general decline in the quality of painting on blue and white wares can be seen in the painting on the large platter dating to about 1775 or 1780 from the Whittle House in Norfolk. The platter has what is often referred to as a Fitzhugh border, taken from a service made for Thomas Fitzhugh, an officer of the Honorable East Indian Company, about 1780. (Illus. 16) The Fitzhugh pattern generated very little interest in Great Britain but was to become enormously popular in the new republic after the American Revolution.

Although Chinese export porcelain with blue and white decoration make up a majority of the shards found on local sites, a few of the polychrome overglazed exportwares dating from after 1760 deserve mention. A partial service in the Collection of Colonial Williamsburg Foundation, decorated with spear border, large famille rose peonies and exotic birds with peacocks' tails on a rock, is like intact pieces with a history of local ownership in the Williamsburg area and shards from Jamestown and Williamsburg. A punchbowl from Wetherburn's Tavern is decorated with a gold chain border and the increasingly whispy floral sprays that characterize post–1760s polychrome wares. The Chinese lady on shards from Claremont Manor, in Surry County, is typical of shards found on numerous plantation sites along the James, including Shirley, and is a basically simple pattern inexpensively produced. (Illus. 17) The polychrome ware found on later eighteenth-century sites is often decorated with a typical floral pattern not unlike that found on a service made about 1770 for a member of the Grigby family (Illus. 20), the flowers rendered with six or eight quick brush strokes of pink, two green leaves, the piece covered with a thick greyish glaze. Many examples can also be found in local archeological collections of porcelain shards decorated with the simple band and star or chain borders found on exportware made about the time of the American Revolution.[53]

The nature of the Chinese exportware found on colonial sites in the

James River basin reveals the provincial status of its owners when compared with wares made for the families of the English upper classes. A few examples must suffice. The nicely painted bowl in the collection of the Association for the Preservation of Virginia Antiquities, with a history of Virginia ownership, is a worthy example of the ware (Illus. 9) but nowhere near as fine as the extremely thinly potted and exquisitely painted tea bowl and saucer made for a member of the Dutch Reverhorst family about 1745. (Illus. 18) An excellent example of the difference between the quality of armorial wares and regular tablewares can be seen in a comparison of the two blue and white plates with inner and outer diaper borders and floral cartouches at the rim. (Illus. 19) The plate on the right was made for a member of the Leuthellier family; it is decorated with a well-painted parrot, the family crest, and the inner border contains exquisitely executed cartouches of a scholar on a terrace gazing at his garden. The plate on the left is identical to many shards found here, including a rim shard from Gloucestertown of virtually identical ware. The brushwork on the armorial plate is considerably finer, the brush strokes more numerous, and the glaze thinner than on the non-armorial plate, whose brushwork is blurred by a thicker glaze. The Chinese imari service made for the English Horsemonden family with Virginia connections — the first Mrs. William Byrd II was a Horsemonden — is in marked contrast to most of the imari wares found in Virginia.[54] The chocolate pot, cups and saucers with the arms of Grigby impaling Bird of about 1770 to 1780 (Illus. 20) are more carefully painted than most of the later wares found on colonial tidewater sites, including a respectably painted punchbowl of about the same date found at Wetherburn's Tavern. The archeological collections of Williamsburg and environs are not, however, totally devoid of armorial porcelain; shards of plates from the service of Lord Dunmore, Virginia's Governor between 1771 and 1775, have been found on several sites in Williamsburg. (Illus. 21)

A comparison of the Virginia shards with the wares found on three eighteenth century wrecks reveals that, despite its relatively mediocre quality, the exportware in Virginia was comparable to the common tablewares imported for the Swedish and Dutch markets in the eighteenth century. A blue and white eight-inch plate with bamboo borders is one of the most prevalent border types from the 1740s found on tidewater Virginia sites (Illus. 21); such wares were also found on the *Hollandia*, an East Indiaman sunk in the mid–1740s, and on the *Goteborg*, sunk near Gothenburg, Sweden, in 1745. To judge from photographs of the *Goteborg's* cargo, it carried a great many wares like those found here.[55]

The recent discovery of a Dutch East Indiaman sunk about 1750 in the

South China Sea has vastly enlarged the comparative scope of the study of mid-eighteenth century Chinese export. The wreck was excavated by Michael Hatcher, a salvage diver based in Singapore, who brought up the ship's bell, dated 1747, with about fifty European stoneware jugs and about forty wine bottles, as well as 126 Chinese gold ingots. The artifacts recovered, as well as the nature of the cargo, have led Christian Jorg, Chief Curator of the Groninger Museum in Groningen, to conclude that Hatcher had found the *Geldermalsen*, a Dutch East Indiaman sunk in 1752.[56] Hatcher salvaged over 162,000 vessels which were sold in Amsterdam in April, 1986.[57]

The recovery of wares from the *Geldermalsen* has provided thousands of intact examples of Chinese porcelain wares identical to hundreds of shards found in the James River basin. At Kingsmill alone, at least five sets of shards identical or very similar to wares from the *Geldermalsen* have been unearthed. The earlier-mentioned tea bowl with cafe au lait glaze on the reverse has the same center scene as dozens salvaged from the wreck, with a giant peony, a large rock and a weeping willow. (Illus. 14) The rim and part of the bottom of an octagonal plate from Kingsmill are similar to a partial set of octagonal plates and platters raised from the *Geldermalsen*, with similar floral cartouches on the rim and a pine tree in the center scene. The plates from the *Geldermalsen* are somewhat simpler, lacking an outer border and having a simpler border on the cavetto. (Illus. 22)[59] A saucer from the same site with sketchy diaper border, skeletal tree branches and a mountain or rock rendered by a quick outline filled in with wash is very much like dozens of tea bowls and saucers from the Dutch East Indiaman. (Illus. 23)[60] A dinner plate found at Kingsmill is of almost identical pattern to dozens from the *Geldermalsen*, with three groups of flowers on the rim, a diaper border with floral cartouches on the cavetto, and chrysanthemums in the center. The example from Virginia is slightly better painted, with lotus leaves carefully rendered with outline and shaded blue wash in the center scene. (Illus. 24)[61] A plate found at Wetherburn's Tavern has a pattern similar to that on tea bowls from the wreck, with sketchy diaper border and a stiffly painted bamboo.[62] These examples are but a few of the possibly hundreds of parallels between the wares in Virginia archeological collections and those salvaged from the South China Sea by Michael Hatcher.

The massed ranks of exportware excavated from the *Geldermalsen* (Illus. 25) provide students of eighteenth-century social history and material culture with a graphic example of the implications of the China trade for western Europe and for Virginia. The increasing availability of Chinese ceremonies during the eighteenth century provided the Virginia colonists with the vessels from which to drink the new and popular beverages, tea, coffee, chocolate and punch. The rising popularity of these beverages occurred at a time when Virginians were experiencing a rising standard of living, and the increasing supply of both the ceramics and the beverages provided the colonists with an outlet for their increasing affluence. Finally, the confluence of these two trends encouraged the gentry and "middling classes" to indulge in the social ceremonies reaching them, as provincials, only after such ceremonies had been established in London. The beauty, availability and durability of Chinese export porcelain makes it one of the most interesting material remains of the complex society that contributed so much to the origins of revolutionary America.

NOTES

1 See, for example, Alice Baldwin Beer, *Trade Goods: A Study of Indian Chintz* (Washington, D. C.: Smithsonian Institution Press, 1970); Ralph Davis, *The Rise of the English Shipping Industry* (London: Macmillan, 1962); Holden Furber, *Rival Empires of Trade* (Minneapolis: University of Minnesota Press, 1976.)

2 T. Volker, *Porcelain and the Dutch East India Company* (Leiden: E. J. Brill, 1970), 48. See also, C. R. Boxer, *The Dutch Seaborne Empire 1600–1800* (New York: Alfred A. Knopf, 1965) and K. N. Chaudhuri, *The Trading World of Asia and the English East India Company, 1660–1760* (Cambridge: Cambridge University Press, 1978) for the rise of the Dutch and English East Indian companies. For shorter accounts, see Christine van der Pijl-Ketel, ed., *The Ceramic Load of the Witte Leeuw* (Amsterdam, Rijksmuseum, n.d.) and Jean Sutton, *Lords of the East: The East India Company and Its Ships* (London: Conway Maritime Press, 1981)

3 For an excellent short account of the Dutch trade in Chinese porcelain see C. J. A. Jorg, *Porcelain and the Dutch China Trade*, (The Hague: Martinus Nijhoff, 1982), 91–140.

4 A. I. Spriggs, "Oriental Porcelain in Western Paintings," *Transactions of the Oriental Ceramic Society* 36 (1964–66). Information on seventeenth-century Dutch inventories obtained by oral communication from Christian J. A. Jorg, Senior Curator, Groninger Museum, Groningen, Netherlands.

5 Julia B. Curtis, "Chinese Ceramics and the Dutch Connection in Early Seventeenth Century Virginia," *Vereniging van Vrienden der Asiatische Kunst*, 15 (1985): 6–13.

6 Julia B. Curtis, "Chinese Ceramics and the Dutch Connection in Early Seventeenth Century Virginia," 6–8. See also, J. Dumas, *Fortunes de Mer* (Paris: Atlas Films, S. A., 1981).

7 John R. Pagan, "Dutch Maritime and Commercial Activity in Mid-Seventeenth Century Virginia," *Virginia Magazine of History and Biography* 90 (1982): 485–501.

8 Hugh Honour, *Chinoiserie: The Vision of Cathay* (New York: E. P. Dutton and Company, Incorporated, 1961), 51.

9 Cited in Linda Schulsky, "Queen Mary's Collection of Porcelain and Delft and Its Display at Kensington Palace Based Upon an Analysis of the Inventory Taken in 1697" (Unpublished Master's thesis, Cooper-Hewitt Museum and Parsons School of Design, 1986), 7, 13–14.

10 See Gordon Lang, *Exhibition of Chinese and Japanese Export Porcelain at Burghley House* (Highfields, Brighton, Sussex: Manor Park Press, [1985?])

11 Quoted in Schulsky, 13.

12 Quoted in Arthur Lane, "Queen Mary II's Porcelain Collection at Hampton Court," *Transactions of the Oriental Ceramic Society*, 1949–50, 25, and Schulsky, 14–15.

13 K. N. Chaudhuri, 406.

14 India Office Library, *Home Miscellaneous Series*, 12: 30–67, 186–223. See pp. 62–65 and 220–21 for types of figures.

15 Quoted in Chaudhuri, 408.

16 India Office Library, *Home Miscellaneous Series*, 14: 196–205.

17 Quoted in Ivor Noel-Hume, *Pottery and Porcelain in Colonial Williamsburg's Archeological Collection* (Williamsburg: Colonial Williamsburg Foundation, 1969), 11.

18 James H. Soltow, *The Economic Role of Williamsburg* (Williamsburg: Colonial Williamsburg, Incorporated, 1965), 15, 48–63.

19 Edmund S. Morgan, *American Slavery, American Freedom: The Ordeal of Colonial Virginia* (New York: Norton, 1975), 158–95, 215–34; Cary Carson *et al.*, "Impermanent Architecture in the Southern American Colonies," *Winterthur Portfolio* 16 (Summer-Autumn 1981): 135–96.

20 Alan Kulikoff, "The Economic Growth of the Eighteenth Century Chesapeake Colonies," *Journal of Economic History* 29 (March 1979): 279–80, 284, 286.

21 Richard L. Bushman, "American High-Style and Vernacular Cultures," *Colonial British America*, Jack P. Greene and J. R. Pole, eds. (Baltimore: John Hopkins University Press, 1984), 366.

22 Bushman, 349, 357–58.

23 Louis B. Wright and Marion Tinling, eds., *William Byrd of Virginia: The London Diary (1717–1721) and Other Writings* (New York: Oxford University Press, 1958.)

24 Louis B. Wright and Marion Tinling, eds., The *Secret Diary of William Byrd of Westover, 1709–1712*, (Richmond: Dietz Press, 1941), hereafter cited as Wright and Tinling, *London Diary*; Maude H. Woodfin and Marion Tinling, eds., *Another Secret Diary of William Byrd of Westover, 1739–1741*, (Richmond: Dietz Press, 1942), hereafter cited as Woodfin and Tinling, *Another Secret Diary*. Other printed diaries consulted yielded little information on changes in habits of consuming tea, coffee, punch and chocolate.

25 Wright and Tinling, *London Diary, 1709–1712*, 160–63.

26 See, for example, Wright and Tinling, *London Diary, 1709–1712*, 76, 106, 115, 127, 273, 325, 483; Wright and Tinling, *Another Secret Diary*, 88, 102, 149, 287, 359, 437, 523.

27 Woodfin and Tinling, *Another Secret Diary, 1739-1741*, 5, 47, 53, 147, 177.

28 See, for example, Wright and Tinling, *London Diary*, 60, 78, 79.

29 See, for example, Woodfin and Tinling, *Another Secret Diary 1739-1741*, 33–38, 46–47, 51, 61, 67, 70–73, 84, 165, 182.

30 See, for example, Wright and Tinling, *London Diary*, 386, 412, 423, 435–43, 456, 528, 466.

31 Woodfin and Tinling, *Another Secret Diary, 1739-1741*, 63. See also 165.

32 Surry County Records, *Deed Book, 1715-1730*, Part 3, 807–10.

33 Surry County Records, *Will Book, 1738-1754*, 438–44.

34 Graham Hood, ed., *Inventories of Four Eighteenth Century Houses in the Historic Area of Williamsburg* (Williamsburg: Colonial Williamsburg Foundation, n.d.), 20. Hereafter cited as Graham Hood, *Inventories*

35 See, for example, Surry County Records, *Deed Book, 1715-1730*, Part 3, "A True and Perfect Inventory . . . of the Estate of Mr. Arthur Allen, Deceased . . . ," 807–10.

36 Graham Hood, *Inventories*, 24; Surry County Records, *Deed Book, 1715-1730*, Part 3, 807–10.

37 Graham Hood, *Inventories*, 20, 24–25. Governor Botetourt had a tea board of silver or plated silver. *Inventories*, 7.

38 Graham Hood, *Inventories*, 6, 7, 21, 29. See also Surry County Records, *Will Book, 1738-1754*, 438–44.

39 See, for example, David S. Howard, *Chinese Armorial Porcelain* (London: Faber and Faber, 1974), 255 (Arms of Husbands, c. 1730), 292 (Arms of Haggard, c. 1732).

40 See, for example, Surry County Records, *Deed Book 1715-1730*, Part 3, 807–10.

41 See, for example, Woodfin and Tinling, *Another Secret Diary, 1739-1741*, 12.

42 Surry County Records, *Will Book, 1738-17*54, pp. 438–39, 541–42; Graham Hood, *Inventories*, 29.

43 Graham Hood, *Inventories*, 6, 9, 22.

44 Mary C. Beaudry, "Ceramics in York County, Virginia, Inventories, 1730–1750: The Tea Service." Paper presented at the Eighth Annual Conference of the Society for Historical Archeology, January 9, 1975, Appendix 3 and p. 6. Hereafter cited as Mary Beaudry, "Ceramics in York County."

45 Mary Beaudry, "Ceramics in York County," Appendix 3.

46 Surry County Records, *Deed Book, 1715-1730*, 807–10; *Will Book, 1738-1754*, 438–44.

47 Graham Hood, *Inventories*, 28, 20–21, 24–25.

48 David S. Howard, *Chinese Armorial Porcelain* (London: Faber and Faber, 1974).

49 Oral communication, Ivor Noel-Hume.

50 I am indebted for much of the information on the shards from the collection of the Virginia Historic Landmarks Commission to Merry Outlaw and Bly Bogley Straub. See also William M. Kelso, *Kingsmill Plantation, 1619-1800* (Orlando: Academic Press, 1984.)

51 C. J. A. Jorg, *Oosterse Keramiek uit Groninger Kollekties* (Groningen: Wolters Noordhoff Grafische Bedrijven, 1982), 64–65.

138 / CURTIS

52 Margaret Medley, *The Chinese Potter* (New York: Scribner's, 1976), 246–47.

53 See, for example, Geoffrey A. Godden, *Oriental Export Market Porcelain* (London: Granada Publishing, 1979), 287, 289, 290.

54 Geoffrey A. Godden, 210. A plate from this service is in the collection of the Colonial Williamsburg Foundation.

55 Stig Roth, *Chinese Ceramics Imported by the Swedish East India Company* (Goteburg: Gothenburg Historical Museum, 1965), 12.

56 C. J. A. Jorg, *The Geldermalsen: History and Porcelain* (Groningen: Kemper, 1986.)

57 Christie's, Amsterdam, *The Nanking Cargo, Chinese Export Porcelain and Gold, European Glass and Stoneware,* 28 April–2 May 1986.

58 C. J. A. Jorg, *The Geldermalsen*, Illus. 47, 66.

59 C. J. A. Jorg, *The Geldermalsen*, Illus. 44, 64.

60 C. J. A. Jorg, *The Geldermalsen*, Illus. 49, 66.

61 C. J. A. Jorg, *The Geldermalsen*, Illus. 61, 74.

62 C. J. A. Jorg, *The Geldermalsen*, Illus. 48, 66.

Chinese Export Porcelain / 139

LIST OF ILLUSTRATIONS

1. Southside Historic Sites Incorporated.
2. Southside Historic Sites Incorporated.
3. Southside Historic Sites Incorporated.
4. Virginia Historic Landmarks Commission.
5. Colonial National Historic Park — Jamestown.
6. Author's Collection.
7. Virginia Historic Landmarks Commission.
8. Virginia Historic Landmarks Commission.
9. Collection of the Association for the Preservation of Virginia Antiquities.
10. Colonial National Historic Park — Jamestown.
11. Colonial National Historic Park — Jamestown.
12. Virginia Historic Landmarks Commission.
13. Colonial National Historic Park — Jamestown.
14. Virginia Historic Landmarks Commission.
15. Colonial National Historic Park — Jamestown.
16. Virginia Historic Landmarks Commission.
17. Claremont Manor.
18. Private Collection.
19. Author's Collection.
20. Private Collection.
21. Author's Collection.
22. Virginia Historic Landmarks Commission.
23. Virginia Historic Landmarks Commission.
24. Virginia Historic Landmarks Commission.
25. Collection of Colonial Williamsburg Foundation. Dinner service from the *Geldermalsen*.

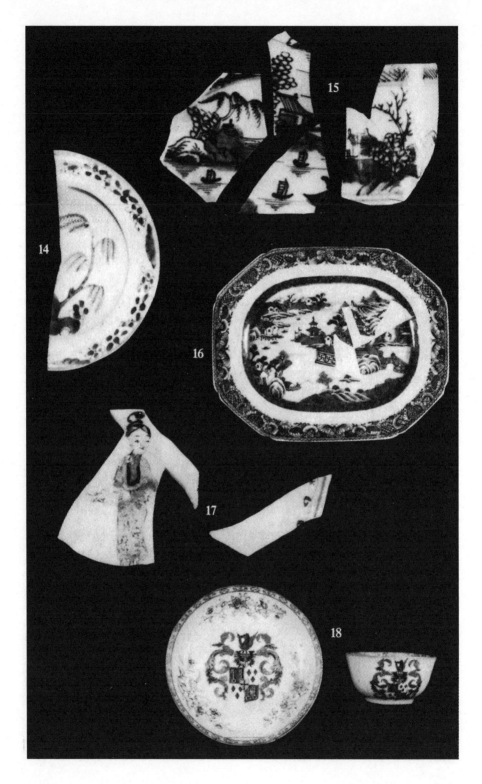

25

3

Strategies for Finding the Northwest Passage: The Roles of Alexander Mackenzie and Meriwether Lewis

Gunther Barth

Alexander Mackenzie and Meriwether Lewis were the first explorers who intentionally crossed North America.[1] Mackenzie's experience as a fur trader and Meriwether Lewis's as an Army officer shaped their searches for the Northwest Passage. Assessing Mackenzie's voyage in the context of a Fur Trade Culture and Lewis's in that of an Army Officer Culture will indicate how both explorers approached their tasks. Such an assessment focuses not so much on what they did, but *how* they did it.

The terms "culture" and "Northwest Passage" appear often in the inquiry and need some explanation. Culture here refers to the physical and mental constructs people create to cope with their environment. The phrase Northwest Passage arose from the search for a water route through North America.

The possibility of a passage through North America had intrigued Europeans since the days of Columbus. Two centuries of searching had eliminated the largest part of the continent from consideration. Only on the Northwest coast, roughly between the forty-second and the sixtieth parallels, did there still seem to be space for a waterway through North America.

---

1. As always Ellen W. Barth has improved my prose and thoughts.

The final searches for the passage were shaped by the 1788 geographic knowledge of the Canadian high north. It depended largely on the ideas of a Detroit-born Canadian fur trader, Peter Pond, who in 1787 as head of the North West Companies' operations spent his last winter in the vicinity of Lake Athabasca. Based on the experience of his travels he speculated that a river which flowed west from the Great Slave Lake, north of Lake Athabasca, emptied into the Pacific in an estuary which Captain Cook's third exploring expedition had sighted on the West coast of North America. Pond imagined that the Rockies came to an end at the sixtieth parallel and that a river ran north of the mountains a relatively short distance to the ocean. He, of course, did not know he underestimated the distance between Great Slave Lake and Pacific by about seven hundred miles.

Alexander Mackenzie, Pond's twenty-five-year old successor as director of the Athabasca district, set out to test this speculation, hoping to improve the economic situation of the Montreal fur trade. A navigable waterway to the Pacific would reduce the North West Company's staggering transportation costs and would also provide links to the North Pacific and China trade. Along such a waterway trade goods and furs could be shipped in bulk between Europe and the Canadian Northwest. The present movement of trade goods over miles and miles of water in small vessels and canoes between Montreal, Grand Portage (at the northwest corner of Lake Superior), and the distant posts of the high north cut heavily into the company's profit.

Mackenzie's introduction into the fur business in a Montreal counting house had acquainted him with the strategic locations of the competing Hudson's Bay Company's depots on the western rim of that bay. They were farther west and north than Grand Portage which gave the competitor the advantage of a much cheaper supply route by sea. The North West Company had to carry its trade goods through churning rapids, hidden rocks, and strenuous portages.

Mackenzie looked for alternatives. On his 1789 expedition he discovered that the river flowing out of the Great Slave Lake in a northwesterly direction soon turned almost due north. It skirted a massive mountain range to the west, a section of the Rockies, and ultimately emptied into the Arctic Ocean. Long before he reached the ocean he realized that his "River of Disappointment," as he called the stream that now carries his name, would not bring him to the Pacific. But rather than return at that point, his fascination with the high north geography lured him to pursue the river to the sea in that brief Arctic Summer. In one hundred and two days, "accompanied by five Canadians & three Indians," Mackenzie covered the 3,000-mile-journey to the Beaufort Sea of the Arctic Ocean and back to Lake Athabasca. "This expedition," he laconically stated after the return, "proved without a doubt that there was not a North West Passage" north of the sixtieth parallel.[2]

In 1792 Mackenzie searched for the Northwest Passage farther south, in the vast expanse west of Lake Athabasca. In the previous year he had bought survey instruments and astronomical tables in London which he used quite successfully to determine his position during the second voyage. Mackenzie followed the Peace River from Lake Athabasca to the range of mountains which had defied his earlier attempt to reach the Pacific. He wintered at Fort Fork, at the juncture of the Peace River and the Smoke River. In the next year, with three fur traders, four voyageurs, and two Indians, he traversed the rugged mountains. In one canoe or on foot, the group followed streams or portaged on Indian trails and trade routes on a course which generally responded to Mackenzie's sense of direction. The Bella Coola River brought them to the ocean, some distance north of Vancouver Island.

"Alexander Mackenzie, from Canada, by land," he wrote on the face of a coastal rock the party had slept on, "the twenty-second of July, one thousand seven hundred and ninety-three."[3] Mackenzie proved that there was no continuous waterway in the north that could qualify as the Northwest Passage. His accomplishment came about two hundred and fifty years after Álvar Núñez Cabeza de Vaca and his three companions first crossed North America far to the South in what was later called the border lands. Both parties succeeded with the help of Native Americans. In Mackenzie's case the Indians were already an integral part of the Canadian Fur Trade Culture.

---

2. T. H. McDonald (ed.) *Exploring the Northwest Territory: Sir Alexander Mackenzie's Journal of a Voyage by Bark Canoe from Lake Athabasca to the Pacific Ocean in the Summer of 1789* (Norman, 1966), pp. 117, 120.

3. W. Kaye Lamb (ed.), "Journal of a Voyage from Fort Chipewyan to the Pacific Ocean in 1793," *The Journals and Letters of Sir Alexander Mackenzie* (Cambridge, 1970), p. 378.

At the turn of the eighteenth century the Fur Trade Culture of the Canadian high north reflected the outcome of a two-hundred-year adjustment of Euro-American and Native American belief and behavior to a constantly changing environment. In the course of the cultural contact, white traders had come to terms with Indian morals and practices just as Native Americans had with Euro-American ones. The mutual adjustments ensured a measure of stability for people who constantly had to cope with an environment altered by circumstances beyond comprehension or control.[4]

The fur trade as a cultural partnership had a special significance for the traders staffing the North West Company's outpost at Lake Athabasca. It was an area of recent contact between traders and Native Americans where Indians not only adapted to the new conditions produced by the trade but also shaped them. At the northern-most fringe of that world, in 1778, Pond had built his post. In the winter of 1787 Mackenzie joined him to take over when Pond returned to his native United States in the spring.

About that time the two traders began their contact with the Subarctic Métis, a Canadian group of mixed descent from Native American and European ancestry who in the mid-nineteenth century established the "Métis Nation" in the Red and Saskatchewan river valleys. One of the Métis, François Beaulieu whose father was either French or Métis and his mother Chipewyan, attested to the multi-cultural world of the high north. As *coureur de bois* he knew Mackenzie and Pond, who had employed his uncle as interpreter. Beaulieu defended the North West Company's interests against the Hudson's Bay Company. As chief of the Yellowknife, he drove the Sekani, who also feared the guns of the Beaver and Cree, into the Rocky Mountains where Mackenzie found them in 1793.[5]

Across the mountains, Mackenzie met another multi-cultural world. Leaving the Parsnip, he crossed the divide to the Fraser River and the country of the Carrier Indians. Although they had never seen a white man before, he found that some already had European iron tools supplied by Shuswap,

4. My understanding of the Canadian Fur Trade Culture has benefited from Dean L. Anderson, "The Flow of European Trade Goods into the Western Great Lakes Region, 1715–1760," Jennifer S. H. Brown, W. J. Eccles and Donald P. Heldman (eds.), *The Fur Trade Revisited: Selected Papers of the Sixth North American Fur Trade Conference, Mackinac Island, Michigan, 1991* (East Lansing, 1994), pp. 93–94.

5. Richard Slobodin, "Subarctic Métis," William C. Sturtevant (ed.), *Handbook of North American Indians*, VI [June Helm (ed.), *Subarctic*] (Washington, 1981), pp. 363–64.

Bella Coola, and Tsimshian Indians who were in touch with the trading ships on the Pacific coast. The Carrier who had suffered from the knives and guns of the Shuswap also fought the Chilcotin to get direct access to the trade goods.[6]

As a young and ambitious fur trader, Mackenzie was finely attuned to and experienced at dealing well in these multi-cultural worlds. He had also mastered the rugged mountains, the dense forests, and the turbulent rivers. He and his men understood well that the advantages gained from trade came only with the skills of survival in the wilderness: and trade and survival were urgent essentials in their culture. Mackenzie embraced the rigors of fur trade life style and culture. He was considered a harsh taskmaster who at times drove his men to the limit of endurance as they battled strong currents and awesome rapids.

Exhausting and speedy travel marked the Canadian fur trade. In the summer of 1824, the Canadian head of the Hudson's Bay Company, George Simpson, traveled by canoe from Hudson Bay to the Oregon Country. His *voyageurs* rose at one in the morning, ate, and then paddled steadily until seven in the evening. In 1750, one of La Vérendrye's sons explained to a minister of Louis XV that his father arduously searched for the Northwest Passage "and made myself and my brothers travel with such a vigor that we should have reached our goal, whatever it was."[7]

When Mackenzie's voyageurs protested his decisions and refused to go on, he argued, berated, and pleaded with them, and they soon accepted the fact that without him they would be in worse shape. Their experience reinforced the customary Fur Trade Culture and told them that a hard-driving leader was needed to reach swiftly the next portage or group of Indians, better yet, both of them at once. On the Pacific Coast rock, the men waited anxiously while Mackenzie took his position and wrote his message on the face of the rock, even though they were surrounded by aggressive Indians in canoes. Their previous experience with coastal traders had taught them to consider white people as enemies and to intimidate them. Mackenzie's men, though shaking with fear of the Indians and anger at his delays stood

6. Catharine McClellan, "Intercultural Relations and Cultural Change in the Cordillera," ibid., p. 388.

7. Lawrence J. Burpee (ed.), *Journals and Letters of Pierre Gaultier de Varennes et de La Vérendrye and His Sons* (Toronto, 1927), p. 503.

their ground with him until he allowed them to climb into the canoe for the return voyage.

Mackenzie treated the Indians he engaged as interpreters like his other employees. He never seemed to have asked himself whether he liked them as long as they did his bidding. During the course of the voyage, however, he insisted on shaking hands with the many Native Americans he met and made sure that his interpreters explained the significance of the gesture. Steeped in the complex culture of the trade, as a sharp trader he kept a sharp eye on his interpreters to be sure that no vital information was kept from him and no deal cut without his approval. He gave sugar regularly to children to gain the good will of their parents and in the same spirit of the trade he collected an impromptu vocabulary of the Carrier and Shuswap languages.

Descending from the divide to the ocean, for the most part he was able to spot and follow well-marked Indian trade and travel routes.[8] Despite the tense encounters, harrowing rapids, and strenuous portages, the spirit of Mackenzie's journal made it clear that mountains, rivers, and trails were part of the world he shared with Native Americans and they with him. Ensconced in the Canadian Fur Trade Culture, he never usurped a part of the common environment by attaching his name or that of one of his companions to a river, mountain, or pass.

Captain Meriwether Lewis, chosen in 1803 by President Thomas Jefferson to lead the first United States exploring expedition from the Missouri via the Columbia to the Pacific Ocean, had little exposure to Native Americans and to a wilderness culture. His West ended at the Army posts in the Ohio Valley. The Army Culture of the opening nineteenth century sustained him and his men. It grew out of Revolutionary War experiences of men and officers and emerged in the two decades which provided the political and economic framework of the young nation.

In the Continental Army, American soldiers learned to support each other to hold a line. Touching the shoulders of a comrade on both sides helped men suppress their fears. Their conduct in combat became a matter of pride, and at times they fought just to uphold their regiment's reputation

---

8. Lamb (ed.), *Journals*, pp. 289–91, 320, 322, 338, 314, 319, 334, 351, 371.

for fortitude. Intrepid officers, dashing forward at the head of the troops, calling to their men to follow, helped soldiers facing likely death.[9]

The Continental Army disappeared in 1783, done in by peace, sectional interests, and the constitutional, economic, political, and ideological malaise of the Confederation. But there still remained, as part of the emerging Army Culture, an obligation of officers to obey their orders and of soldiers to follow their officers through thick and thin and to stand with their comrades.

The post-war officers created an unhappy image. Many young ones, with their wartime exploits fresh on their mind, boasted of their roles as patriots and officers. They bragged that their Army service as officers had achieved American independence. Citizens who treasured the egalitarian and libertarian potential of the Revolution regarded the swaggering ex-officers as remnants of European authoritarianism and militarism. In 1786, when Shays's Rebellion dramatized the military impotence of the Confederation, the Congress relied on the subterfuge of Indian danger in western Massachusetts to raise troops to deal with rebellious farmers.[10]

After the Federal Republic replaced the Confederation in 1789, the Federalists and Republicans gave voice to their different ideas of the nature of a standing Army. The Republicans were dismayed when the Federalists who controlled the executive branch and the Congress used a series of military crises to create a national military establishment. The Republicans held the Federalists responsible for the actual and imagined threats that a standing Army represents to a free society. Some members of the new Army officer corps, however, thought of themselves not as a professional elite but as citizens-officers, based on the Cincinnatus model. They were a presence the Republicans welcomed when they came into office in 1801.

When Meriwether Lewis joined the U.S. Army as an ensign in 1795, officers were trained to urge their men to follow them facing death, and men followed their duty to do just that. Although Lewis embraced the Army Cul-

---

9. Robert Middlekauff, *The Glorious Cause: The American Revolution, 1763–1789* (New York, 1982), pp. 502–04.

10. Richard H. Kohn, *Eagle and Sword: The Federalists and the Creation of the Military Establishment in America* (New York, 1975), pp. 41, 54, 89; Charles Royster, *Light-Horse Lee and the Legacy of the American Revolution* (New York, 1981), pp. 30–34.

ture, he personally never led a thinning line of soldiers against anyone. The following year, after he was transferred to the First Regiment of Infantry, he was either on furlough, recruiting men, or visiting the Army forts of the Ohio Valley as the regimental paymaster. He did well with his promotions. An ensign in 1795, he became lieutenant in 1799 and captain in 1800. His commanding officer, John Francis Hamtramck, had advanced on a slower track. He was captain in 1776, became major in 1786, lieutenant colonel in 1796, and colonel in 1802.[11] One year earlier, when the French Canadian veteran of the Revolutionary War angled for a higher rank, a Federalist friend reminded him that the party now in power offered little hope of becoming a brigadier.[12]

Lewis's quasi-civilian Army background may have been among the attributes which in 1801 attracted Thomas Jefferson to the young Virginian whom he knew as son of an Albemarle County neighbor. His career proved useful to Jefferson who during the campaign of 1800 had promised to reduce the size of the Army. As the President's private secretary Lewis's personal knowledge of the officer corps help Jefferson to trim the Army officer roster without losing Republican officers or competent ones with no party allegiance.[13]

In 1803, when Jefferson appointed Lewis as leader of an overland expedition, the Army Culture of the opening nineteenth century enabled Lewis to resolve the great problem that met the expedition in its planning stage. The civilian component of the Army Culture allowed him to create a command of two captains as co-leaders. He wanted to accommodate William Clark whom Lewis and Jefferson had promised a captaincy if he joined the expedition. The Army, however, claiming that there was no opening in that rank, commissioned Clark a second lieutenant of artillery.

Lewis insisted that Clark would nevertheless be in every respect his equal. Ignoring the official rank, Lewis introduced Clark as captain and al-

---

11. Francis B. Heitman (comp.), *Historical Register and Dictionary of the United States Army, from Its Organization, September 29, 1789, to March 2, 1903*, 2 vols. (Urbana, 1965), I, 496, 631. This is a facsimile reprint of the original edition published in 1903.

12. Kohn, *Eagle and Sword*, pp. 295–96.

13. Donald Jackson, *Thomas Jefferson & the Stony Mountains: Exploring the West from Monticello* (Urbana, 1981), pp. 117–19.

ways shared responsibility equally. He thus forged a partnership which was fundamental to the cohesion of the expedition and its ultimate success. It rested on a device from the world of business, sustained by an Army Culture with room for the citizen-officer, and it yielded results far greater than each man might have achieved alone.

The solution did credit to Lewis's intricate personality. His journal entries reveal him as a man of sudden mood changes who slipped quickly from euphoria to gloom. Eloquence and silence marked the poles of his perceptive mind. Some of his journal entries are like soliloquies reflecting not only the range of his mind but also identifying him as the citizen-officer who could fill the complex role of leader *and* partner.

As a newly formed Army unit in search of appropriate procedures, the expedition could look to the Continental Army precedents. These spelled out the chain of command, the regulations enforcing discipline, and the punishment for violating the rules; in short, the conduct of troops garrisoned in the U.S. military posts. The Corps' area of operation, however, would not be tied to a base in the United States. Its field of action stretched through parts of the continent unknown to captains and men, thus placing the new unit outside any Army convention. The Corps' orders to be at peace with everyone clearly set it apart from units and soldiers whose commitment and pride were recharged in combat.

Lewis and Clark took charge of their special, newly formed Army unit while continuing to assess what constituted appropriate military conduct for the expedition. They gradually shaped the motley party into an intrepid Corps of like-minded men. They combined the conventional tools of military authority with the spontaneity of expeditionary leadership using the citizen-officer as a model. One practice inherited from the Continental Army, courts-martial were considered a standard part of Army discipline. With the help of six courts-martial, the captains molded the mixed lot of soldiers, backwoodsmen, and guides into a special Corps, with sensible discipline, total loyalty, and respect for the captains' judgment. This latter was tested severely at the confluence of the Marias and the Missouri. Unsure which river to follow, Lewis and Clark did extensive reconnaissance which eventually supported the captains' strong convictions and led to the correct decision. Although their explanations at the time of doubt did not convince the men, they "said very cheerfully," Lewis recorded in his journal, "that they were ready to follow us anywhere."[14]

The shared hardships of the trail and the requisite self-sufficiency of the group also altered Army routine. Adapting regular procedure, Lewis and Clark insisted that enlisted men sit on the courts-martial while a sergeant presided, except in trials involving crimes punishable by death, when the captains took over. The first winter camp and the severe North Dakota temperatures enforced the physical closeness of the expedition. The arrivals and departures of Indian chiefs and white traders at the fort impressed the men with the special status of their Corps. The four months of shared experiences in tight quarters strengthened their loyalties to each other, their compliance with regulations, and their commitments to the goals of the expedition. Once they left Fort Mandan courts-martial were not again needed on the voyage.

The captains as citizen-officers found that a somewhat egalitarian approach to discipline united the expedition. At their request, two days after Sergeant Floyd's death on August 20, 1804, the soldiers held an election for his successor, and Private Gass was duly promoted sergeant. On another occasion, November 24, 1805, all members of the expedition, including York and Sacagawea, were given the chance to vote on the location of the winter quarters on the Pacific coast. Clark even recorded each vote in his account of the election.

Lewis acquitted himself superbly as citizen-officer in his vital encounter with the Shoshoni, while Clark was bringing canoes and most explorers up the last navigable stretch of the Beaverhead River. The Shoshoni were the first Indians the expedition had seen in three months and the only possible source of horses for crossing the Rockies. After their first contact with Lewis they became apprehensive, fearing they were being led into an ambush. They threatened to disperse before horse trading could be conducted with the goods that Clark was bringing. The dual nature of the citizen-officer helped to solve the crisis. Lewis as army officer acted decisively to counter the Indians' suspicions; as citizen he was unencumbered by concerns for an

14. Reuben Gold Thwaites (ed.), *Original Journals of the Lewis and Clark Expedition: 1804–1806*, 8 vols. (New York, 1904–05), II, p. 136.

officer's honor and free to entrust his gun to the Shoshoni chief Cameawhait. Thus, Lewis could make himself a hostage pledging the peaceful aims of the expedition, as did his three companions.

The expedition's sense of mission derived from its role as the first United States exploring expedition. It was the brainchild of President Thomas Jefferson. A high point in his fascination with the American West, the expedition produced the first officially deliberate encounter with the nature, people, and resources of a large part of the continent unknown to the young nation. The mouth of the Columbia, however, had already been explored by the turn of the eighteenth century. Jefferson's idea that only a short portage separated the Missouri from the Columbia was more than the last phase of a long search for the Northwest Passage. It was the harbinger of new geopolitical aspirations of the United States.

The expedition matched Jefferson's far-reaching instructions to Lewis. The Louisiana Purchase treaty of April 30, 1803, added major diplomatic tasks. Lewis and Clark derived pride from the President's charges. And so did the men. "Our little Community," as the citizens-officers called the party, was a distinct contrast to the solitary traders, free-wheeling trappers, canny interpreters, and cagey representatives of the Montreal-based North West Company whom the explorers encountered. Each of these men were pursuing their interests or those of their employers.

The explorers officially served their nation's policy. Their success indicated that the Army culture had created a strong expeditionary force by infusing a democratic spirit into military routine. Their practical adaptations gave scope to the men's creativity and sustained their confidence in each other. The Army culture linked the diverse groups of explorers into a national expedition. Fusing diverse men and methods, the captains exposed their search for unity as the essence of the American experience.

Alexander Mackenzie pursued his own design. He sought to solve the North West Company's need for a feasible water way to the Pacific which would reduce the operating cost of its far-flung western posts. Mackenzie directed just one canoe with nine employees of the Montreal fur company to the ocean and back without governmental support. In 1807, an open letter to Lewis by the publisher of Patrick Gass's journal snidely questioned the large size and support structure of Lewis's expedition comparing it to the small size of Mackenzie's, but made no mention of the larger goals and tasks of the U.S. expedition.[15]

Despite of its small size and private nature, Mackenzie's voyage eventually became a part of a commercial and political development that provided Canada with a major share of the Pacific Northwest coast. His arduous exploring and trading venture supplied the geographic base for dreams of a Canadian continental destiny. Fortuitously, the fur trade culture which sustained Mackenzie and subsequent Canadian explorers acted for a while to shield Indian nations in the Canadian West from the sudden onslaught of land-hungry settlers.

Two decades after Mackenzie's voyage to the Pacific, the North West Company profited greatly from his discovery as it thwarted the efforts of the rival Hudson's Bay Company to find a convenient water route to the Pacific. During the War of 1812, employees of the North West Company purchased Fort Astoria at the mouth of the Columbia in October, 1813. They were inspired by rumors of approaching British men-of-war assigned to seize the post established by John Jacob Astor's Pacific Fur Company in 1811 as the pivot of his projected world-wide fur empire. When an arriving British naval captain, chagrined to see his target already in the hands of his countrymen, raised the Union Jack over Fort Astoria he turned the acquisition into a conquest. And as such it was returned to the United States in accordance with the peace Treaty of Ghent of December, 1814, which annulled all territorial conquests of the belligerents. The captain's territorial escapade thus diminished the British claims to the mouth of the Columbia, although the North West Company still owned Fort Astoria and called it Fort George.

The Convention of 1818 between the United States and Great Britain guaranteed equal rights to the citizens of both nations in the Oregon country and further weakened the British dominance in the area. Three years later, the balance shifted when the Hudson's Bay Company absorbed the North West Company and skillfully protected the Mackenzie legacy of its former rival.

---

15. Donald Jackson, *Letters of the Lewis and Clark Expedition with Related Documents: 1783–1854*, 2 vols. (2nd, rev. ed., Urbana, 1978), II, 401–02.

Faced with the American determination to hold on to the Oregon Country below the 49th parallel, the invigorated Hudson's Bay Company stripped the country of its fur resources and in the early 1840s started a slow retreat to Victoria, B. C. When the Treaty of 1846 between Great Britain and the United States extended the existing boundary of the 49th parallel across the Rocky Mountains to the Pacific, Great Britain retained its coastal possessions between that line and the 54th parallel, the southern limit of the Russian territory in North America. Thus Mackenzie's vision finally materialized with the emergence of British Columbia as the Canadian gateway to the Pacific.

Mackenzie's familiarity with the Fur Trade Culture enabled him to move men, provisions, Indian presents, arms, ammunition, and three thousand pounds of baggage in a lightly built canoe, twenty-five feet long inside, twenty-six inches deep, and four feet nine inches wide, to the divide of the Rockies, portaging the divide, backpacking and canoeing to the ocean. In one hundred and eight days his men covered the two-thousand-three-hundred-mile distance from Fort Fork to the Pacific and back.

Meriwether Lewis, facing a much more complex task assigned by Jefferson, applied his knowledge of the Army Culture to forge a motley group of men into the first United States exploring expedition. Together with his co-captain and partner, William Clark, he set an example as citizen-officer who instilled a sense of mission into the twenty-nine man core of the expedition: two captains, fourteen Army regulars, nine young men from Kentucky, the interpreter, two French Canadian river men, and Clark's black servant York. A French Canadian interpreter, his Shoshoni wife Sacagawea, and their baby were added to the expedition at the Mandan villages. In eight hundred and sixty-three days (two years, four months, and ten days), the co-captains led the expedition of discovery and diplomacy on a seven thousand-mile voyage from the Mississippi to the Pacific and back.

The discoveries of the Lewis and Clark expedition turned a western wilderness of guesswork and rumor into a distinct part of the continent. Even though it demolished the last hope for a convenient water passage through North America, the Corps found a route from the Mississippi to the Pacific. By exploring the breadth of the Louisiana Purchase, the explorers proved its significance to the future of the young republic.

Unwittingly, the expedition reinforced the destruction of Native American nations. Following Jefferson's instructions, the captains tried hard in many, many Indian councils to bring Native Americans peacefully into white society through commerce. As a prerequisite for commerce, they repeatedly urged Indians to live in peace with each other and with white Americans. Lewis and Clark, of course, faced a hopeless task given the role of peace and war in Indian societies and the complex trade relations among Indian nations. The two successfully carried out their instructions in many other areas. They increased the sum of useful knowledge through collecting ethnological, geographical, zoological, and botanical information and traced the course of a future continental empire.

The expedition buttressed the United States claim to the entire Columbia basin. In subsequent decades, Americans derived their title to the "Oregon Country" to a great extent from the explorers' topographical descriptions and maps. Their reports about natural resources drew migrants to the Columbia. Trappers, traders, and settlers added to the legal niceties about "the rights of discovery" the brawn of conquest.

Guided by the Fur Trade Culture and the Army Culture Mackenzie and Lewis accomplished their tasks. They knew how to do them, and they did them well.

4

The Legacy of Old Canton

Jacques M. Downs

The Persistence of Canton Culture

A perspicacious reader might ask, "Why study any dead community at such length?" An answer to this question must necessarily be complex. Certainly the Canton firms produced business, financial, and lifestyle leaders among the American wealthier classes, especially in the northeast. Equally clear is the fact that among the American residents of old Canton lay the origin of American policy toward China. Because the community was so extraordinary, an acquaintance with its composition, activities, and attitudes is necessary for an understanding of that group and that policy. The life of the foreign enclave and the manner in which business was conducted shaped American attitudes, along with those of all foreigners on the China coast, and Americans, with their unusual democratic, New World orientation re-acted in ways, which may have been unique among Western residents. In any case those attitudes continued throughout the nineteenth century.

Because the opium trade was the economic foundation of the community (and particularly of the more important American firms), it has received extended attention (too much so according to one critic). It may have been that tea or silk was equally influential, but I do not believe it. Moreover I am convinced that this traffic was a major influence in molding American opinion, and it gave especial importance to such issues as extraterritoriality and the official blindness concerning the illegal commerce.

Of course for the most part, while they were in China, Americans blended into the larger foreign community, making whatever adjustments in habit and outlook that seemed appropriate to the attainment of their primary (i.e., generally business) goals. Although they adapted easily both in Canton and at the treaty-ports, Americans were self-consciously distinct from the other Westerners—they had come with peculiar values and ideas which set them apart. These values and concepts underwent changes at the treaty-ports, just as they had in old Canton, and these changes would later appear in the pressures on American policymakers, missionary boards, and other people who attempted to represent the United States in that very different part of the world. Professor Fairbank notes:

"There are no pure 'Sino-American' relations in China. The Americans are part of a 'foreign' community . . ., members of a class of privileged 'foreigners' who

322

form an additional stratum of the local ruling class." Yet, "the American in his self-image . . . is an anti-imperialist (and therefore anti-British) democrat, but he cannot live in China except as the British do, as a member of the elite. . . ." Thus, The American in China was obliged to be a democrat manqué, a ruler with qualms of conscience, in a world he never made but found seductively enjoyable. . . . The Englishman fitted into China's ruling class with less tension between his ideals and his actions.[1]

Additionally these (psychologically) uncomfortable expatriates were the effective agents in transferring whatever was moved from China to America and vice versa—goods, people, and influences. In the peculiar culture of the treaty-ports, Americans appear to have exerted an extraordinary leverage. Just after the turn of the century one writer commented that Shanghai was more American than British in tone, despite the greater number of British residents. It was young, growing, informal, very busy, and imaginatively enterprising, unlike the more traditional cities of the United Kingdom,[2] a condition at least in some degree due to the example of its American residents.

Canton Culture Spreads North

The more one pursues the subject, the clearer it becomes that most of what we know as "treaty-port culture" had been in existence years before the treaty-ports were created. The "unequal treaties" opened the northern ports, but they did not create the communities and their special style of life, attitudes, and institutions. These dated back at least to the end of the Napoleonic Wars and some went still further into the past.[3] Yet whatever its earlier history, treaty-port culture was an extension of old Canton.

Despite its unfavorable location, Canton remained the most important foreign trading center in China for a decade after the Opium War. Even the 20 percent lower shipping costs at Shanghai did not divert most tea from Canton until the Taiping Rebellion disrupted the old trade routes. As both the principal port for trade and the first Chinese city that Western vessels touched, Canton served as a gateway. China was so different from anything Americans and other Westerners had ever known that, even had the dynasty adopted free trade, newcomers would still have been dependent on the old hands for their introduction to China. Missionaries, eager to take advantage of their newly opened opportunities, crowded into the Canton area and taxed the resources of the Mission and its friends. Like the merchants they continued to approach China through Canton, because there was no practical alternative. During that critical period when the new ports were being opened, the Canton community, which now included Hong Kong, remained the only established Western settlement on the coast where non-Chinese might find fellow countrymen, friends, or even people whose language they could speak. The newcomers were apt students of what the community had to teach about their new environment. There they put on the old attitudes and mores as easily as they donned the typical dress and adopted the seductive lifestyle of the old system.

Not only merchants and missionaries but also their Cantonese compradors and servants carried northward the views, the business methods, and the well-worn habit patterns of Canton. Because these southerners had skills the northern Chinese lacked, they were the natural go-betweens, and they soon established an important place for themselves in the treaty-ports. In actuality what was new on the Chinese side was principally the forms of things. Although the Cohong, the Consoo Fund, and the innumerable charges of the old system were abolished by the Treaty of Nanking, much of the substance remained. And more kept appearing as both Westerners and Cantonese reestablished the old ways up and down the China coast. The ex-Hong merchants continued to do the lion's share of the business at Canton,[4] and all sorts of people, displaced by the abolition of the Canton system, found niches for themselves and their skills. Compradors, linguists, shroffs, and other typically Cantonese occupations appeared at every port. The ubiquitous coolies, the swarms of personal servants, and the tea, silk, porcelain, and *chow chow* merchants continued largely as before. Vested interests of all nationalities worked to perpetuate as much of the old system as served their purposes.[5]

Another very strong reason for the reestablishment of Canton institutions in the treaty-ports was simple drift. The treaties abolished the old system, but efforts to set up new institutions were directed toward a defense of what Westerners had won. The Chinese were too inexperienced to organize a workable new system. At the most elementary level, therefore, the absence of foreign initiative was a prescription for chaos. The situation was not improved for a decade after the Cushing Treaty, when, paradoxically, the pursuit of traditional business in traditional ways finally forced change. The international Maritime Customs Service was the result of British and American official exasperation with the breakdown of the Shanghai customs and was secured over the opposition of many merchants as well as the foot-dragging of Chinese officialdom.[6]

For many years even the composition of the treaty-ports' population remained similar to what it had been at pretreaty Canton. It was a strongly masculine community, dominated by the British and Americans, with the former outnumbering the latter more than two to one in the late 1850s and three to one by 1870. The only significant new national element was the Germans, who numbered 138 at Shanghai by the latter date. Among American merchants New Yorkers and Bostonians still predominated, and New England was disproportionately represented among the missionaries.[7] Continuing the unacknowledged educational function of old Canton, the treaty-ports introduced newly arrived Westerners to China, inculcating ideas,

324

roles, business methods, pidgin, and lifestyles in much the same fashion as in the earlier days. Alterations in the community ethos came slowly and in the form of accommodations to the changing realities of trade and the clash of Western power and knowledge with Chinese impotence and inexperience. But for the most part, continuity was more striking than innovation, and in attitudes, institutions, tastes, even in geography and architecture, the treaty-ports resembled old Canton.

Understandably, most scholars have emphasized the qualitative difference resulting from the shift of power in East Asia from China to the Western nations. In the new settlements this shift was reflected in the recognition that the British Consulate was the center of potential power, particularly as H.M. officials learned how to employ their advantages. But the similarities to old Canton are at least as important as this difference. Perhaps they are less noticeable, because diary keepers, letter writers, and journalists generally record news, which is to say change, rather than the many continuities. If foreign consuls were the focus of power in the treaty-ports, the tone of the community was more often set in the local (British) chamber of commerce. The members were firms and individual proprietors—representatives of business. The large concerns tended to dominate the group as they had before the Opium War. The Americans, remaining out of the organization, were nevertheless influenced by the chamber's decisions. They usually followed the lead of the British, just as they had done in old Canton after 1821.

Earlier writers have noted the manner in which the treaty-ports resembled each other topographically. Each was near, yet separated from, a Chinese walled city. The foreign quarter often included "a defensive screen of water."[8] Most were located upriver from the sea near an anchorage where ships might remain for extended periods. Although Captain Elliot had picked Hong Kong, it was British and American merchants themselves who first decided to settle in strategic positions at Amoy, Foochow, and Shanghai. All Westerners had similar motives in going to the new ports, and they had similar needs and fears about remaining there. As soon as the number of foreigners became large enough, the settlements asserted their autonomy. The Chinese living there were chiefly servants, compradors, refugees, and other dependents on the foreign community.[9] In each of these particulars, one sees the shadow of pretreaty Canton.

Although Hong Kong was not, properly speaking, a treaty-port, in many ways it resembled one. Isolated from the Chinese hinterland even more than the other settlements, the new crown colony partook fully of the culture that was common to all foreign enclaves on the coast. From a merchant's point of view, Hong Kong was an extension of the outside anchorages. Originally it offered merely a safer harbor than Lintin, and later it became the first dry-land storeship—the largest and most secure smuggling base in China.

The creation of Hong Kong had been the work of Charles Elliot, whose devotion to the commerce is well known. In fact he went so far to avoid interrupting the trade that most British merchants in China were outraged and accused him of everything from cowardice to treason. They were convinced that he was pro-Chinese and/or was the creature of James Matheson. Whatever their opinion Elliot's one lasting contribution was Hong Kong, and despite some early problems, the settlement soon proved its worth.

The Hong merchants, alert to their own interests, did not regard the new settlement with friendly eyes.[10] Like Elliot they realized that possession of the island-entrepôt meant the end of Canton as they knew it. Henceforth the foreigners held the cards. Trade restrictions, tariffs—any kind of commercial legislation could now be circumvented. Why, indeed, go seventy miles up the river with all the attendant regulations, expenses, and dangers, when a perfectly good and legal marketplace now existed outside? From the standpoint of the Chinese government, Hong Kong was immediately a disaster. Every regulation or tax tended to drive trade from Canton to Hong Kong. Canton's problems were Hong Kong's opportunities, and there was absolutely nothing any mandarin could do about it. Even extraterritoriality, provided for in the British treaty, became almost unnecessary, when legal problems could be handled locally. A mere exchange of prisoners solved most criminal problems. For the Americans, with their demand for equal treatment and their anti-imperial views, the crown colony's existence had ensured that extraterritoriality was among the first matters defined in their negotiations with China. Moreover once so delineated, the right would extend British privileges still further because of the most-favored-nation clause. The same was true of other newly negotiated rights—transshipment of goods, revisions in the tariff, missionary rights, etc. And the settlement of Chinese nationals in Hong Kong would raise the question of jurisdiction in a new way. The extension of British citizenship to include Chinese residents of Hong Kong would be impossible for China to oppose. The cession of Hong Kong was critical, and the most-favored-nation clause, which had been Chinese policy (under very different circumstances), began the century-long erosion of Chinese sovereignty.

The composition of both incoming and outgoing cargoes remained about the same in the years after the treaties. The volume increased substantially, however, and the beginnings of major changes were visible. Opium and bills were still the leading imports, and tea remained the principal export. The rhythm of tea production still dictated work hours and seasons, making the first flexible and the latter alternately strenuous and leisurely.

The big four American firms at Canton in the 1840s and 1850s were Russell & Co. (founded 1824), Wetmore & Co. (founded 1834), Olyphant & Co. (founded ca. 1828–30), and Augustine Heard & Co. (founded 1840). Only the last had not been in existence at least a decade when the Cushing Treaty was signed, but both of its founders were graduates of Russell & Co. Thus all the well-established American firms were products of old Canton. Even

326

many of the smaller concerns of the postwar years were led by the pretreaty generation. Bull, Nye & Co (under several names), J. D. Sword & Co., Rawle, Duns & Co., and other companies were the creations of men with years of experience under the old system. The same was true of the British firms, most notably, of course, Jardine's and Dent's. These men and organizations and others like them had grown and prospered in the pretreaty environment, and they continued to operate in much the same manner as they had before the "new system."

Many Canton ways of doing business were accepted without question. They were simply very convenient. Among the most obvious were sale by chop and muster, the contracting of housekeeping functions to a comprador, bookkeeping systems, letter writing, and so forth. In most important respects even countinghouse organization was recognizable as that of pretreaty Canton though more extended, growing in ways and directions begun under the old system. As firms became larger, the partners began to dine apart from the employees, and specialization of labor increased. The largest hongs became departmentalized by cargo—tea, silk, opium, cotton goods, etc. Each of the several experts, tea-tasters, silk-inspectors, and bookkeepers, enjoyed a certain distinction for his expertise and possessed a variety of titles—English, pidgin, and slang—for his profession.[11]

The development of physical facilities was similar. The factory grew into a compound (yamen?), but the residence halls and the business offices remained in the same building. Go-downs, compradors and their employees, shroffs, and servants were housed nearby. Even the appearance of these structures was familiar. The "compradoric style" of architecture included exterior colonnades, arcades, verandas, and other features characteristic of the old thirteen factories at Canton.[12] The kitchen and dining arrangements, the heating, and the disposal facilities were also very familiar to those who had known the old system.

Even the subsidiary businesses that cropped up in the treaty-ports resembled those in prewar Canton. Ship chandlers, contractors, hotel keepers, shipbuilders, and the rest were to be found in Shanghai directories as soon as such publications appeared. Missionaries continued to dominate the hospitals, schools, charities, and scholarship. The Chinese Repository continued publication until 1851 and served as a common source of information until a spate of newer (generally lay) journals took its place.

Recreational facilities proliferated with the newly acquired freedom of movement. All of the pastimes of old Canton found counterparts in the northern ports, and, in addition, those pursuing activities, which had been forbidden or inconvenient at Canton, often coalesced into organizations, especially at Shanghai. There was The Club, around which social life revolved. All Westerners except the Germans, who had their own, belonged to this organization. The German club admitted all foreigners to its excellent theater productions. Community members also supported the race track, a

Russell & Company, Shanghai, c. 1875. Watercolor on paper by unidentified artist. Note the colonnaded verandas, the extensive gardens, and the general "compradoric" architectural style. Courtesy of the Peabody & Essex Museum. Photo by Mark Sexton.

bowling alley, a racquet club, a yacht club, rowing clubs, cricket clubs, other athletic organizations, and lending libraries. There were churches, a seamen's chapel, a hospital, and at least one and often two newspapers each representing one of the mutually antagonistic divisions of the settle· ment. Even the internecine feuds resembled the petty bickerings in the older community.

Even the less-formalized recreations resembled those common under the old system. Perhaps most evident were cards. Loo, poker, whist, and other gambling games were everyday amusements. Music, horseback riding, billiards, and hunting all had their devotees. Bird hunting became something of an obsession with some traders. In the prewar era, it had been possible only on a few offshore islands, but, especially at Shanghai, it was extremely popular. Years after they had returned home, merchants wrote extensively and with great zest of their hunting exploits in the delta. The custom of huge meals and frequent banquets, noted at Canton, was stimulated as settlements were planted in and near the lushly productive Yangtze Basin with its varied and unusual foods and its access to the products of central and north China.[13] Only the tea-tasters, who had to preserve the acuteness of their tastebuds, and those in training for the numerous athletic events, exercised discipline at the table. Like Canton residents before the war, treaty-

328

port merchants dined and often drank with Falstaffian gusto. The stress on violent daily exercise made for large appetites, despite the often enervating climate.

With the release from the old Eight Regulations and the acquisition of space, amenities formerly available only at Macao were moved to the foreigners' factories. The gardens,[14] pets, and aviaries, previously found only in the old Portuguese colony, were located inside the walled company compounds at the northern ports. Life for the foreign resident became easier, more comfortable. And yet, as before, the inhabitants complained of boredom. If, as Clyde Kluckhohn says, "each different way of life makes its own assumptions about the ends of human existence," what can be said for the premises of life at the treaty-ports or, indeed, at old Canton?

As in all preindustrial societies, this leisure and opulence were paid for, in several ways, by the lower classes. One does not have to subscribe to Marx's theory of surplus value to understand this truth. The common Chinese provided the market for opium, the cheap labor to produce the teas and silks, the servants for the Westerners' factories, and, later on, even the commodity for the coolie trade. Like slum dwellers in areas bordering on wealthy sections of modern cities, they were easily displaced by the richer Westerners whenever they wanted more land and facilities. "The style of living amongst the better class of Europeans has resulted in many inconveniences to those below them in worldly means and position," commented three writers about Amoy in the late 1860s.[15]

The Transmutation of Ghetto Attitudes

These "inconveniences" were physical evidence of a set of attitudes that became common at the treaty-ports—attitudes that had been inherited from old Canton, but which now lacked the restraints of the old Canton system. In the ghettos of medieval Europe, Jews developed a number of characteristically negative images of the Gentiles who surrounded them. The outside world was both fatefully attractive and dangerous, at times even threatening the safety of the ghetto itself. Regarded as aliens, and compelled to live under oppressive regulations apart from the rest of the population, European Jews developed conceptions of the *Goyim* that were markedly defensive. Similar conditions often make for similar attitudes.[16] Residents of the metaphorical ghetto of old Canton had begun to project upon the Chinese their fears and needs in a series of negative views that survived the power revolution of the Opium War and took root in the new settlements on the coast. In this way ideas, which grew out of fearful impotence, became stereotypes held by a powerful, exploitive elite—an odd and ominous situation. The Jews never acquired any share of their oppressor's power to demonstrate what could happen when such ideas become the basis for action. With foreigners in China after 1842, matters took a very different turn.

Long before the Opium War released it from restrictions, the Canton community had developed its own culture and continuity, borrowing heavily from British India, the Dutch in Java, and from the Chinese themselves. It was, as others have noted, a hybrid, and it exhibited the vigor frequently associated with hybrids. Yet it was dependent upon an illegal commerce condemned as immoral by the community's own spiritual leaders. The drug traders knew, of course, that like the rest of the community, their critics needed the very trade they censured. From a mere handful of residents before the War of 1812, the foreign settlement had evolved into a flourishing establishment of over one hundred permanently resident traders and missionaries, and the number of annual transients ran into the thousands. All this growth had been made possible only because the China trade had grown, and the China trade rode on the back of opium. It is remarkable, under the circumstances, that there are so few expressions of guilt in the correspondence, especially because the drug traders were often men of upright character. Perhaps the explanation of this puzzling phenomenon lies partly in the fact that the commerce had developed over several decades in tandem with other more or less questionable trades and in time of world war.

In traditional society wartime commerce almost compelled merchants to skirt the edges of the law. Dodging blockades, flying false colors, trafficking in contraband, and even privateering were simply part of mercantile life during an international conflict, even for otherwise law-abiding citizens. Seen in the light of the disturbed conditions of wartime, the American drug trade in China appears as part of a larger pattern. It was only one of a great number of imaginative and sometimes deviant ways to solve the difficult trading problems of the time. The period of its gestation—the 1790s to the early 1820s—was an era of war in all parts of the world, followed by residual conflicts especially in Latin America, the eastern Mediterranean, and Southern and Central Asia. The problem of what to take to China in exchange for teas, silks, and cottons was particularly perplexing. For people who had been evading wartime restrictions all over the globe for twenty-five years, the opium trade must have appeared relatively innocuous. Once begun the trade was revealed as a bonanza, and it soon provided the solution for which China traders had long searched. With the import bottleneck broken, the legitimate trade boomed, and the Canton community grew until it burst its bounds.

Thus conceived in sin and dependent upon smuggling for its economic life, the Canton foreign settlement's development could hardly be anything but skewed. The community's very needs impelled Americans, like other residents, toward behavior and attitudes that were selfish, exploitive, and, in practice if not intent, racist. The prosecution of the opium trade, after all, presumed something about the seller's regard for the user. It became

330

psychologically necessary for the merchant to define the Chinese as persons to whom it was appropriate to sell opium.

The Opium Trade Resumes

Not waiting for the conclusion of a treaty (which ignored them in any case), drug merchants returned to the trade as soon as it was relatively safe. It is not clear which American firm reentered the opium trade first, but certainly the British never left it. Even before the end of the captivity, James Matheson and Andrew Jardine were arranging for their drug traffic to be conducted through their Manila affiliate, Otadui & Co. (of which firm, the American John Shillaber, was a partner), ordering opium on the firm's account from Bombay, and otherwise preparing to capitalize on the new situation.[17] Although mightily harassed by Chinese officials, the British coastal trade continued despite depressed prices, a condition that was not relieved until British forces crushed Chinese resistance. While prices were low and enforcement effective, however, there was little incentive for most Americans to break their promises not to traffic in opium.

Several individual traders may have been the first Americans to reappear in the drug trade. One George W. Fraser (also known as Frazer), captain and nominal owner of Jardine's one hundred-ton schooner *Ariel*, flew the American flag as a means of avoiding British jurisdiction. Commodore Lawrence Kearny's attempt to prevent the abuse of the flag by seizing the little clipper made him the target of considerable abuse for "enforcing Chinese law" in the correspondence of members of both Heard's and Russell's.[18] A partner in the latter firm, Robert Bennet Forbes, was the builder of the vessel, and Heard's was Jardine's agent at Canton. Besides by that date, both firms were again dealing in opium themselves.

Heard and Company

Although the date of Augustine Heard & Company's entry into the trade is uncertain, it took place well before the end of the war, probably in the spring or summer of 1841. George Basil Dixwell, the firm's opium man, had arrived by May. Previously he had been a supercargo in the Bengal trade, and in November Coolidge asked Matheson to assist the young man in drug matters. Dixwell was at that time on his way to Macao "to inspect several parcels of opium consigned to us from Bombay." The letter bearing the request also carried the note in Matheson's hand, "I will advise him concerning opium."[19] Thereafter the letters from Dixwell contain much information on the firm's drug business. Early in 1842 Coolidge even offered Matheson the services of his concern in selling opium at Whampoa.[20]

At first Heard & Co. ventured in English ships, but it soon acquired its own vessels. It sent the *Don Juan,* a chartered schooner, up the coast with opium in August 1844 and made "splendid sales" at prices far above those of the sluggish Canton market.[21] By the following summer, the firm was running three vessels in the coastal trade and had purchased a fourth as a storeship but kept her under the British flag.[22] At that time the opium traffic was Augustine Heard & Company's most profitable business. Dixwell wrote Heard, "The Indian [opium] business is so much the best we have that it seems as if no effort should be spared to foster and increase it."[23]

Russell and Company

The more important of the two remaining American companies that had pledged themselves to refrain from carrying on the narcotics traffic was Russell & Co. That firm had cited in its correspondence at least four good reasons to stay clear of the illegal commerce: first it was dangerous and illegal; second it was "disreputable and immoral"; third the firm had given its word not to trade in opium; and fourth (and probably most crucial) the market was very poor so long as the Chinese continued to enforce their domestic laws. The first and the fourth reasons had now been eliminated by the British expeditionary force. The only inhibitions left were legality, morality, and honor. Balanced against these three imponderables were the weightier concerns of security and money. Once again the opium trade was by far the safest and most profitable commerce in China. Whatever the importance of other considerations at other times and under other circumstances, economic rationality very plainly dominated the thinking of the partners of Russell & Co. in 1842.

The firm remained true to Green's pledge during the period of hostilities, but, once the war was over, Russell & Co. wasted little time in resuming its opium business. Edward Delano, whose diary for 1841 contains a number of entries very clearly expressing his distaste for the drug commerce, notes laconically on 26 October 1842, "Had conversation with Mr. [Edward] King about Opium trade—he says we shall go into it on the 1st January—recommends ordering a ship of 3 or 350 tons from U.S. to which I agree." Early in 1843 Russell & Co. again was actively dealing in the narcotic, and Howqua's death in September removed a major obstacle to this part of the firm's business. Two partners, Joseph Gilman in 1842 and Edward Delano in 1843 and again in 1844, went to India. Although the purpose of Gilman's first voyage is not absolutely clear, Delano was instructed to buy opium and his references to opium production and sales in both Calcutta and Bombay make it evident that promoting Russell & Company's drug business was never far from his mind during his visits to the subcontinent.

It is also quite evident that the partners recognized the continuing odium attached to the trade for, whenever they were compelled to say anything public about the traffic, they lied about it. Possibly the most glaring of these

332

denials was that of Paul S. Forbes. Because he was also American Consul, Forbes was obliged to remain free of illegal dealings, especially within the territory of the host country. Secretary of State Legare had reminded Forbes on 2 June 1843 that his connection with an opium-trading firm was impermissible for a U.S. official.[24] Forbes denied the charge, though the participation of Russell & Co. in the drug traffic by early 1843 is established beyond doubt.

The other partner in Russell & Co. who perjured himself was the redoubtable Robert Bennet Forbes, who claimed in his *Personal Reminiscences:*

> Russell & Co. considered it important to keep the pledge made by Mr. Green, and for a long time had nothing to do with opium; certainly not within my time, between 1840 and 1844, when my interest ceased for a time.[25]

Forbes also neglects to mention that he was a partner from 1849 to 1854, when the firm was admittedly back in the trade. Moreover, although Forbes returned home in 1840 when the firm was out of the trade, he immediately began building opium clippers, the first of which was the schooner *Ariel*. She was built for sale in the trade, and she was sold to Jardine, Matheson & Co. early in 1842.[26] Clearly one claiming some kind of self-justification because of his lack of connection with the drug trade should hardly have been constructing opium vessels. Also before 1844 Forbes sent out several other such craft. These were not for sale but were the property of Russell & Co.[27]

There appears little reason to press the point. Russell & Co. obviously would not have ordered or purchased the ships unless it had a reason to use them. Forbes wrote his memoirs years after the fact, but his pride in his ships did not permit him the convenience of forgetfulness. He lists all the ships, which he had a hand in building, in the appendix to his book. One can only conclude that, like his cousin, Bennet Forbes lied.[28]

The Nature of the New Opium Trade

There was good reason to lie about participating in this latter-day drug traffic, for it differed considerably from the comparatively tranquil commerce of the early years under the Lintin system. From 1837 onward the risk was high. Additionally in breaking Chinese resistance, the British also destroyed what maritime policing existed, and piracy reappeared in more virulent form than ever. Under these conditions, only the most desperate and best organized Chinese brokers remained in the trade. By 1839, Jardine found it necessary to warn his coastal captains, "Lay it down as a rule not to be deviated from . . . Never trust one of the low fellows who accompany you along the Coast, one dollar. . . . The men sent in the Ships are generally low, unprincipled characters, not to be trusted."[29] Heavily armed Western craft made the deliveries, and the level of violence was higher than ever before. The character of the trade thus began to appear even more disreputable. The vicious behavior of some of the crews contrasted with the fact that the officers of opium vessels, whether British or American, were generally young men of excellent families.[30] Protected by Western guns and the Chinese underworld, the trade went wherever there was demand.

And it certainly was profitable, despite the lamentations about low prices. In the midst of the Opium War, James Matheson wrote Andrew Jardine, "Do not be afraid of wanting money. We have ample for every purpose. . . . Morgan sells . . . a Lac a month—Davis and Scott [captains in the coastal trade] perhaps half a Lac a month. . . . Morgan's balance on 1st May was nearly 6 Lacs."[31] Even allowing for the high wages paid in the smuggling trade, two hundred thousand dollars gross for a month was a comfortable profit for a single ship.

In 1842 the Canton newspapers carried a number of articles deploring the "licentiousness of the crews of the Opium vessels at Whampoa."[32] The *Register* commented editorially,

> everyone must know what sort of a community is likely to be formed by a body of seafaring men pursuing an illegal trade at the mouth of their own guns; their success in trading depending upon sharp competition one with the other and their security being in their united might.[33]

Actually this was prophecy. The Canton estuary was to become the scene of some of the most brutal actions in the history of the trade.[34]

When the Americans returned to this commerce, they were compelled to adopt its operative procedures, including violence and disregard of Chinese life and property. The most grievously hurt by this turn of events, as always, were the most inoffending—Chinese fisherman, small traders, and boat people. A British seaman engaged in the drug trade casually noted the attitude of the smugglers: "We always make a practice of running over the Chinese fishing boats by night, for they will not get out of our way."[35] The *Canton Register* further noted the futility of Chinese resistance to this ugly business. Because no fleet that the Chinese could muster could match the weaponry and speed of the smuggler's vessels, the only path of defense open to the Chinese authorities was shore batteries, but this alternative would have been both ineffective and a violation of the newly signed Treaty of Nanking. British naval vessels stationed in the area would have intervened. Thus the continuation of the traffic was insured and protected.[36]

All this data was common knowledge in the foreign community, particularly among those interested in the trade. The partners of Augustine Heard & Co. and of Russell's were fully aware of the implications of their actions when they made their separate decisions to reenter the opium trade in the months after the Chinese capitulation.

334

The North Coast

But this was in the Canton estuary. In the increasingly important markets established at the various stations along the East Coast, things may have been more peaceful, at least at first. Certainly plenty of ships were coming and going to the Coast and to India, Manila, and Singapore. Houses at Canton and Hong Kong took pride in the comfortable passages, the rakish lines, and the astonishing speed of their opium clippers. Their names indicate something of the owners' feelings: the *Ariel,* the *Red Rover,* the *Antelope,* the *Zephyr,* the *Coquette,* the *Will-of-the-Wisp,* and the various bird schooners—the *Kestrel,* the *Lark,* the *Swallow,* the *Petrel,* the *Falcon,* and so on. Letters and diaries left by Canton residents continually refer to the arrival and departure of these sinister but lovely vessels, and who knows if the merchants who plied this trade from the safety and luxury of Canton and the treaty ports gave even a second thought to the misery they brought to thousands of harmless people?

Meantime the regularity of the commerce and the speed and security of the clippers made them the common carrier of mail, persons and valuable goods. The cash surplus the trade generated made narcotics traders the bankers and insurers of the rest of the community during the early years at the new ports. For a number of such important services as well as for their commercial base, the treaty-ports were even more heavily dependent upon the drug traffic than old Canton had been. Consequently the influence of the opium trade persisted and probably increased. In fact it was an arch-symbol. It represented the triumph of economic necessity over moral imperatives, exemplifying many merchants' basically predatory attitude toward Asia and the inability of China to resist them.

Rationalizations notwithstanding the issue was reasonably clear, for some firms declined to deal in opium for moral reasons, although they realized that they were placing themselves at an economic disadvantage in so doing. James Matheson was not telling his London correspondent any secret when he wrote, "it is the command of money which we derive from our large Opium dealings and which can hardly be acquired from any other Source [that] gives us important advantages."[37]

The Moral Implications of the Traffic

Yet even those who did not take part in the traffic accepted, to some degree, the premises on which the trade was based, for nonsmugglers were a part of the community that opium had created. Thus all benefited from the illegal commerce, and all Westerners were affected by community opinion. The treaty-ports produced a frame of mind that has become notorious. There is a continuous line of development from the beginning of the drug trade to the emergence of that poisonous set of attitudes sometimes called the "Shanghai mind."[38]

To the economic necessity and the symbolism of the opium trade must be added the primary motivation of every American China merchant. He was there to acquire a "competency" as quickly as possible. In the acquisitive atmosphere of old Canton and at the treaty ports, secondary motivations were kept in check. Here, if anywhere, the "economic man" of the classical economists was to be found in the flesh. China traders were rational, profit-maximizing entrepreneurs in Canton, where few pressures from family, custom, religion, or law restrained them. They had come to seek a fortune; they would wrest it from China and go home to practice their ethics.

One of the most brutal expressions of this commercial errantry, with all its power and [acknowledged!] possibilities for evil, was reported some years later in Shanghai when a mercantile resident remarked to the famous British consul, Rutherford Alcock:

> No doubt your anticipations of future evil have a certain foundation. . . . They *will* probably come, when those who then may be here will see abundant cause to regret what is now being done. . . . But it is my business to make a fortune with the least possible loss of time . . . in two or three years at farthest, I hope to realise a fortune and get away and what can it matter to me, if all Shanghai disappear afterwards, in fire or flood? You must not expect men in my situation to condemn themselves to years of prolonged exile in an unhealthy climate for the benefit of posterity. We are money-making, practical men. Our business is to make money, as much and as fast as we can;—and for this end all modes or means are good which the law permits.[39]

It may be that the danger of such destructive attitudes is built into all capitalist enterprise unrestrained by a strong moral strictures and an enforced legal code. It has recently been noted that Adam Smith found the same attitude among East India Company servants.[40] But the "Shanghai mind" was not merely greedy self-concern. It also involved an ignorant contempt for Chinese values and life. This attitude took time to develop and to become a part of the common mental equipment. It required a change in the power structure and habituation to cruelty. So long as the foreigners remained few in number and Chinese power went unchallenged, factory denizens remained respectful, or at least bigots did not dare parade their prejudices.

The antiopium campaign of the late 1830s increased the community's familiarity with violence, and the war brought appalling massacres as masses of Chinese soldiers confronted modern weaponry for the first time. Brutality became casual.

> The slaughter of fugitives is unpleasant, but we are such a handful in the face of so wide a country and so large a force, that we should be swept away if we did not read our enemy a sharp lesson wherever we came in contact.[41]

336

Such was the justification of one British soldier. During the Opium War the contrast between the traditional fierce posturing of Chinese soldiers before a battle and the heaps of corpses after a "battle" made for an anomalous response from the American observers. They were at once sympathetic, contemptuous, amused, and horrified. Although Edward Delano pitied the Chinese, he also was exasperated at their weakness and "cowardice." To this was added a tendency to ridicule. Delano's diary contains a story that even today retains its pathos and desperate humor.

> Capt Eyres of H.B.M. Sloop of war "Modeste" came on board. He was agreeable. Says that during the engagement, or previous to the engagement at Anc..ghoy fort, a linguist came on board his ship begging him not to be in too much haste in discharging the guns, and further stated that if the English would not put any iron or lead in their guns, he would not! This said the Chinese would give them time to escape.[42]

The manner of handling accidental killings of Chinese reinforced cultural attitudes. For years such incidents had been quieted by a payment to the family of the deceased. Sums that seemed enormous to a coolie's widow were paltry to a merchant used to daily dealings in kegs of specie.[43] The consequent disgust of traders at the "venality" of the Chinese was as natural as it was unfair, and it served to strengthen the conviction that the Chinese set a very low value on human life.[44] This kind of accident became more common at the treaty-ports. Avid bird hunters at Shanghai sometimes accidentally shot peasants on whose land they were stalking game. A few dollars to the family and an appeal to the local authorities brought immunity from any retribution. "Which of us has not had this experience?" asked Dyce with startling frankness in 1906.[45]

Missionary Attitudes

The missionaries were no exceptions. They struck up friendships with merchants whose livelihood they despised, they cashed letters of credit with opium merchants, accepted their services in missionary institutions, and used smuggling craft to journey up and down the coast and to carry their mail. Merchants and missionaries wrote for each others' publications, shared accommodations, and joined each others' organizations and social gatherings. Small wonder that they developed similar interests and attitudes.

At least part of this identity of viewpoint is to be expected. Even more than merchants the missionaries tended toward rigidity in their cultural values and a corresponding contempt for Chinese culture and customs. Some see a major racist component in the missionaries' opinion of the Chinese, and, because most Westerners probably shared a low opinion of nonwhite peoples generally, they were probably not exempt.[46] Nevertheless missionary publications and correspondence, as a rule, seem to show less racial feeling than do mercantile writings, and there is much evidence of a very different nature. The early missionaries made strong efforts to love the Chinese. They accepted them as fellow beings with equal claim to Christian concern. This regard clearly was a function of the missionaries' more profound allegiance to the universalist teachings of Christianity. It was to be the instrument of saving these otherwise hopeless creatures, after all, that the missionaries had come to China.[47]

Yet to speak of saving others presumes at least cultural superiority over them. The missionaries could not regard the Chinese as equals so long as they remained in their graceless condition.[48] As with the merchants, the nature of the missionaries' contacts with the Chinese made this attitude almost inevitable. Although sympathy and affection were encouraged by the faith and were explicitly recognized as missionary methods as well as virtues, it is notable that they were largely directed toward children, servants, or patients, that is, people identified as inferiors or petitioners for help. Incidentally they were also the most likely to accept the faith.

It was a rare missionary who protested against the extraterritorial or other "unequal" clauses in the new treaties. On the contrary there was considerable attraction for many in the "forward policy" adopted by the British. A contemporary clergyman put the contradiction nicely. The war, he noted,

> was regarded by the religious public, both in England and in this country, as one whose objects were wholly unjustifiable, and whose results would probably tend still further to alienate the empire from all Christian nations. . . . The result was hailed with thankfulness and joy.[49]

It was one thing to deplore the war and the hatred it would arouse, but it was quite another to ignore the opportunities for evangelism that the "unequal treaties" opened up. It was for this, after all, that the members of the Mission had been praying ever since they had begun their labors in the very limited vineyard of Canton and Macao. They could hardly be expected to reject the benefits of the changed political situation. That the ways of God are inscrutable, and that he works his purposes even through the evil doings of sinful men were axioms to men of the cloth. In this fashion they had the best of both worlds: they could condemn the war and welcome the fruits of victory.

The Survival of the Ghetto

Dead institutions, especially once they come to be regarded as immoral, are often a mystery to generations that have never experienced them. Insti-

338

tutionalized evil, after all, is somehow more tolerable than radical, novel wickedness. Like the traditional church, most people come to live with ancient sins, though not necessarily approving of them. Gradually, however, cannibalism, human sacrifice, slavery, racism, imperialism, and all kinds of exploitation have come under the ban of an increasingly sensitive humanity. Most of the vast and largely unexplored ethical revolution has taken place in the past two hundred years. Hence the present generation's understandable but regrettable bias against the past. The good old days are now the bad old days, and with this growing sense of horror at the sins of our ancestors has come more than a little self-righteousness.

I do not wish to be either a moralist or an apologist, but an historian is trapped by his profession. Judgment may be the Lord's, but avoiding judgment on an immoral act seems immoral in itself. Even the most objective writer cannot avoid stating facts, which often indict unless explained away. There are temptations in both directions—either to defend the people one has begun to understand (and one meaning of understanding is sympathy) or to condemn the evil. The line is difficult to discern, let alone to hold. I hope I have not succumbed to my dilemma.[50] I have found in the opium trade a key to the understanding of the early American community in China and to the shaping of our first official China policy. Thus, I have given the drug traffic special attention. It may be that tea or silk was equally influential, but I do not believe it.

Under almost any circumstances, people far from their homes behave differently from more sedentary folk. They also are changed by their experiences. When they return to the place of their origin, they often carry back in their luggage strange ideas, tastes, and perspectives. They are marginal, not quite fully integrated into any culture, but they sometimes have shown great capacity for changing things, both at home and abroad. Few of the Canton residents individually were movers and shakers, but collectively the community was the agency of momentous historical action. In addition a number of Canton nabobs became leaders in the American industrial revolution after their return home. Many were known for their exotic tastes, sumptuous living, and, oddly, their conservative business ethics.

Except for a handful of lately arrived clergymen and an occasional doctor or naval officer, the only Americans who went to China before the Opium War were businessmen. Even the consuls were primarily merchants, as Congress scrimped and cut corners to ensure that the Foreign Service cost as little as possible. Thus it was that the American community, which grew up in the only port in China open to them, was a mercantile community. I do not wish to slight the missionaries. Although few in number, they were most important, and some very competent scholars are currently investigating them. Yet the community's soul was commercial, and in their backgrounds, day-to-day requirements, and attitudes, merchants and missionaries were not strikingly different.

339

The Americans were a comparatively large group at Canton, second only to the British, and they were self-consciously distinct. Most importantly they were the effective agents in transferring whatever was moved from China to America or vice versa—goods, people, ideas, or influences. It has long been clear that America did not cut her China policy out of whole cloth but received it pretty nearly complete from her nationals resident in Canton. It is only by understanding these people that we can begin to comprehend their needs and concerns. I have attempted to describe the Americans' origins, daily lives, their business methods and organizations, their later lives, and their relation to the some of the great events that took place on the coast of China during the sixty years of the old China trade. I have done so in the hope that others will become interested in this and other examples of what might be called "private international relations." Just as it was a critical element in the origin of official relations in the 1840s, it was also important elsewhere in what has come to be called the Third World, and it remains important today.

Moreover its influence on China continued long after Caleb Cushing went home. One of the most significant lines of continuity between old Canton and the treaty-ports was that of opinion. Beginning with the ghetto psychology of Canton and extending to racial attitudes, exploitive frames of mind, the confusion of luxury and necessity—in fact, with most of the alterations of traditional democratic and Protestant values, the treaty-ports strongly resembled Canton before the Opium War.[51]

It will be recalled that the isolation of foreigners was originally a Chinese idea, begun and continued as a means of preventing contamination of China by the barbarians. The same motive led to the ban on alien women, to the prohibition against learning foreign languages, or to teaching the outsiders Chinese and the Eight Regulations generally. Gradually members of the foreign community came to accept and even to value their segregation. Perpetuated and legitimized by the "unequal treaties," the ghetto became a place of privilege and a target for Chinese xenophobia. As the foreigners' fear of the Chinese developed, they grew increasingly concerned for the security of their persons and property. "Their position . . . on the very edge of a teeming continent, exposed to a hostility which was more cultural than political . . . created an underlying solidarity among the foreign residents."[52] As Manchu authority deteriorated and disorder increased, this solidarity grew proportionately. It reached something of a peak, or rather a plateau, in 1853, when the Shanghai community raised its own troops and barred all Chinese soldiers, rebel (Taiping) or imperial, from the settlement. Thereafter the barbarians were regularly united by the strongest of motives—self-defense.

Luxury, isolation, fear, local hostility, the "natives" visible only as menials, the universality of avarice, and the acceptance of the narcotics trade made the treaty-port a breeding ground for vicious myth and cavalier arro-

340

gance. Because the existence of the opium traffic had already identified the Chinese as exploitable, they became available for other dubious trades. With the beginning of the Taiping Rebellion and the uprising of the Triads at Shanghai, Americans sold arms, food, and services to both sides. As the practice of competitive convoying and the coolie trade developed (the latter especially at Swatow), it was clear that the old disregard for the Chinese, especially those of the lower orders, had not only survived but had taken root elsewhere and had produced new and more malignant growths. The ricksha, which some see as a symbol of the "cultural miscegenation"[53] of the treaty-port, also represented the white Shanghailander's view of his position in East Asia. It converted the coolie into a beast of burden in the service of the Westerner.

Living as a privileged minority in well-upholstered comfort, insulated from, but extracting fortunes from various kinds of exploitation, Americans in the treaty-ports could hardly be expected to develop enlightened social attitudes. Because they saw their residence as temporary, and they knew that a fortune was self-justifying at home, Americans were the less willing to disturb the mores of treaty-port culture. It would have been surprising, given this milieu, had more humane or more democratic views prevailed. When they became used to the workings of extraterritoriality, foreign residents' irresponsibility and arrogance grew proportionately. The ultimate product of this development was the granitic "Shanghai mind" that came to characterize many residents of the treaty-ports. Americans who became absorbed into this community not infrequently adopted its mentality, and because American merchants were a continuing force in American foreign policy, it is scarcely necessary to note that U.S. flexibility was probably impaired by the residence of American citizens at the treaty-ports. To say that many of these attitudes and customs clashed harshly with both the national and the Protestant creeds is also to say that the mercantile influence on American foreign policy often worked against the dictates of both, as well as against any larger view of the common national interest.

Thus comparatively well-educated Americans, with democratic and Christian ideals, joined a very pleasant, comfortable community which became the means for altering or even of sloughing off these ideals. The Canton community and its heir, treaty-port culture, provided an easy way of transvaluing both the ideology of the Declaration of Independence and the Christian imperative. Through the Canton community, both merchants and missionaries met the problems of imperialism and racism together with the rest of Western civilization. The compromises these American exiles made with their ideals were to return to haunt this nation and to frustrate its policies and purposes.

341

"The American Consul's Four-in-Hand," from a stereoscope photograph. Notice the unusual construction of the sedan chair. The bearers carry it Indian file, not abreast. While this arrangement undoubtedly facilitated getting through narrow streets and crowds, it must have been difficult to turn sharp corners. Courtesy of the Peabody & Essex Museum.

453

The Legacy of Old Canton

1. John K. Fairbank, "The American Approach to China, ca. 1840–1860," draft paper for the January 1970 Cuernavaca Conference on American East Asian Relations, 16.

2. Charles M. Dyce, *Personal Reminiscences of Thirty Year's Residence in the Model Settlement, Shanghai, 1870–1900* (London: Chapman & Hall, 1906), 46–48.

3. The similarity of treaty-port institutions to those of British India is a commonplace. See John King Fairbank, *Trade and Diplomacy on the China Coast, 1842–1854* (1953, one vol. ed. Cambridge: Harvard University Press, 1964), 157, and Rhoads Murphey, "Traditionalism and Colonialism: Changing Urban Roles in Asia," *Journal of Asian Studies* 29 (November 1969). See also such works on British India as Percival Spear's *The Nabobs* (London: H. Milford, Oxford University Press, 1932), and Dennis Kincaid, *British Social Life in India, 1608–1937* 2d ed. (Port Washington: New York: Kennikat Press, 1973). More recent is George Woodcock's *The British in the Far East* (New York: Atheneum, 1969).

4. Chang Chung-li. *The Income of the Chinese Gentry* (Seattle: University of Washington, 1982), 167–68.

5. Fairbank calls it the "Cantonization" of the newer ports. See especially his chap. XXI, 383–409. Discussion of at least part of the process went on at the time it was happening. Bridgman, for example, considered the linguists "indispensable," and said so in the *Repository* XII (September 1843): 500. See also Woodcock, *British in the Far East*, 16–17, *passim*.

6. On the origins of the Maritime Customs Service, see Fairbank, *Trade and Diplomacy*, 438–68, and Stanley F. Wright, *Origin and Development of the Chinese Customs Service, 1843–1911* (1936; reprint, Shanghai: Privately printed, 1939).

7. Dyce, *Personal Reminiscences*, 31 and Anonymous, *The Englishman in China* (London, 1860), 49 and 192.

8. C. A. Montalto de Jesus, *Historic Shanghai* (Shanghai: Kelly & Walsh, 1909), 35; Fairbank, *Trade and Diplomacy*, 156–57, and Rhoads Murphey in *The Chinese City Between Two Worlds*, Mark Elvin and G. William Skinner, eds. (Stanford, Calif.: Stanford University Press, 1974), 19–20.

9. Refugees flocked in especially with the Taiping Rebellion. See Rutherford Alcock, *The Capital of the Tycoon* (London, 1863), I: 38. Incidentally in the treaty-ports as in old Canton, it was the Chinese who insisted upon segregation. See Montalto, *Historic Shanghai*, 37.

10. James Ryan to JM, 17 June 1841, Canton Letters, JMA.

11. Fairbank notes that a tea-taster was called a *cha-see* or an "expectorator"; a silk inspector was a *tsze-tsze* or "grub"; a bookkeeper was called "books"; and so forth. See Fairbank, *Trade and Diplomacy*, 160.

12. Dyce describes the typical layout as well as anyone. Inside the walled compound, he notes that the residence hall-countinghouse was two stories high with thick walls and interior halls in the form of a cross, meeting in the center of the building, where the staircase was located. There were four very large rooms on each floor and a veranda on both floors running around all sides of the building. In the compound's walls, there were two gates, the front entrance, and a more modest rear exit. See Dyce, *Personal Reminiscences*, 33–35. Montalto calls the architectural mode, "Italian villa style or orientalised by the addition of verandahs, and generally with gardens where, amidst thriving home flowers, pheasants were to be seen sometimes." Montalto, *Historic Shanghai*, 41–47. Cf. W. F. Myers, N. B. Dennys, and Charles King, *The Treaty Ports of China and Japan* . . . (London, 1867), 378.

13. See the customary Shanghai dinner described in Fairbank, *Trade and Diplomacy*, 160–61.

454

14. Only two of the factories at Canton had gardens, and they were comparatively small.

15. Meyers, Dennys, and King, *Treaty Ports*, 118.

16. It is instructive to read Louis Wirth's classic *The Ghetto* (1928; reprint New York: MacMillan & Co., 1956) with old Canton (and the treaty-ports) in mind. The points of similarity are striking: the ghetto was a method of social control of a "dissenting" (read "foreign") minority, of achieving tolerance and security through prophylaxis. There was "partial autonomy" in the ghetto, and its residents were seen as a source of income by the leaders of the majority. Residents were subjected to a series of regulations on their residence, mobility, and occupations and were frequently abused by the populace if they violated any of these rules. The ghetto was generally near the marketplace, because Jews were frequently involved in trade, money-lending, and other service occupations that revolved about the market. One of the strongest forces in ghetto cohesiveness was the treatment of Jews as a community by the majority. Typical institutions included the synagogue (church), cemetery, schools, hospitals, and other philanthropic organizations. "The ghetto is not only a physical fact; it is also a state of mind" and so on. Wirth even goes so far as to suggest that "the whites in the cities of China" constituted a kind of ghetto (282). Clearly the idea is not an extraordinary one.

17. JM to T. W. Henderson, Bombay, 5 and 11 May 1839, and to WJ, 8 May 1839, JM Private LB, JMA.

18. AH to PCB, 15 June 1843, HP; Paul S. Forbes, "Journal," 26 May 1843; FP and JH to parents, 14 June 1843, HP. Although it is probably impossible to prove that individual merchants preceded the firms into the drug trade, people like Fraser and Sturgis certainly had the motives and plenty of experience. Moreover their names appear in the trade very early, and at least Sturgis seems to have stayed in the trade. Edward Delano noted on 2 January 1844 that Sturgis had despatched the *Don Juan* "for the East Coast with Drugs" (ED's diary). Tyler Dennett states simply that Sturgis was "implicated in drug smuggling" (*Americans in Eastern Asia* [1922; reprint, New York: Barnes & Noble, 1941], 124).

19. JC to JM, 26 November 1841, Canton Letters, JMA.

20. JC to JM, 2 January 1842, JMA.

21. Dixwell to AH, 3 September 1844 and 17 November 1844, HP. Fairbank says merely, "Augustine Heard and Company of Boston began to act as Jardine's agents in Canton in 1840, and soon were distributing Indian opium on their own account" (*Trade and Diplomacy*, 226).

22. Dixwell to AH, 27 July 1845, HP. This was the brig, *Snipe*, William Endicott, master.

23. Ibid.

24. Legare to Forbes, 2 June 1843, U.S. Department of State, Instructions to Consuls, X: 191–92.

25. *PRs*, 161. In a letter to his wife dated 17 October 1839, Forbes had taken a somewhat different stand. Musing over the loss of his first fortune in 1837, he wondered if "perhaps Providence took away my fortune because I made it in Opium. What I make this time will be free from that stain," FFP.

26. ED reported the sale in his diary (for twelve thousand dollars), and regretted that she would be used in the drug trade under American colors, but he fails to give the name of the purchaser. See also his admiring description of the Forbes-built *Zephyr* in his diary, 4 September 1842.

27. And he was still a partner in that prospering firm. RBF, *PRs*, appendix. See also Basil Lubbock, *The Opium Clippers* (Boston: Charles E. Lauriat, 1933) 247 and 258. Building fast, well-armed vessels (generally schooners) for the opium trade was

not a new business. As early as the mid-1820s, Americans were so engaged. See testimony of Sir Charles Marjoribanks, 23 February 1830, First Report on the East Indian Company's Affairs, H/C, 1830, V., questions 858 and 859, and THP to JPC, 15 January 1825, SCP. See also letters from the Perkinses in May-June 1826, J.E.C., "Extracts."

28. Interestingly when R. B. Forbes was preparing a history of Russell & Co. for the second edition of his *Personal Reminiscences*, he encountered considerable resistance from the partners to printing anything whatever about the firm. His brother, John Murray, and Paul S. Forbes were particularly disturbed. Ultimately John Forbes bought the copyright in order "to use scissors wherever he chooses in cutting out objectionable parts." Thus it may have been the influence of others that restrained the usually candid "Black Ben." See RBF to WD, 28 February 1879, FAD Papers, DP. See appendix for excerpts from family letters concerning this affair.

29. To Captain Jauncey, *Governor Findley*, 11 January 1839, WJ Private LB, JMA. The hand is Henry Wright's, but the voice is Jardine's.

30. Fairbank, *Trade and Diplomacy*, 226, and Lubbock, *Opium Clippers*, 18–19.

31. 4 May 1841, Macao Letters, JMA. In the difficult months from June to December 1839, when Chinese enforcement was at its most effective and the opium trade (supposedly) depressed, Captain John Rees, who continued selling on the coast for Jardine's, reported sales of nearly $1.2 million worth of the drug. See Rees's Account Sales Book, JMA. A much higher figure is indicated by the rough accounts current from 1840 to June 1841. By this time the coastal trade was over twice the size of the Canton-area sales. Indeed the figure given is so high as to stretch one's credulity— $4,365,662.09! JMA. Joseph Coolidge had written Heard on 29 November 1839, "The opium trade is flourishing vigorously. Patna is selling at $900 which costs at Singapore 150—and large quantities are arriving from Bombay and Calcutta. Jardine Matheson & Co. is said to have made 1,000,000 dls in opium in Septr.—This sounds large—but there must be some foundation for it for I heard it from an enemy," HP. See also RBF to SC, 3 March 1840, SCP.

32. E.g., *CPress*, 2 July 1842.

33. *CReg*, 5 July 1842.

34. A letter to Lord Aberdeen in the British Foreign Office, dated 6 April 1843, describes the evils of the new smuggling methods and their perpetrators: "I do not believe that there is a Gang of Burglars and Highway Robbers in England more relentless, more unfeeling and more cruel in their occupations, more thoroughly lost to all our common feelings of humanity than these British semi-pirates upon the Canton River, and upon some portions of the China coast" (quoted more fully in Fairbank, *Trade and Diplomacy*, 71–72, n. e).

35. Fairbank, *Trade and Diplomacy*, 72, n. e.

36. *CReg*, 5 July 1842.

37. To John Abel Smith, 8 September 1841, JM Private LB, JMA. A decade later another British merchant commented sourly that in his firm's refusal to handle opium, "We seem to have placed ourselves here in altogether a false position, by assuming an establishment, and an expenditure corresponding . . . with the leading Houses English and American, while by excluding opium . . . we are precluded from those sources of profit which *may* justify them in their large expenditure." See W. S. Brown, Shanghai to William Rathbone, Jr., Liverpool, 3 July 1851, quoted by S. G. Checkland, "An English Merchant House in China after 1842," *Bulletin of the Business Historical Society*, 27 (1953): 189, n. 85.

38. Cf. Rhoads Murphey, who believes the attitude was the product of decades of Western frustration with Chinese failure to change: "The treaty port mind, evolving from early expectations through frustrations and becoming in later decades more

456

and more bitter." *The Outsiders: The Western Experience in China and India* (Ann Arbor: University of Michigan Press, 1977), 137.

39. Alcock, *Capital of the Tycoon*, I: 37–38. This passage is partially quoted in Fairbank, 161, n. c. Cf. Robert Bennet Forbes's less strident phrasing, "I did not come here for my health, neither to effect a reform, moral or political, but to get the needful wherewithall to be useful & happy at home." RBF's LB, 7 August 1839, reel 1, frame 335, RBFP.

40. *Wealth of Nations* (London, 1776), 605, quoted by Rhoads Murphey, Changing Urban Roles," 78.

41. A. S. H. Mountain, *Memoirs and Letters* (London, 1857), 199.

42. ED's diary, "off Tiger Island," 11 March 1841.

43. ED's Diary, 17 and 18 January 1841.

44. Such payments may well have looked very different to Confucian Chinese. There were "many exceptions and special circumstances" that were recognized in Chinese law. Moreover "the total role of formal law in ordinary life was limited . . . by the prominence of the customary (and largely unwritten) law of clan, guild, council of local gentry and other extra-legal organs." Derk Bodde, "Basic Concepts of Chinese Law," *Proceedings of the American Philosophical Society* 107 no. 5 (October 1963): 393.

45. Dyce, 149.

46. Wu Chao-kwang (also known as Chao-kwang Wu), *The International Aspects of the Missionary Movement in China* (1930; reprint, AMS Press, 1977), 239–40, and S. Y. Teng, "The Predisposition of Westerners in Treating Chinese History and Civilization," *The Historian* 19 (1953): 319.

47. Woodcock states, "If, between 1840 and 1949, the Christian missionaries played a major role in the spread of western education and of western medicine in China it was due in the greater part to American effort. While until 1940 the British remained the most important western power in China politically and commercially, in the field of religion, and particularly of practical Christianity, they lost the lead almost in the beginning and never regained it." Woodcock, *The British in the Far East*, 104.

48. The missionaries commonly blamed the evils they saw (and fancied) all around them in China—lying, stealing, fornication, infanticide, brutality, etc.—to the absence of the Light. The conversion of China, therefore, would go further than any other single reform to help China solve its problems. Modernization was identified with Christianization. See Stuart Creighton Miller, *The Unwelcome Immigrant* (Berkeley and Los Angeles: University of California Press, 1969), especially chap. IV, "The Protestant Missionary Image, 1807–1870," 57–80.

49. William Gammell, *A History of American Baptist Missions* (Boston, 1849), 197–98. See also Peter W. Fay, "The Protestant Mission and the Opium War," *PHR* 40 no. 2 (May 1971): 145–61, especially 161, and Stuart Creighton Miller, "Ends and Means: Missionary Justification of Force in Nineteenth Century China," in John K. Fairbank, ed., *The Missionary Enterprise in China and America* (Cambridge: Harvard University Press, 1974), 251–57. The latest and most complete study of the missionaries will be coming out this year. See Murray Rubenstein, *Origins of the Anglo-American Missionary Enterprise in China, 1807–1840.* (Metuchen, N.J.: Scarecrow Press, ATLA Monograph Series #33, 1994).

50. I suspect Peter Fay believes I have. See Forword.

51. Woodcock traces this disrespect and the freebooting activities that it spawned among the British directly back to the opium trade of the 1830s (*The British in the Far East*, 19).

52. Fairbank, *Trade and Diplomacy* 159.

53. Ibid., *Trade and Diplomacy*, 466.

5

American Continentalism: An Idea of Expansion, 1845–1910

Charles Vevier

IDEOLOGY is the means by which a nation bridges the gap between its domestic achievement and its international aspiration. American continentalism, as the term is used here, provided just such an order of ideology and national values. It consisted of two related ideas. First, it regarded the United States as possessing identical "national and imperial boundaries." These were located within the physical framework of a "remarkably coherent geographic unit of continental extent." Second, it viewed much of North America as a stage displaying the evolving drama of a unique political society, distinct from that of Europe and glowing in the white light of manifest destiny.[1] This attitude sharpened the practice of American foreign policy. Encountering the opposition of Europe's powers, it asserted that the United States was engaged in a domestic and therefore inevitable policy of territorial extension across the continent. American diplomacy in the nineteenth century thus appeared to demonstrate national political and social worth rather than acknowledge its active involvement in international affairs. Relying on its separation from the Old World, the United States redefined the conventional terms of foreign relations by domesticating its foreign policy.

But sharp and immediate disengagements in history are rare. Professor Norman Graebner has argued persuasively that the acquisition of Oregon and California—conventionally set within the background of territorial expansion to the west and guaranteed by manifest destiny—was due predominantly to martime influence and executed by a President whose party repre-

---

* Mr. Vevier presented this essay under its original title "Imperial Aspects of American Continentalism" at the annual meeting of the American Historical Association in Washington, D. C., on December 28, 1958. An associate professor at the University of Wisconsin-Milwaukee, the author's major interest is the history of American foreign policy and his major publication is *The United States and China, 1906–1913* (New Brunswick, N. J., 1955).

[1] Bernard De Voto, *The Course of Empire* (Boston, 1952), xiii and Albert K. Weinberg, *Manifest Destiny* (Baltimore, Md., 1935), 1–2, 8. For an over-all definition of continentalism, see Charles A. Beard, *A Foreign Policy for America* (New York, 1940), 12–35. The argument presented in this paper is not in support or opposition to Beard as such; in fact, I have derived a considerable portion of the argument by reversing the order of Beard's term continental Americanism, in order to demonstrate that his insulationist outlook is also subject to an expansionist interpretation. See Max Lerner, *America as a Civilization* (New York, 1957), 887–88, who raises this issue in a mild way without intending to pursue it further.

Charles Vevier

sented the agrarian expansionism of Jefferson.[2] In spite of its apparent territorial insularity, American continentalism was bound to an older doctrine that had been overshadowed by the record of land acquisition of the 1840's. In these years, and in the 1850's as well, there were some men who were affected by the outlook of American continentalism and who adapted for their own ends the great objective of European expansion that dated from the age of Columbus and the Elizabethans. They sought to deepen commercial contact with Asia, an ambition that added a maritime dimension to the era of territorial expansion preceding the Civil War.

Students of American Far Eastern policy have already pointed out the rough coincidence of the westward movement across the continent with the rising activity of American interest in the Pacific Ocean and trade in China.[3] By the early 1840's, Hawaii had already shifted into the continental orbit.[4] Exploration of the Pacific Ocean had been undertaken by the government beginning with the Wilkes expedition in 1838 and concluding with the Ringgold voyages to the northern Pacific in 1853–1859.[5] The Cushing Treaty with China in 1844 and the opening of Japan by Perry a decade later reflected the attraction of Far Eastern trade markets to American merchants on the Atlantic seaboard. The gold strike of 1849 stimulated railroad passage across the Isthmus of Panama, encouraged shipping operations between New York and California,[6] and suggested continuation of this traffic to the Orient. The wider commercial possibilities implied by these forces meshed with an older American interest in the Caribbean, particularly in Cuba and the picket line of West Indian islands that ran down to Latin America. In an age of the clipper ship and the steady reduction of the tariff at the behest of agrarian elements, these developments drew taut the strand of national mercantile expansionist ambition that seemingly had lain slack while the territorial lines of American continentalism were cast westward across North America. This added tension suggested to some that the United States was linked to the historic expansionism of Europe westward to Asia, that it was the fulfillment of the long search for a "passage to India," and that a great

[2] Norman Graebner, *Empire on the Pacific* (New York, 1955), 3, 218; Robert G. Cleland, "Asiatic Trade and American Occupation of the Pacific Coast," *Annual Report, American Historical Association, 1914* (2 vols., Washington, D. C., 1916), I, 283, *passim.*
[3] Eldon Griffin, *Clippers and Consuls* (Ann Arbor, Mich., 1938), 9–12 and Tyler Dennett, *Americans in Eastern Asia* (New York, 1922), 175–76, 178.
[4] Harold Whitman Bradley, "Hawaii and the American Penetration of the Northeastern Pacific 1800–1845," *Pacific Historical Review*, XII (Sept. 1943), 286–87.
[5] Allan B. Cole, "The Ringgold-Rodgers-Brooke Expedition to Japan and the North Pacific, 1853–1859," *ibid.*, XVI (May 1947), 152 ff.
[6] John Haskell Kemble, "The Panama Route to the Pacific Coast, 1848–1869," *ibid.*, VII (Feb. 1938), 1 ff.

American Continentalism 325

mercantile empire could be developed on the basis of Asian commerce.[7]

Historians have been prone to examine American expansionism in terms of conflicting mercantile and agrarian interests.[8] They have overlooked the presence of a unifying view of American world geographical centralism that was grounded in a "geopolitical" interpretation of American continentalism and its place in the history of Europe's expansion to Asia. What emerged was a combination of two deterministic patterns of thought reflected in the outlook of such men as William Gilpin, Asa Whitney, Matthew Fontaine Maury, and Perry McDonough Collins. These men shaped an expectation of commercial empire as an end in itself as well as a means of developing the internal continental empire. Today, after the bitter experiences of its practice in the 1930's, geopolitics deservedly has an unsavory reputation. Although it did not exist in any organized form or established theory before the Civil War, it was, nevertheless, a conceptual instrument whose economic implications projected American continentalism onto the world scene and anticipated in some respects its greater use by the expansionists of 1898.

William Gilpin, "America's first Geopolitician,"[9] declared that the unifying geographical features of the North American continent, particularly the Mississippi Valley, contrasted favorably with Europe and Asia. A summary of his views in the period 1846–1849 reveals his belief that the physical environment of America promised the growth of an area equal in population and resources to that of the entire world. A Jeffersonian democrat and a devotee of the writings of Alexander von Humboldt, he believed in the inevitable westward march of an agrarian civilization to the Pacific Ocean. He also associated westward expansion with American commerce and whaling enterprise already established there. During the Oregon crisis in 1846, Gilpin advised congressmen, as he may have suggested to President James Polk,

---

[7] Henry Nash Smith, *Virgin Land: The American West as Symbol and Myth* (Cambridge, Mass., 1950), 3–51. Smith's work has been very helpful in this study.

[8] In his book *The Idea of National Interest* (New York, 1934), 50, Beard states: *"For the sake of convenience in tracing the application of the national interest conception* in the external relations of the United States, those relations may be divided into territorial and commercial, *although in practice the two are seldom, if ever, divorced."* My point here in citing Beard is not to raise the issue of the over-all validity of the approach to the problem that he employed. His is a great work that attempted to lay out a theoretical framework for the study of American foreign policy. In this instance, I am more interested in the agreement of belief enforced by ideology and the considerations included in it rather than in the differences fostered by economic interest and their political expression. By italicizing Beard's own qualfications above I have tried to indicate my own use of them in approaching the problem. See also footnote one.

[9] Bernard De Voto, "Geopolitics with the Dew on It," *Harper's Magazine,* CLXXXVIII (Mar. 1944), 313. De Voto's piece is brilliantly suggestive and should be read in conjunction with Smith, *Virgin Land,* 35–44. See also Maurice O. Georges, "A Suggested Revision of the Role of a Pioneer Political Scientist," *Frances Greenburg Armitage Prize Winning Essays: Armitage Competition in Oregon Pioneer History, Reed College* (2 vols., Portland, Ore., 1945–46), and James C. Malin, *The Grassland of North America* (Lawrence, Kan., 1947), 177–92.

Charles Vevier

that settlers moving into Oregon from the Mississippi Valley, the geographically favored heart of the continent, would make the mouth of the Columbia River an outlet for the export of American farm produce to Asia. Since agriculture sought through commerce an "infinite market of consumption" in the Far East, Oregon became the "maritime wing of the Mississippi Valley upon the Pacific, as New England was on the Atlantic."[10] A strong bid for Asian trade, therefore, depended on the construction of a transcontinental railroad from the Mississippi to the Columbia River that would link the agricultural heart of the North American continent with the Pacific Ocean. By developing the interior, thereby gaining access to the coast, the United States might become the center of a new world traffic pattern. America's "intermediate geographical position between Asia and Europe . . . invests her with the powers and duties of arbiter between them," he wrote in 1860. "Our continent is at once a barrier which separates the other two, yet fuses and harmonizes their intercourse in all relations from which force is absent."[11]

The Pacific railroad, in fact, was closely identified with the career of Asa Whitney, who had returned from China after a successful career as a merchant and who had campaigned from 1845 onward for the construction of a railroad from the upper portion of the Mississippi Valley to Oregon. It was Whitney's project that dominated for five years the great American debate over this vital internal transportation scheme.[12] Unless Oregon was bound to the rest of the country by a transcontinental railroad, Whitney warned, the nation would be forced to engage in a balance-of-power diplomacy in the European manner, an eventuality that he thought would destroy the continental homogeneity of America. In presenting his Pacific railway scheme, he proposed to connect Oregon with the rest of the country, open oriental trade marts to American commerce and agriculture, particularly if the railroad was tied to a Pacific Ocean shipping line, and provide an instrument for the internal development of the nation-continent that would serve as "the means, and only means, by which the vast wilderness between civilization and Oregon can be settled." Thus he exalted the continental potential

[10] Gilpin to James Semple, Mar. 17, 1846, in *Report* (*Senate Executive Document*, 29 Cong., 1 sess., V, No. 306), 21, 44, 23, 30; "Speech on the Pacific Railroad," Nov. 5, 1849, in William Gilpin, *The Central Gold Region: The Grain, Pastoral and Gold Regions of North America* (Philadelphia and St. Louis, 1860), 20–21; Gilpin to David R. Atchison, Jan. 23, 1846, in *Report* (*Senate Executive Document*, 29 Cong., 1 sess., IV, No. 178), 4.

[11] De Voto, "Geopolitics," 319; Gilpin to Atchison, Jan. 23, 1846, *Report* (*Senate Executive Document*, 29 Cong., 1 sess., IV, No. 178), 6, 7; Gilpin to Semple, Mar. 17, 1846, *ibid.*, V, No. 306, 25, 30; Gilpin, *Central Gold Region*, vi.

[12] Margaret L. Brown, "Asa Whitney and His Pacific Railroad Publicity Campaign," *Mississippi Valley Historical Review*, XX (Sept. 1933), 209–24; George L. Albright, *Official Explorations for Pacific Railroads 1853–1855* (Berkeley, Calif., 1921), 10–18.

American Continentalism 327

of producing "the most necessary and important products of the earth—bread stuffs and meat," and stressed the value of an international "commerce of reciprocity—an exchange of commodities." The railroad, he insisted, would "revolutionize the entire commerce of the world; placing us directly in the centre of all . . . , all must be tributary to us, and, in a moral point of view, it will be the means of civilizing and Christianizing all mankind."[13]

Matthew Fontaine Maury, hydrographer of the United States Navy and adviser on railroad and international commercial problems to southern businessmen and politicians, was also interested in the relationship of the Pacific railroad issue to the old dream of the "passage to India."[14] But he formulated a wider geopolitical conception of the North American continent by linking it with Latin America as well as with Asia. He agreed that a Pacific railroad was needed to develop the continental interior as a means of raising land values, encouraging settlement of the western lands, and providing for the continental defense of the nation. He, too, shared the conviction of the importance of the Asian trade and, faithful to the interests of the South, he pressed for the construction of a transcontinental railroad from Memphis to Monterey.[15]

Maury, however, was influenced by an old geographical-historical idea that river valley civilizations were the most enduring and fruitful forms of society. In his view, the basins of the Mississippi and the Amazon Rivers were united in a vast continental-maritime complex that depended upon American supremacy of the Gulf of Mexico and the Caribbean Sea, the "American Mediterranean" as he called it. Aware of the potential of an age of steam, he believed that conventional ideas of geographical relationships had to change. Maury urged Americans to think of ocean navigation around the globe in terms of great circle travel rather than of routes laid out on the Mercator projection. This placed his Memphis-Monterey transcontinental railroad project that was to service the Mississippi Valley close to the great

[13] Cole, "Ringgold-Rodgers-Brooke," 152; *Memorial of Asa Whitney*, Feb. 24, 1846 (*Senate Executive Document*, 29 Cong., 1 sess., IV, No. 161), 8–9, 1, 6, 2, 5.

[14] Cole, "Ringgold-Rodgers-Brooke," 153; Smith, *Virgin Land*, 153–54; Henry F. Graff, *Bluejackets with Perry in Japan* (New York, 1952), 45; Merle Curti, *The Growth of American Thought* (New York, 1943), 321, for mention of Maury's religiosity. See R. S. Cotterill, "Memphis Railroad Convention, 1849," *Tennessee Magazine of History*, IV (June 1918), 83 ff., for an account of the South's view of the Pacific railroad issue. Maury was also elected a vice-president of the National Railroad Convention that met in St. Louis before the opening of the Memphis convention. He represented the Board of Directors of the Virginia and Tennessee Railroad. *Proceedings of the National Railroad Convention which Assembled in the City of St. Louis on the Fifteenth of October, 1849* (St. Louis, 1850).

[15] Maury to John C. Calhoun, Mar. 29, 1848, in J. D. B. De Bow, ed., *The Industrial Resources, etc., of the Southern and Western States . . .* (3 vols., New Orleans, 1852–53), I, 257, 259; Maury to T. Butler King, Jan. 10, 1847, in *Steam Communication with China, and the Sandwich Islands* (*House of Representatives Reports of Committees*, 30 Cong., 1 sess., III, No. 596), 23 ff.

circle running from Central America to Shanghai at a point off the coast of California. Cut a canal through the Isthmus of Panama that would link the Pacific Ocean with the "American Mediterranean" and the shortened route to Asia would force European commerce to use a passageway that Maury insisted should never be under the control of a foreign power since it violated traditional American policy to allow foreign interference in the Western Hemisphere. "I regard the Pacific railroad and a commercial thoroughfare across the Isthmus as links in the same chain, parts of the great whole which...is to effect a revolution in the course of trade....Those two works ... are not only necessary fully to develop the immense resources of the Mississippi valley ... but ... their completion would place the United States on the summit level of commerce. . . ." In effect, Maury extended the line of American continental interest south from the Mississippi in order to command the same degree of geographic centralism that had marked the ideas of Gilpin and Whitney. The canal, taken in conjunction with the Pacific railroad, demonstrated his ambition for the United States to overcome the "barrier that separates us from the markets of six hundred millions of people—three-fourths of the population of the earth. Break it down . . . and this country is placed midway between Europe and Asia; this sea [Gulf of Mexico and the Caribbean] becomes the centre of the world and the focus of the world's commerce."[16]

This doctrine of geopolitical centralism was reflected in the activity of Perry McDonough Collins, whose career had been shaped by the westward movement, experience with steamship operations on the Mississippi, and the California gold rush. Living on the West Coast in the 1850's, he not only absorbed the impact of the nation's new geographical position on the Pacific but also read about Russia's explorations of the northern Pacific Ocean and its expansion into eastern Siberia. Quickly he "fixed upon the river Amoor in Eastern Siberia as the destined channel by which American commercial enterprise was to penetrate the obscure depths of Northern Asia."[17]

[16] Maury to Calhoun, Mar. 29, 1848, De Bow, *Industrial Resources*, 365, 373, 369, 370; Maury to King, Jan. 10, 1847, *Steam Communication (Report, House of Representatives*, 30 Cong., 1 sess., III, No. 596), 20, 23; William L. Herndon and Lardner Gibbon, *Exploration of the Valley of the Amazon (Senate Executive Document*, 32 Cong., 2 sess., VI, No. 36), 190, 191, 193, testifying to Maury's influence in urging this expedition and in coloring the conclusions regarding the linkage of the Amazon and the Mississippi Valleys; T. Butler King, Jan. 16, 1849, *Railroad Across the Isthmus of Panama (House of Representatives Reports of Committees*, 30 Cong., 2 sess., I, No. 26), 2–3, citing Maury on the importance of an isthmian railroad to link the Caribbean Sea and the Pacific Ocean; F. P. Stanton, *Railroad to the Pacific (House of Representatives Reports of Committees*, 31 Cong., 1 sess., III, No. 439), 32, 14, 27.
[17] I have drawn upon my article "The Collins Overland Line and American Continentalism" in the *Pacific Historical Review*, XXVIII (Aug. 1959), 237–53. The quotation is in Perry Mc-Donough Collins, *A Voyage Down the Amoor* (New York, 1860), 1. A valuable contribution

American Continentalism 329

Supported by President Franklin Pierce and Secretary of State William Marcy, Collins traveled throughout Siberia in 1856 and saw there elements of the American West. He felt himself to be a "pioneer in these wilds in the shape of a live Yankee," encountering many of the "difficulties that all western men who have blazed the first trail in a new country know by experience." Russian expansion in this region he interpreted as similar in objective and spirit to that of American continental expansion. Russia, he predicted, would move into Manchuria just as the United States had gone into Louisiana. The Amur River in eastern Siberia he likened to the Mississippi in North America. In his mind the spirit of the American frontier had international and historical significance: the emergence of the United States in North America was the first vital step in linking Europe and Asia. "The problem of a North Western passage to India . . . , which has occupied the great minds of Europe for some centuries, has been solved by the continuous and onward march of American civilization to the West . . . the commerce of the world will find its path across this continent. . . ."[18]

Collins inspired Western Union's project for the construction of an international overland telegraph system through British Columbia, Alaska, and Siberia in 1865 which was to be linked with Russia's own network to Europe. Basic to the whole scheme was the anticipation that the transcontinental telegraph line to the Pacific built by Western Union in 1860–1861 would be in the center of the vast enterprise. "Consequently," ran one of the company's circulars, "when the extension line of this company shall be completed the commerce of the whole of Europe, Asia, and North America, radiating from their great commercial centers will be tributary to it."[19]

The outlook formulated by these various opinions suggests the existence of two related American worlds. The first was the nation-continent created through the interaction of foreign policy and territorial expansion that resulted in the acquisition of contiguous territory in North America. In

---

to knowledge of Collins' career and activities has been made by Vilhjalmur Stefansson in his book *Northwest to Fortune* (New York, 1958), 243–53.

[18] Perry McDonough Collins, Feb. 28, 1857, *Extract from Notes* (*House of Representatives Executive Document*, 35 Cong., 1 sess., XII, No. 98), 50; Collins to Marcy, Jan. 31, 1857, *ibid.*, 16–17, 19–20; Perry McDonough Collins, "Overland Telegraphic via Behring Strait and Across Asiatic Russia to Europe," in Western Union, *Statement of the Origin, Organization and Progress of the Russian-American Western Union Extension, Collins Overland Line* (Rochester, N. Y., 1866), 164.

[19] Western Union, *Statement of the Collins Overland Line*, 15. The company also hoped to run extensions from Russia's trunk system to China and Japan. This explains the grandiose vision of telegraphic supremacy in Asia. In addition, Collins began negotiations with Latin American governments to unite their lines with the American trunk system. In this sense, one should read "Western Hemisphere" for "North America" in the passage quoted in the company's prospectus.

turn, it projected the concept of the second American world, the continental domain that was fated to extend its influence over the entire world through the expansion of commerce and control of international communications The relations of both worlds were reciprocal. All this, however, depended upon realizing the economic implications of the central position conferred upon the United States through its expansion in North America and the significance of this event in the general expansionist history of the European world.

By the middle of the 1850's, aspects of this informal system of geopolitical thought had made its impression upon public discussion, affecting debates over internal communication and transportation as well as foreign policy.[20] It is true, however, that the notion of an American "empire" based on the idea of the United States as the great land bridge to Asia had given way to the growing tension of the sectional debates over federal policy dealing with the development of the continental interior.[21] Nevertheless, the fund of ideas that had projected American continentalism onto the world scene were restated and maintained by William Henry Seward, an expansionist, a worshipper of the continental tradition established and exemplified earlier by John Quincy Adams, and a man whose outlook[22] matched the geopolitical determinism exhibited by Gilpin, Whitney, Maury, and Collins.

Ten years before Seward became Secretary of State, he advocated the construction of a Pacific railroad and telegraph in the debates over the admission of California to the Union. Americans who understood the benign future of the American continent, Seward argued, had to prevent a division between the North and the South in order to overcome the more portentous split between East and West caused by the expansion of the United States. Centralized political unity, the economic welfare of the continental

---

[20] The standard work dealing with this phase is Robert R. Russel, *Improvement of Communication with the Pacific Coast as an Issue in American Politics, 1783–1864* (Cedar Rapids, Iowa, 1948), 18–19, who asserts that from the 1850's onward the emphasis shifted to discussion of internal affairs and development. Smith, *Virgin Land,* 282, note 28; James C. Malin, "The Nebraska Question: A Ten Year Record, 1844–1855," *Nebraska History,* XXXV (Mar. 1954), 14, for an interesting discussion of the global perspective of Stephen Douglas; Richard W. Van Alstyne, "Anglo-American Relations, 1853–1857," *American Historical Review,* XLII (Apr. 1937), 493, for an incisive critique by John F. Crampton of American ambition in a letter to Lord Clarendon; James G. Swan, *The Northwest Coast* (New York, 1857), 403, linking affairs in China and Russia with the Washington territory, and his article "Explorations of the Amoor River: And Its Importance on the Future Great Inter-Oceanic Trade Across the American Continent," *Hunt's Merchant's Magazine,* XXXIX (Aug. 1858), 176–82.

[21] Smith, *Virgin Land,* 29.

[22] "Neither politicians nor statesmen control events. They can moderate them and accommodate their ambitions to them, but they can do no more." Seward to Charles Francis Adams, Nov. 4, 1862, *Papers Relating to Foreign Affairs of the United States* (Washington, D. C., 1862), 231; Seward to Thurlow Weed, Apr. 4, 1847, Thurlow Weed Papers, University of Rochester, for a sample of Seward's veneration of John Quincy Adams.

empire, and mastery of the seas that bounded the great land mass between two worlds—these were required if the United States was to take effective advantage of its geographical position to direct commerce with Europe and "intercept" trade with the Far East. He charged the South with obstruction of the American primacy on the world stage that was promised by its domestic development. "This nation is a globe," he cried, "still accumulating upon accumulation, not a dissolving sphere."[23] "Even the discovery of this continent [North America] and its islands, and the organization of society and government upon them," Seward stated, "grand and important as these events have been were but conditional, preliminary, and ancillary" to the great goal of European expansion for four hundred years, the attainment of the seat of all civilization—Asia.[24] The revolts of 1848 and the strain of maintaining the "crazy balance of power" forecast the destruction of Europe, and it fell to the United States to seize the torch and light the way. Because the United States was writ large on the sphere of world geography and history, it had the obligation to extend by means of its institutions the "civilization of the world westward ... across the continent of America," across the Pacific to Asia, on through Europe until it reached "the other side, the shores of the Atlantic Ocean."[25]

This rhetoric was not separated from the realities that Seward encountered as Secretary of State. The continent under American dominion, he reported, "like every other structure of large proportions," required "outward buttresses" that were strategically favorable to the United States. Thus the policy of attempting to buy naval installations in the Caribbean after the Civil War reflected his conviction at the outbreak of the conflict that Spanish intrusion in the region partially justified the launching of a propaganda counterattack throughout Latin America as well as war against Spain. In 1864, he insisted that commerce and communication in North America were centralized in the United States and had to be extended as a means of uniting domestic and foreign commerce and encouraging the development of American "agricultural, forest, mineral, and marine resources." It was Seward who wrote the vital provisions of the Burlingame Treaty of 1868 with China that provided for the importation of Chinese coolies to work on the transcontinental railroad and western mining undertakings. He also contributed to the continental basis of the argument used by Senator Charles Sumner, who supported the purchase of Alaska by pointing out that the new

---

[23] *The Works of William H. Seward*, ed. George E. Baker (5 vols., New York, 1853–84), I, 91.
[24] *Ibid.*, 247–49.
[25] *Ibid.*, IV, 124; *Cong. Globe*, 36 Cong., 2 sess., 251 (Jan. 5, 1861).

territory rounded off the continental domain and permitted contact with Far Eastern markets by the shortest possible sea route from the West Coast. Later Seward made his meaning more clear to Canadians when he implied that the Alaskan purchase was a portent of "commercial and political forces" that made "permanent political separation of British Columbia from Alaska and the Washington territory impossible."[26] And, it was Seward's system of roughhewn continental geopolitics and beliefs cut out of the American grain that gives depth to the vigor with which he pursued American interests in the Far East. Much of his ambitious program, however, was not fulfilled because, as he said, "no new national policy deliberately undertaken upon considerations of future advantages ever finds universal favor when first announced."[27] But Alfred Thayer Mahan countered this argument when he remarked in 1902 that "all history is the aggressive advance of the future upon the past, the field of collision being the present."[28]

Mahan might well have added, however, that it was his geopolitics as well as that of Brooks Adams that defined the "field of collision." For the serious domestic crisis in the United States occurring in the 1890's within the context of a global economy and an international transportation revolution forecast a pessimistic future. Each, in his own way, attempted to swamp it with a conception of the past that he carried with him. Both Mahan's quest for a new mercantilism and Adams' propaganda for a new empire illustrate a retreat into history for a model that might avert disaster. One theme emerged—the extension of the nation's economic power from the line of the West Indies, Panama, and Hawaii to Asia. Here, the expansionist projection of the American continental experience that was developed in the pre-Civil War period acquired some relevance in the outlook of Brooks Adams. Viewing the expansion of Europe and of the United States as complementary developments, he turned to geopolitics to explain the nature of the problem.[29]

The Germans and the Russians appeared ready to march to the East. This move would reverse the historical westward trend of the exchanges that

[26] Charles C. Tansill, *The United States and Santo Domingo, 1798–1863* (Baltimore, Md., 1938), 227; Frederick W. Seward, comp., *William Henry Seward: An Autobiography* (3 vols., New York, 1891), II, 535; Seward to Chandler, May 14, 1864, Western Union, *Statement of the Collins Overland Line*, 51; Dennett, *Americans in Eastern Asia*, 530; James Alton James, *The First Scientific Exploration of Russian America and the Purchase of Alaska* (Evanston and Chicago, 1942), 19, 35, 27; for Sumner's argument advocating the purchase, see *Charles Sumner, His Complete Works*, ed. George F. Hoar (20 vols., Boston, 1900), XV, 36 ff.; Baker, *Seward*, V, 574.

[27] Seward to Yeaman, Jan. 29, 1868, in Seward Papers.

[28] Alfred Thayer Mahan, "Subordination in Historical Treatment," in *Naval Administration and Warfare* (Boston, 1908), 269.

[29] I have drawn upon my article "Brooks Adams and the Ambivalence of American Foreign Policy," *World Affairs Quarterly*, XXX (Apr. 1959), 3–18.

American Continentalism 333

formed the basis of world power. Obsessed by the belief that control over Asia and its resources was the issue between the Russo-German bloc and what he believed to be a weakened England, Adams called for an Anglo-American rapproachement. This would allow the geographical center of the exchanges to "cross the Atlantic and aggrandize America." The result? "Probably," Adams suggested, "human society would then be absolutely dominated by a vast combination of peoples whose right wing would rest upon the British Isles, whose left would overhang the middle province of China, whose centre would approach the Pacific, and who encompass the Indian Ocean as though it were a lake, much as the Romans encompassed the Mediterranean."[30] Specifically, Adams, Mahan, and the imperial expansionists who clustered around Theodore Roosevelt urged upon the United States the "large policy of 1898," which revived the Caribbean-Panama-Pacific Ocean relationship that had been sketched out in the 1840's and 1850's and publicized by Seward.[31] But by 1909, the outer edges of this grandiose empire were frayed by abrasive realities in Asia. The failure of the open door in China, the knowledge that the Philippines could not be defended, the growing tension with Japan over Manchuria—all this was complicated by the existence of the ideological *Realpolitik* of Theodore Roosevelt, who claimed American manipulative power over affairs in Asia but who was cautious enough to realize that he did not have it. Roosevelt's refusal to carry out completely Adams' program drove Adams back to examine his own nationalist assumptions in a biography of his grandfather that he never completed.[32]

At this point in his quest, the traditional elements of American continentalism received a full statement—geographical determinism, political and social separation from Europe, and independent action in foreign affairs. Nevertheless, Adams, like Mahan, continued to interpret the history of American continentalism as an expression of eighteenth-century mercantilist imperialism. Just as Asia appeared in his own time to be the principal objective that would guarantee survival through expansion, so North America had appeared to the European powers. "Men believed that he who won

[30] Brooks Adams, *America's Economic Supremacy* (New York, 1900), 196, 13, 190, 12, 25.
[31] Julius Pratt, "The Large Policy of 1898," *Mississippi Valley Historical Review*, XIX (Aug. 1932), 233, 229–30, for Albert Shaw's agreement with Bryan on this as well as the statement by Senator William E. Chandler; Alfred Thayer Mahan, *The Interest of America in Sea Power* (Boston, 1897), 260, and *The Problem of Asia* (Boston, 1900), 7–9, for his remarks on the preparation for imperialist expansion that had occurred earlier in American history on the basis on this geographical outlook.
[32] Arthur Beringause, *Brooks Adams* (New York, 1955), 304 ff.; Brooks Adams, "Unpublished Biography of John Quincy Adams" in the Massachusetts Historical Society (microfilm copy by courtesy of Mr. Lyman Butterfield and the Massachusetts Historical Society).

America might aspire to that universal empire which had been an ideal since the dawn of civilization."[33] Franklin, Washington, and John Quincy Adams had understood the need for a consolidated, unified, and expansionist state strong enough to establish itself in North America. In 1823, the Monroe Doctrine confirmed what the American Revolution had already demonstrated: the leadership of the westward march of the exchanges would pass from a divided Europe to a unified America. "It was the first impressive manifestation of that momentous social movement which has recently culminated in the migration of the centre of the equilibrium of human society across the Atlantic."[34] Here the nationalist met the imperialist when the expansionist projection of continentalism made clear that America, the prize of empire in the eighteenth century, had to become an empire in the twentieth century.

Contemporary students of the United States foreign policy that developed at the turn of the century are confronted with a problem of perspective. From the standpoint of the expansionist projection of American continentalism revealed in the pre-Civil War era, the imperialism of McKinley and Roosevelt was not a new departure in American history. It was not an "aberration" of national behavior which has been loosely defined as the emergence of the United States to world power. The geopolitical suggestions of Mahan and Brooks Adams helped American statesmen to install the United States as such a power. It was also a startling demonstration of the adjustment of the new ideological justifications of the 1890's to an older nationalistic expansionist base formulated by men of an earlier generation.[35] Gilpin, Whitney, Maury, and Collins had sensed the meaning of the new technology, its effect upon geographical relationships, and the interrelations between aspects of the economic system at home, and these men were captured by a desire to assume the leadership of an entire Western civilization in order to make a lasting impression upon Asia.

Historians who are sensitive to the relationship of foreign and domestic affairs as well as to the play of ideas upon foreign policy might do well to reexamine and explore the concept of American continentalism as an ideology of overseas expansion. Conventionally employed to explain the separatist and isolationist quality of the American outlook on world affairs

---

[33] Adams, "Unpublished Biography of John Quincy Adams," 130.

[34] *Ibid.*, 299.

[35] Julius Pratt, "The Ideology of American Expansion," in *Essays in Honor of William E. Dodd,* ed. Avery Craven (Chicago, 1935), 347, for a comment that stresses manifest destiny rather than American continentalism as employed in this essay. See also the judgment of Seward's biographer regarding the continuity of the expansionist impulse in Frederic Bancroft, "Seward's Ideas of Territorial Expansion," *North American Review,* CLXVII (July 1898), 79 ff.

American Continentalism 335

in the nineteenth century, American continentalism also possessed a geopolitical character—natively derived in large measure—that was contrary to
its own spirit. The only virtue of geopolitics is that it draws attention to
the facts of political geography; its greatest vice is that it lends itself to
almost mystical judgments of national purpose in international affairs.
Seemingly dealing with reality, it becomes a refuge for unclear and unful-
filled aspirations. Geographers long ago learned this bitter lesson. Historians
of American foreign policy might profit by investigating further the active
presence in nineteenth-century America of this aspect of thought, not as
a justification for foreign policy but as an important stimulus of nationalist
expansionism.

6

James Polk

Norman A. Graebner

"Who is James K. Polk?" demanded the Whigs contemptu-ously of their Democratic opponents during the presidential canvass of 1844. In feigning astonishment at the Democratic choice, these men were exploiting a dilemma which long characterized Polk's political career. Except among his close associates he was unloved and unappreciated in his own day; throughout the nineteenth century Americans all but ignored him. Perhaps the reason is clear. Men are remembered for their unique qualities, and Polk had none. In oratory he lacked the elegance of Daniel Webster; in intellect, the preciseness of John C. Calhoun. In reputation he was no match for the Whig party's gallant hero, Henry Clay. Not even in personality or appearance was he conspicuous. He was below average in height, with thin face and piercing grey eyes. He wore his hair long and brushed back behind his ears. He was an uncompromising Presbyterian—a man honest and incorruptible, thoughtful and meditative, slow and measured in speech, methodical and industrious. Polk's personal attributes were worthy, even admirable, but they hardly conveyed distinction.

Yet Polk's gradual eclipse during the decades that followed his presidency resulted as much from historic as from personal factors. His identification with the Texas and Mexican War issues made him appear to post-Civil War historians as the chief proponent of slavery expansion. These writers consigned him, along with Calhoun, to that large and seemingly contemptible category of southern leaders whose aggressiveness allegedly plunged the nation into civil war. But the publication of his diary in 1910 quickened an interest Polk at a time when historians no longer accepted the abolitionist interpretation of the forties uncritically and were willing to judge the Tennessean by the evidence of his written record. Since that time few scholars have doubted that Polk was the most significant figure in the presidency between Andrew Jackson and Abraham Lincoln.

Polk was forty-nine years old when he entered the presidential office in March, 1845—the youngest incumbent of the White House up to that time. If he was not marked for greatness, his success was neither inconsequential nor accidental. His political experience was deep and long, giving him a knowledge of party behavior as thorough as that of any of his contemporaries. He achieved his first political prominence in Congress when, as a Representative from Tennessee, he joined the vanguard in the attack on the Maysville Road bill and the Bank of the United States early in Jackson's presidency. His devotion to the Jacksonian cause led him eventually into the camp of Martin Van Buren and two successful terms as speaker of the House of Representatives. His leadership in the House brought him a wide acquaintance and revealed his remarkable capacity for detail. Polk followed his Congressional career with a term as governor of Tennessee. A vigorous campaigner, a thorough Jacksonian, a man of parts in national Democratic circles, Polk had become by 1842 a man mentioned widely for the vice-presidency. This did not presage his nomination and election to the White House two years later, but it indicated that his "availability" was clear.

Polk's nomination was largely accidental. Former President Van Buren had been the titular head and front-running candidate of the Democratic party before the Baltimore convention of 1844. But the New Yorker faced the determined opposition of two groups. Southern Democrats attempted to put Calhoun in contention for the nomination by exploiting the powerful Texas issue in the South. But another Democratic clique, led by Lewis Cass of Michigan, Robert J. Walker of Mississippi, James Buchanan of Pennsylvania, and William L. Marcy of New York, quickly nationalized the Texas issue with appeals to "manifest destiny," and forced the question on the party as a national concern. Van Buren's anti-slavery leanings caused him to balk at immediate annexation. This hesitancy permitted his Southern and

JAMES POLK

national opponents to join forces against him, prevent his nomination with the two-thirds rule, and eventually secure the nomination of a compromise candidate—Polk of Tennessee. For the moment Polk's Jacksonianism satisfied the Van Burenites just as his stand on Texas appealed to Southerners. Under Polk, however, it was the national Democratic faction that reached new heights of power and influence, both in Congress and in the Cabinet. During his four years in office this group comprised the core of Democratic power.

Polk had more than experience and an ambitious party bloc behind him. He had an unsuspected feel for leadership. He accepted the dictum of Alexander Hamilton that the American system provides no substitute for energy in the executive. Not long after he entered the presidency, one Washington editor said of him: "Few men are capable of the labors which he encounters; and few in his place would devote themselves with the same assiduity to the public service. He works from 10 to 12 hours in every 24. He holds two Cabinets a week. He sees visitors two hours every day when the Cabinet is not employed. . . . He is also in frequent communion with his secretaries."

So persistently did Polk remain at his official tasks that during his term he was outside the capital only six weeks. He spent one day at Mount Vernon early in his administration. In the summer of 1846 he vacationed briefly at Old Point Comfort. In May and June, 1847, he visited the University of North Carolina from which he graduated in 1819. Later that summer he toured New England for two weeks; and, lastly, in August, 1848, he rested for ten days at Bedford Springs, Pennsylvania. Shortly before he left office, Polk explained this devotion to duty: "No President who performs his duty faithfully and conscientiously can have any leisure. If he intrusts the details and smaller matters to subordinates constant errors will occur. I prefer to supervise the whole operations of the Government myself rather than intrust the public business to subordinates, and this makes my duties very great."

Polk was guide and master of his administration. Ten weeks before his inauguration he wrote to Cave Johnson of Tennessee, later to become his postmaster general, ". . . I intend to be myself President of the United States." Polk demanded absolute cooperation from members of his Cabinet, and required assurances that they would retire at the moment they became aspirants for the presidency. For Polk this appeared essential, for his announce-

115

ment, at the time of his nomination, that he would not seek re-election raised the issue of the succession even before he entered the White House. In Cabinet sessions Polk encouraged free discussion. He listened attentively, but seldom abandoned his convictions. Gideon Welles, never an admirer of the President, reported early in Polk's administration that several Cabinet members "have been at particular pains to tell me that the President has his own way . . . does as he had a mind to." Later the reluctant Welles admitted that Polk "had courage and determination and shrank from no labor or responsibility." Judge John Catron wrote to Andrew Jackson in the spring of 1845: "Our friend is very prudent, and *eminently* firm, regardless of consequences. He came here to be—THE PRESIDENT—which at this date is as undisputed as that you was The GENL at N. Orleans." Jackson discovered how little he could influence Polk when the new President, ignoring the General's admonition, removed Francis P. Blair and the *Globe*, and established the Washington *Union* under Thomas Ritchie as the official organ of the Administration.

George Bancroft, the eminent historian and Polk's first secretary of the navy, has left the most impressive testimony of Polk's administrative capacity. Fifty years after the events of the 1840's, he recalled that Polk, on his inauguration day, informed him that he had four key objectives as President: tariff reduction, reestablishment of the Independent Treasury, the settlement of the Oregon boundary, and the acquisition of California. That Polk achieved these goals led Bancroft to the conclusion that he was "one of the very foremost of our public men and one of the very best and most honest and most successful Presidents the country ever had." Polk's administration succeeded, Bancroft added, "because he insisted on being its centre, and in overruling and guiding all his secretaries to act so as to produce unity and harmony."

Polk's rigid control of his administrative machinery accounts only partially for his success. Every aspect of his program required the eventual approval of Congress. That he achieved Congressional majorities on his pet measures has been written off by some historians as a simple expression of public opinion. Had he tried to dominate Congress, say his critics, his lack of color would have proved fatal. Only as a mirror of Jacksonianism was he equal to the task. But public opinion is never clearly defined or easily converted

JAMES POLK

into policy. Polk's Democratic party was no longer united in 1845 on any philosophy. Throughout the expanding industrial and commercial centers of the North were powerful Democratic voices which sounded less and less Jacksonian as they demanded that the Federal government underwrite the economy with a variety of special dispensations. In both houses of Congress were determined Whig minorities that maintained a persistent attack on Polk's leadership. Against his enemies the President commanded the allegiance of only a segment of the party which had elected him.

Van Buren's followers were sullen. Since the Texas issue had carried Polk into the White House, they predicted logically that the friends of annexation would dominate the new administration. When Polk's Cabinet appointments favored "Texas" men, the Van Burenites concluded that the President had sold out to their enemies.

Actually, Polk, knowing the magnitude of their power as well as their discontent, made repeated efforts to pacify the Van Buren clique with a Cabinet post. He proffered the Treasury to Silas Wright, who declined because of his election to the New York governorship. Van Buren, in return, recommended another New Yorker, Benjamin F. Butler, for the State Department, and either Azariah C. Flagg or Churchill C. Cambreleng for the Treasury. Instead, the President incurred the wrath of the Van Burenites by placing Buchanan in the State Department, and, in deference to the South and Vice President George M. Dallas, he tendered the Treasury Department to Walker. For New York he now reserved the War Department. He offered this post to Butler, who refused to accept anything but the Treasury. Polk then decided on Marcy, also of New York but Van Buren's chief rival in New York politics. At the eleventh hour Butler reversed his decision, but his acceptance arrived in Washington too late.

Neither was Calhoun's powerful Southern faction represented in the Cabinet. Party spokesmen had prophesied that if the South Carolinian were not retained as secretary of state he would bolt the party, and that to dismiss him while the Texas negotiation was pending would be an irreparable insult. Calhoun professed delight at his return to private life in March, but the astute Webster observed that the Southern leader stood "at the head of the aggrieved." The Calhounites, in voicing their animosity toward the Administration, erroneously accused the President of bowing to the Van Buren group. Calhoun had but one explanation—"that I stood in the way of the restoration of the old Jackson Regime." Whatever the motive behind the Cabinet appointments, Polk, as president, faced resentment in two of the three important factions of his party. It was doubtful in March, 1845, if the Democratic organization was sufficiently united to carry any measure against a resolute Whig minority. Thomas Corwin, the partisan Ohio Whig, saw the Administration's dilemma clearly. "The truth is," he wrote, "Polk is not far from the category of Tyler. He is like Tyler an accident. He knows this. His friends know & feel it, and if his friends were United they would compel him to many a wild & wicked freak. But his friends are not united."

Polk was unawed by this opposition. When Congress met in December, 1845, he not only confronted it with a carefully-prepared program but he also made it clear that he was determined to carry this program into law. From the moment that Congress assembled, he exerted continuous pressure on key Democrats in both Houses through personal interviews or through members of the Cabinet. To Polk every administration proposal was a party measure to be forced through Congress as a matter of party responsibility.

Such determination merely reflected the President's deep conviction. Early in his career Polk had imbibed the philosophy of Thomas Jefferson. He entered political life an enemy of Clay's American System, and never ceased to condemn the protective tariff, the national Bank and credit system, internal improvements, and the distribution of Federal surpluses among the states. "I would keep no surplus revenue there to scramble for, either for internal improvements, or for any thing else," he once remarked. "I would bring the Government back to what it was intended to be, a plain economical Government." Even as President he never compromised with these beliefs.

Southern Democrats had led a continuous, if unsuccessful, assault on the high Whig Tariff of 1842. Polk renewed the attack in his message to Congress in December, 1845. He admitted that Congress had the power to levy taxes and could institute a tariff for that purpose. "But care should be taken," he added, "that all the great interests of the country, including manufactures, agriculture, commerce, navigation, and the mechanic arts, should . . . derive equal advantages from the incidental protection which a

JAMES POLK

just system of revenue duties may afford." Taxes, he said, should
be imposed on all classes according to their ability to pay. The
existing tariff was wrong because it imposed "heavy and unjust
burdens on the farmer, the planter, the commercial man, and those
of all other pursuits except the capitalist who has made his invest-
ments in manufactures." Secretary of the Treasury Walker prepared the new tariff bill, mildly protective but proposing a general
reduction of rates. In addition, the Walker bill introduced a sim-
plified form by separating all dutiable goods into groups and providing *ad valorem* rates for each classification.

Opponents of tariff revision declared repeatedly throughout
the ensuing debate that they comprised a majority in Congress,
but Polk and Walker, aided by George Dwight, a little-known
Massachusetts Whig, maintained a steady pressure on Congress.
Dwight occupied a large parlor in one of the capital's leading
hotels and there dispensed generous, if discriminate, hospitality
as an agent of British manufacturing and mercantile interests.
When the President in March learned that the Committee on
Ways and Means was prepared to introduce specific duties on
iron, he called in its chairman, James I. McKay of North Carolina, and extracted from him a promise to report the bill in its
original form. Late in April word reached the White House that
the Whigs in the Senate had managed to postpone action on the
tariff bill. Polk reminded Dixon H. Lewis, chairman of the Senate
Finance Committee, of the recommendations of the annual message. "I told him," the President recorded in his diary, "that I
considered them as administration measures and that I intended to
urge them upon Congress as such, and that I considered the public
good, as well as my own power and the glory of my administration, depended in a great degree upon my success in carrying
them through Congress." So occupied was Polk with Congressional affairs that seldom did he miss having evening callers when
Congress was in session.

July was the critical month for the tariff. Shortly before the
House vote was taken on July 3 the President reminded Daniel
Dickinson of New York that the vote would be close and that the
fate of the measure lay with the Democratic delegation from his
state. Dickinson left immediately for the Capitol while Polk dispatched other members of Congress to exert similar pressure on
doubtful votes. That afternoon Dickinson was able to report the

successful passage of the bill in the House. The Senate decision remained doubtful. Scores of lobbyists had invaded Washington to defeat the measure. "The absence of a single democratic Senator will probably enable them to effect their object," observed the President. "I considered the passage of the bill before the Senate the most important domestic measure of my administration, and therefore I take so great an interest in it."

So tightly were the lines drawn on the tariff that everyone in Washington knew the Senate decision hinged on every vote. Polk learned that James Semple of Illinois was about to leave Washington on business. After a long conversation Polk secured Semple's agreement to remain. As the Senate vote neared all attention was focused on two men, William H. Haywood of North Carolina and Spencer Jarnagin of Tennessee. Haywood, a Democrat, balked at voting for tariff reduction. Polk warned him that he would be the only Southern Democrat voting against the measure and that he "would strike a severe blow upon my administration, inflict grave injury on the country, and . . . would ruin himself." Haywood resigned his seat rather than vote against his conscience or his party.

Now the fate of the new tariff was in the hands of Jarnagin, a Whig under instructions from the Tennessee legislature to vote for tariff reduction. Polk dispatched Hopkins Turney, a Tennessee Democrat, to encourage Jarnagin to obey his instructions. Webster, leader of the protariff forces in the Senate, brought the full weight of his prestige to bear on Jarnagin, but at the White House the Tennessean promised Polk that he would vote for the Walker bill and thereafter refused to discuss the matter with the Whigs. During the fateful session, Jarnagin stalked from the Senate chamber and permitted Vice President Dallas to cast the deciding vote for engrossment. Then the Tennessee Whig returned to vote for the final passage. Executive leadership was decisive throughout.

Polk achieved his second legislative ambition a few days later when his Independent Treasury bill passed Congress by a narrow party vote. His recommendation for the graduated reduction of Federal land prices, a measure favored earlier by both Jackson and Van Buren, failed through the combined votes of Whigs and Northern Democrats. But Joshua Giddings, the Ohio Whig and bitter opponent of the Administration, complained of the presence

JAMES POLK

of members of the Administration on the House floor during the final vote on the bill. "Discussion had ceased," he recalled,

> they did not therefore attend to listen to our debates; yet we saw the Secretary of State, the Secretary of War, the Secretary of the Treasury, the Secretary of the Navy, the Postmaster General, the editor of the Executive organ, and the President's private secretary, busily engaged with individual members of the dominant party, with every indication of exerting their influence to induce gentlemen to vote for that Executive measure. . . . It was a shameless prostitution of the Executive character, which may well cause a blush upon the cheek of every American who feels an interest in the honor of his country, or in the purity of our institutions. . . .

Demands throughout the North and Northwest for river and harbor improvement at Federal expense had been accumulating for several years when Congress began to debate the River and Harbor bill of 1846. This was neither an Administration nor a party measure, and the debate on internal improvements, unlike the debate on the tariff and the Independent Treasury, revealed a sectional rather than a party cleavage. The South, representing the Jacksonian tradition, stood firm against the measure whereas Northern Whigs and Democrats tended to support it. Polk remained noncommittal, reminding callers at the White House that when he was in Congress he had voted against all such measures. To the astonishment of many Democrats, Polk greeted the passage of the River and Harbor bill early in August with a resounding veto. There was bitterness in the Northern reaction, for only Southern Democrats had voted in a bloc against the measure. Here was evidence, charged Polk's critics in the North, that the President was playing a Southern game.

Undaunted by such sectionalism, Polk was prepared to veto every internal improvement bill that reached his desk. Perhaps his most uncompromising lecture to Congress on that issue came in December, 1847, when he declared that the power of Congress to improve inland waterways must be conceded completely or must be denied altogether. "If it be admitted," he said, "how broad and how susceptible of enormous abuses is the power thus vested in the

General Government! There is not an inlet of the ocean or the lakes, not a river, creek or streamlet within the States, which is not brought for this purpose within the power and jurisdiction of the General Government."

Polk's tenacious control of domestic policies through White House interference and executive veto increasingly embittered his opponents. Some accused him of wielding so much authority over Congress that he was undermining the American democratic system itself. The pent-up resentment of one Whig finally exploded on the floor of Congress early in 1848:

> What great measure, whether of a financial or of any other character, has not been originated by the President or one of the heads of department who may have been selected to do his pleasure? I detest and abhor this one-man power. I am utterly opposed to a consolidated government. What honeyed language do we not hear on this subject from gentlemen on the other side? How eloquently they can declaim against the threatening dangers of a consolidated government, yet what else is our government at this hour? All power, the whole Government, is now virtually in the hands of the President, and he wields and exercises that power just as he pleases. Let a man have the boldness to differ from his views, and let him have the temerity to avow that difference on this floor, and he is denounced in the [Washington] Union before the next twenty-four hours. Forthwith he must walk the plank. He has but one alternative, either to stand on the platform with the Executive, or be pushed into the sea. . . . The President is elected by the people, and measures are willed by the President; *ergo*, whatever measures he wishes are the measures of the people, and his will is the will of the people. That is the will of the people. That is the argument. But I go for a truly popular government; by which I mean a government in which all great measures of public policy originate with the people themselves.

Polk's Jacksonianism became more militant as his administration progressed. During the summer of 1848, while Congress was in session, he kept a veto message in readiness. "Should another veto become necessary," he confided to his diary, "I desire to make it a strong paper, so that if I should be over-ruled, as I may

JAMES POLK

be, by a united Whig vote and a part of the Democratic members, making a vote of two thirds, I may leave my full views on record to be judged of by my own countrymen & by posterity." His last night in office, March 3, 1849, Polk carried that message to the Capitol to be prepared if any river and harbor bill pending before the Senate should pass. But Congress never forced the President to read it.

To Polk internal improvements were the key to the entire American System of Henry Clay. Every aspect of that program had been overthrown—the Bank, the protective tariff, the distribution of the proceeds of Western lands, and internal improvements. But if the last principle were revived, he feared, all other aspects of the system would be revived also. Against this danger there was no defense except that of the Presidential veto. To make this clear, in his message of December, 1848, he lectured the Whigs on the nature of the American constitutional system: "Any attempt to coerce the President to yield his sanction to measures which he cannot approve would be a violation of the spirit of the Constitution . . . and if successful would break down the independence of the Executive department and make the President, clothed by the Constitution with the power to defend their rights, the mere instrument of a majority of Congress. . . . If it be said that the Representatives in the popular branch of Congress are chosen directly by the people, it is answered, the people elect the President. . . . The President represents in the Executive department the whole people of the United States as each representative of the legislative department represents portions of them." This message reveals how completely Polk's concept of the presidential office was Jacksonian.

Polk's distinction as president rests even more on diplomacy than on the management of his domestic program. Of the two expansionist issues (Texas and Oregon) raised by the campaign of 1844, Texas offered no challenge to his leadership. It had been an independent republic for almost a decade when Congress, through the Joint Resolution of early March, 1845, invited the region to join the United States. The Texas convention, called the following summer, accepted the invitation of Congress. In December, 1845, Texas became a state in the Union. Yet annexation had one troublesome result. In the spring of 1845 Mexico carried out its threat to break diplomatic relations with the United States if this nation ever voted to annex the former Mexican province.

Oregon was the more serious challenge, but the difficulties it presented the President were largely self-imposed. The traditional American diplomatic offer of the forty-ninth parallel had been eminently reasonable, but under the stimulation of manifest destiny doctrines Western Democrats demanded all of Oregon to the Alaska boundary and forced their platform on the Democratic party in 1844. If this stand had some appeal politically, it was impossible diplomatically. There was no apparent way in which the nation could gain the line fifty-four forty without more or less fighting. Yet Polk in his inaugural reaffirmed the party's conviction that the American title to Oregon was "clear and unquestionable." He was in no mood to challenge the Western Democrats by abandoning the campaign platform. Nor did he run much risk of antagonizing his expansionist friends in his subsequent negotiations with Great Britain during the summer of 1845. Actually only two minor issues still separated the two nations, those of Vancouver Island and the navigation of the Columbia. Privately both Polk and the British government had arrived at the necessity of reaching an agreement at the forty-ninth parallel, but Polk was still too encumbered politically to pursue details. He assured his secretary of state that his party commitments would not tolerate another offer of compromise. "I told him," Polk recorded, "that if that proposition had been accepted by the British Minister my course would have met with great opposition, and in my opinion would have gone far to overthrow the administration; that, had it been accepted, as we came in on Texas the probability was we would have gone out on Oregon."

Polk, still clinging to the Baltimore platform, raised the fifty-four forty issue again in his message to Congress in December, 1845. He warned the nation that the British rejection of his July offer, which he assured the Democrats had been made only in deference to his predecessors, was evidence enough that "no compromise which the United States ought to accept, can be effected." Upon Polk's recommendation that it was time to terminate the convention of joint occupancy in Oregon (renewed by England and the United States in 1827 in lieu of a diplomatic settlement), Congress proceeded to debate a resolution to extend the necessary twelve-month notice to England. Immediately the President found himself trapped by the enormous discrepancy between his political

JAMES POLK

commitments to his party and the diplomatic realities in the Oregon situation. Since any Congressional action would convey to the Executive a mandate for a prompt and final settlement of the Oregon dispute, it made considerable difference to members of Congress how the President would use his authority.

William Allen of Ohio, chairman of the Foreign Relations Committee in the Senate, rushed to the defense of the notice, assuring Congress that the President would settle for nothing less than the whole of Oregon. Southern Democrats, led by Calhoun, challenged the Western bloc and argued that the President's message actually cleared the way for a settlement at the forty ninth parallel. Nothing, declared Walter T. Colquitt of Georgia, could be "clear and unquestionable" that had been in dispute for thirty years. Haywood of North Carolina reasoned that Polk had accepted the necessity of compromise once and would do so again. But the Democrats were divided, and as late as April, 1846, John C. Rives wrote to Silas Wright, the Democrat governor of New York: "The 54° 40 & the 49° men both allege that the President is with them, certain; & I suspect that both are about half right. They both say they can prove it if necessary."

Polk's Whig opponents recognized his self-inflicted dilemma and plotted to embarrass him. "The Democratic leaders," observed William C. Rives, "have gotten themselves into a narrow defile, between warring sections of their own party, with a solid phalanx of the public arrayed against them—a position from which no art can rescue them, retreat and advance being alike impossible or fatal." What gave the Whigs such broad latitude for political maneuvering was the general conviction that the Executive would avoid war at all costs. They noted that neither the President nor the extremists in Congress were making any provision for the defense of the country.

Whig strategy demanded that the Administration be held responsible for an Oregon settlement, so that the President could not escape his commitment to fifty-four forty without first divesting himself of his political advantage. Polk, at the moment of settlement, must be made to face the full fury of the super-patriots in Democratic ranks. "The question of peace or war is with the Administration," observed Thurlow Weed's Albany *Evening Journal*, a powerful Whig publication, early in January, 1846. "If England is disposed to settle the question upon fair terms, the President can close the matter at once. He 'opened the ball' in his

Inaugural. His organ and party have been making political capital out of it quite long enough. They have had what there is of glory in the alarm—let them now take the responsibility of their own issue." By appearing to take an uncompromising stand against England, the Whigs hoped to force the Administration to carry the complete burden of diplomatic responsibility between war and peace. In one case it would face the country; in the other, the extremists within its own party. In either case the President would suffer the consequences of taking the nation to the brink of war. As Weed wrote in February, "The Administration must settle the question or stand guilty of blundering as well as of crime, in the eyes of the world."

In Congress the Whigs attacked and ridiculed the President for causing confusion in Congress. They observed that week after week he neglected to throw any light on the question of his future action. Senator Jacob W. Miller of New Jersey observed that the President's stand seemed "like the mercury in the barometer, to go up and down according as gentlemen placed their fingers on the bulb. When touched by the warm hands of the Senators from Indiana, from Illinois, and from Ohio, it immediately went up to 54° 40'; but when the cool and distinguished Senator from North Carolina put his finger upon it, it fell as quickly to 49°." Alexander Barrow of Louisiana declared with considerable truth, "There never was, before, a period when some one in the Senate was not authorized to speak for the Executive, made regularly acquainted with his views, and ready to put right those who misconstrue his plans or language." Whigs insisted on knowing how the President planned to dispose of the Oregon question. "I want light," shouted George Evans of Maine, "I want further assurance how the notice is to be used if we pass it."

These Whig jibes sent a constant stream of Democrats to the White House to seek the President's views. Polk refused to commit himself. When early in January, 1846, James A. Black of South Carolina sought the President's opinions, Polk recorded: "I told him that my opinions were contained in my message, that they had been well considered, and that I had not changed them; that I had recommended the Notice and thought it ought to be given." Such an answer was hardly satisfactory when Congress could not agree on the meaning of the message, but it served Polk's purpose and was repeated. When Turney sought to ascertain the Administration's intentions to better govern his own con-

JAMES POLK

duct in Congress, Polk discreetly referred him to the message. Still the compromise views of Calhoun could not be ignored. Polk assured him privately that he would submit any fair British proposal to Congress for its previous advice before rejecting it.

It was Haywood who stimulated the extremists into action early in March when he professed in Congress to speak the views of the Administration. The exasperated Edward Hannegan of Indiana prophesied that if this were true, the President "would sink so deep that the Trumpet of the Angel of Resurrection would not reach him!" The Indianan stormed into the Executive office and demanded a clear-cut decision. "I answered him that I would answer no man what I would do in the future," the President hedged, "that for what I might do I would be responsible to God and my country and if I should hereafter do anything which should be disapproved by himself and others, it would be time enough to condemn me." Similarly he informed the inquisitive Cass that his views on Oregon were contained in his message. Allen argued logically with Polk that he required the authority to speak for the Administration if he were to regain his position as the Senate's spokesman on foreign affairs. He presented to Polk a prepared statement for his endorsement, but the President would not be trapped. "I told him I could give no authority to him or any one else to say anything in the Senate," replied the President, "that I had given no such authority to Mr. Haywood and I would give none such to him; that I did not wish to be involved in the matter & that what he said he must say on his own responsibility." Polk refused to believe that he was responsible for the confusion in Congress, and attributed the party divisions rather to personal ambitions. "The truth is," he wrote in April, "that in all this Oregon discussion in the Senate, too many Democratic Senators have been more concerned about the Presidential election in '48, than they have been about settling Oregon either at 49° or 54° 40'."

Gradually Polk's duplicity antagonized all factions of his party. At the White House Calhoun reminded the President repeatedly of his promise to avoid war, but he could wrest no assurance from Polk that the Administration would accept a compromise settlement. In April the Senator wrote to his son, "The Oregon negotiation has been wretchedly managed. The differences ought to have been adjusted long since; as it is, it is so entangled, that much uncertainty still hangs over it." So completely did Polk avoid a showdown with the extremists that Calhoun believed to the end that the final settlement was achieved against the influence of the Executive.

During the spring the Van Burenites in Congress joined Calhoun in demanding a compromise arrangement. But this faction, too, found the Administration unfathomable. Thomas Hart Benton of Missouri, who gradually took the lead in denouncing the Western Democrats, complained that he was assailed daily in the *Union* for attempting to carry out what the President had asked the night before. To John A. Dix of New York, an important member of the faction, Polk's persistent effort to create the illusion that compromise was being achieved against his will while he secretly favored it was nothing short of treachery. "The whole matter of the Oregon question," he wrote in June, "has been scandalously mismanaged from the President down. . . ."

Polk was saved further embarrassment by the rapid shift in public and Congressional sentiment. By late spring it was quite obvious that the extremists had been isolated by Congressional argument, newspaper editorials, and the wearing out of public emotion. Even for the calculating Weed the time had come to join the general movement toward compromise. Whigs and Democrats alike could rejoice at the passage of the resolution for notice, for a peaceful settlement was now assured. England seized the diplomatic initiative and proposed an acceptable boundary along the forty-ninth parallel. Polk, through the device of seeking the prior approval of Congress, managed not only to rid himself of a political dilemma but also to escape the condemnation of all but the most extreme. Allen resigned his post as chairman of the Senate Committee on Foreign Relations; a few Western Democrats professed humiliation at what they termed a loss of national honor. But the Oregon settlement was so satisfactory that even the extremists were soon willing to permit the fifty-four forty issue to rest. Little of the nation's approbation was reserved for the President. Polk, refusing to face a divided party, had permitted the question to drift. Exerting no leadership himself, he was unable to associate his Administration with the final triumph in the minds of his contemporaries. That victory belonged to Calhoun and other Congressional leaders.

Even while Oregon negotiations were pending Polk involved himself in the question of California. The key to this significant

JAMES POLK

diplomatic maneuver was the American declaration of war against Mexico in May, 1846. Behind that decision lay months of semi-obscure negotiation with Mexico over a series of unsettled issues—the claims of American citizens against the Mexican government for property stolen or destroyed in Mexico, the Texas-Mexican boundary, and the future of such California harbors as San Francisco, Monterey, and San Diego. Polk had attempted to reopen diplomatic relations with Mexico through the John Slidell mission of November, 1845, instructing Slidell to secure a satisfactory boundary line which would include the Rio Grande and as much of the coveted California coast as possible. In exchange, the United States would assume all American claims against the Mexican government and pay additional millions, the precise amount depending on the extent of ocean frontage which Mexico might concede to the United States.

Slidell was not recognized by the government in Mexico City, and Polk, to strengthen his diplomatic arm, dispatched General Zachary Taylor with an American force to the region of the Rio Grande. To Mexico this had all the appearance of aggression, and with a few scattered shots in that distant wilderness the uneasy peace vanished. With the notice of hostilities, the Cabinet agreed unanimously on war. On May 13 Congress accepted the President's request for a formal declaration.

Polk did not want war. In his diplomacy with Mexico he had hoped to secure California by purchase. His eagerness had provoked a clash of arms, but having become involved in war, he was determined to prolong the conflict until he could drive Mexico into a cession of California. To admit such war aims publicly, the President feared, would be fatal. The principle of indemnity, clearly recognized under the law of nations, was acceptable only to those Americans who placed responsibility for the war on Mexico. What disturbed Polk was the refusal of the Whigs to do so. His own action in sending Taylor to the Rio Grande left sufficient doubt in the minds of his opposition that it elicited an unending review of the war's causes. Politicians who attacked the war could hardly approve the annexation of California as the fruit of that struggle. Polk did not want to be accused of conducting a war of conquest. To the American public and members of Congress, therefore, he remained silent on the subject of California. Benton knew the Administration well and saw its predicament clearly when he wrote:

AMERICA'S TEN GREATEST PRESIDENTS

It is impossible to conceive of an administration less warlike, or more intriguing, than that of Mr. Polk. They were men of peace, with objects to be accomplished by means of war; so that war was a necessity and an indispensability to their purposes. They wanted a small war, just large enough to require a treaty of peace, and not large enough to make military reputations, dangerous for the presidency. Never were men at the head of government less imbued with military spirit, or more addicted to intrigue. How to manage the war was a puzzle. Defeat would be ruin: to conquer vicariously, would be dangerous.

In his conduct of the Mexican War, Polk faced a challenge of major proportions. To achieve California he had to keep the nation involved until Mexico was ready to negotiate. Yet how could he prevail upon Congress to furnish the sinews of war without revealing his purpose in continuing the struggle? Polk admitted simply that his aim was a just peace. In his war message he declared it his desire "not only to terminate hostilities speedily, but to bring all matters in dispute between this Government and Mexico to an early and amicable adjustment." Official policy, noted the Washington *Union*, was that of seeking peace through war. In a circular to American ministers and consuls the Administration declared its military objectives in Mexico as the conquest of an "honorable and permanent peace." Fearing that no administration in Mexico that ceded California could remain in power unless it received, at the moment of the treaty, sufficient funds to support an army, Polk requested two million dollars from Congress to overcome the chief obstacle to peace. This, he said, was "the adjustment of a boundary between the two republics." In his message to Congress in December, 1846, he again declared his purpose in demanding additional troops to be that of obtaining "an honorable peace and thereby secure *ample indemnity* for the expenses of the war, as well as to our much injured citizens. . . ." Yet he carefully avoided any precise definition of that indemnification.

What embarrassed Polk was his need of pursuing the war against an ephemeral enemy that continued to lose all the battles but refused to ask for terms of peace. If the purpose of the war was peace, at what stage in the progression of American victories would a peace be conquered? In complete disgust, Giddings at-

JAMES POLK

tacked the President's message of December, 1846: "The people of the nation are demanding of the Executive a statement of the objects of the war. What are the ulterior designs of the government in its prosecution?" The Ohioan recounted the successes of American arms in Mexico, professedly achieved in the name of defense, and continued: "What estimation must the author of this message have placed upon the intelligence of this body, and of the nation, when he penned these statements? Such absurdities defy argument." Despite the logic of such attacks, the Whigs ultimately voted additional troops and equipment under the conviction that if they gave the President enough rope he would eventually hang himself.

But the challenge to the President's equanimity ran deeper. The Whig party never forgot, nor permitted the nation to forget, that Winfield Scott and Zachary Taylor, the two leading generals in the war, were Whigs. Polk observed Taylor's unique capacity to attract favorable attention to himself from all segments of the American public. The President believed him unfitted for military command. In September, 1846, he complained that Taylor "simply obeys orders and gives no information to aid the administration in directing his movement." But the beleaguered President continued, "After the late battles, which were well fought, the public opinion seems to point to him as entitled to the command." Although he trusted Scott even less, Polk offered him command of the Vera Cruz expedition late in 1846. Eventually the President attempted to resolve the question of partisanship in the military command by obtaining the appointment of Benton as a lieutenant general to serve as supreme commander over the American forces in Mexico. The Senate defeated the President's proposal. Without the power to replace them, Polk followed the actions of the two Whig generals with mounting fear and agitation. "I am held responsible for the conduct of the War," he complained, "and yet Congress refused to give me a commander in whom I have confidence, & I am compelled to employ the officers whom the law provided, however unfit they may be."

Some Democrats joined the Whigs in opposing the wartime Administration. Many of the Van Burenites rejected Polk's rationalization for the war, yet they supported the President as a party obligation. Calhoun deserted the Administration completely and openly used his prestige in Congress to undermine and embarrass it. He charged the President with bungling American diplomacy with Mexico, for if Texas annexation alone were the cause of the war, the burden would fall on the South Carolinian as the author of the treaty of annexation. Calhoun accused the Administration of stupidity in involving the country in a war which would furnish popular Whig presidential candidates for a decade. Calhoun and his friends joined the Whig minority to defeat one wartime measure after another. In one succinct paragraph of February, 1847, Polk summarized the many political pressures beating against his wartime leadership:

> It is now in the third month of the Session and none of my war measures have yet been acted upon. There is no harmony in the Democratic party. . . . In truth faction rules the hour, while principle & patriotism is forgotten. While the Democratic party are thus distracted and divided and are playing this foolish and suicidal game, the Federal party are united and never fail to unite with the minority of the Democratic party, or any faction of it who may break off from the body of their party, and thus postpone and defeat all my measures. I am in the unenviable position of being held responsible for the conduct of the Mexican War, when I have no support either from Congress or from the two officers highest in command in the field. How long this state of things will continue I cannot foresee.

Slavery added another dimension to the political confusion of Congress. David Wilmot, a little-known Pennsylvania Democrat, anchored the question of slavery expansion to the Mexican War with his Proviso of August, 1846, which declared that slavery should not exist in any territory acquired from Mexico as the result of the war. Polk was dismayed at the ensuing debate over slavery, for he insisted that it had no connection with the war. He reminded members of Congress that the institution could exist in neither New Mexico or California. "The state of things in Congress is lamentable," he noted early in 1847. "Instead of coming up to the mark as patriots and sustaining the administration and the country in conducting a foreign war, they are engaged in discussing the abstract question of slavery. . . ." Abolitionists attacked the war savagely because they regarded it as the conspiracy of slaveholders to expand the area of slavery at Mexico's expense.

JAMES POLK

Whig conservatives, fearful of the impact of the slavery issue on the Union, accepted as their wartime program Senator John Berrien's proposed amendment of February, 1847, which declared that "the war with Mexico ought not to be prosecuted by this Government with any view to the dismemberment of the republic, or to the acquisition by conquest of any portion of her territory."

Polk's resourcefulness was equal to the occasion. While politicians and editors attacked the Mexican War and demanded its immediate cessation, the President in April, 1847, dispatched Nicholas P. Trist, chief clerk in the State Department, to join Scott's headquarters in Mexico and attempt to establish direct negotiations with the Mexican government. Trist's instructions were specific, for the President knew precisely what he wanted. He had made that clear in his earlier instructions to Slidell and in his Cabinet deliberations following the outbreak of war. He would settle for no less than the acquisition of San Diego bay and the entire California coast to the north of it. Trist was told to run the boundary down the Colorado "to a point directly opposite the division line between Upper and Lower California; thence due west, along said line, which runs north of the parallel of 32° and south of San Miguel, to the Pacific Ocean. . . ." This line, Polk believed, would bring San Diego bay into the United States. Trist was committed to absolute secrecy, but the news of his mission leaked to the press, and by June the *New York Herald*'s Washington correspondent had secured a copy of the Administration's boundary proposals. Thereafter it was futile for the President to deny his war aims.

Through Trist, Polk eventually escaped his wartime dilemmas and achieved his territorial objectives in the Southwest. But even this diplomatic achievement was gained without his approval, for he had recalled Trist from Mexico as early as October, 1847. During a brief armistice with the Mexicans in August, Trist had agreed to forward to Washington a Mexican proposal that would have conceded all California ports except San Francisco to Mexico. Polk explained his decision to recall Trist in one diary notation: "Mr. Trist is recalled because his remaining any longer with the army could not, probably, accomplish the objects of his mission, and because his remaining longer might, & probably would, impress the Mexican Government with the belief that the United States were so anxious for peace that they would ultimate[ly]

133

conclude one upon the Mexican terms. Mexico must now first sue for peace, & when she does we will hear her proposition."

Unknown to the President, Mexico complied with these conditions when it asked Trist to remain in Mexico and conclude a peace treaty. Having been assured by the Mexicans in advance that they would concede a boundary along the thirty-second parallel, Trist agreed to ignore his instructions. During January, 1848, he negotiated the treaty of Guadalupe Hidalgo which conveyed California and New Mexico, including the port of San Diego, to the United States. Polk knew that Trist was involved in treaty negotiations but took no measure to terminate his efforts until late in January when the decision could have no effect on events in Mexico. Polk accepted the treaty, but he rejected Trist, for his agent had become a close friend of Scott and, after January, the President could only interpret Trist's actions as an effort to embarrass him and his administration.

Peace had become a prime requisite. Despite the succession of American victories in Mexico, it required over eighteen months to terminate the war. "It was not brief, cheap, and bloodless," observed Benton. "It had become long, costly, and sanguinary." Polk demanded that the Senate examine only the treaty, not the circumstances surrounding the negotiation. This assured its ratification. The treaty became the law of the land, but Polk refused even to compensate its author for his expenses in Mexico. Benton recalled regretfully, "Certainly those who served the government well in the war with Mexico fared badly with the administration. . . . Trist, who made the treaty which secured the objects of the war, and released the administration from its dangers, was recalled and dismissed."

Polk's achievements in diplomacy were among the most remarkable in American history. If his own role was often confused, his fundamental demands on other nations were so precise and limited that he could achieve them despite the enormous domestic pressures under which he labored. In his message of December, 1847, he declared that the bay of San Francisco and other harbors on the California coast "would afford shelter for our navy, for our numerous whale ships, and other merchant vessels employed in the Pacific ocean, [and] would in a short period become the marts of an extensive and profitable commerce with China, and other countries of the East." Polk was concerned primarily with frontage on the Pacific, and even after the ratification

JAMES POLK

of the treaty with Mexico he defined his diplomatic gains in no other terms.

Polk's career raises fundamental questions concerning political success and its conditions. That singleness of purpose which made possible his presidential triumphs also exposed his Administration to endless criticism. He pressed toward his goals, unmindful of consequences. So narrow and all-consuming were his policies that he was probably never fully conscious of the bitter sectional controversy which they created. He never perceived the relationship between the acquisition of California and the rise of freesoilism in the nation. In this Polk was sincere, for he was convinced that terrain and climate would bar slavery from the Southwest. But for millions of Americans the relationship between slavery and territorial expansion was distressing indeed. It was not the President's actions alone that laid the foundations of civil strife; it was primarily his refusal to recognize their impact on the American consciousness.

Unfortunately Polk's deviousness almost matched the dexterity which he revealed in the management of his office. Vice President Dallas once observed that Polk suffered from the same defects of character that applied to Charles I. To the President he applied the words of Macaulay's History of England: "He was, in truth, impelled by an incurable propensity to dark and crooked ways. It may seem strange that his conscience, which, on occasions of little moment, was sufficiently sensitive, should never have reproached him with this great vice. But there is reason to believe that he was perfidious, not only from constitution and from habit, but also on principle. He seems to have learned from the theologians whom he most esteemed . . . that, *in every promise which he made, there was an implied reservation that such promise might be broken in case of necessity, and that of the necessity he was the sole judge.*" Dallas was especially disturbed at Polk's habit of announcing one purpose publicly and pursuing another privately. To him it was an administration of "frauds and falsehoods . . . brought home by undeniable evidence." Cunning, the Vice President added, so completely dominated Polk's actions that even his "most devoted friends could not refrain from complaining to each other, with bitter grief and shame, of his crooked politics. His defeats, they said, gave them less pain than his intrigues."

AMERICA'S TEN GREATEST PRESIDENTS

For Polk a successful presidency, measured by his own standards, required both a vast expenditure of energy and a high degree
of expediency, for he had few genuine political assets. He lacked
the magnetism and popularity to build a large personal following.
The public almost ignored him. When he visited Chapel Hill in
May, 1847, for example, no one came to see him off. "You would
be surprised to see how little attention the President or his family
receives here," wrote one Washingtonian, "—if it were not for the
office-hunters, he would hardly receive any." Polk's journey to
New England produced little enthusiasm, and whatever cheers he
received were meant for the President, not the man.

Nor was Polk successful in building political support through
the Federal patronage. Perhaps the distribution of offices won
some key votes in Congress, but the President's insistence on making appointments himself sent a wave of discontent through Democratic ranks. Politicians who had campaigned enthusiastically for
the party felt dismayed and abused at the denial of public offices.
Some Democratic leaders took offense at almost all of Polk's diplomatic appointments since they appeared to serve no party purpose.
The *New York Tribune* concluded that Polk's patronage policy
was "deplorably odious to a vast majority of the leading Democrats of the country." Calhoun asserted in November, 1846, that
the President through his patronage decisions had "distracted and
divided and disheartened and alienated the party to an extent unknown heretofore."

Federal patronage brought no greater satisfaction to the President than it did to the disaffected members of his party. Polk saw
clearly that it was a source of presidential weakness. He had been
in office scarcely four months when he wrote to Governor Silas
Wright of New York, "I sincerely wish I had no office to bestow."
On his first anniversary in the White House he noted in his diary
that the absence of patronage "would add much to the happiness
and comfort" of his office. By January, 1847, he felt the pressures
of the system so keenly that he predicted defeat for any president
who sought re-election if he were forced to wield the Federal
patronage. Polk wrote of the trials of the system: "In every appointment which the President makes he disappoints half a dozen
or more applicants and their friends, who . . . will prefer any
other candidate in the next election, while the person appointed
attributes the appointment to his own superior merit and does not
even feel obliged by it." Polk recognized one basic principle in

JAMES POLK

the distribution of patronage—that the withholding of office might garner support, but that offices once bestowed are no guarantee of future loyalty.

Polk's insistence on wielding the selective power brought to his office a monotonous stream of office-seekers who nearly drove him to distraction. His lamentation so dominates his diary that historians have noted little besides this aspect of his patronage experience. He admitted that he had utter contempt for the hordes who took his time to set forth their merits and claims. "It is a great and useless consumption of my time, and yet I do not see how I am to avoid it without being rude or insulting, which it is not in my nature to be," he noted with complete resignation. On March 4, 1846, he recorded that all was not pleasant at the White House: "I am ready to exclaim, will the pressure for office never cease! It is one year to-day since I entered on the duties of my office, and still the pressure for office has not abated." During the Mexican War the President wrote that the begging for rewards was "not only disgusting, but is almost beyond endurance." Even after the war ended, he declared that it required "great patience & self command to repress the loathing I feel towards a hungry crowd of unworthy office-hunters who often crowd my office."

Occasionally members of Congress sought to protect themselves from their constituents by submitting applications to the President and then instructing him privately to ignore their candidates as unworthy of public office. One day David R. Atchison of Missouri voted against his own applicant in the Senate and quickly proposed another name to Polk. When the irate President demanded of him why he had opposed his first nominee, the Senator replied simply that "we are obliged to recommend our constituents when they apply to us." Polk recorded in his diary that he was tired of the trickery and treachery practiced on him by some members of Congress. He threatened to prepare a treatise on the evils of the Federal patronage as a warning to his successors. "If God grants me length of days and health," he wrote in January, 1847, "I will, after the expiration of my term, give a history of the selfish and corrupt considerations which influence the course of public men, as a legacy to posterity. I shall never be profited by it, but those who come after me may be."

Polk, never physically strong, declined markedly under the burdens of office. Long before his term expired, his friends detected his shortened step, his air of languor and exhaustion.

AMERICA'S TEN GREATEST PRESIDENTS

Charles J. Ingersoll, the noted Democratic politician, warned Mrs. Polk that her husband was wearing himself out—that unless he had some recreation he would die in office. He suggested that she order her carriage and demand that the President accompany her on an occasional drive. "I did so," she replied, "and the carriage waited and waited, until it was too late. It would have been obliged to wait all day, for somebody was always in the office, and Mr. Polk would not, or could not, come. I seldom succeeded in getting him to drive with me." So completely did his official cares dominate his being that Polk found no relaxation in entertainment or anecdote.

For Polk the price of leadership came high. He had never sought the presidency; throughout his last year in the White House he looked forward to his retirement to private life. "I have now passed through two-thirds of my Presidential term," he observed in November, 1847, "& most heartily wish that the remaining third was over. . . ." On March 3, 1848, he noted in his diary, "This day closes my third year in the Presidential office. They have been years of incessant labour, anxiety, & responsibility." On the day that he left the White House he recorded, "I feel exceedingly relieved that I am now free from all public cares." But with leisure did not come the recuperation of body and serenity of mind he required. The labors and anxieties of the past had been too exhausting. His health continued to fail, and he died on June 15, 1849, three months after leaving office.

7
Matthew Calbraith Perry: Antebellum Precursor of the Steam Navy

John H. Schroeder

Between the War of 1812 and the Civil War, the peacetime role of the U.S. Navy expanded dramatically. The primary peacetime mission of the Navy continued to be the protection of American overseas commerce, but accelerating American economic activity around the world transformed the operational definition of that duty by creating an array of additional demands and pressures for increased naval support. In the years after 1815, the protection of commerce meant that the Navy combated pirates, policed smuggling, showed the flag in major ports around the globe, maintained a continuous presence on various overseas stations, and performed limited diplomatic duties. Government officials and most politicians, regardless of their partisan faction, believed the Navy should play a limited peacetime commercial role and defined that mission in a rather narrow and defensive manner. Americans also assumed that most of the Navy's activities would occur in the Caribbean, the Mediterranean, and the Atlantic. To perform its role, the Navy Department maintained a small, active force of fewer than two dozen wooden sailing warships and existed on a budget that averaged less than $4 million per year.

By the 1850s the protection of commerce had been redefined and meant a great deal more than it had three decades earlier. The Navy now played a positive and expansive role in the nation's burgeoning overseas commerce. It not only protected and defended American lives, property, and trade overseas; it now also helped identify new markets, collected valuable commercial and nautical information, concluded diplomatic agreements, and opened new areas to American enterprises. In the Navy, the Mediterranean Squadron continued to be the most prestigious duty station, but American naval forces in Latin America, the Pacific, and the East Indies now carried out activities that were more challenging and more valuable to American overseas commercial interests. The Navy's far-flung activities required an active force of steam as well as sail vessels numbering between forty and fifty, and an annual budget

4   FROM SAIL TO STEAM

Matthew Calbraith Perry. Portrait by William Sidney Mount in 1835. *Courtesy of the Naval Academy Museum.*

of more than $12 million per year. On the eve of the Civil War, the Navy still had fundamental problems, and it hardly resembled the modern naval force of the late nineteenth century; but the nation's staggering overseas commercial expansion had already transformed the Navy's peacetime mission. And in the process, the Navy had assumed an important diplomatic and commercial role in shaping the nation's overseas economic development.

The naval career of Matthew Calbraith Perry spanned this period, and he stands as a key transitional figure between the navy of the early nineteenth century and the new commercial navy that was beginning to emerge by the

Civil War. His early career embodied the values and the traditions of the old navy, dominated by its magnificent wooden sailing warships. At the same time, Perry was an early proponent of the type of technological innovation and naval reform that would transform the peacetime role of the Navy and the character of its warships by the end of the century.

Matthew Calbraith Perry was born into a distinguished American naval family. His father had been a naval officer in both the American Revolution and the undeclared Naval War with France; his four brothers also joined the Navy, and one, Oliver Hazard, became one of the fighting heroes of the War of 1812. Matthew himself entered the Navy at age fourteen and served under the legendary John Rodgers and Stephen Decatur in the War of 1812. He subsequently served on various duty stations, mastered the intricacies of seamanship in wooden sailing vessels, rose to the rank of captain, and eventually commanded the Africa Squadron. During the Mexican War, Perry commanded the Gulf Squadron and distinguished himself in battle during several engagements, including the expeditions against Tabasco and the capture of Vera Cruz. By 1850 Perry, or "Old Bruin" as he was known, had compiled an impressive record of command and service similar to other top naval officers in the Age of Sail.

Unlike most of his naval peers, however, Perry had long been an energetic proponent of technological innovation, improved education, and progressive reform within the Navy. In a navy of wooden sailing vessels, Perry had become an early advocate of steam power and explosive ordnance. Throughout his career, he had demonstrated a notable intellectual curiosity and wide range of educational interests. Perry had also compiled an exceptional record of diplomatic experience in different capacities. Yet these attributes might well have represented nothing more than interesting sidelights to an impressive and traditional antebellum naval career had Perry not been chosen to command the American expedition to Japan. His selection permitted him to combine and fully utilize his varied naval, diplomatic, and intellectual talents in commanding an undertaking that developed into a major diplomatic expedition. The dramatic success and far-reaching significance of the expedition captured the nation's imagination and elevated Perry to his place as one of the Navy's most distinguished nineteenth-century officers. In retrospect, Perry's understanding of the broad significance and implications of his Far Eastern exploits as much as the achievements themselves made the commodore an exemplary harbinger of a coming epoch when the Navy and its officers would play an instrumental role in forging an overseas colonial empire for the United States.[1]

Born on 10 April 1794, in Newport, Rhode Island, Matthew Calbraith Perry was one of the eight children of Christopher Raymond and Sarah Wallace Perry. Christopher Perry was a seafaring man who served in several ships and was taken prisoner four times during the Revolution. Later he served in the American merchant marine and, in June 1798, he entered the Navy as captain in command of the yet unfinished frigate *General Greene*. During the naval war with France, the warship helped suppress pirates, conveyed American merchantmen, and patrolled the Caribbean. In 1801, Perry returned to the merchant service, but he later received a temporary appointment as commandant of the Charlestown Navy Yard.

Matthew Calbraith was the fourth child and third son of the family. All five of the boys became naval officers, and two of the three daughters married naval officers. Matthew entered the Navy as a midshipman in January 1809 and served on the schooner *Revenge* under the command of his brother Oliver Hazard Perry. In the next six years, Matthew also served under Commodores John Rodgers and Stephen Decatur, but he was not involved in any of the dramatic naval engagements of the War of 1812. In fact, the British blockade bottled up Decatur's frigate *President* in New York and allowed Perry enough time ashore to court and marry Jan Slidell, the daughter of a prominent New York merchant, in December 1814. The marriage was a happy one, providing Perry with nine children as well as important political contacts through his brother-in-law John Slidell, an influential Jacksonian Democrat during the 1830s and 1840s. One of Perry's sisters, Anna Maria, provided another family tie of professional importance through her marriage to the younger brother of Commodore John Rodgers.[2] These family connections aided Perry's social stature and professional career. And later his social connections were further enhanced by the marriage in 1848 of his daughter Caroline to August Belmont, the wealthy, German-born financier who was active in New York Democratic Party circles.

After a brief tour of duty with the Mediterranean Squadron in 1815, Perry took a furlough from the Navy and commanded merchantmen owned by his in-laws, before returning to the Navy in 1819. In the next eleven years, Perry received several assignments, including his first two commands, and his career progressed steadily. He served with the naval squadron that escorted a group of free blacks to West Africa to found a free colony at the site of Monrovia at Cape Mesurado. He served with the West Indies Squadron in the effort to end piracy in the Caribbean. He also received valuable experience as first lieutenant or executive officer of the 102-gun *North Carolina*.

In 1830, the Navy Department ordered Perry to assume command of the new sloop *Concord*. This assignment proved to be a frustrating but worthwhile experience for Perry as he was first forced to deal with the personal demands of an eccentric politician and later allowed to view firsthand the effect that naval power could have on diplomatic disputes. Perry's initial assignment on board the *Concord* was to convey John Randolph of Roanoke to Russia as the republic's new Envoy Extraordinary and Minister Plenipotentiary. The cruise provided a trying but useful lesson in patience and self-restraint for the thirty-six-year-old officer. Randolph embarked with a mountain of luggage, an entourage of personal servants, and his well-known cantankerous personality. The new minister insisted that Perry make several stops en route, and once Randolph reached Russia, he remained there only briefly before having Perry convey him and his entourage back to England.[3]

When finally rid of Randolph, the *Concord* joined the Mediterranean Squadron where Perry served for the next two years. Here Perry was able to pursue his intellectual interests in the culture and history of the region as well as to play an instructive role in resolving a claims dispute with Sicily in 1832. When discussions stalled, Commodore Daniel T. Patterson entrusted temporary command of the squadron to Perry. In concert with the *Brandywine* and the *Constellation*, Perry sailed to Naples in July 1832, then departed, and reappeared in September in command of the *Concord*. With the sloop *John Adams* already in port, all this naval activity had the desired effect, and a treaty resolving the claims issue was signed in October 1832.[4]

By the mid-1830s, Perry found himself among a number of energetic and farsighted younger officers who wanted to introduce various progressive ideas into the Navy. Perry, his brother-in-law Alexander Slidell MacKenzie, Robert Stockton, and Franklin Buchanan were officers whose further advancement and ideas for change had been stifled by the Navy's seniority-based promotion system and by the number of officers in their sixties and seventies who clung to positions of power in the department because there was no retirement system. These senior officers dominated the Board of Navy Commissioners which directed naval affairs, and generally opposed progressive reform and technological innovation because they held very traditional ideas about the Navy and its role. For example, the board conceded a limited place for steam power in the Navy, but detested the very thought of a navy dominated by cumbersome steam vessels that did not demand a high level of seamanship and created endless noise and dirt.[5]

In contrast, the younger group of career naval officers advocated extensive changes to improve the Navy and urged the application of steam power and other technological advances. These officers admired the changes then beginning in Europe where serious experiments had begun with steam power, iron hulls, and explosive shells. Perry, Slidell, and others also sought a much expanded peacetime diplomatic and commercial role for the Navy. To protect and extend American commerce, they wanted more ships deployed overseas and engaged in an increased array of peacetime activities. Thus Perry, Charles Wilkes, Matthew F. Maury, and other officers actively supported the proposed naval exploring expedition to the South Seas. In endorsing the project, these officers emphasized that the gathering of scientific, commercial, and nautical information would immeasurably enhance the nation's overseas maritime and economic interests in the Pacific. In essence, they sought an active role for the Navy in the creation of an overseas American commercial empire.[6]

Perry soon emerged as a leader in the group. During a decade as second in command and then as commandant of the Brooklyn Navy Yard, Perry advocated an array of reforms and innovations. He sought improvement in the recruiting of seamen and in the education of officers. He had long taken the shipboard instruction of officers seriously and now supported the establishment of a naval academy. In 1833, he was instrumental in founding the United States Naval Lyceum, an organization formed "to promote the diffusion of useful knowledge, (and) to foster a spirit of harmony and a community interest in the service." For officers in New York, the Lyceum held regular meetings and lectures, recorded weather data, and maintained a library. Perry served as its first curator and later became its president. He also helped found the *Naval Magazine*, served on its editorial board, and contributed occasional articles. When the Naval Academy was founded in 1845, Perry served on the board of officers that organized the new institution and designed its first curriculum. During this period, Perry developed an interest in the improvement of coastal lighthouses as important aids to navigation. In 1837, he wrote a report that recommended improvements in navigational aids for the New York area. Then after a trip to Europe and England in 1838, he prepared a report recommending the creation of an independent lighthouse board and the application of the superior lens of Augustin-Jean Fresnel to replace the older reflectors then in use in American lighthouses. Although his recommendations were practical and well advised, they were not widely adopted in the United States until the 1850s.[7]

Perry had a more immediate impact in the area of naval technology. He had long been interested in steam power and wanted to develop a genuine steam warship rather than the harbor-bound floating steam batteries authorized by Congress and favored by some senior officers. After the construction of a steam warship was authorized in 1834, the Navy Department placed Perry in charge of construction of the *Fulton II*, which was launched in 1837. Although serious problems existed with the vessel, Perry worked hard to demonstrate the practicality of an ocean-going steam warship. In 1838, he sailed the *Fulton II* to Washington where the President and numerous congressmen toured the ship. Resistance to steam power remained intense in the Navy and the Van Buren administration, but this venture helped persuade numerous politicians of the potential of steam power and proved to be one factor in Congress's 1839 decision to authorize three war steamers, including two, the *Mississippi* and the *Missouri*, that followed Perry's designs. For his efforts, Perry has been credited with being the "father of the steam navy." Although the label is perhaps an exaggeration, Perry nevertheless deserves recognition as the founder of the Navy's engineering corps, whose organization he outlined and championed. In 1839 and 1840, Perry also experimented with different cannons and types of shells. As a result, he demonstrated the superiority of the Paixhans type 64-pound shell artillery and the comparative inaccuracy of grape shot. Perry also advocated the use of iron warships and endorsed construction of the propellor-driven, steam frigate *Princeton*, which was built under the supervision of Robert Stockton.[8]

Many of the ideas of the Navy's progressive young officers were embodied in an influential 1837 article "Thoughts on the Navy," published in the *Naval Magazine*. Although it bore the name of Perry's brother-in-law Alexander Slidell, the article was coauthored by Perry and expressed his ideas about the need for a more modern, efficient, and powerful American navy. Its authors asserted that "all of our misfortunes as a nation, from the day we became one," have proceeded from the "mistakes and disasters of the past," and the nation must establish the principle that attacks on our commerce and "our national honor shall be prevented at the time by a prompt display of power . . . ." To accomplish this, the United States needed to build a navy commensurate with the "extent and value" of its commerce in "relative proportion" to the navies that other maritime nations maintained to protect their respective foreign trades. The Navy could then "follow the adventurous trader, in his path of peril, to every sea with cruisers ready to spread over him the protecting flag of the republic!" The United States had the world's eighth largest navy, but to meet its peacetime responsibilities,the Navy would need to be expanded to three times its size, a goal that Slidell and Perry endorsed enthusiastically.[9]

In spite of Perry's vision and achievements, relatively little progress had been made in the movement for naval reform by the early 1840s. The Van Buren administration remained indifferent to the need for changes in the Navy. Secretaries of the Navy Mahlon Dickerson and James K. Paulding both held very conservative naval attitudes and opposed technological innovation. The administration also demonstrated little interest in the peacetime commercial and diplomatic potential of the Navy. For example, the United States Exploring Expedition, which had been authorized during Andrew Jackson's presidency, almost did not sail at all, owing to administration inertia and indifference, before finally departing in 1838.

In early 1843, orders to command the Africa Squadron ended Perry's term of shore duty. The assignment was a difficult one, not highly coveted by experienced naval officers, because service in African waters was characterized by bad weather, difficult conditions, the constant threat of yellow fever, and the absence of recreational or leisure outlets for the men. The squadron under Perry was dispatched to police the slave trade in accord with the recently negotiated Webster–Ashburton Treaty, to protect the black settlements established by the American Colonization Society, and to provide "all the aid and support" that lawful American trade required. "It is the chief purpose, as well as the chief duty of our naval power," wrote the Secretary of the Navy, "to see that these [commercial] rights are not improperly abridged, or invaded."[10]

In Africa, Perry attempted to police the slave trade in a conscientious manner, but the size of his four-ship squadron limited its effectiveness. The commodore had much better fortune in combating yellow fever among his crews. He instituted a number of measures that dramatically reduced the effect of the disease. All men were required to wash their bodies every week, to wear a flannel undershirt during nights as well as days, and to sleep in a cloth jacket and pants. In addition, fresh air was dried and circulated below the decks of the ships, and smudge pots were burned to repel insects.

Under Perry's leadership, the Africa Squadron provided effective naval support for American commerce along the West African coast. In previous years, legitimate American trade and black American settlements had been subjected to constant danger and periodic attacks by various native African tribes. In 1841, at the village of Little Berebee on the Ivory coast, the American schooner *Mary Carver*, carrying a cargo valued at $12,000, had been captured and her crew murdered. Although the Secretary of the Navy had issued instructions in August 1842 for Commodore William Ramsey to obtain reparation, it was Perry who finally took action. On 13 December 1843, Perry's entire squadron anchored off Little Berebee. Two hundred sailors and marines landed and pitched a tent on the beach so that the Americans would not have to enter the hostile village to hold a conference with the local ruler, King Ben Krako. Krako, a man of great size and strength, attended the meeting accompanied by several subordinates and an interpreter. In regard to the *Mary Carver* outrage, Krako provided an explanation that Perry found preposterous, and a general melee ensued. The American sailors killed the king and several natives in the scuffle and burned the village. The following day, Perry proceeded to Grand Berebee and held a conference with several other local chiefs, all of whom disclaimed any part in the *Mary Carver* attack and praised the killing of the feared King Krako. To appease Perry, local authorities signed a treaty specifying that natives in the area would not plunder trading ships or molest missionaries.[11]

In September 1845, several months after Perry returned to the United States from Africa, Secretary of the Navy George Bancroft informally offered Perry command of the Gulf Squadron. The deterioration in Mexican–American relations and the likelihood of war made this command highly attractive, but complications soon arose. The Secretary did not identify a specific date for the appointment to become effective, and indicated that Perry would take over as soon as Commodore David Conner relinquished his command of the Gulf Squadron. Since Perry sought additional time at home in 1845 and Conner was known to be in poor health, neither Perry nor the Navy Department anticipated any problem with the transition of commanders. However, in spite of his health, Conner had no intention of relinquishing his choice command and, in fact, remained as commodore of the squadron until he was finally removed in March 1847, more than eighteen months after Bancroft had first offered the command to Perry. In the meantime, Perry languished in the United States until August 1846 when he received command of the steamer *Mississippi* and joined the Gulf Squadron. Once on station, Perry flew the red broad pendant of vice commodore until he finally took full command of American naval forces in the Gulf in March of 1847.[12]

Once hostilities with Mexico began in May 1846, the U.S. Navy played an essential military role in the war. American naval forces prevented Mexican gunboats and privateers from disrupting American commerce, captured a number of Mexican seaports, transported troops, carried supplies, and provided additional logistical support for the American armies of Zachary Taylor and Winfield Scott. Although the enemy's weak naval forces proved to be no match for the United States, the U.S. Navy's achievement was rendered more impressive by the severe obstacles that had to be surmounted. In Washington, the Polk administration had not prepared for naval warfare and provided minimal support once hostilities began. The administration never assigned high priority to the Navy, and Congress responded to the Navy's needs in a piecemeal manner. Officers complained frequently of inadequate supplies, poor facilities, and long delays in the arrival of war material. The Navy also required more warships, and many of those provided were unsuitable for effective use in the shallow waters along the Mexican coast.[13]

After he joined the Gulf Squadron in September 1846, Perry assumed an active part in the war effort. In October, he led the first Tabasco expedition which produced the easy conquest of Frontera and a seventy-mile expedition up the Grijalva River to Villahermosa. Although he could have occupied the town, Perry withdrew after a brief truce and limited fighting because he lacked sufficient forces to occupy and hold the town. After participating in several other actions including the capture of Tampico, Perry returned briefly to Norfolk and Washington, D.C., in early 1847. This visit finally produced the Navy Department's decision to remove Conner and install Perry as commander of the Gulf Squadron. Although Conner had proved to be rather ineffective as a fighting commander, his removal produced bad feeling among his own partisans and criticism of Perry's presumed political machinations in Washington.

Conner's removal was especially controversial because it came in the midst of the American offensive against Vera Cruz on 20 March 1847. The overall operation was commanded by General Winfield Scott, who relied on the Navy for logistical support and control of the coast. In addition, Scott urgently needed artillery, but Perry insisted that naval forces would provide the guns that Scott required only if the gun crews came as well. In this way, Perry ensured a significant combat role for naval forces in the invasion and capture of Vera Cruz. His well-drilled gun crews fought valiantly and earned special praise from Scott himself. Subsequently, Perry's forces captured Tuxpan in April and then returned to Tabasco in June. There with the river approach blocked by enemy forces, Perry led a naval landing force that marched overland several miles and forced the surrender of the town of Villahermosa.[14]

By the end of the war, Perry had achieved a reputation as one of the Navy's

Capture of Tabasco. On 14 June 1847 Perry led nine ships and forty-seven boats up the Tabasco River (top). Two days later he personally led a naval brigade ashore (bottom) to occupy the city of Tabasco (present-day Villahermosa). These lithographs, published by Sarony & Major in New York in 1848, were based on watercolors by eyewitness Lt. Henry Walke, U.S.N. *Courtesy of the Naval Academy Museum.*

most capable officers. Known as "Old Bruin" for his gruff way of barking out orders, Perry was widely respected for his diligent, serious and efficient manner. "In many respects he is an astonishing man," wrote fellow officer Franklin Buchanan in 1847, "the most industrious, hardworking, energetic, zealous, preserving, enterprising officer of his rank in our navy. He does not spare himself or *anyone* under him. . . . his great powers of endurance astonish everyone; all know he is by no means a brilliant man but his good common sense and judgment, his sociable manner to his officers, no *humbuggery* or *mystery*, make him respected and esteemed." Never a dashing or romantic figure, "Old Bruin" inspired neither great love nor hero worship. Instead, he earned the respect and admiration of his contemporaries through hard work, sound judgment, and effective performance.[15] Although his family ties and political connections might have been resented, Perry's talent and achievements could not be denied.

After he returned to the United States and was honored for his wartime exploits, Perry relinquished command of the Home Squadron in the fall of 1848 and began more than three years of shore duty as general superintendent of mail steamers. Perry's most important responsibility in his new role was to supervise construction of government-financed mail steamers being built for several private steamship lines. Congress had approved subsidies for the steamers with the specification that the ships would be built in such a way that they could be converted to naval vessels in wartime. But Perry's instructions and authority were vague, and he exercised little control over the new steamships in spite of the energy and commitment he brought to the assignment. Although Perry was an enthusiastic proponent of steam warships, he doubted that the new mail steamers could ever be converted into effective steam fighting ships.[16]

Near the end of 1851, the Navy Department selected Perry to command the East India Squadron and to lead a major diplomatic mission to Japan. Although the East Asian assignment provided an opportunity that led to Perry's greatest professional achievement, Perry preferred command of the prestigious Mediterranean Squadron. An exotic, remote, secluded land in Asia, Japan had long held a fascination for Europeans and Americans. After initial contact with Westerners, the Japanese suppressed Christianity and excluded all foreigners during the seventeenth century. The only contact occurred at the small island of Deshima, off Nagasaki, where the Dutch maintained a small settlement that provided the few items Japan sought from the outside world. During the Napoleonic Wars, the Dutch chartered a number of American ships to fly their colors and visit Deshima, but this early and trifling American commerce with Japan ended once the Dutch resumed trade in their own ships in 1813. For the next three decades, Americans had virtually no contact with Japan.

During the 1840s, American interest grew in Asia and Japan in the aftermath of the signing of the Treaty of Wanghia with China. In 1845, the Polk administration dispatched Alexander H. Everett to exchange treaty ratifications with China and to negotiate a treaty with Japan. When Everett died en route, his naval escort, Commodore James Biddle, continued the mission, exchanged ratifications with China, and then proceeded to Japan in the 90-gun *Columbia* accompanied by the sloop of war *Vincennes*. Arriving in the Bay of Yedo (Tokyo) in July 1846, Biddle achieved little and committed a number of blunders in the process. He permitted dozens of armed guards to surround his ships and Japanese sailors to board and inspect them. Without an interpreter, he dealt directly with minor Japanese authorities, showed himself freely on board, and entrusted the President's official letter to one such minor official. The Japanese refused to accept the letter and ordered the American ships to depart with a curt note from a local official. To receive the reply, Biddle boarded a Japanese guard boat and in the process was rudely pushed or bumped by a Japanese sailor. Although the Japanese offered to punish the offender, the damage was done. Lacking explicit instructions that would have permitted retaliation, Biddle departed with the embarrassing assistance of a tow from the Japanese. In 1849, the Navy sent Commander Thomas Glynn to Nagasaki to pick up fifteen American whalemen who were being held there. Unlike Biddle, Glynn demanded respect for the American flag and the return of the Americans. He sailed his *Preble* through a cordon of guard boats and anchored within cannon shot range of the city. In subsequent negotiations, he threatened to bombard the city if the Americans were not released; and they were freed within two days.[17]

When he returned to the United States in 1851, Glynn urged the Fillmore administration to send another mission to Japan and in the process added his name to a growing movement to open relations with the Japanese. By this time, the United States had emerged as a Pacific power eager to expand its political influence in the Pacific Basin, increase its economic activity in the area, and establish close ties with the Far East. Although various factors were involved, the main pressures were economic and commercial, as different American interests sought to protect the nation's extensive whaling fleet, expand existing trade, and open new markets. The Treaty of Wanghia had only quickened American commercial interest in Asia and whetted the American appetite for the fabled commercial wealth of the Orient. In response to active lobbying, the Fillmore administration agreed in 1851 to send a new mission to Japan and selected Commodore John H. Aulick for the assignment. With a squadron of three ships, Aulick experienced difficulties soon after his departure, quarreled with one of his captains, suffered a breakdown in health in Canton, and ended up being removed from his command in November 1851.[18]

Perry's selection as Aulick's replacement was exceptional. Perry's vision, initiative, experience, and influence transformed the mission into a major naval and diplomatic project of far-reaching significance for the United States. Although he would have preferred command of the Mediterranean Squadron, Perry informed the Navy Department that he would accept command of the East India Squadron if the sphere of action and size of the squadron were "so enlarged as to hold out a well grounded hope of its conferring distinction upon its commander."[19]

From the outset, Perry's command contrasted sharply with that of his predecessor Aulick because of the great care, time, and energy Perry devoted to preparations for the expedition. He also requested and received a much enlarged squadron with three additional ships assigned immediately and others to follow. Eventually, Perry would command ten ships, an American squadron of unprecedented size in Asian waters. He also selected first-rate officers whom he had known previously to assist him including Commanders Franklin Buchanan, Sidney S. Lee, and Joel Abbot, who commanded the *Susquehanna*, the *Mississippi*, and the *Macedonian*, respectively.

During 1852, Perry collected as much information and learned as much about Asia and Japan as he could. He met with naval officers who had sailed in the western Pacific and visited New Bedford, Massachusetts in April to talk to whaling captains familiar with the area. He read extensively and conferred with German scholar Philipp Franz von Siebold. As a result, Perry was exceptionally well versed in the history, culture, and customs of the Japanese by the time he sailed. Perry also took great care in purchasing various presents for the Emperor and other Japanese dignitaries. He selected gifts to demonstrate the culture and technological advancement of American civilization. In addition to volumes by John J. Audubon, Perry included an assortment of champagne, cordials, and perfumes. More important were the gadgets and machine products, including rifles, pistols, carbines, farming implements, a daguerreotype camera, a telegraph, and a quarter-size railroad complete with locomotive, tender, coach, and track.

Perry also reshaped the expedition by convincing the administration to make the mission to Japan his primary duty, in contrast to Aulick's instructions which specified that the Japan mission was supplemental to his regular duties as commander of the East India Squadron. After receiving general instructions in March 1852, Perry conferred with Secretary of the Navy John P. Kennedy and Secretary of State Daniel Webster, who suggested that the commodore be permitted to draft his own diplomatic instructions. When he departed, Perry carried detailed instructions from Kennedy, diplomatic instructions from the State Department, and a letter from the President to the Emperor of Japan.[20]

Most specific in regard to Japan were the instructions Perry himself had written for the State Department. Signed by Acting Secretary of State C. M. Conrad, this document outlined the background, three main objectives, and conduct of the mission to Japan. First, the treaty was to provide protection for American seamen and ships wrecked or endangered by weather in Japanese waters. Second, the agreement should permit American vessels to obtain provisions, water, and fuel, and, if necessary, to refit in Japanese ports. Third, the treaty should allow American vessels to use one or more Japanese ports to trade their cargoes. In addition, the squadron was instructed to explore and survey the coastal waters of Japan. To achieve these objectives, the Navy authorized Perry to use his "whole force" but reminded him that the mission was to be of a "pacific character." The commodore's conduct was to be "courteous and conciliatory, but at the same time, firm and decided." He would resort to force only in "self defense" or "to resent an act of personal violence" against himself or one of his men.[21]

In November 1852, after months of preparation, Perry sailed in his flagship, the *Mississippi*, and arrived at Hong Kong via the Cape of Good Hope route in April 1853 to find three of his ships already in port. To his chagrin, the *Susquehanna* had sailed to Shanghai to protect American merchants under the threat of violence from the Taiping Rebellion. When he reached Shanghai, Perry ignored pressure from the merchant community and the American minister to remain there with his squadron. Although he agreed to leave a sloop at Shanghai, Perry transferred his flag to the *Susquehanna* and departed for Naha on Great Lew Chew (Okinawa) in the Ryukyus in mid-May. Earlier, Perry had written to the Navy Department emphasizing the importance of establishing "ports of refuge and supply" as bases for the mission to Japan. Lew Chew seemed an ideal choice for such a base because the harbor was good, and it was accessible to Japan. Although nominally under Japanese control, the islands were semiautonomous. Moreover, the people were docile, unarmed, and backward, with their only defense being their considerable ability to evade, procrastinate, and ignore foreigners and their demands. The proximity of Lew Chew to Japan ensured that Perry's actions and the size of his squadron would be reported to the Japanese. Lew Chew, then, provided an excellent place for a dress rehearsal.[22]

At Naha, Perry refused to meet with natives or local officials who met the American ships. Only when the regent for the ruler of the island visited the *Susquehanna* did Perry receive him and announce that he would visit the royal palace at Shuri. The horrified officials of Lew Chew attempted without success to divert Perry. On the appointed day, Perry and an impressive entourage landed, rejected further attempts to divert them, and proceeded to Shuri. The commodore rode in an elaborate sedan chair constructed for the occasion to emphasize his exalted station. After visiting the palace and feasting at the regent's residence, Perry and his party returned to the American ships. In the next two weeks, the Americans visited Naha frequently, procured a shelter for

Americans on shore, and dispatched a party to explore the island while other Americans surveyed the coastal waters.

In early June, the *Susquehanna* and the *Saratoga* sailed for the Bonin Islands to the northeast. At Port Lloyd, Perry found a small colony of thirty-one residents headed by Nathaniel Savoy, a native New Englander who had settled the island with a small group from Hawaii. Although he had no intention of using the islands as a base for his Japanese operations, Perry understood the potential value of the port, which stood directly on the great circle route from Hawaii to the south China ports. Perry himself purchased a small tract of land to serve as a possible waterfront coal depot. He also raised the American flag, drew up a code of laws, and had Savoy elected chief magistrate. Later, Perry would assert an official American claim to the islands and recommend establishment of an open port for whalers, steamers, and merchant ships of all nations. Perry then returned to Naha, where he drilled American forces on shore and dispatched more parties to collect a range of information on the islands. As subsequent events would demonstrate, the commodore intended Lew Chew and the Bonins to serve as much more than a temporary base for his own mission. He believed that he had taken the initial steps in establishing two permanent American "ports of refuge and supply" for American whalers, merchantmen, transpacific steamers, and naval vessels.[23]

On 2 July 1853, the flagship *Susquehanna* and three other warships departed on a six-day journey to Japan. At the entrance to the Bay of Yedo, Japanese junks and guard boats immediately appeared and surrounded the American ships. But the Japanese ships were prevented from tying lines to the American ships, and Japanese sailors were not permitted to board. Only when a man identified as the vice governor appeared, was he permitted to board the *Susquehanna*, where he was received by Perry's subordinates rather than the commodore himself. The Americans informed the Japanese that Perry had a letter from the President for the Emperor, and they refused to deliver the document at Nagasaki as the Japanese specified. Operating through his subordinate officers, Perry insisted that the President's letter be delivered to appropriate authorities at Uraga, indicating that the American fleet would proceed directly to Yedo and the royal palace if the Japanese refused. To underline his claims, Perry had already initiated surveys of the area.

Finally, the Japanese agreed to receive the President's letter in special ceremonies at Kurihama near Uraga. At daybreak on 14 July, the *Susquehanna* and the *Mississippi* steamed into the bay at Kurihama, anchored, and positioned themselves to command the Japanese shore fortifications. Since thousands of Japanese troops congregated on shore, Perry sent 250 armed marines and sailors in several launches. Once they were ashore, the ceremony itself was brief. The American couriers opened the elaborate box containing the American document and received a Japanese scroll in return. The Japanese reply acknowledged receipt of the President's letter, explained that negotiations could not occur at this spot, and informed Perry that he could now depart. In response, the commodore explained that he would sail in two or three days and would be pleased to convey any messages to Lew Chew or Canton. When the Japanese did not reply, Perry explained that he planned to return the following spring with at least four naval vessels and possibly more. The conference then ended, the Americans returning to their ships without incident. The next day, Perry transferred to the *Mississippi* and steamed up the bay to the outskirts of Yedo before turning back. A final ceremony was held on 16 July, in which small presents were exchanged, and the American squadron departed for Naha the following day.[24]

Perry based his decision to return to Japan later rather than wait for the Japanese response to the President's letter on several considerations. By departing for China, Perry could reprovision his squadron, add warships, give the Japanese time for deliberation, and address any problems that might have arisen in China. When he left Japanese waters, Perry could take considerable satisfaction in his initial achievements. He had avoided Biddle's earlier mistakes and established contact with the Japanese on a basis of equality without provoking an incident or engaging in hostilities. He had insisted on proper respect for his official authority, refused to deal directly with lower Japanese officials, and delivered the President's letter in an appropriate ceremony. Perry had also refused to permit Japanese to swarm over his ships, insisted that all provisions be paid for, and exchanged gifts with the Japanese only on an equal basis. In addition, American forces had navigated the Bay of Yedo without hindrance, conducted surveys of the area, and approached the outskirts of the capital. His firmness, careful preparation, and conciliatory manner also left the unmistakable message that he was a determined man who would not be easily diverted by traditional Japanese tactics.[25]

Back at Naha, the reports he received displeased Perry. During his absence, provisions had proved difficult to obtain, and numerous spies and police plagued Americans on shore. At a dinner on 28 July, Perry insisted that a free market be established, that Americans be left unmolested on shore, that use of a rest house be continued, and that a coal shed be erected for use by Americans. When the regent demurred, Perry replied that he would again march to the palace at Shuri unless he received a satisfactory response within twenty-four hours. For effect, he dispatched a carpenter to inspect and repair the sedan chair he had used on his initial visit. However, the regent complied with each request the next day, and Perry departed for China on 1 August.

In China, the arrival of additional naval vessels strengthened Perry's forces, and by the end of 1852 his squadron numbered ten ships. Although he had originally planned not to return to Japan until the spring of 1854, rumors in China led Perry to fear that a Russian squadron was preparing to visit Japan before he returned, and he hastened his departure. By late January 1854, his entire squadron had assembled at Naha, where it remained for two weeks.

Perry found relations with the natives at Naha more amicable but protested to the regent about various difficulties. The commodore also recommended American occupation of Great Lew Chew should his mission to Japan fail. In February the squadron departed for Japan and anchored near Uraga where Perry prepared for a long stay.

Local Japanese officials welcomed the Americans hospitably and informed them that five Japanese commissioners had been appointed to negotiate with Perry at Uraga. Perry countered by suggesting the negotiations be held at the Japanese capital. Thus began several weeks of disagreement over exactly where the formal negotiations would be held. Finally, the Japanese proposed and Perry accepted Yokohama, fifteen miles south of the capital, as the site.

Formal negotiations began with an elaborate ceremony on 8 March 1854, after Perry with an entourage of three bands and 500 marines, sailors, and officers came ashore. In the initial meeting, the Japanese delivered the Emperor's reply and agreed to protect shipwrecked Americans and American ships in distress as well as to provide provisions, water, and coal to American ships at one designated harbor. According to the Japanese, preparation of the harbor would take five years, and, in the meantime, coal would be available at

"Comm. Perry meeting the Imperial Commissioners at Yokohama." On 8 March 1854 Commodore Matthew C. Perry led a party of 500 men ashore at Yokohama. Amid pomp and ceremony he received Japan's answer to the letter from President Millard Fillmore that he had delivered the previous year. Lithograph by Sarony & Company after a painting by W. Peters. *Courtesy of the Naval Historical Center.*

Nagasaki. The Japanese also agreed to sell or barter anything ships might want that could be furnished from their empire.

Negotiations continued through March as Perry and the Japanese differed on the extent of commercial privileges and the number of ports to be opened. On 13 March, Perry formally presented the American gifts to the Japanese and provided a full demonstration of the miniature railroad and telegraph. On the 24th, the Japanese reciprocated with gifts of their own as relations between the two groups continued to be cordial and free of hostility. Finally, on 31 March 1854, the Treaty of Kanag·····a was signed in a formal ceremony. The agreement guaranteed protection for shipwrecked American sailors and American ships in distress and specified that the ports of Shimoda and Hokadate would be open to American ships to purchase wood, water, coal, and provisions at a fair price. At these two ports, shipwrecked American sailors were also permitted to reside temporarily and to move freely within designated areas. In addition, the treaty included a most-favored-nation clause and allowed the United States to send "consuls or agents" to reside at Shimoda anytime after eighteen months.[26]

Although the concessions granted in the treaty did not approximate those enjoyed by the United States in its relations with China, the agreement constituted a dramatic achievement. Not only had Perry accomplished the basic objectives outlined in his instructions; the commodore had also placed diplomatic relations between the two nations on a formal and equal basis. Such status had never been granted to the Dutch at Nagasaki or to any other nation. Subsequently, the commercial concessions would prove to be inadequate for the United States, but Perry's treaty nevertheless provided the basis for later expansion of commercial privileges.

As soon as the treaty was signed, Perry dispatched Commander H. A. Adams to the United States in the *Saratoga* with a copy of the treaty while the main body of the expedition remained in Japanese waters, continued to survey the coastline, and visited the treaty ports of Shimoda and Hokadate. In July, Perry returned to Naha and signed a treaty of friendship with the regent. The commodore then returned to Hong Kong before leaving for the United States in September 1854.

Although contemporary attention focused on the "opening" of Japan, Perry's own goals and achievements were not limited to the treaty with Japan. He himself conceived of his mission in broad strategic terms and attempted to provide the basis for an American commercial empire in the western Pacific. In addition to the concessions wrested from Japan and the substantial scientific and nautical activities of the expedition, Perry sought American maritime superiority in the area. In the Lew Chew Islands, he had insisted on a treaty that guaranteed water, wood, and provisions for American ships, native pilots to guide American captains safely into the harbor, land access for Americans on Great Lew Chew, an American burial ground there, and construction of an

American coal shed. In the Bonin Islands, Perry had formally asserted an American claim to the islands, helped establish a small independent community headed by a native New Englander, and purchased land at Port Lloyd to serve as a coaling station. He also dispatched two vessels to investigate reports that shipwrecked American sailors were being held captive on Formosa and to explore coal deposits there. Although no sailors were found, the coal proved to be abundant. The treaty with Japan, then, represented but a part of Perry's visionary Far Eastern program.[27]

Perry used the period after his return to the United States to outline his views on the nation's Far Eastern policy in two articles, as well as an address to the American Geographical Society. Like many other Americans of his time, Perry predicted a new era of commercial enterprise for the United States in the Pacific basin. The recent treaty with Japan represented only a "preliminary" step toward a more advanced commercial agreement that could be concluded once Japan was better prepared to enter the international community. To encourage American commerce, Perry urged formal diplomatic and commercial treaties with Siam, Cambodia, Cochin China, and parts of Borneo and Sumatra. Perry also endorsed creation of a government-supported steamship line from the Pacific ports of the United States to China, Japan, and the main islands in between. Finally, Perry emphasized the value of naval power in Asian diplomacy. "In all negotiations with China and other eastern nations," wrote Perry, "the display of a respectable armed force is necessary . . . in most cases, the mere presence of such force will answer the purposes desired . . . ."[28]

Although such views were popular during the 1850s, Perry went far beyond his contemporaries in advocating the creation of a European-style empire in the Pacific. He believed that the United States should take control of Lew Chew and the Bonin Islands, and he wanted the United States to take the initiative on the "magnificent island" of Formosa by establishing an American colony at the port of Kelung. Once established through a land grant, the American settlement would soon increase its area, wealth, and power until it rivaled the ports of Hong Kong and Singapore in importance. In addition to the rich coal deposits on Formosa, American settlement there would provide an "entrepot for American trade" in Asia and give the United States an excellent "naval and military position . . . directly in front of the principal ports of China." Like most other Americans of his day, Perry also embraced the idea of American intervention in the internal affairs of Asia as part of the "responsibilities which our growing wealth and power must inevitably fasten upon us." Because "the advance of civilization and the industrial arts" could only be achieved when the Asian peoples joined the "new family of commercial" nations, the commodore argued that military intervention might "be fully justified," to force "the empires of China and Japan into the family of nations."[29]

Perry envisioned continued American expansion in the Pacific as Americans reached for their ultimate destiny by settling the remote islands of the Pacific and creating their own governments there. But Perry well understood that the development of an American empire in the Pacific would not be a benign process. Forceful military and political action would be necessary to combat European rivalry and establish American supremacy. Eventually, the American people would extend "their dominion and their power until they shall have . . . placed the Saxon race upon the eastern shores of Asia." There, predicted Perry, the American "exponents of freedom" would eventually confront the Russian representatives of "absolutism" in a "mighty battle" that would determine "the freedom or the slavery of the world."[30] These visionary ideas placed Matthew Perry far ahead of his time and attracted little serious support in the 1850s. In this respect, the commodore's prescience made him much more an ideological contemporary of Alfred T. Mahan's generation than of his own antebellum era.

In the United States, Perry received a hero's welcome and lavish praise for the expedition's achievements. Congress gave Perry a vote of thanks and a $20,000 grant for serving as the diplomatic envoy as well as the naval commander of the expedition. The commodore received a gold medal from the merchants of Boston and a 381-piece silver service from the New York Chamber of Commerce. In a ceremony in June 1855 at Newport, the governor and the General Assembly of Perry's native Rhode Island presented him with a large silver salver. In the meantime, Perry had begun work on the official narrative of the expedition, with Volume I appearing in 1856 and Volume II in 1857. By the end of 1857, Perry seemed ready for a new assignment, and he was rumored to be the next commander of the Mediterranean Squadron. But in early 1858, Perry caught a severe cold, became seriously ill, and died on 4 March.

Although his death denied him the chance for further distinctions in the upcoming Civil War, Matthew Calbraith Perry's legacy was already secure. In nearly a half century of service, he had distinguished himself as a professional officer, wartime commander, naval reformer, and effective diplomat. The breadth of his achievements was unmatched in the antebellum Navy. As a professional naval officer and commander, Perry was one of the best of his day. He was courageous in battle, and during the Mexican War he proved to be an energetic and effective commander. But in addition to these attributes, Perry also distinguished himself as a naval reformer and diplomat. Throughout his career, he sought ways of modernizing and improving the efficiency of the Navy and better educating its men. Perry also became a skilled diplomat during his career, and the combination of his personal talent, energy, and intelligence was largely responsible for the spectacular success of the expedition to Japan. Equally important is the fact that Perry fully understood the long-term significance of his activities in the Far East. He realized that he was not merely opening formal relations with one island nation but was helping to shape a maritime empire as well. Thus representing the very best qualities of the old navy, Matthew Calbraith Perry also manifested the very attributes that would be demanded by the navy of the new American empire several decades later.

FURTHER READING

The standard scholarly biography of Perry is Samuel Eliot Morison, *"Old Bruin": Commodore Matthew C. Perry, 1794–1858*. In spite of some distracting digressions, Admiral Morison's biography is typically well written and extensively researched, and presents a full account of Perry's life. An old, still useful, but inaccurately titled study is William E. Griffis, *Matthew Calbraith Perry: A Typical American Naval Officer*. A more recent biography of little value is Edward M. Barrows, *The Great Commodore: The Exploits of Matthew C. Perry*.

Aspects of Perry's career have also been treated in a number of studies. His contributions to antebellum naval development are analyzed in John H. Schroeder, *Shaping a Maritime Empire: The Commercial and Diplomatic Role of the American Navy, 1829–1861*. Perry's service in the African Squadron is discussed in Donald R. Wright, "Matthew Perry and the African Squadron," Clayton R. Barrow, Jr., ed., *America Spreads Her Sails: U.S. Seapower in the 19th Century*. K. Jack Bauer, *Surfboats and Horse Marines: U.S. Naval Operations in the Mexican War, 1846–1848* is an excellent study that details Perry's role in the conflict.

On the development of steam power in the United States, see Frank M. Bennett, *The Steam Navy of the United States: A History of the Growth of the Steam Vessel of War in the U.S. Navy and of the Naval Engineer Corps*; see also, David B. Tyler, *Steam Conquers the Atlantic* and John G. B. Hutchins, *The American Maritime Industries and Public Policy, 1789–1914*.

On the expedition to Japan, an abundant literature exists, but good starting points are Morison's *Perry*, Schroeder's *Shaping a Maritime Empire*, and Arthur Walworth, *Black Ships off Japan: The Story of Commodore Perry's Expedition*. Perry's own account is found in the official narrative, F. L. Hawks, ed., *Narrative of the Expedition of An American Squadron to the China Seas and Japan*. Also insightful is Earl Swisher, "Commodore Perry's Imperialism in Relation to America's Present-day Position in the Pacific," in the *Pacific Historical Review*. Perry's difficulties in China are detailed in Curtis T. Henson, *Commissioners and Commodores: The East India Squadron and American Diplomacy in China*.

NOTES

1. Although the study is not directly cited in the notes, this article is based to a considerable extent on the research and material in John H. Schroeder, *Shaping a Maritime Empire: The Commercial and Diplomatic Role of the American Navy, 1829–1861*. For detailed treatments of Perry's life, see Samuel Eliot

24   FROM SAIL TO STEAM

Morison, *"Old Bruin": Commodore Matthew C. Perry, 1794–1858* and William E. Griffis, *Matthew Calbraith Perry: A Typical American Naval Officer*.

2. Detailed treatments of the Perry family and Matthew's early years are found in Morison, *"Old Bruin"* and Griffis, *Perry*.

3. Morison, *"Old Bruin,"* 104–17. Also, William Cabell Bruce, *John Randolph of Roanoke, 1773–1833: A Biography Based Largely on New Material*, I: 634–61.

4. Morison, *"Old Bruin"* 121–23.

5. W. Patric Strauss, "Mahlon Dickerson" and "James K. Paulding," in Paolo E. Coletta, ed., *American Secretaries of the Navy*, I: 160–62, 165–71.

6. *House of Representatives Report No. 94. 23rd Cong., 2nd Sess.* (1834–35).

7. Morison, *"Old Bruin"*, 124–39.

8. Ibid., 127–32. Also, Frank M. Bennett, *The Steam Navy of the United States: A History of the Growth of the Steam Vessel of War in the U. S. Navy and of the Naval Engineer Corps*.

9. "Thoughts on the Navy," *Naval Magazine*, II (1837): 5–42.

10. Abel P. Upshur to Perry, 30 March 1843, Letters Sent by the Secretary of the Navy to Officers, 1798–1868, Naval Records, R.G. 45, National Archives, vol. 34.

11. Donald R. Wright, "Matthew Perry and the African Squadron," in Clayton R. Barrow, Jr., ed., *America Spreads Her Sails: U.S. Seapower in the 19th Century*, 80–99.

12. Morison, *"Old Bruin,"* 179–89.

13. K. Jack Bauer, *Surfboats and Horse Marines: U.S. Naval Operations in the Mexican War, 1846–1848*.

14. Ibid.; Morison, *"Old Bruin,"* 230–38.

15. Description by Buchanan as quoted in Charles Lee Lewis, *Admiral Franklin Buchanan: Fearless Man of Action*, 121–22.

16. David B. Tyler, *Steam Conquers the Atlantic*, 204–7.

17. David F. Long, *Sailor-Diplomat: A Biography of Commodore James Biddle*, 209–20; Merrill L. Bartlett, "Commodore James Biddle and the First Naval Mission to Japan, 1845–1846," *American Neptune*, 61 (1981): 25–35.

18. Charles O. Paullin, *American Voyages to the Orient, 1690–1865*, 123–24.

19. Perry to W. A. Graham, 3 December 1851, as cited in Griffis, *Perry*, 289–91. Perry's preparations for the expedition are described in detail in Morison, *"Old Bruin,"* 270–90. Also, Arthur Walworth, *Black Ships off Japan: The Story of Commodore Perry's Expedition*.

20. John P. Kennedy to Perry, 13 November 1852, C. M. Conrad to Kennedy, 5 November 1852, Fillmore to His Imperial Majesty, The Emperor, *Senate Executive Document No. 34*, 33rd Cong., 2nd Sess. (1854–1855), 2–11.

21. Conrad to Kennedy, 5 November 1852, ibid., 4–9.

22. Perry to Kennedy, 14 December 1852, ibid, 12–14. Perry's own account of the expedition is F. L. Hawks, ed., *Narrative of the Expedition of an American Squadron to the China Seas and Japan.*

23. Earl Swisher, "Commodore Perry's Imperialism in Relation to America's Present-day Position in the Pacific," *Pacific Historical Review*, 16 (1947): 30–40; "Extracts from the Rough Journal of Commodore Perry, 24 June 1853," *Senate Executive Document No. 34*, 33–39; "Report of an Examination of the Bonin Group of Islands," Hawks, ed., *Narrative of the Expedition*, II: 127–33.

24. "Notes Referring to . . . the preliminary negotiations of Commodore M. C. Perry with the authorities of Japan in July 1853," *Senate Executive Document No. 34*, 45–57.

25. Morison, *"Old Bruin,"* 336; Walworth, *Black Ships off Japan*, 115.

26. Perry to J. C. Dobbin, 25 January 1854, Dobbin to Perry, 30 May 1854, *Senate Executive Document No. 34*, 108–10, 112–13.

27. Hawks, ed., *Narrative of the Expedition*, I: 343–92; Perry to Dobbin, 1 April 1854, *Senate Executive Document No. 34*, 145–50. A copy of the treaty is contained in ibid., 174–75.

28. "Extracts from the Rough Journal of Commodore Perry, 24 June 1853," ibid., 39; Hawks, ed., *Narrative of the Expedition*, II: 153–54, 167–70, 180. Volume II of the *Narrative* contains various reports on aspects of the expedition including "Remarks of Commodore Perry Upon the Expediency of Extending Further Encouragement to American Commerce in the East," 173–82, and "Remarks of Commodore Perry upon the Probable Future Commercial Relations with Japan and Lew Chew," 185–87.

29. Ibid. 178, 180, 177, 176.

30. *A Paper by Commodore M. C. Perry, U.S.N., Read Before the American Geographical and Statistical Society . . . March 6, 1856.*

8

The Sale of Alaska in the Context of Russian American Relations in the Nineteenth Century

N. N. Bolkhovitinov

The sale of Russian America has attracted the attention of both Soviet and foreign researchers for a long time. In 1939, the now deceased Professor S. B. Okun' published a monograph in which he gave, for the first time in Soviet literature, an adequately detailed and documented account of the general history of the Russian American Company and the 1867 sale of Alaska. "It was impossible to preserve our colonies in case of war, it was impossible to protect them from the consequences of widespread rumors concerning the presence of gold there . . . and finally, there was a transfer of Russian interests to the Asian mainland—these were the reasons that nudged the tsar's government toward selling Alaska." The most significant factors, in Okun's opinion, were the awkward position of the Russian American Company, which "was able to exist only with the support of the government," the serious financial problems of that government, and several international considerations. "Attempting to strike a blow against English power in North America and to force a collision between the United States and the British Empire, Russia decided to put Alaska up for sale. Yet, it was this drive for supremacy on the American continent that compelled the United States to acquire it."[1]

Later on, in a fundamental work, A. L. Narochnitskii offered a detailed interpretation of the expansion of European powers and the United States in the North Pacific, specifically the active involvement of the American traders, whalers, and smugglers in Rus-

*Translated from the Russian by Mina A. Jacobs, Anchorage, Alaska. The basis of this paper is taken from the book by the author entitled *Russian-American Relations and the Sale of Alaska, 1834-1867* (Moscow: Nauka, 1990).

[1]S. B. Okun', *Rossiisko-amerikanskaia kompaniia* (Moscow and Leningrad, 1939), 234-235, 242, and others.

sia's American possessions in the 1850s and 1860s.[2] A small, and unfortunately, rather tendentious work about the American expansion into the North Pacific and the sale of Alaska was published by T. M. Batueva, while R. V. Makarova devoted an article to the history of the liquidation of the Russian American Company.[3]

A significant number of books and articles about Russian American relations and the sale of Alaska has been published outside the Soviet Union, particularly in the United States and Canada, as well as in Mexico and Japan (J. Gibson, O. W. Gerus, R. J. Jensen, H. I. Kushner, D. H. Miller and others).[4]

As a result of successful international collaboration, a collection of articles was published in 1987 under the title, *Russia's American Colony*, which included papers by N. N. Bolkhovitinov, "Russian America and International Relations"; J. R. Gibson (Canada), "The Sale of Russian America to the United States"; and H. I. Kushner, "The Significance of the Alaska Purchase to American Expansion." This book contains a useful survey of new literature about the whole history of Russian America.[5]

---

[2] A. L. Narochnitskii, *Kolonial'naia politika kapitalisticheskikh derzhav na Dal'nem Vostoke, 1860-1895* (Moscow, 1956), 154-195.

[3] T. M. Batueva, *Ekspansiia SShA na severe Tikhogo okeana v seredine XIX v. i pokupka Aliaski v 1867 g.* (Tomsk, 1976); R. V. Makarova, "K istorii likvidatsii Rossiisko-amerikanskoi kompanii (Moscow: Probl. istorii i etnografii Ameriki, 1979), 264-274.

[4] R. J. Jensen, *The Alaska Purchase and Russian-American Relations* (Seattle, 1975); H. I. Kushner, *Conflict on the Northwest Coast; American-Russian Rivalry in the Pacific Northwest, 1790-1867* (Westport, 1975); D. H. Miller, *The Alaska Treaty* (Kingston, 1981); O. W. Gerus, "The Russian Withdrawal from Alaska: The Decision to Sell," *Revista de Historia de America* 75-76 (1972-1973): 157-178; J. R. Gibson, "The Sale of Russian America to the United States," *Acta Slavica Japonica* 1 (1983): 15-37. For a detailed analysis of these works, see N. N. Bolkhovitinov, "Zarubezhnye issledovaniia o Russkoi Amerike," *SShA—ekonomika, politika, ideologiia* 4 (1985): 87-95; as well as *Zarybezhnye isseldovaniia o zakliuchitel'nom periode deiatel'nosti Rossiisko-Americanskoi Kompanii i prodazhe Aliaski v 1867 g.* and *Zarubezhnye issledovaniia po istorii Russkoi Ameriki*, ed. by N. N. Bolkhovitinov (Moscow, 1987), 78-100.

[5] N. N. Bolkhovitinov, "Russian America and International Relations," in S. F. Starr's, *Russia's American Colony* (Durham, 1987), 251-270, 405-408; also J. R. Gibson, "The Sale of Russian America to the United States," in

158   *Pacifica*, Vol. 2, No. 2, November 1990

Along with these serious works by scholars, unfortunately, there have also appeared derivative works frequently using invalid hypotheses and assumptions. For example, M. I. Belov published a jubilee article in 1967. Among the author's bold and interesting ideas, he suggests that "Alaska was sold by Russia fifty years before its official sale." However, he does not go so far as to provide detailed support for this assertion. He simultaneously offers overly emotional and inadequately supported conclusions. He asserts, for example, that several people "within the tsar's entourage" had been bribed, that the Russian government "got involved in a dishonest deal" on account of the danger of war with the United States and finally, that "the initiative for selling Alaska, if one can put it so mildly, belonged completely to the United States of America."[6]

A weak acquaintance with the literature and sources is reflected in the popular works of A. I. Alekseev, particularly in the book, *The Destiny of Russian America*: ". . . neither notes nor preliminary protocols of the discussions have reached us," the author categorically asserts.

> We have found them neither in the personal archives of the Tsar nor in the archives of the chancellor, A. M. Gorchakov, who carried on negotiations regarding the sale of Alaska, one on one, eye to eye, without leaving any official documents . . . . Certainly, to reach such a decision was not at all simple: yet right up until the actual deed of sale, none of the government officials , nor any of the heads of the Russian American Company had raised the question of selling Russian territories. But as with all these foreign policy affairs, the shortsighted tsarist government, pushed by the governments of the United States, England and France arrived at this shameful decision.[7]

Starr, 271-294, 408-414; H. I. Kushner, "The Significance of the Alaska Purchase to American Expansion," in Starr, 295-315, 414-419; and P. Polansky, "Published Sources on Russian America," in Starr, 319-352.

[6]M. I. Belov, "K stoletiiu prodazhi Aliaski," *Izv. VGO.* 4 (1967): 297, 299. See also M. I. Belov, *Osvoenie russkimi liud'mi Dal'nego Vostoka i Russkoi Ameriki do kontsa XIX veka* (Moscow, 1982), 131.

[7]A. I. Alekseev, *Sud'ba Russkoi Ameriki* (Magadan, 1975), 312.

It is not at all clear in which archives Alekseev was working. If he had turned to the principal archives, which preserve material on the Russian American Company and Russian foreign policy, then without too much difficulty he would have discovered documents in the tens and hundreds. Among them are numerous documents concerning preliminary discussions on just this issue which occurred within the highest governmental circles of St. Petersburg and Washington, beginning as early as the 1850s, continuing throughout the course of the negotiations, and concluding with the signing of the treaty dated March 18 (30), 1867, in the American capital.

In addition, to comprehend the actual circumstances which led up to the conclusion of the 1867 treaty, it is not necessary to turn exclusively to archival documents. A large amount of important material has already been used by S. B. Okun' (USSR) and Victor J. Farrar. Many documents have been introduced into scholarly circulation, published either in whole or in part, and are accessible to researchers in microfilm.

A weak knowledge of the sources, inaccuracies, which may at first glance seem harmless, mistakes, and unfounded assumptions, all lead the reader to an incorrect and even distorted understanding of the essential interrelationship between Russia and the United States in the North Pacific. It might even seem that informed people sometimes "construe" that the United States "actually forced" the tsarist government to conclude the treaty of 1867, and that "the doubtful character of the act is confirmed by archival material which points to bribery of several people having an influence on the tsar and all sorts of encouragements to conclude this treaty."[8] More than this, in the weekly publication, Za rubezhom [Abroad], A. Sergeev wrote about the 1867 treaty as an "act of thievery," concluded by a Belgian baron Stoeckl. "Opposed to this shameful and dishonest act was the eminent Russian navigator, Ferdinand Petrovich Wrangell."[9]

It is hardly worthwhile to consider similar pearls of bold journalistic opinion if they did not create completely distorted assumptions, not only about the fate of Alaska, but on all the history of

---

[8]G. Voitolovskii, "Po raznye storony Beringova proliva," *Mirovaia ekonomika i mezhdunar. otnosheniia* 6 (1986): 38.

[9]A. Sergeev, "Provokatsiia s geografiei," *Za rubezhom* 7: 1336 (1986): 6.

Russian-American relations. It is not mere chance that the editorial sections of newspapers and journals contain letters received from readers with questions. When will it be time to take Alaska back? Will it be taken back gradually so that over the course of time "the loan" will revert this territory? Assertions also appear: The treaty is a "loan" that expires in the year 2000; it has a "temporary character," and so on.

It turned out that the press was not entirely precise with the details but essentially gave a correct reply. "Russian America (now the state of Alaska) was sold by the tsarist government and not loaned; the treaty was not signed with a temporary intent but 'for all time.'"[10]

The clamor over this "act of thievery," in my opinion, not only distorts the character and sense of the events during the last century, but may also inflict direct damage on our current relations between the Soviet Union and the United States. An American journal has already published an article by M. I. Belov which cannot help but arouse distrust of the Soviet Union.[11]

At the same time, a completely objective and documented study of the history of the sale of Russian America could contribute to a mutual understanding and trust between both countries. It was with this particular aim in mind that I began the research on this problem in the early 1980s.

The academician, A. A. Guber, correctly identified the major difference between western European and imperial Russian colonial policy: the former was maritime, the latter was continental. The Far Eastern and the Pacific interests of Russian politics accordingly played an immeasurably lesser role at this time and were subordinated to the general political situation in Europe.[12] The influential tsarist expert, Count Ia. O. Lambert, emphasized as early as 1817 that, "in consequence of her geographic location, Russia was not

---

[10]Argumenty i fakty 9-15 dek. (1986): 5. The author has emphasized A. I. Alekseev's reply.

[11]M. I. Belov, "Sale of Alaska," *Alaska Review* (Spring-Summer 1967): 3-19; H. R. Huttenbach, "Sale of Alaska: Reply to a Soviet Commentary, *Alaska Review* (Spring-Summer 1970): 33-45.

[12]"Politika evropeiskikh derzhav v Iugo-Vostochnoi Azii: 60-e gody XVIII v. - 60-e gody XIX v. " A. A. Guber and others, eds., *Dokumenty i materialy* (Moscow, 1962), 10.

destined to be a large developed marine power." She should treat the notion of increasing trade in the outlying areas, away from her main ports, with great circumspection. The conservative character of Russia's feudal-serf policies toward the Pacific and northwest America at this time is manifested in a number of ways: by the skeptical reaction toward P. Dobell's projects concerning the growth of trade ties between Kamchatka, Russian America, the Philippines, California, and Canton; by the refusal of a request by the "owner of the Sandwich Islands" Kaumuali'i, for Russian citizenship, and by the categorical refusal to support Georg A. Schäffer's proposal to annex the Hawaiian Islands in 1818 to 1819.[13]

Those supporting the expansion of Russian influence in the Pacific basin and North America at the beginning of the 1820s (N. P. Rumiantsev, N. S. Mordvinov, I. B. Pestel', and others), gradually began to lose ground. On the opposing side were the more influential figures like K. V. Nesselrode and Ia. O. Lambert. Accordingly, conservative and protective tendencies began to dominate the Russian policy in northwest America, and for the most part, complaints from the Russian American Company were given little attention.

The tsarist government and the Russian American Company strongly disagreed during the signing of the conventions of 1824-1825, when the company, strengthened by the influence of Decembrists, specifically K. F. Ryleev, openly quarreled with the Department of Foreign Affairs. Numerous notes and protests were sent to the government, pointing out that the convention of April 5 (17), 1824, by granting the Americans free trade and fishing rights in the Russian possessions for a period of ten years, not only violated the privileges of the company but threatened its welfare and its very

---

[13]See the notes of Ia. O. Lambert, January 2 (14), 1817 and the commentary of M. A. Saltykov on the proposal of P. Dobell, 1816-1817 "Politika evropeiskikh derzhav....", 477-490. AVPR [Arkhiv vneshnei politiki Rossii, hereafter cited as AVPR] F. K., d. 13378, l. 165-173 [Fond Kantseliarii, memorandum 13378, sheets 165-173] ; K. V. Nesselrode - Aleksandru I, "maiia - dnia 1819 goda", AVPR, F. Gl. arkh. 1-10, op. 9, d. 1, l. 131-135 [Fond Glavnogo arkhiva. 1-10, description 9, memorandum 1, sheets 131-135] ; N. N. Bolkhovitinov, "Vydvizhenie i proval proektov P. Dobella (1812-1821)," Amerikanskii ezhegodnik (1976): 264-282.

existence.[14] In the summer of 1826, the leadership of the Russian American Company once again requested intercession by asserting that "the company finds itself in such a dubious and even unfortunate position that not only its own existence is threatened but all the local areas mentioned above would face certain destruction."[15]

All these protests and complaints encountered the resistance of the Department of Foreign Affairs, particularly K. V. Nesselrode who maintained that the conventions of 1824-1825 actually benefited the company because they established recognized borders for Russian possessions in America by international agreements. Free trade and navigation by foreign competition was limited to the ten-year period. Nesselrode reiterated this opinion in a wordy report to the tsar in the autumn of 1826. According to the agreement, the Americans themselves recognized that "over the course of several years, we will have the legal power to effectively prevent them from trading and fishing in this whole area," wrote the Minister of Foreign Affairs. To change the text of the conventions and "have it out politically" with the United States and England, Nesselrode not only considered this premature, but thought it contrary "to the dignity of our court and to all the interests of the company itself."[16]

As we see, despite the repeated complaints and protests, the Russian American Company did not succeed in obtaining a reconsideration of the 1824-1825 conventions. However, the company's firm position did have some impact. After the ten-year period expired, the unfavorable free trade conditions for the United States and England in Russian America were not continued. This occurred in the mid-1830s, after a lengthy, but ineffectual diplomatic correspon-

---

[14]See AVPR. T. 13. S. 460-462, 493-497, 556-561 [Arkhiv vneshnei politiki Rossi, vol. 13. pages 460-462, 493-497, 556-561] and particularly the material presented by Emperor Nicholas I together with the papers of K. V. Nesselrode from October 27 (November 8), 1826, AVPR, F. K., 1826 g., op. 468, d. 2995, l. 5-191. [Fond Kantseliarii, 1826, description 468, memorandum 2995, sheets 5-191.]

[15]RAK - Nikolaiiu I, 29 iiulia (10 avgusta) 1826 g. [Russian American Company - Nicholas I, July 29 (August 10), 1826.] Same as above, sheet 10.

[16]K. V. Nesselrode - Nikolaiiu I, 27 oktiabria (8 noiabria) 1826 g. [K. V. Nesselrode - Nicholas I, October 27 (November 8), 1826]. Same as above, sheets 154-180; see also Mémoire D. B. (Dmitri Bludow). Same as above, sheets 192-199.

dence that led to the well-known (although not very prolonged) reorientation of the Russian American Company's relations with its foreign competitors.

One of the results of my research is the corroboration of a thesis regarding the expansionist character of United States politics (similar, by the way, to those of tsarist Russia), about which Soviet specialists were already writing in the 1950s,[17] and which was developed in the works of radical American historians in the 1960s and 1970s (books and articles of W. A. Williams, W. LaFeber, H. I. Kushner and others).[18] Numerous documents in AVPR, the Central Archives in Moscow and Leningrad; material in the National Archives and the Library of Congress in Washington, D. C.; and the papers of W. Seward, W. Gwin, and other American political figures; representatives in business circles, all explicitly testify to American expansionism in the North Pacific and Russian-America's opposition to it.

But this is only one side of the question. The same archives and libraries contain many documents that demonstrate the mutually advantageous business ties between Russia and the United States and the cooperation of Russian *promyshlenniki* with the Boston whalers delivering American provisions to Russian America.

Which of these tendencies prevailed? There does not seem to be a single answer to this question. At the beginning of the 1820s and in the mid-1830s, opposition and rivalry intensified, threatening at times to seriously affect the relations between the two governments. During the mid-nineteenth century, United States whaling reached its height in the North Pacific. With the beginning of the Crimean War, on the other hand, fruitful business contacts and joint ventures were enriched and intensified. Americans brought war munitions, provisions, sea vessels, and a variety of equipment to Russian America, to Kamchatka, and to the Amur region. During the years of the American Civil War (1861-1865), the United States was not particularly interested in foreign expansion. G. V. Fox's triumphant

---

[17]A. L. Narochnitskii, see above, 154-195.

[18]W. A. Williams, *The Roots of Modern American Empire* (New York, 1964); W. LaFeber, *The New Empire: An Interpretation of American Expansion, 1860-1898* (Ithaca, 1963); E. V. Paolino, *The Foundation of the American Empire: William Henry Seward and U.S. Foreign Policy* (Ithaca, 1973); and Kushner, cited above.

mission to Russia in the summer of 1866 was the culmination of Russian-American rapprochement. It was during this time that Alaska and Siberia entered into a joint venture to construct a telegraph line to connect Europe and America. It was precisely at this time that the decision was made to sell Russian possessions in America to the United States, during a "special meeting" which took place on December 16 (28), 1866, and in which Emperor Alexander II, A. M. Gorchakov, Grand Prince Konstantin, M. Kh. Reutern, H. K. Krabbe, and E. A. Stoeckl all participated.

Emperor Alexander II (1855-1881).

When discussing the reasons for the sale, allusions are often made to the difficult situation of the Russian American Company. Documents testify that the company's position was indeed difficult but not critical. The decision to prolong the company's period of operation had essentially been made and the government decided to accept the responsibility of providing it financial assistance. More important, though not the deciding factor, was the external threat to the colony and the impossibility of defending it in the event of war.[19] Although United States expansion was more a potential threat than a real one, Russia undoubtedly took this into account. (Notes of Grand Prince Konstantin, A. M. Gorchakov, E. A. Stoeckl, and others).

From these documents, it is obvious that the main reasons were to eliminate a potential hotbed of future conflict, to consolidate a

---

[19]In addition, it became known that gold had been discovered in northwest America. The Russian American Company was left with practically no means to protect its possessions from the invasion of foreign adventurers. See Okun', 230-234.

true alliance between the two countries, and to redirect Russian attention to strengthening its position in the Far East (particularly in the Amur river region).

The check for $7,200,000 which paid Russia for its territory in North America. The check is dated almost a year after the formal transfer of powers took place in Sitka, as the House of Representatives, which must approve all money bills, hotly debated the amount and was further delayed by the impeachment proceedings against President Andrew Johnson. The check is made out to Edouard de Stoeckl, Russia's minister in Washington and endorsed by him and the president of Riggs Bank.

Other more general causes which were closing the future of Russian America: the remnants of a serf system, the smallness of the Russian population in the colonies (maintained at a level between six hundred and eight hundred people), the Indian factor, the independence of the Tlingits, and so forth. These general causes, however, are not specifically discussed in the documents of the "special meeting."

Neither contemporary nor earlier researchers have turned their attention to the fact that Russia, by yielding its ownership to the United States, turned out to be the first European power to actually relinquish its overseas colonies voluntarily. In connection with this, it is interesting to recall that in 1788, Catherine II, while rejecting a request from G. Shelikhov and I. Golikov, had emphasized, "The examples of American settlements were not flattering, and moreover not advantageous for the motherland . . . . A great dispersion into the Pacific will not be beneficial." To trade is one thing, "but to take possession is another."[20] The long held idea of a continental and not a maritime future for Russia, the rejection of annexation of distant overseas territories, and the concentration on strengthening her position in the Far East, Siberia, and Central Asia all acquired, in the long term, a greater meaning. In the mid-1860s, these ideas found expression in the decision to sell Russian America to the United States.

The mission of G. V. Fox to Russia in the summer of 1866 and the subsequent sale of Alaska in the spring of 1867 gave rise to many rumors about the unusual Russian-American rapprochement, even suggestions of an alliance. In Russia, delays in the United States payment temporarily cooled the ardor of the overly enthusiastic proponents of such an alliance. Speculation about an alliance soon resumed. During the course of debates in Congress, there were many allusions to the friendly position of Russia during the years of the American Civil War. In July of 1868, almost simultaneously with the disbursement of the funds for the purchase of Alaska, the imperial palace decided to ask the president to hasten the revocation of all obstacles "for the passage of trade and war vessels through the straits."[21] (This was one of the main goals of Russian foreign policy after the Paris Peace Conference in 1856.)

In August of 1867, the visiting United States squadron, commanded by Admiral David Farragut,[22] was joyously welcomed in St. Petersburg. Within one year, Admiral Farragut, on the flagship *Franklin,* received permission to cross the Black Sea straits. It is interesting that the American sailors greeted the Russian ambassador in Constantinople, Count N. P. Ignat'ev, with particular affection. He, in turn, held a reception in honor of the famous American admiral. It was precisely these events (the decision of the House to grant the request for free passage through the Bosphorous

---

[20]A. I. Andreev, ed., *Russkie otkrytiia na Tikhom okeane i Severnoi Amerike* (Moscow, 1948), 281-282; AVPR, f. RAK, d. 36, l. 1-2 [folio RAC, memorandum 36, sheets 1-2] (autograph).

[21]GG 40th Congress. Second Session. (July 6, 1868) 3764.

[22]Tsentral'nyi gosudarstvennyi arkhiv Voenno-Morskogo Flota SSSR, f. 283, op. 3, d. 2185, l. 1-57. [f. 283, description 3, memorandum 2185, sheets 1-57], hereinafter cited as TsGAVMF.

and Dardanelles and the visit of Admiral Farragut to Constantinople) that the American consul in Moscow, E. Schuyler, singled out when he mentioned the growth in Russian amicability toward the United States.[23] Once again, articles appeared in the press about a Russian-American alliance.

It is significant that, in its September 1868 issue, the magazine *Birzhevye vedomosti* [*Exchange Register*] featured a comprehensive article about the traditions and perspectives of Russian-American relations. Reviewing the fundamental landmarks of the two countries relations since the Crimean War, this influential organ of Russian business circles came to the conclusion that "rapprochement between Russia and North America, these two colossi on either side of the ocean, was not only possible but also in both their best interests."

The magazine ranked the "goodwill concession" of the sale of Russian possessions to the United States "the most important and successful act by our government in the area

The signature page of the treaty which concluded the sale of Alaska to the United States. Signators are William H. Seward, U.S. Secretary of State, and Edouard de Stoeckl, Russia's minister in Washington.

[23]R. J. Jensen, 133-134; E. Schuyler - U. S'iuardu, 19 sentiabriia 1868 g., no. 39 [E. Schuyler-W. Seward, September 19, 1868, No. 39] NARS [National Archives and Record Service, Washington, D. C.] RG 59. CD, Moscow, r. 1.

of external politics." As a result, Russia "lost little of her political importance, her prestige" but took the "first step toward Russian-American alliance," a step which "eliminated every cause for future conflict which might have arisen between Russia and the United States." The article concludes, "In the whole world we know of no other two governments which would be able to arrive at a means for promoting co-existence between themselves, in friendship and in union, as Russia and the United States of North America and for this reason, this union serves with a guaranty of true civilized progress for each of these powers."[24]

Now it is hardly necessary to argue with the optimistic evaluation and charitable hopes of the *Birzhevye vedomosti* editorial. A more sober judgement was expressed by one of a few principal opponents to the sale of Russian America, P. N. Golovin: "Regarding the strengthening of friendly relations between Russia and the United States, it can be said positively that the sympathy of Americans toward us will continue as long as they are not obliged to do something and it continues to be advantageous; the Americans will never sacrifice their interests for simple convictions."[25]

Although the old myth about the existence of a Russian-American alliance is long-standing, it seems necessary to decisively reject it, since I do not agree with the widespread opinion in the literature about the serious break which allegedly occurred in Russian-American relations after 1867. (E. H. Zabriskie, E. J. Carroll, J. L. Gaddis, and others.)[26] Professor Gaddis, the father of contempo-

---

[24]Birzhevye vedomosti 13 (25) sent. No. 242 (1868): 1-2. [September 13 (25). No. 242 (1868)]. E. Schuyler was particularly interested in this article. He had an English translation made of it and sent it to W. Seward. See E. Schuyler - U. S'iuardu, 29 sentiabriia 1868 g., no. 39 [E. Schuyler-W. Seward, September 29, 1868, No. 39]. NARS [National Archives and Record Service. Washington, D. C.]. RG 59. Moscow, r. 1.

[25]Doklad P. N. Golovina vel. kn. Konstantinu, 20 oktiabria 1861 [The report of P. N. Golovin to Grand Prince Konstantin, October 20, 1861]. Ts-GAVMF, f. 410, op. 2 , d. 2515, l. 255. [folio 410, description 2, memorandum 2515, sheet 255].

[26]E. H. Zabriskie, *American-Russian Rivalry in the Far East* (Philadelphia, 1946); E. J. Carrol, "The Foreign Relations of the United States with Tsarist Russia, 1867-1900," doctoral dissertation, Georgetown

rary post-revisionists, characterizes the period after 1867 as a time of intensification of opposition and "diverging interests" in contrast to the "heritage of harmony" of 1781 to 1867. He observes that "the good relations" during the first half of the nineteenth century were determined by "the absence of conflicting interests" and the existence of a common competitor, Great Britain; these gave way to an intensification of competitiveness in the Far East and Manchuria. "Ideology began to make a difference; questions began to be raised as to whether democracy could, or should, maintain friendly relations with the most autocratic nation in Europe?"[27]

So it was that in the last years of the nineteenth century the general arrangement of powers in the international arena began to change, and there can be no doubt that disagreements between Russia and the United States began to gradually intensify. Incidentally, the period before 1867 was not only characterized as a time of "harmony" but also one of colliding interests, disagreements, and even conflicts (specifically in the northwest of America). Even the sale of Alaska was partly a result of these disagreements. For a time, at least, it had eliminated or assuaged these difficulties (if the whole of the North Pacific is taken into consideration). In any case, it is quite impossible to assert that after 1867 these conflicts grew. Ideological conflicts had existed for a long time before 1867. The reforms of the 1860s to some extent mitigated them but they were not eliminated.

In his book, G. P. Kuropiatnik demonstrates that the relations between Russian and the United States remained highly favorable in the 1870s, particularly during the period of the eastern crisis and Russo-Turkish war of 1877 to 1878.[28] At the turn of the 1870s to 1880s, in the opinion of the author, "The active cooperation of the two countries came to an end. It was no longer possible to overshadow the differences, pretensions and series of unpleasant incidents. Another phase had begun, when the growth of Russian-American relations was, for the most part, determined by, the new social strengths of the two bourgeois governments, gradually trans-

---

University, 1953); J. L. Gaddis, *Russia, The Soviet Union and the United States: An Interpretive History* (New York, 1978); and others.

[27] Gaddis, 27.

[28] G. P. Kuropiatnik, *Rossiia i SShA: ekonomicheskie, kul'turnye i diplomaticheskie sviazi, 1867-1881* (Moscow, 1981), 192-331.

forming them into imperialist powers."[29] Quite definitely, revived conflict between Russia and the United States, first in Manchuria and then in the Far East, was already apparent at the end of the nineteenth century and the beginning of the twentieth.

But even during these years, both countries retained old features in their relationship. They continued successfully to develop social-political, trade, scientific, and cultural contacts. In the last ten years of the nineteenth to the beginning of the twentieth, there was a sharp increase in emigration from Russia to the United States,[30] but all this is too far removed from our theme to deal with it effectively at this time.

The historic significance of the 1867 treaty rests first in the fact that it served as a basis for the formation of Russia's Asiatic-Pacific Ocean borders, which are roughly unchanged to this day. The treaty eliminated any foundation for claims or disagreements regarding territorial questions and established a basis for cooperation and not conflict in the North Pacific.

The timeliness of the study of the Pacific Ocean aspect of Russian-American relations is also connected with one more event—the 500th anniversary of the discovery of America by Columbus (1492). It should be kept in mind that representatives of various countries have participated in the discovery and opening up of America—Spain, Portugal, England, Holland, and France. To Russia belongs the credit of discovery and penetration into the northwest part of the American continent. Incidentally, 1991 marks the 250th anniversary of the V. Bering-A. Chirikov expedition (1741) that in effect, began the actual opening up of the northwest part of North America. Outer space is being studied today through international efforts. In a similar way, American mainlands were also opened up and made known by representatives of various countries and peoples; it is not chance that on the ground of North America, in its time, there existed New Spain, New England, New France, and subsequently Russian America. The discovery and colonization of America was not a single event, but a lengthy process.

---

[29]Kuropiatnik, 339.

[30]A. S. Sokolov, *Russkie v Amerike v kontse XIX v.* (Leningrad: Dis. Kand. ist. nauk., 1985); N. L. Tudorianu, *Ocherki rossiiskoi trudovoi emigratsii perioda imperializma* (Kishinev, 1986), 117-270.

Sale of Alaska—Russian American Relations   171

The final stage of this process began at the end of the eighteenth and the first part of the nineteenth century when, on the western shores of North America (California and Oregon), several colonizing clans met—the Russians from the North, the Spanish from the South, the Americans and English from the east. This powerful process was completed when the United States conquered the firmest position on the Pacific seacoast of North America.

PHOTO CREDITS

Page 164 Alexander III, courtesy Sitka National Historical Part, National Park Service.
Page 165 Check for $7,200,000, the National Archives, Washington D. C.
Page 167 Treaty, the National Archives, Washington D. C.

9

The Independent Minister: John M.B. Sill and the Struggle against Japanese Expansion in Korea, 1894–1897

Jeffery M. Dorwart

Most students of United States diplomacy consider the Russo-Japanese War of 1904–1905 to have been the critical turning point in official American attitudes and policies toward Japan.[1] Prior to this war, these scholars contend, the United States government adhered to a strict policy of Japanese-American friendship. Japan seemed to share a common concern to keep the Far East open to all foreign contact, and the government in Washington and its representatives in East Asia sympathized with Japan's efforts to revise its unequal treaties with the Western powers. American officials also looked with favor upon Japan's victories over China in 1895 and Russia in 1905, since now Korea and China would be

---

[1] See Edwin O. Reischauer, *The United States and Japan* (Cambridge, Mass., 1965), 20; Payson J. Treat, *Diplomatic Relations Between the United States and Japan* (3 vols., Gloucester, Mass., 1938), III, 270–277; Foster Rhea Dulles, *Yankees and Samurai: America's Role in the Emergence of Modern Japan, 1791–1900* (New York, 1965), 249; Raymond A. Esthus, *Theodore Roosevelt and Japan* (Seattle and London, 1966), 3; Charles E. Neu, *An Uncertain Friendship: Theodore Roosevelt and Japan, 1906–1909* (Cambridge, Mass., 1967), 20.

more accessible to U.S. businessmen, travelers, and missionaries. But after Japan had driven Russia out of Korea in 1905, only the United States challenged Japanese supremacy in that area. Growing tensions between the competitors threatened to destroy a half century of amity. For the first time since Commodore Matthew Perry had opened Japan to the West, scholars argue, government officials looked upon Japan as a threat to American interests in East Asia and the Pacific Ocean, and they recommended opposition to Japanese expansion.[2]

A decade before the Russo-Japanese War of 1904–1905, however, at least one American diplomatic representative in Asia had already informed Washington of irreconcilable Japanese-American differences, and had labored for three years to block Japanese expansion in Korea. This diplomat was John M. B. Sill, United States minister and consul general to Korea from 1894 to 1897. During his tenure at the Seoul legation, John Sill was the only American standing against Japan's drive to make Korea part of the Japanese empire and close it to American trade, travel, and missionary enterprise. He upheld American treaty rights in the area and advocated a formal Open Door policy several years before the State Department adopted such a program. Sill formulated policy, made independent and often controversial decisions, and defended his policies against a clique of timid American naval officers and remote Washington bureaucrats. When he thought his government had failed to take steps to stop Japanese expansion, he would ignore what he termed shortsighted and uninformed instructions from distant Secretaries of State.

Although Sill did more to inform Washington of conditions in Korea and to resist Japanese expansion in East Asia during the last decade of the nineteenth century than any other American, his activities have been largely ignored by historians.[3] This neglect seems to stem at least in part from the emphasis they have placed on

---

2 There were some Americans, such as expatriate writer Lafcadio Hearn, who, as early as 1893, predicted eventual hostility between the United States and Japan, but no U.S. government official publicly expressed such views. Dulles, *Yankees and Samurai*, 252.

3 See, particularly, Fred Harvey Harrington, *God, Mammon and the Japanese: Dr. Horace N. Allen and Korean-American Relations, 1884–1905* (Madison, 1944); William Elliot Griffis, *Corea, The Hermit Kingdom* (London, 1905); Walter LaFeber, *The New Empire: An Interpretation of American Expansion, 1860–1898* (Ithaca, N.Y., 1963).

The Independent Minister   487

Sill's legation secretary, Horace N. Allen, a Presbyterian medical-missionary, diplomat, and entrepreneur. Allen entered Korea in late 1884 and immediately made himself a favorite at the Korean court by saving the life of the queen's nephew, Min Yong-ik, who had been slashed by an assassin's sword. For years Allen served as an intimate adviser to the weak king, even leading a mission to Washington, D.C., to establish a Korean legation.[4]

Allen became the most famous American in Korea and at the same time a leading contact for State Department officials, newspapermen, and business promoters. Third Assistant Secretary of State William W. Rockhill, syndicated columnist Frank George Carpenter, and Delaware businessman General James Harrison Wilson were all close friends of Allen.[5] The Allen-Carpenter relationship was especially warm, and the reporter never tired of publicizing Allen's work in Korea. "Dr. H. N. Allen, the Secretary of the American legation, will go down into history," the journalist wrote in 1894 in the *Atlanta Constitution*, "as one of the greatest of our diplomats."[6]

Carpenter's evaluation of Allen was repeated by later writers. Missionary-historian William Elliot Griffis, considered the nation's foremost expert on Korea at the end of the nineteenth century, praised Allen as "the chief guardian of American interests in Corea" during the 1890s.[7] Griffis arrived at this conclusion after studying documents which Allen had provided the author in order to assist him in the preparation of a Korean history. "My special obligations are due to our American Minister, H. N. Allen," Griffis wrote in the preface to his 1905 book on the Hermit Kingdom.[8] Admitting his debt to Griffis's work, Arthur Judson Brown, author of numerous books on the Far East during the first decades of the twentieth century, presented an identical view of Allen.[9] So, too, did Allen's biographer, historian Fred Harvey Harrington. Citing

---

4 For a discussion of Allen's career, see Harrington, *God, Mammon and the Japanese, passim.*

5 See the Horace Allen Papers, Korean Collection, box 2, press copy books 5 and 6, New York Public Library.

6 *Atlanta Constitution,* Sept. 2, 1894, p. 2.

7 Griffis, *Corea,* 490.

8 *Ibid.,* viii.

9 Arthur Judson Brown, *The Mastery of the Far East: The Story of Korea's Transformation and Japan's Rise to Supremacy in the Orient* (New York, 1919), 59, 62, 199, 502.

488   PACIFIC HISTORICAL REVIEW

many documents in Allen's own "Korean Collection" (on deposit in the New York Public Library), Harrington concluded that his subject was the most influential Westerner in Korea between 1884 and 1905.[10]

On the other hand, these same authors devoted little space to Sill, and when they did mention the minister, it was to condemn him. Carpenter, echoing Allen's opinion of Sill, dismissed him as being merely another political appointee.[11] Harrington was sharply critical, and relied for his judgment on Allen's evaluation of his boss. Allen had criticized Sill for being "an old man in his dotage," who had come to Korea to have "a nice vacation studying the fauna and flora."[12]

Admittedly, Allen's influence on Korean-American relations, as Harrington has suggested, was immense. Allen helped establish formal diplomatic relations between the two countries, persuaded the Korean government to hire American advisers, and wrested lucrative mining concessions from the king. But acknowledgment of Allen's accomplishments does not require one to view Sill as a cantankerous, old man puttering around in the shadow of his subordinate from 1894 to 1897. The evidence suggests that Sill made important contributions in his own right.

When President Grover Cleveland appointed Sill to the Seoul legation in 1894, he did so at the request of Don Dickinson and Edwin F. Uhl. Both men had engineered Cleveland's successful campaigns in Michigan and had been rewarded with posts of their own, Dickinson with the position of Postmaster General during Cleveland's first term and Uhl with an appointment as Assistant Secretary of State in 1894.[13] To these men, Sill, who was an ordained minister, former superintendent of Detroit public schools, and loyal party worker, also deserved a reward. The President agreed, and in January 1894 appointed Sill as the U.S. minister and consul general to Korea. Uhl took particular delight in forwarding to his friend a letter of introduction to "His Majesty the King of

---

10 Harrington, *God, Mammon and the Japanese, passim.*

11 *Atlanta Constitution,* Sept. 2, 1894, p. 2.

12 Harrington, *God, Mammon and the Japanese,* 98, 171–172.

13 Shirley W. Smith, "John M. B. Sill," in *Michigan and the Cleveland Era: Sketches of University of Michigan Staff Members and Alumni Who Served the Cleveland Administrations, 1885–89, 1893–7,* edited by Earl D. Babst and Lewis Vander Velde (Ann Arbor, 1948), 230.

The Independent Minister **489**

La Chosun" and wishing him the best of luck at his new diplomatic post.[14]

Sill needed such encouragement since he arrived in the Hermit Kingdom without any prior diplomatic experience and immediately confronted one of the most complex and trying periods of Korean history. During his first year in Seoul, he saw Korea become a battleground between China and Japan for supremacy in East Asia and a center of international intrigue where Russia, Great Britain, France, and Germany used the Sino-Japanese War of 1894–1895 to increase their own influence in the area.[15] The nature of Korean-American relations in 1894 further complicated the new minister's assignment. The United States in 1882 had been the first Western nation to sign a treaty with the Koreans. This Treaty of Amity and Commerce had unofficially recognized Korea as an autonomous political unit and thereby ignored China's traditional tributary relationship with Korea. Formal recognition came in 1887 when a fully-accredited American minister had established residence in the capital at Seoul. The first American diplomatic and commercial representatives encouraged the Korean struggle for autonomy, expecting, as a result, to increase their own influence in Korea. Washington, however, had no intention of aiding or defending Korean independence with force. Even so, Korean officials, encouraged by Allen who had been in Korea since 1884, employed American advisers and asked for American assistance in upholding their country's independence.[16]

This was the delicate situation that faced Sill when he landed in Korea during the latter part of April 1894. He had little time to analyze the problem, however, since almost immediately he was confronted with a rebellion that threatened the lives of eighty Americans in the capital. At first, Sill followed Allen's strategy of cooperating with the Korean king to preserve order. The veteran missionary had established a close friendship with the young mon-

---

14 Uhl to Sill, Jan. 26, 1894, Diplomatic Instructions of the Department of State, 1801–1906: Korea, Vol. 1, National Archives, Record Group 59 (hereafter cited as Korea Instructions, NA, RG 59).

15 C. I. Eugene Kim and Han-Kyo Kim, *Korea and the Politics of Imperialism, 1876–1910* (Berkeley and Los Angeles, 1967), 74–84.

16 For a good survey of Korean-American relations during the period from 1866 to 1887, see Yur-Bok Lee, *Diplomatic Relations Between the United States and Korea, 1866–1887* (New York, 1970).

490   PACIFIC HISTORICAL REVIEW

arch and with a pro-Japanese clique at the Korean court so that he might increase his influence in the kingdom and win concessions for American missionaries and businessmen. Disorder weakened the present regime and hence Allen's own effectiveness in keeping Korea open to American commercial and religious activity. Finally, in May 1894, Allen advised the Korean government to request an American warship to help it maintain order in the kingdom. Sill promptly endorsed his legation secretary's action and asked Washington for a gunboat.[17]

Allen viewed Sill's deference to his suggestions as evidence of the professor's meekness. Sill was a powerfully built man, weighing nearly two hundred pounds, but his eyes and face were gentle and scholarly. "Mr. Sill is a nice old gentleman" with "a kind heart," Allen wrote Third Assistant Secretary of State Rockhill in 1894.[18] But the tough Presbyterian missionary-diplomat soon discovered that he would be unable to dominate his new boss as he had expected to do. Sill, he quickly learned, was a strong willed individual and used to making decisions and leading men.

Even during his first month in Seoul, Sill had expressed independent judgment, questioning Allen's close friendship with the Korean king. Sill was not impressed with the nervous little monarch and never established any rapport with him. From the outset, Sill believed he should follow an independent course and not tie American interests too closely to the Korean government, and he assured Washington that he would do nothing to entangle the United States in Korean affairs.[19]

But events in Korea during 1894 moved too rapidly for Sill to pursue a restrained policy. An insurrection against the government by a nationalist religious sect known as Tonghak convulsed the countryside and soon threatened the capital. The king could not maintain order, and both China and Japan prepared to intervene to protect their extensive interests on the peninsula. Once again Sill summoned an American man-of-war. This time the minister sent his inquiry to Rear Admiral Joseph Skerrett, commander of American naval forces in East Asia. But the admiral rejected Sill's

---

17 Sill to Secretary of State, May 17, 1894, Despatches from United States Ministers to Korea, Vol. 10, NA, RG 59.

18 Allen to Rockhill, May 25, 1894, Rockhill Papers, Houghton Library, Harvard University.

19 Sill to Secretary of State, May 17, 1894, Korea Despatches, 10, NA, RG 59.

The Independent Minister 491

appeal. The diplomat's concern was unfounded, Skerrett wrote from his secure quarters in Nagasaki, because small disturbances occurred constantly in Korea and the local ..uthorities always protected Americans. Sill disagreed. "The King has absolutely no adequate means of restoring quiet by force of arms," he retorted, "and Seoul may at any time become the centre of revolution and a most dangerous place for the 70 or 80 Americans residing there."[20] Skerrett refused to move.

The incensed Sill reported the admiral's obstinance to Washington. The United States Navy, Sill insisted, must provide protection for Americans in Korea. British, French, Chinese, and Japanese warships had already arrived in Chemulpo harbor to defend their nationals, Sill cabled Secretary of State Walter Q. Gresham, but the American community remained at the mercy of any armed group that might attack them.[21] On June 1, 1894, Gresham forwarded the minister's communication, along with a plea for assistance from the Korean legation in Washington, to Secretary of the Navy Hilary A. Herbert. A naval vessel should be sent to Korea, Gresham noted in a cover letter, "for the protection of our Legation and citizens of the United States residing there."[22]

Sill's entreaty, combined with Gresham's advice, convinced Herbert to send Skerrett to Chemulpo. Following department directions, the aged admiral left Nagasaki aboard his flafiship, the *Baltimore*, a 4,400-ton cruiser. The warship steamed into the muddy Korean harbor several days later and dropped anchor, whereupon Skerrett invited Sill to visit him aboard his ship and report on conditions in Seoul. The minister obliged and met with the flag officer in his comfortable cabin. Sill told Skerrett that a legation guard might be needed to prevent rioting and looting around the American compound. The minister repeated his fears to the State Department several days later. "As it now stands," he wrote Gresham, "the Japanese are here and they probably believe they cannot leave without 'losing face'; they might possibly like an opportunity to assert their fast fading influence in Korea." More-

---

20 Sill to Skerrett, June 1, 1894, enclosure in Sill to Gresham, June 1, 1894, Korea Despatches, Vol. 11, NA, RG 59.

21 Sill to Gresham, June 1, 1894, *ibid.*

22 Gresham to Secretary of the Navy, June 1, 1894; Ye Lung Loo to Gresham, June 1, 1894, Area File of the Naval Records Collection, 1775–1910: Area 10, National Archives, Record Group 45 (hereafter cited as Area 10 File).

over, Sill continued, "some irresponsible outrage committed upon a Chinaman by a Japanese, or vice versa, might be the beginning of a deplorable contest on Korean ground."[23]

Washington heeded Sill's warning. On June 22 Assistant Secretary of State Uhl cabled that the President had authorized Sill "to use every possible effort for the preservation of peaceful conditions."[24] Cleveland's order did not explain what was meant by using "every possible effort for the preservation of peaceful conditions," but Sill assumed he had been given a free hand to work for peace and good order on the peninsula, even if this necessitated ventures into domestic politics, collaboration with other Western powers, or even confrontations with Chinese and Japanese authorities. Following Cleveland's exhortation, Sill explored available diplomatic and military avenues to prevent war. He consulted with Russian, French, and British representatives in Seoul. When these "Caucasian" diplomats dispatched a note to Japanese and Chinese officials, calling for mutual withdrawal of troops from the peninsula, Sill added his signiture to the document.[25] The American minister also considered using military force to preserve peace. He received Skerrett's promise to retain a warship in Chemulpo harbor and to prepare some armed men for possible deployment in Seoul. "We shall have a considerable territory to guard," Sill asserted, "for I am likely to put adjoining American property under our flag."[26]

Sill had faith in the naval officer's assurance of support. Consequently, he prepared his legation quarters as a refuge for any Western or Korean official who might find his life endangered. The admiral, however, had no intention of remaining at Chemulpo. The *Baltimore*'s supplies were low, and Skerrett longed to return to his wife and daughter at Nagasaki. As Sill readied his legation haven, the American cruiser slipped quietly from its anchorage.

Sill cabled Secretary Gresham at once. The admiral's hasty departure, he complained, had left him "in a humiliating and most perilous position."[27] Washington responded by promptly relieving Skerrett of his command. Fortunately, the officer's indiscretion did

---

23 Sill to Gresham, June 18, 1894, Korea Despatches, 11, NA, RG 59.

24 Uhl to Sill, June 22 and 23, 1894, Korea Instructions, 1, *ibid.*

25 Note enclosed in Sill to Uhl, June 25, 1894; Sill to Gresham, July 18, 1894, Korea Despatches, 11, *ibid.*

26 Sill to Skerrett, June 26, 1894, Area 10 File.

27 Sill to Gresham, July 8, 1894, Korea Despatches, 11, NA, RG 59.

The Independent Minister 493

not endanger American lives in Seoul. The capital remained calm and soon the decrepit, unseaworthy gunboat *Monocacy,* which had participated in the shelling of Korean fortifications several decades earlier, replaced the departed *Baltimore.*

Sill now believed that the critical situation was over, but new complications developed in Washington for the American minister. Determined to discover actual conditions in Korea, Secretary Gresham called Gozo Tateno, the Japanese minister in the United States, to the State Department on July 7, 1894. Gresham inquired about Japan's motives in Korea and was stunned by Tateno's reply. "Our situation at home is critical," the Japanese diplomat explained, "and war with China would improve it by arousing the patriotic sentiment of our people and more strongly attaching them to the Government."[28] Tateno's frank admission that Japan would violate its treaties with Korea and upset the peace in East Asia in order to stabilize its own government shocked the highly legalistic Secretary of State. Prompted more by moral outrage than by any concrete policy to stop Japan, Gresham rushed a note to the American minister in Tokyo, Edwin Dun, criticizing Japan's conduct. "You are instructed to say to the Government at Tokyo," Gresham cabled Dun, "that the President will be painfully disappointed should Japan visit upon her feeble and defenseless neighbor the horrors of an unjust war."[29] On July 9 Gresham sent Sill a copy of the same note, and as Sill's actions would soon indicate, the minister believed that the United States government expected him to direct his energies against Japanese expansion in Korea.[30]

The Cleveland administration, however, had no desire to further antagonize Japan. It had maintained friendly relations with the Asian kingdom and intended to continue these relations. Washington did not consider Japanese policies in Korea a threat to American interests, and Gresham's statement was merely a hasty response to Tateno's startling revelations.[31] But unaware that Gresham's sentiments did not represent American policy, Sill em-

---

28 Tateno's private secretary kept a complete transcript of the Tateno-Gresham talks on July 7, 1894. For a copy, see Notes from the Japanese Legation in the United States to the Department of State, 1858–1906, Vol. 5, NA, RG 59.

29 Gresham to Dun, July 7, 1894, Diplomatic Instructions of the Department of State, 1801–1906: Japan, Vol. 4, *ibid.*

30 Gresham to Sill, July 9, 1894, Korea Instructions, 1, *ibid.*

31 For Cleveland-Gresham policies in East Asia, see Jeffrey M. Dorwart, "The Pigtail War: The American Response to the Sino-Japanese War of 1894–1895" (Ph.D. dissertation, University of Massachusetts, 1971).

494   PACIFIC HISTORICAL REVIEW

barked on a program designed to obstruct Japanese policies in Korea.

Sill initiated his anti-Japanese crusade several days after reading Gresham's note to Dun. When, on July 15, Japanese soldiers molested British Consul C. T. Gardner, his wife, and a legation secretary on a Seoul street, the American minister acted. He met with Russian, French, and German representatives in the capital, advising them to inform their respective governments of Japan's disruption of peaceful conditions in Korea. Japan, Sill insisted, must investigate the outrageous incident. And after the local military commander coldly rejected Sill's protest, in what the minister called "an obvious sneer inconsistent with diplomatic courtesy," Sill complained directly to Tokyo.[32] Japanese officials in Tokyo ignored Sill.

Sill next turned his attention to new and much more severe Japanese provocations. On July 22 Japanese soldiers, intent upon seizing control of the Korean government, occupied the royal palace and imprisoned the king. Korean political refugees poured into the American compound through its unguarded gates. Unable to control the mob, Sill rushed an urgent plea for assistance to the two American warships now anchored just off the Korean coast. He asked Captain Benjamin F. Day of the recently returned *Baltimore* and Commander Robert E. Impey of the *Monocacy* for a legation guard. Neither officer appeared anxious to commit troops to Korean territory. Day, a career officer promoted through the ranks, opposed sending his men into the heat and disease of the local countryside. Moreover, he disliked missionaries and refused to endanger his personnel to protect them. "In event of war between Japanese and Chinese," he wrote Sill, "there would seem to be no reason for apprehending danger to Americans provided they attend to their own affairs."[33] For his part, Commander Impey urged Sill to employ Japanese soldiers as a legation guard and use them to keep order.[34]

Sill deplored this lack of naval cooperation. He labeled as "very unjust" Day's insinuation that American missionaries endangered their own lives by mixing in Korean politics. He accused the officers

---

32 Sill to Dun, July 19 and 21, 1894, Korea Despatches, 11, NA, RG 59.
33 Day to Sill, July 20, 1894, Area 10 File.
34 Sill to Gresham, July 24, 1894, Korea Despatches, 11, NA, RG 59.

of being pro-Japanese and of hindering his attempts to preserve peaceful conditions. "I would be violating my instructions and laying myself open to severe and merited disapproval from my Government," Sill argued, "if I should ask for a Japanese guard when I may just as well apply to my own Government forces for protection."[35] The minister indicated that, if Day and Impey refused to help, he would cable Washington directly for assistance.

Day finally agreed to dispatch fifty armed men for the protection of the legation. Unable to locate a pilot for his steam-launches, Captain of Marines George F. Elliott marched a mixed contingent of marines and sailors overland the thirty-one miles to the capital rather than risk navigating the uncharted Han River. At 7 P.M. on the evening of July 23, American military personnel, each man armed with forty rounds of ammunition, began an eleven-hour march through Korean territory. A Japanese guide assisted the men along narrow footpaths, over deep sand, and through muddy rice fields. When the small column of sailors and marines arrived at the legation, the Japanese at the head of the group rode his horse through the compound gates, creating the impression among the Korean crowds that the United States supported Japan in its attack against the Korean monarchy.[36]

Though Sill now had his legation guard, he condemned the manner in which it had arrived. He criticized Day for permitting a Japanese horseman to lead Americans into Seoul, and he cautioned the officer against further displays of sympathy toward Japan. "This act added intensity to a growing anti-American feeling," Sill informed the captain.[37] Day denied pro-Japanese sentiments. "I don't care what nationality he is," the officer replied bitterly, and "for his bad manners in riding his horse through the Legation gate I am in no way responsible, nor do I regard the fact that he did so a matter of political or any other consequence whatever."[38]

While the two Americans bickered, a series of naval and land encounters between Japan and China led finally to Sino-Japanese

---

[35] *Ibid.*

[36] G. F. Elliott, "Marines in Seoul, Korea," *Annual Report of the Secretary of the U.S. Navy, 1895* (Washington, D.C., 1895), 523–529; Day to Sill, July 24, 1894, Area 10 File.

[37] Sill to Day, Aug. 1, 1894, Area 10 File.

[38] Day to Sill, Aug. 3, 1894, *ibid.*

declarations of war on August 1, 1894. After several months of fighting, Japan drove China out of Korea, gained control of the seas around the kingdom, and tightened its grip on the Korean monarchy. Various cliques struggled to dominate the government, and Japanese agents stirred up unrest in the capital. Sill followed closely the reports of these events. "While we are now relieved from any apprehension on account of the probable coming of the Chinese army to this point," he informed Rear Admiral Charles C. Carpenter, newly appointed commander of the Asiatic squadron, "the whole kingdom has never been in a more complete state of anarchy and confusion, and the factions in Seoul have never been more alert and dangerous."[39]

Carpenter agreed to keep a guard at the legation until peaceful conditions were restored, but soon regretted this decision. In November 1894, Acting Secretary of the Navy William McAdoo ordered the admiral to investigate rumors that his men had committed immoral acts in Seoul.[40] Evidently some local missionary had written the department, accusing American marines and sailors of drunken debauchery and the outrage of a Korean woman. Carpenter asked Sill to discover the source of these charges, and Sill detailed the task to his legation secretary. Allen traced the damaging correspondence to Rose Ely Moore, the wife of an American missionary. She had not personally observed the alleged excesses, Allen reported after his interview with Mrs. Moore, and probably had been overly sensitive to gossip.[41] There was no evidence to substantiate the charges, Allen told Sill, and the minister forwarded this finding to Carpenter.

Carpenter cleared his men of wrongdoing, but the Navy Department decided to remove its armed party from Seoul to avoid further embarrassment. When Sill learned of this decision, he begged the Navy Department to reconsider and insisted that neither Koreans nor Japanese could keep order in the rebellious provinces around the capital. "The repressive and restraining force of our guard here is very great," he wrote Captain William M. Folger of the gunboat *Yorktown*, recently anchored in the nearby harbor.

---

39 Sill to Carpenter, Sept. 26, 1894, *ibid.* Similar sentiments are expressed in Sill to Gresham, Nov. 2, Dec. 4 and 18, 1894, Korea Despatches, 11, NA, RG 59.

40 McAdoo to Carpenter, Nov. 19, 1894, Area 10 File.

41 Carpenter to Sill, Jan. 15, 1895; affadavit of Rose Ely Moore, witnessed by Allen, enclosed in Sill to Carpenter, Jan. 19, 1895, *ibid.*

The Independent Minister 497

"It may never be called to active defense of American interests," Sill continued, "but its presence make[s] powerfully for good order and against the necessity for active defense."[42] As a last resort, he warned Admiral Carpenter in March 1895, ::e would complain directly to the President if the navy failed to provide adequate protection.

The Navy Department gave in to Sill's pressure and left the guard until the last days of the Sino-Japanese War. The war, in fact, lasted only another month, until April 1895. Japanese forces pushed into Manchuria, captured the Chinese strongholds at Port Arthur and Weihaiwai, and threatened to overrun Peking. The corrupt and decadent Manchu government, fearing dissolution of the empire, sued for peace. Sino-Japanese representatives then concluded a partial cease-fire and finally a peace treaty at Shimonoseki, Japan, on April 17, 1895. The Treaty of Shimonoseki left Japan in virtual control of the Korean peninsula.[43]

Sill struggled desperately to maintain American influence in the kingdom against the victorious Japanese. Japan must be curbed, Sill told Washington, or it would close Korea to all American contact. Japan was demanding a fifty-year franchise over Korean railroads and complete control over Korea's telegraph and postal services, he warned Gresham in April 1895. Sill complained about Japan's desire to control the Korean mining industry, particularly since his legation secretary, Horace Allen, had recently wrested a concession from the king for the Unsan gold mines.[44] The minister outlined for Washington Japan's program to establish monopolies over Korean fishing, transportation, and banking concerns. Japanese advisers had infiltrated every branch and department of the Korean government, Sill wrote, and had expelled all other foreign employees, including Americans. Japan's postwar policies in Korea, he concluded, infringed upon U.S. treaty rights and violated the most-favored-nation doctrine.[45]

Sill organized the foreign representatives in Seoul to protest

---

42 Sill to Folger, March 13, 1895, *ibid.*

43 *Documentary History of the Peace Negotiations between China and Japan, March–April 1895* (Tientsin, 1895), 1–29.

44 Spencer J. Palmer, "American Gold Mining in Korea's Unsan District," *Pacific Historical Review*, XXXI (1962), 379–391; Harrington, *God, Mammon, and the Japanese, 156.*

45 Sill to Gresham, April 17, 1895, Korea Despatches, 11, NA, RG 59.

498   PACIFIC HISTORICAL REVIEW

monopolistic Japanese practices. Accompanied by the Russian chargé d'affaires, he called on the Korean minister of foreign affairs on May 4, 1895. In this meeting, Sill presented what clearly could be called an Open Door policy for Korea.

not really this is liner boiler boilerplate

> We feel that we are enunciating the views of our respective Governments when we state that nothing is claimed for our manufacturers and merchants in foreign markets but the opportunity of fair and open competition and in doing so we are merely echoing the spirit of the most favored nation clause of the Treaties with Foreign Powers.
> All we wish to emphasize is the principle that as foreign commercial interests in this country develop, those concerned should not find themselves hampered in the wholesome race of open competition by exclusion from privileges secured by people earlier in the field.[46]

Sill received little encouragement from the Japanese-dominated Korean bureaucrat, and sought other means to ensure an open door policy on the peninsula. As a first step, he advised Washington to reassess its Korean policies. The United States government, he cabled Gresham in May 1895, should resist Japanese domination of Korea.[47] Remembering Gresham's blunt note to Japan in July 1894, Sill hoped the Secretary continued to view Japanese actions in Korea as unjust and would listen to his recommendations to curb Japanese power. But, unfortunately for Sill, Gresham died suddenly and was succeeded by former Attorney General Richard Olney, who warned the diplomat to stop protesting Japanese expansion. "In all its dealings with this Government in connection with the late war," the new Secretary of State cabled, "Japan has frankly and freely disclaimed all imputation of actual or ulterior designs of conquest over Korea, and declared as its purpose the independence of Korea. . . ."[48] Washington still considered Japanese-American friendship essential for stability in East Asia, Olney implied, and Sill should do nothing to upset this policy.

Sill stood alone in his condemnation of Japanese aggressive and monopolistic schemes. Involved in Latin American complications and convinced that cooperation with Japan could best protect American interests in East Asia, the Cleveland administration

---

46 Enclosure in Sill to Gresham, May 11, 1895, *ibid.*
47 Sill to Gresham, May 11, 1895, *ibid.*
48 Olney to Sill, June 21, 1895, Korea Instructions, 1, *ibid.*

turned its back on Korean affairs. It withdrew warships from the area and ordered Sill to find other ways to protect Americans at his legation. Acting Secretary of State Alvey A. Adee, one of the most influential men in the State Department, instructed the minister to stop calling for U.S. Navy gunboats and to ask that the Korean government defend Americans under its 1882 treaty obligations. If Sill refrained from censuring Japan, the acting secretary added, there would be far less danger to Americans in Seoul. The United States government did not object to increased Japanese influence in Korea and neither should its minister to Korea.[49]

Despite his government's pro-Japanese policies, Sill refused to sit by idly as the Japanese manipulated Korean politics. His resolve to resist Washington's directives became even stronger after Japanese agents entered the royal palace, murdered the anti-Japanese queen, and burned her mutilated body. Sill urged the Cleveland administration to condemn Japanese complicity in the atrocity and, at the same time, issued his own denunciation of a Japanese-inspired edict which degraded the assassinated queen. He also voiced concern for the life of the king, believing that the Japanese wished to destroy the entire royal family and replace it with a government subservient to Japan. He would collaborate with British, French, and Russian representatives, Sill wrote Washington, to protect the monarch.[50]

Sill went even further in his attempt to check Japanese destruction of the Korean government. He provided refuge in his own quarters for Korean officials opposed to Japan, and he asked Captain Folger of the *Yorktown* to send an armed party to protect them.[51] When Secretary Olney learned of Sill's behavior, he promptly disavowed the minister's actions. "Intervention in political concerns of Korea is not among your functions and is forbidden," he cabled Sill on November 11, 1895. "Refugees cannot be sheltered by you against officers of *de facto* government charged

---

[49] Adee to Sill, July 8 and 17, 1895, *ibid.*

[50] Sill to Secretary of State, Oct. 10, 1895; Sill to Olney, Oct. 26 and Nov. 9, 1895; Allen to Secretary of State, Oct. 13, 1895, all cited in Spencer J. Palmer, *Korean-American Relations: Documents Pertaining to the Far Eastern Diplomacy of the United States* (2 vols., Berkeley and Los Angeles, 1963), II, 357–362; see also M. Frederick Nelson, *Korea and the Old Orders in Eastern Asia* (Baton Rouge, 1945), 229–231.

[51] Palmer, *Korean-American Relations*, 362–366.

500   PACIFIC HISTORICAL REVIEW

with apprehending them as violators of the laws of their country."[52] The Secretary forbade the employment of the *Yorktown* to protect Koreans and ordered Sill to reserve his legation only for American citizens.

Sill defended his behavior by citing President Cleveland's message of June 22, 1894, which had directed him to use "every possible effort for the preservation of peaceful conditions" in Korea. Olney brushed aside this argument, explaining that the President's directive no longer applied. "This instruction only referred to events which were then occurring," Olney cabled Sill in December 1895, "and was not, as you appear to think, a standing instruction."[53] The Secretary sent new orders to Sill on January 1, 1896, commanding him to cease anti-Japanese activity and to advise other Americans in the area to refrain from adventures in local politics.[54] But the minister ignored Olney and persisted in his support of anti-Japanese elements in the capital. Believing that Washington misunderstood the situation, Sill refused to change his approach to the Korean question.

The Cleveland administration left Sill alone during its last months in office. A presidential election year and domestic problems precluded interest in remote overseas complications. Besides, since the minister's dispatches now alluded only to the granting of a railroad concession to an American syndicate, Olney apparently assumed that Sill had carried out his last departmental directive to stop criticizing Japan.[55]

The new Republican administration of William McKinley soon learned about Sill's failure to comply with Olney's January note. John Sherman, McKinley's new Secretary of State, scolded Sill, and in March 1897 ordered him to distribute a circular among American missionaries explicitly proscribing political activity. Disregard of departmental directions, the Secretary warned, might lead to Sill's recall.[56]

Actually the McKinley administration had already decided to discharge Sill. Months earlier, Horace Allen had initiated a campaign to undermine support for Sill in the United States. He

---

52 Olney to Sill, Nov. 11, 20, and 21, Dec. 2, 1895, Korea Instructions, 1, NA, RG 59.
53 Olney to Sill, Dec. 31, 1895, *ibid.*
54 Olney to Sill, Jan. 11, 1896, *ibid.*
55 Olney to Sill, May 21, 1896, *ibid.*
56 Sherman to Sill, March 30, 1897, *ibid.*

The Independent Minister 501

coveted his superior's post, and when his Ohio neighbor, William McKinley, had been elected president, Allen expected to get Sill's position. "I think I deserve it," he wrote W. W. Rockhill, "and I have done the whole work for seven years."[57] The clever missionary-diplomat mobilized Ohio cronies to press his case upon the President. Headed by Judge George K. Nash, Congressman Archibald Lybrand, and Captain C. W. Everett, the Ohio clique convinced the new executive to remove Sill and appoint Allen in his place. Judge Nash, whose son lived near Allen in Korea, rendered the most service. He met personally with McKinley on March 14, 1897. "I told him that I had but one pet lamb which I wished to save," Nash wrote to his son in Seoul, "and his name is Allen."[58]

Allen employed public opinion, as well as these influential contacts, in his quest for the Korean post. Aware of official Washington sympathy for Japan, he publicized Sill's anti-Japanese policies in an effort to discredit the minister. "Last winter in his enthusiasm he went so far against the Japanese and the instruction he had received," Allen wrote to James R. Morse of the Korean Mining and Development Company, "as to get such a reprimand from the Department by telegraph that he thought the only course left him was to resign."[59] Allen next asked his journalist friend, Frank G. Carpenter, to print information about Sill's emnity toward the Japanese.[60]

Allen's efforts were not altogether necessary. The Japanese government had already voiced opposition to Sill's continued presence in Korea. For several years the indefatigable minister had resisted Japan's attempts to absorb Korea into its growing Asian empire, and with the change in American administrations, Japan saw an opportunity to remove the bothersome diplomat. Sill had blocked Japan's efforts to restore peace in war-torn Korea, Tokyo informed the United States government, and he should be recalled.[61] This pressure to oust Sill, even at the risk of having the champion of Korean independence, Horace Allen, replace him, attested to the concern with which Japan viewed the minister's influence in the capital.

---

[57] Allen to Rockhill, Dec. 29, 1896, box 2, book 6, Allen Papers.
[58] Nash to his son, March 14, 1897, *ibid.*
[59] Allen to Morse, Nov. 20, 1897, book 5, *ibid.*
[60] Allen to Carpenter, May 8, 1897, book 6, *ibid.*
[61] Sill to Sherman, May 8 and 7, 1897, Korean Despatches, 13; Sherman to Sill, May 6 and 7, 1897, Korea Instructions, 1, NA, RG 59.

502   PACIFIC HISTORICAL REVIEW

Sill had never been Allen's pawn, and no one realized this more than the legation secretary himself. "He [Sill] is quit. contrary," Allen wrote to his sister Jennie in February 1897, "and has gone his own course. . . ."[62] Neither was Sill a retiring, old gentleman, collecting flowers on some Korean hillside, and he does not deserve to be ignored by historians. True, Allen was the most important American in Korea when Sill arrived in 1894, and Allen was the most powerful American after Sill returned to his native Michigan in late 1897. Yet during his three years as minister and consul general in Korea, John M. B. Sill dominated American diplomacy on the peninsula. He advocated a reappraisal of American foreign policies in Korea, particularly the assumption that Japanese-American friendship would preserve an open door for trade, travel, and missionaries. He suspected that one day Japan would force all Americans out of the area, and he urged Washington to resist Japanese domination of Korean affairs.

John Sill failed to alter American policies or attitudes toward Japan. He never convinced his government of the dangers to American interests in East Asia posed by increased Japanese power. American leaders for the next decade continued to believe that Japanese-American friendship would lead to peace and stability in the Far East and in the Pacific Ocean. This did not mean, however, that Sill failed to contribute anything to American diplomacy. He enunciated a clear statement of the Open Door policy several years before W. W. Rockhill and Secretary of State John Hay published their famous notes. Sill's predictions of a future Japanese-American confrontation, if the United States did not change its traditional Asian policies, were on record in the State Department long before similar warnings from more seasoned diplomats and officials. Sill would doubtlessly not have been surprised at the growing tensions between the United States and Japan after the Russo-Japanese War of 1904–1905, nor perhaps with the Japanese attack on Pearl Harbor years later.

---

[62] Newt Allen to Jennie Allen, Feb. 25, 1897, box 2, book 6, Allen Papers.

10

Assessing Public Opinion: Editorial Comment and the Annexation of Hawaii – A Case Study

George F. Pearce

T HE QUESTION of annexing the Hawaiian Islands sparked the first national debate in American history on imperial expansion and in many ways presaged the outcome of the subsequent controversy over the retention of the Philippines.[1] The debate continued intermittently in the Congress and in the nation's press for a period of five years. Finally, on July 6, 1898, in the midst of the Spanish-American War, the Senate passed a joint resolution annexing the Hawaiian Islands to the United States. This political action inaugurated an expansionist foreign policy that reaped an empire in less than a year.

Historians have long debated the reasons why the United States suddenly cast aside its traditional and anticolonial policy for outright annexation of insular territories and alien peoples. The Senate had rebuked, and the public had ignored, attempts by Secretary of State William H. Seward in the 1860s and by President Ulysses S. Grant in the 1870s to acquire colonial possessions. Indeed, as late as

[1] One American diplomatic historian has described the debate on the joint resolution for annexing Hawaii as "something of a dress rehearsal for the 'great debate' that lay seven mon.hs ahead." Thomas J. McCormick, *China Market: America's Quest for Informal Empire, 1893–1901* (Chicago, 1967), 112.

April 1898 the anticolonial tradition seemed strengthened by the congressional resolution for war with Spain. To silence those who suspected American intentions, Congress had called for Cuban independence and had renounced any intention of exercising sovereignty over that island. The war resolution implied that the politicians believed Americans would go to war to free the Cubans, but not for the purpose of acquiring territory. Paradoxically, in less than three months, this same body consented to the annexation of the Hawaiian Islands.

Some historians have concluded that the explanation for the change in attitude can be found in an upsurge of popular expansionist sentiment within the nation. They argue that expansionist sentiment had grown throughout the 1890s and that the annexation of Hawaii demonstrated this growing sentiment. The favorable vote on the joint resolution, Albert K. Weinberg argues, merely mirrored the voice of the American people who demanded such action.[2] However, historians who draw such conclusions do so without careful assessment of the complicated nature of public opinion.

Too often, interpretive works on late nineteenth-century American imperial expansion have equated newspaper editorial opinion with public opinion. The purpose of this study is to determine the extent to which editorial opinion about the Hawaiian annexation issue actually reflected popular opinion. Recent studies dealing with public opinion and the structure of American foreign policy will be analyzed and their findings applied to the situation in the 1890s so as to suggest new tools for assessing the delicate interrelationship of public opinion and policy.

For the most part, attempts by historians to relate editorial opinion to public opinion have been unconvincing. The practice goes back at least to 1931 when diplomatic historian Eber Malcolm Carroll established the precedent "of using the newspaper editorial as . . . [a] major tool for uncovering public opinion."[3] Since then,

---

2 Albert K. Weinberg, *Manifest Destiny* (Gloucester, 1935), 269. Sylvester K. Stevens claims that "a majority of the American people in the feverish days of 1898" favored annexation. Sylvester K. Stevens, *American Expansion in Hawaii, 1842–1898* (New York, 1968), 295. Commenting on the vote for annexation, Thomas A. Bailey states that "the time had finally come when the American people concluded that an independent Hawaii, like Texas of an earlier day, was . . . an anachronism. . . ." Thomas A. Bailey, *A Diplomatic History of the American People* (8th ed., New York., 1969), 435.

3 Melvin Small, ed., *Public Opinion and Historians* (Detroit, 1970), 17.

numerous other historians have accepted Carroll's rather simplistic inference that there is a direct relationship between the contents of editorials and the opinions held by the newspaper subscribers. But their failure to provide any statistical data or references to studies establishing that editorials either mold or reflect the opinions of their readers makes the validity of such inferences highly questionable. Although one analyst has concluded that in the editorial column the newspaper "employs direct suggestion to shape attitudes of its subscribers," he also acknowledged the great difficulty in determining the extent to which editorials influence or reflect individual opinion.[4] Nonetheless, many historians naively assume that public opinion is identical with public presentation of opinion. This "journalistic fallacy," as one expert on public opinion calls it, "is the illusion that the item which one sees represented in print as 'public opinion' . . . really has . . . wide-spread importance and endorsement." It is a "naive error," he contends, to think that "editorial clippings from different sections of the country," supporting or opposing "popular or legislative action," represent public opinion on the issue.[5]

Despite such warnings, historians have tended to personify public opinion by not infrequently referring to it as the "voice of the people" and the "public conscience." Metaphors of this sort merely propagate the myth that public opinion is "some kind of being which dwells in or above the group, and there expresses its view upon various issues as they arise."[6] Thus, experts on public opinion disagree with historians and insist that a personified public is not a reality, though they admit that it is a convenient label, since "any kind of opinion may be attributed to it without the possibility of checking the assertion."[7]

---

[4] Julian Laurence Woodward, *Foreign News in American Morning Newspapers: A Study in Public Opinion* (New York, 1930), 15. Studies on editorial readership exist, yet any attempt to establish an editorial-opinion relationship on the basis of their findings would be pure conjecture. See Dean C. Baker and James C. McDonald, "Newspaper Editorial Readership and Length of Editorials," *Journalism Quarterly*, XXXVIII (1961), 473–479; and Ralph K. Martin, Garrett J. O'Keefe, and Oguz B. Nayman, "Opinion Agreement and Accuracy between Editors and Their Readers," *Journalism Quarterly*, XLIX (1972), 460–468.

[5] Floyd H. Allport, "Toward a Science of Public Opinion," *Public Opinion Quarterly*, I (1937), 12.

[6] *Ibid.*, 7.

[7] *Ibid.*, 8; see also V. O. Key, Jr., *Public Opinion and American Democracy* (New York, 1964), 8–9.

Public opinion is, of course, an elusive concept; its elusive nature is compounded by the fact that it can be expressed in many ways by many different segments of the public. Furthermore, those members of the public who express common opinion on a particular issue are not necessarily the same members of the public who express common opinion on a different issue. For any number of reasons, a portion of the public may reach a common opinion on a certain issue and then realign as the issues change.[8] The opinions held by many publics, then, make up public opinion. Of course, some members of the public never form opinions on public issues.

While it is difficult to gauge public opinion, it is even more difficult to determine its effect on officials and politicians. Admittedly, there is no way to determine accurately what politicians in the 1890s considered their most effective gauge for measuring the public climate on foreign policy issues, or, for that matter, what elements of opinion most influenced their positions on such issues. Nor can we know precisely the kind of opinion that politicians looked for or listened for within their constituencies when calculating the most popular position to take on an issue. To reconstruct an individual performance would be most difficult. Yet, this study rests upon the assumption that politicians had some method for measuring opinion on divisive issues.

Who most likely would have comprised the public that held opinions on the question of annexing Hawaii? Gabriel Almond claims that "the characteristic response of Americans to questions of foreign policy is one of indifference."[9] He sees this indifferent attitude as being particularly strong during the greater part of the nineteenth century. During this period a relatively stable world political situation existed, and most Americans were intensely involved with private interests.[10] Almond's view is supported by James N. Rosenau, who also believes that the mood of the mass public toward

---

[8] In the first issue of *Public Opinion Quarterly*, public opinion was described by Floyd H. Allport, editor of the *Quarterly*, as follows: "The term public opinion is given its meaning with reference to a multi-individual situation in which individuals are expressing themselves, or can be called upon to express themselves, as favoring or supporting (or else disfavoring or opposing) some definite condition, person, or proposal of widespread importance, in such a proportion of number, intensity, and constancy, as to give rise to the probability of affecting action, directly or indirectly, toward the object concerned." See Allport, "Toward a Science of Public Opinion," 23.

[9] Gabriel A. Almond, *The American People and Foreign Policy* (New York, 1965), 53.

[10] *Ibid.*, 54.

foreign affairs is one of "indifference and passivity." Except during acute "crises (and not always then)," Rosenau claims, "the mass public is usually unmoved by the course of world events. Few of its members are likely to have more than headline acquaintance with public discussions of foreign policy issues. . . ."[11]

A recent study in public opinion estimates that the number of Americans showing an interest in foreign policy in the 1890s "numbered between 1.5 and 3 million, or something between 10 and 20 percent of the voting public."[12] Considering the educational opportunities in the 1890s, it is surely unlikely that over ten percent of the voting public concerned itself with foreign affairs. Most of those who did, according to Ernest R. May, "would have come from the 500,000 or so who had graduated from colleges and the 1 to 1.5 million who had graduated from high school."[13] May's opinion is supported by V. O. Key, Jr., who states that "on questions of foreign policy the disinclination to express an opinion is especially marked among persons wth only grade-school education."[14] Among those who express opinion on foreign policy to the pollsters, May has found that "the proportion of professional men and businessmen runs very high; that of clerical and skilled workers less high; that of unskilled workers and farmers markedly low."[15] The wealthier and better educated also have a higher representation in the foreign-policy public than in the voting public. In makeup, then, the foreign-policy public is far less representative of the total population than is the voting public. The findings of the above studies indicate that public opinion concerning territorial expansion in the

---

11 James N. Rosenau, *Public Opinion and Foreign Policy* (New York, 1961), 36. Another student of public opinion and foreign policy contends that many members of the American voting public "show only a limited interest in foreign affairs; for them foreign policy is a remote, unintelligible abstraction." Cabell Phillips, "The Mirror Called Congress," in Lester Markel, ed., *Public Opinion and Foreign Policy* (New York, 1949), 85. Based on a Gallup Poll taken in February 1948, "eighty-eight percent of voters with less-than-average incomes, . . . [and] 82 percent with above-average incomes, could not cite the purpose of the Marshall Plan." Martin Kriesberg, "Dark Areas of Ignorance," *ibid.*, 54.

12 Ernest R. May, *American Imperialism: A Speculative Essay* (New York, 1968), 24.
13 *Ibid.*

14 Key, *Public Opinion and American Democracy*, 333. A Gallup Poll taken in February 1948 revealed that 29 percent of the population "with grammar schooling or less . . . [were] unaware of the Marshall Plan, compared with 3 percent of the college graduates." Kriesberg, "Dark Areas," in Markel, ed., *Public Opinion and Foreign Policy*, 56.

15 May, *American Imperialism*, 22; see also Almond, *The American People and Foreign Policy*, 122–135.

1890s would be represented by what was being said, written, and done about it within this "comparatively well-to-do, well educated, well read, and politically active public, numbering less than 3 million and living mostly in cities."[16] Reference to public opinion on colonies in this paper, therefore, refers only to that comparatively small portion of the population which May shows was "specially interested" in the matter.[17]

How do the few members of the public who show an interest in foreign affairs arrive at the position they take on foreign-policy issues? Two political scientists, George Belknap and Angus Campbell, argue convincingly that affiliation with a political party largely determines the positions taken on foreign-policy questions. That is, "the party serves as a reference point to which they look . . . for their position on foreign policy questions."[18] If Belknap and Campbell's conclusion is sound, then most Americans who comprised the foreign policy public in the 1890s would have held views that were dictated by their perception of their political party's position on matters of foreign policy.[19] One would assume, therefore, that they relied heavily upon the prime news medium of the day—the newspaper—for information to reinforce their position on foreign policy issues. Yet they often could not obtain that information because a trend in the evolution of the American newspaper in the 1890s largely precluded the possibility of giving wide coverage to foreign affairs.

During the 1890s newspaper consolidation forced the enlarged papers to attract more subscribers and advertisers. And, although it was a time when the United States was emerging in world affairs, it is unlikely that editors of the "new journalism"—those who "shared the appetites, the successes . . . of their fellow magnates in rails, and oil . . ."[20]—would have elected to increase the amount of news or editorials pertaining to foreign affairs and to decrease the coverage

---

16 May, *American Imperialism*, 24. May's label—"foreign policy public," which he applies to that segment of the American public which shows an interest in, and holds opinion on, foreign affairs—is used in this study. A contemporary newspaper defined popular opinion even more narrowly: "Popular opinion" equals "men conspicuous in public, professional, and business life." *Chicago Inter-Ocean*, Oct. 10, 1898, p. 6, quoted in McCormick, *China Market*, 213.

17 May, *American Imperialism*, 21.

18 George Belknap and Angus Campbell, "Party identification and Foreign Policy," *Public Opinion Quarterly*, XV (1951–1952), 618.

19 *Ibid.*, 621; see also V. O. Key's appraisal of "Party as Opinion Maker," in Key, *Public Opinion and American Democracy*, 449–452.

20 Bernard A. Weisberger, *The American Newspaperman* (Chicago, 1961), 122.

of other topics. Such a decision would have been inconsistent with the general trend among editors of adapting the newspaper "to the interest, standards, and pastimes of a mass public that was lightly educated and in the market for diversion and amusement."[21]

Even if editors had elected to publish more news on foreign affairs in the regular news columns and to increase the number of editorials that had a foreign "news peg," the readership of such news would most likely not have increased significantly. Contemporary studies reveal that, in spite of increased educational opportunities and national prosperity, less than ten percent of Americans reading newspapers read any significant amount of news on foreign affairs.[22] We can assume that in the 1890s this percentage was probably lower. However, subscribers who did read this material during that decade were most likely to represent public opinion on the Hawaiian annexation.

On January 17, 1893, the Hawaiian monarchy was toppled in a bloodless coup, and overtures by the provisional government to annex the former island kingdom to the United States were set in motion. News about the Hawaiian revolution arrived in the United States on January 28, 1893. The first reaction from the press indicates that, irrespective of their political inclinations, most editors agreed that American annexation of Hawaii was preferable to letting the islands come under foreign domination. Journals with a Republican affiliation were generally more favorable to annexation, however.[23]

---

21 Bernard C. Cohen, *The Press and Foreign Policy* (Princeton, 1963), 249. Walter Lippmann says that "the . . . press of the 19th century escaped the tutelage of government only to fall under the tutelage of the masses. It found support and profit in serving the whims and curiosity of the people." Quoted in William Albig, *Modern Public Opinion* (New York, 1956), 376.

22 A readership survey of fifty-one newspapers taken by the American Institute of Public Opinion in 1953 reveals that adults read about half a column of foreign news daily and devote an estimated two and one-third minutes to reading this material. Cohen, *The Press and Foreign Policy*, 251. Using data from a readership survey, V. O. Key states that "day in and day out the odds are that less than 10 percent of the adult population could be regarded as careful readers of the political news." Key, *Public Opinion and American Democracy*, 353. Bernard C. Cohen claims that the number of careful readers of foreign news would be several percentage points lower. Cohen, *The Press and Foreign Policy*, 257.

23 During the two weeks following the arrival of the first news about the Hawaiian revolution, *Public Opinion* reprinted thirty newspaper editorials on the topic. Of the 14 editorials in the Republican newspapers, 10 favored and 3 opposed annexation, and 1 remained undecided. The 16 editorials in the Democratic papers divided 9 to 7 in favor of annexation.

As the Hawaiian annexation episode began to unravel, the nature of the editorials about it became increasingly partisan. Within a fortnight editoral opinion had largely undergone a realignment along political lines.[24] The evidence suggests that, in this early editorial division on the Hawaiian question, an editor's political affiliation was most likely to determine his position. He had little official information upon which to form his opinion; and in such a short time he had no way of gauging public opinion on the subject. His political party became for him, in effect, a device for instant and declarative knowledge. New developments which finally revealed the administration's sympathetic view toward annexation solidified this partisan division among editors.

The story of how the American minister to Hawaii, John L. Stevens, had used United States military forces to aid the revolution broke in the press on February 11, 1893.[25] Four days later President Benjamin Harrison sent a Hawaiian annexation treaty to the Senate. At that time only thirty-two days had elapsed since the overthrow of the Hawaiian queen.

Knowing that a two-thirds majority vote on the treaty depended upon obtaining some Democratic votes, administration officials endeavored to secure Democratic support. At the request of the President, Secretary of State John W. Foster conferred with Democratic Senators John T. Morgan and A. P. Gorman about prevailing opinion on the treaty among their party colleagues. Both senators assured Foster "that they anticipated no serious opposition to the treaty from their side of the chamber. . . ."[26] Events soon changed these optimistic predictions of quick confirmation for the treaty.

While not unalterably opposed to the acquisition of Hawaii, some Democrats questioned the tactics employed by the Harrison administration to secure the treaty. Furthermore, the treaty had the appearance of a partisan Republican measure, and Democrats

---

24 From the middle of February 1893 until Cleveland's inauguration on March 4, 1893, twenty-six editorials on the Hawaiian issue appeared in *Public Opinion*. Twelve of the thirteen editorials from Republican newspapers favored annexation, while nine of the thirteen editorials from Democratic newspapers opposed annexation.

25 Stevens's sympathy with the revolutionary forces was well known. Former Secretary of State James G. Blaine had appointed Stevens as minister to Hawaii. Both had been friends and neighbors in Augusta, Maine, and both were on record as favoring Hawaiian annexation to the United States. Alice Felt Tyler, *The Foreign Policy of James G. Blaine* (Hamden, 1965), 216.

26 John W. Foster, *Diplomatic Memoirs* (2 vols., Boston, 1909), II, 168.

looked to President-elect Grover Cleveland for guidance.[27] When Cleveland met with some of his cabinet appointees on February 22, 1893, at Lakewood, New Jersey, "the case of the Hawaiian Queen" was a topic of discussion.[28] There is no record of the conversations or decisions, but shortly after this meeting the Democrats in Congress learned that Cleveland desired "that the treaty be left for the new administration to deal with."[29] By the end of February 1893, apparently enough opposition to the annexation treaty had developed to make the Harrison administration believe it inexpedient to force a test vote. President Harrison's term in office ended on March 4, 1893, with Senate action on the treaty pending.

On March 9, 1893, President Cleveland sent a special message to the Senate withdrawing the treaty.[30] Two days later Cleveland appointed James H. Blount, a former Georgia congressman and chairman of the House Committee on Foreign Affairs, as his special commissioner to Hawaii. Blount had instructions to investigate all matters touching on the recent revolution in Hawaii and to report his findings to the President.[31] Blount submitted his report to Secretary of State Walter Q. Gresham on July 17, 1893. Apparently, Blount's report confirmed the administration's suspicions about Stevens's part in the revolution and prompted doubts about support for the revolution among native Hawaiians. Cleveland thereupon formed his Hawaiian policy on the conviction that anything short of restoring the legitimate government would be an injustice.[32]

The state of affairs in Hawaii caused Cleveland much anxiety, and by early December 1893, he had reached the end of his patience in waiting for the deposed queen (Liliuokalani) to accept his conditions for restoration of the monarchy. In a cabinet meeting on December 7, the President resolved to "lay the whole matter before

---

27 Julius W. Pratt, *Expansionists of 1898* (Baltimore, 1936), 122.

28 Matilda Gresham, *Life of Walter Quintin Gresham, 1832–1895* (2 vols., Chicago, 1919), II, 684.

29 Pratt, *Expansionists of 1898*, 122.

30 Cleveland stated that "for the purpose of re-examination I withdraw the treaty of annexation between the United States and the Provisional Government of the Hawaiian Islands. . . ." James D. Richardson, comp., *Messages and Papers of the Presidents, 1789–1905* (11 vols., Washington, D.C., 1898), IX, 393.

31 U.S. Dept. of State, *Foreign Relations of the United States, 1894* (Washington, D.C., 1895), Appendix II, "Affairs in Hawaii," 467–469.

32 Pratt, *Expansionist of 1898*, 138.

Congress."[33] On December 18, President Cleveland sent a 6,000 word special message to Congress commending the "subject to the extended powers and wide discretion of the Congress."[34]

Where did editorial opinion stand on the Hawaiian question and how did it relate to public opinion? Editorial comment during Cleveland's attempt to impose a strictly moral solution to the rancorous Hawaiian political problem generally followed political lines. Slightly over eighty-five percent of the Republican journals opposed Cleveland's policy of withdrawing the treaty of annexation and ordering an investigation of the affair, while just over eighty percent of the Democratic journals favored it.[35] A contemporary newspaper complained that "this discussion of our relations with the Sandwich Islands is not a political canvass; . . . yet the partisan papers are arrayed against each other on this topic with all the heat and rancor of a sharply fought election contest."[36]

During the remainder of Cleveland's administration the Senate approved two proposals which stated that the United States should refrain from interfering in Hawaii's internal affairs and should provide the islands with an external protective shield against foreign aggression. Despite these resolutions, Cleveland's Hawaiian policy came under increased attack by both the Democratic and Republican press. An analysis of editorial comment on the Hawaii problem in *Public Opinion* during the period shows that ninety percent of the editorials in Republican journals favored annexation or, in some way, were critical of Cleveland's handling of the matter. Thirty-three percent of the editorials in Democratic journals attacked Cleveland's policy because it lacked resolution and because his attempt to restore the deposed queen to the throne ignored reality. The increasing likelihood that the Republican party could capture the White House in the 1896 presidential election, and the

---

33 Henry James, *Richard Olney and His Public Service* (New York, 1923), 92.

34 Richardson, *Messages and Papers,* IX, 472.

35 From Cleveland's inauguration until the end of 1893, *Public Opinion* carried forty-one editorials from Republican journals and forty-six editorials from Democratic journals commenting on Cleveland's Hawaiian policy. Thirty-five editorials from Republican journals opposed Cleveland's policy while six favored it. The editorials from Democratic journals divided thirty-seven to nine in favor of Cleveland's policy.

36 *Philadelphia Telegraph,* Nov. 21, 1893, as cited in *Public Opinion,* XVI (1893), 213.

growing hostility to Cleveland's domestic policy within the Democratic party, probably did more to influence the increased editorial criticism of Cleveland's Hawaiian policy than did any upsurge in popular sentiment for annexing Hawaii.[37]

On June 16, 1897, President William McKinley submitted a Hawaiian annexation treaty to the Senate. It embodied practically the same features as the 1893 treaty.[38] Although during the ensuing months the Senate supporters of annexation did not relax their efforts to accomplish their objective, they had agreed not to press for a vote on the treaty. During February 1898, they even let it be known that they supported dropping the treaty, and early in March McKinley consented to abandon it.[39] By this time the Cuban affair had practically pushed the Hawaiian annexation issue off the editorial pages. Finally, after George Dewey's victory at Manila Bay on May 1, the Hawaiian Islands were annexed by a joint resolution of Congress on July 6, 1898.[40]

A survey of newspapers during the months preceding annexation does not reveal any appreciable change in proannexationist sentiment. In July 1898, the *Literary Digest* summed up the general positions that the nation's newspapers had taken on the issue of expansion: "The leading Republican Party papers of the cities, with few exceptions, advocate a policy of expansion and territorial acquisition. . . . Among regular Democratic papers which commit themselves there seems to be a general opposition to expansion."[41]

The newspaper was the primary news medium in the 1890s. In-

---

37 Cleveland's use of troops in the Pullman strike figured as a major issue in the 1894 congressional elections which brought Republican control of the House. Harold U. Faulkner, *Politics, Reform and Expansion* (New York, 1959), 181. This action further divided the Democratic party. Cleveland already had driven a wedge in the party by supporting the repeal of the Sherman Silver Purchase Act and by preferring gold over silver coinage. Moreover, the administration had antagonized many of its mugwump supporters when it failed to secure reductions in the tariff. When Cleveland enlarged the civil service and vetoed pension bills, he displeased other groups of voters and editors.

38 *Sen. Rept. 681*, 55 Cong., 2 sess. (1897), 96–97. On June 24, 1897, *Public Opinion* carried editorial comment about the annexation treaty. Of the five editorials from Republican journals, all favored passage of the treaty. The editorials from Democratic journals divided seven to two against passage of the treaty.

39 One historian interprets the decision not to force a test vote on the treaty as an indication "that Senators sensed some effective opinion against annexation." May, *American Imperialism*, 181.

40 Some Republicans who had earlier opposed annexation were apparently won over by a combination of party loyalty and the patriotic fervor that flowed in the wake of Dewey's victory.

41 "The Newspapers and the Issue of 'Imperialism,'" *Literary Digest*, XVII (July 9, 1898), 32–33.

deed, it provided the sole reading material available to most of the country. Still, although newspapers were widely circulated, they devoted relatively little space in their columns to news and editorials on foreign affairs. Newspaper editors apparently detected that a small percentage of their subscribers read such news, a view, as already noted, substantiated by recent analyses of public opinion. Since an indifferent attitude toward foreign affairs existed among the American people during the 1890s, it is unlikely that editorial opinion about Hawaiian annexation would have either created or reflected mass popular opinion on the issue.

What about the small segment of the American public—the foreign policy public—that did concern itself with such matters. As previously established, the members of this public, much like many editors of newspapers, often let their political affiliation determine their position on the issue of annexation. In all probability, therefore, members of the foreign policy public read editorials on the annexation issue in newspapers that took the same position on the question as their own. The relationship of public opinion to foreign policy towards Hawaii thus became a matter of editors reinforcing, rather than molding, the opinions held by those subscribers who were counted as being part of the foreign policy public. Of course, even if the newspaper is not successful "in telling people what to think, . . . it is . . . successful in telling its readers what to think about."[42]

Admittedly these conclusions are based on informed conjecture and, therefore, cannot be stated unequivocally. They do not preclude the possibility that communication in some form took place between editors and attentive readers of news and editorials on foreign affairs. There is no way of knowing to what extent these readers communicated their opinions to editors, or to what extent such opinions when communicated were reflected in editorials. Yet it seems safe to surmise that such expressions of opinion occurred relatively infrequently and, when they did occur, had little influence on the shape of editorials.[43]

---

42 Cohen, *The Press and Foreign Policy*, 13.

43 It is impossible to say whether the trend toward absentee ownership in journalism made the editorial column any less reflective of the opinions of subscribers. Even in the days of personal journalism, the views of the editor apparently did not lead, did not reflect, and often did no more than give his views. At least we have no evidence of what the linkage was between editor and public. Writing in 1898, journalist E. L. Godkin claimed that "the effect of newspaper editorial writing on opinion is small, so far as one can judge." "Do People Read Editorials in the Paper?" *Review of Reviews*, XVII (1898), 100–101.

336   PACIFIC HISTORICAL REVIEW

This paper reveals that the historian cannot facilely equate edi- /tuh
torial opinion with public opinion on the issue of Hawaiian annexation. The historian must treat editorial opinion on the question as
nothing more than opinion expressed publicly.[44] Such opinion may
have reflected the opinions held by a segment of those who constituted public opinion on the issue. Still, an analysis of this opinion
reveals nothing in the way of a measurement of the number of
Americans who supported a particular editorial position on the annexation question, or of what part of the American public held
opinions on the question.

If newspaper editorials are to be discounted as a measure of public
opinion, are there other sources as yet overlooked which could help
the historians to gauge public opinion and its impact on foreign
policy in the 1890s?[45] A careful reading of the protracted Senate
debate in the *Congressional Record* produces no evidence that senators were influenced by public sentiment, for the debates make almost no mention of the impact of public opinion on annexation.
By way of exception, Senator Samuel McEnery, mirroring the view
of the sugar interests, expressed concern for the sugar growers in his
state and in the nation at large. The Louisiana Democrat feared
that annexation would mean the removal of sugar duties. Free sugar, he claimed, would "destroy a promising industry in over twenty
states of this Union."[46] McEnery's concern for the sugar interests
was not shared by other senators, however. Most of them justified
their positions on strategic, moralistic, or historical grounds. Senator George F. Hoar of Massachusetts best described the passive
attitude Americans had toward the Hawaiian affair. In describing
his support for the annexation of Hawaii, Hoar later observed: "My
approval of it was then, I suppose, well known. Certainly no friend

---

44 Bernard C. Cohen has recently quoted an Assistant Secretary of State as saying:
"I watch the editorials, but I do not consider them as reflections of anyone's opinions
other than the man who writes them." Cohen, *The Public Impact on Foreign Policy*
(Boston, 1973), 110.

45 While attempting to gauge American expansionist sentiment toward annexing
Hawaii in another study, the writer of this article found himself relying heavily on
the newspaper and periodical press as sources of public opinion. This predicament
instigated a search for sources which contained additional evidence about public
opinion on annexation and its communication to politicians. The search uncovered
other (see below) sources containing relevant empirical data on the subject. George
F. Pearce, "American Expansionist Sentiment and the Annexation of Hawaii" (D.A.
dissertation, Carnegie-Mellon University, 1970).

46 *Cong. Rec.*, 55 Cong., 2 sess. (1898), 6303.

of mine, and nobody in Massachusetts, so far as I know, in the least objected or remonstrated against it."[47] Likewise, a perusal of the available biographies and autobiographies of those congressional leaders[48] who actively participated in the debate reveals a similar lack of references to public opinion. In only one of these works is public opinion directly mentioned in connection with the annexation question. Texas Congressman Joseph Bailey was an opponent of annexation. Bailey's biographer, Sam H. Acheson, regards Bailey's position on annexation as out of step with public opinion on the issue.[49] But if such a favorable expansionist sentiment existed, apparently Bailey and the two senators from Texas were either unaware of it or could afford to ignore it.[50]

Although the *Congressional Record* for the years 1893 to 1898 contains fifteen memorials, petitions, and resolutions on the question of annexation from special interest groups, private clubs, chambers of commerce, groups of private citizens, and state legislatures, this small demonstration of opinion surely had a negligible impact on the course of the debate, the more so since eleven of the fifteen petitions were received during 1893 and 1894. Another source of opinion on Hawaiian annexation is contained in state House and Senate journals. These records provide data on the number of resolutions passed urging congressional delegations to support particular positions on domestic and foreign affairs. An examination of these journals for fifteen states that held legislative sessions in 1897 or 1898 show that two legislatures passed resolutions pertaining to Hawaiian annexation, one rejecting and one supporting annexation. During this time most of the legislatures passed resolutions urging their congressional delegations to take a certain stand on such national issues as tariff legislation and direct election of senators. Of the foreign issues that did attract their attention, Cuban independence was more important than the ques-

---

47 George F. Hoar, *Autobiography of Seventy Years* (New York, 1903), 306.

48 Senators Arthur P. Gorman, Thomas C. Platt, Shelby M. Cullom, Henry C. Lodge, Joseph B. Foraker, Orville Platt, Marcus A. Hanna, Richard F. Pettigrew, Benjamin R. Tillman, Nelson W. Aldrich, William E. Chandler, and George F. Hoar. Congressmen Joseph Cannon, Champ Clark, Thomas B. Reed, and Joseph Bailey.

49 Sam Hanna Acheson, *Joe Bailey, The Last Democrat* (New York, 1932), 115.

50 Bailey voted against the joint resolution for annexing Hawaii when it came to a vote in the House. The vote on the resolution in the Senate reveals that Senator Horace Chilton voted against it, and that Senator Roger Q. Mills, an avowed opponent of annexation, was paired and did not vote. *Cong. Rec.*, 55 Cong., 2 sess. (1898), 6712.

tion of annexing Hawaii.[51] It is likely that senators looked to resolutions of state legislatures as an important criterion of public opinion in pre-Seventeenth Amendment times. If we can assume that legislative resolutions were a reliable gauge of public opinion, once again we must conclude that the politicians got a negative reading on popular support for Hawaiian annexation.

The party platforms drawn up at the state Democratic and Republican political conventions held in the spring and summer of 1898 provide still another index of expansionist opinion at the time of the vote on annexing Hawaii. By this time the future political status of the Philippines had sparked a foreign policy controversy. Surely, the politicians who served on the platform committees had attempted to get a sounding on expansionist sentiment prior to the conventions. The Literary Digest compiled the positions taken by twenty-seven Republican and twenty-four Democratic conventions, or nearly 57 percent of all the state conventions held, concerning overseas expansion. Of the 24 Democratic party platforms, 12 contained no expressions on the Philippine issue, 7 were positively opposed to extending American sovereignty to the Philippines, 2 indicated that they favored retaining a portion of the islands, and 3 took ambiguous positions on the question.[52]

There were no statements on the Philippine question in 8 of the 27 state Republican party platforms. Thirteen platforms contained planks that indicated they favored keeping part of the islands. Planks in 6 platforms expressed a willingness to leave the issue in the hands of the administration. The Ohio (President William McKinley's home state) platform best expressed the latter position: "The people can safely leave the wise and patriotic solution of these great questions to a Republican President and a Republican Congress."[53] None of the state platforms of either party supported extending American sovereignty to the entire group of the Philippine Islands. In only two states (California and Nevada) did the platforms of both the Democratic and Republican parties indicate that they favored keeping part of the Philippines. The Nevada and New Jersey Republican platforms were the only two that mentioned the annexation of Hawaii; both supported this action.[54] Thus, a sum-

---

51 Pearce, "American Expansionist Sentiment," 136–137.
52 "Party Platforms and the Philippines," Literary Digest, XVII (Oct. 22, 1898), 481–482.
53 Ibid.
54 Ibid.

mary of "public opinion" on expansionism derived from state political conventions confirms that politicians felt free to ignore it. It
can be assumed that the politicians in Washington soon became
familar with the foreign policy plank in their state party platforms,
and viewed these weak expressions, or lack of expressions, on expansion as a fairly accurate gauge of the American public's imperialistic ambitions.

Still another source of opinion on expansion were views expressed by organized labor. John C. Appel has shown that organized labor was at first indifferent about the movement to annex
Hawaii. But after President McKinley submitted a treaty of annexation to the Senate in June 1897, a few local bodies threw their official support against annexation.[55] Fearing that annexation would
bring about an influx of cheap Chinese labor, officials of the Coast
Seamen's Union in California protested such action. Spokesmen for
some railroad brotherhoods, on the other hand, argued that expansion would cause their special craft to boom. In a speech on the floor
of the House, Congressman Charles H. Grosvenor of Ohio quoted
statements made by a brotherhood official expressing this sentiment.[56] But on the whole, American labor was so immensely preoccupied with organizational matters and with its demands
against industry that it gave scant attention to foreign affairs. The
Iron Molders Journal cogently summed up labor's attitude toward
Hawaiian annexation: "The fate of Hawaii, judging by the amount
of interest displayed in it by the majority of the trades-unionists, is
looked upon with indifference."[57]

Farmers were even less interested than labor in the Hawaiian affair. Claiming that he voiced the feelings of a million American
farmers, businessman-editor Herbert Myrick sent a plea to the
chairman of the House Committee on Agriculture calling for him
to inform the members of the House that annexation would ad-
versely affect American agricultural interests.[58] Late in 1897 the
Beet Sugar Association of Nebraska sent out "circulars urging the
people to oppose annexation and to write to their congressmen to

---

[55] John C. Appel, "American Labor and the Annexation of Hawaii: A Study in
Logic and Economic Interest," *Pacific Historical Review*, XXIII (1954), 5.

[56] *Ibid.*, 16.

[57] Quoted in *ibid.*, 5.

[58] Merz Tate, *The United States and the Hawaiian Kingdom* (New Haven, 1967),
290–291. Myrick was editor of *American Agriculturist*, but "its 1893 and 1897–98
issues . . . carried no articles or letters of disapproval [of annexation]." *Ibid.*, 291.

that effect."[59] Thus, the farmers, too, were indifferent and hardly constituted effective public opinion on the issue. One historian concludes that "the opposition from American farmers [to expansionism] was certainly insignificant and ineffectual."[60]

The executive branch of the government took little part in the debate, but the public's indifference to annexation was manifestly apparent in the volume of correspondence addressed to the White House on the matter. When President McKinley submitted an Hawaiian annexation treaty to the Senate on June 16, 1897, he confided to close associates that he "wished to gauge opinion while the treaty was debated."[61] McKinley failed to elaborate upon his expectations. If he expected letters from the public, these did not materialize. In the ensuing thirteen months from the time the treaty was submitted to the Senate until the joint resolution for annexation was passed, McKinley received only one letter on the subject.[62] Indeed, there is evidence that the number of letters on the affair directed to the chief executive actually declined as the debate progressed. When President Cleveland sent an address to Congress on December 18, 1893, in which he stated that he would not again submit the treaty of annexation to the Senate, he received six letters relating to the speech within a week. Each of the writers praised the stand he had taken on the matter of Hawaii.[63] Even so, McKinley's action in resubmitting an annexation treaty to the Senate earmarked it as an administration measure which, in the long run, led to its passage.

That the Hawaiian question had acquired a politically partisan nature by 1898 is reflected in the Senate vote on the joint resolution for annexation. The resolution passed on July 6, 1898, with a vote of 42 to 21, and 26 paired and not voting. Only one Republican, Justin Morrill, joined the Democrats to vote nay. Six Democrats (A. Gorman of Maryland, J. Morgan and F. Pettus of Alabama, W.

59 *Ibid.*, 292.

60 *Ibid.*, 291.

61 H. Wayne Morgan, *William McKinley and His America* (Syracuse, N.Y., 1963), 295.

62 James F. Rusling to McKinley, June 18, 1897, McKinley Papers, Library of Congress, Washington, D.C.

63 Charles S. Fairchild to Cleveland, Dec. 19, 1893, Cleveland Papers, Library of Congress, Washington, D.C.; George Hunter Smith to Cleveland, Dec. 20, 1893, *ibid.*; S. H. Sterall to Cleveland, Dec. 20, 1893, *ibid.*; C. M. Anderson to Cleveland, Dec. 21, 1893, *ibid.*; Vaughan S. Collins to Cleveland, Dec. 21, 1893, *ibid.*; Oscar S. Straus to Cleveland, Dec. 23, 1893, *ibid.*

Sullivan and H. Money of Mississippi, and J. McLaurin of South Carolina) voted yea with the Republicans.[64] Party commitment, rather than an increase in favorable expansionist sentiment, was the dominant influence determining the outcome of the vote.[65] If mass public opinion had supported annexation, it would likely have transcended party affiliation, forcing the politicians, in many instances, to abandon their party's position on the issue. Probably such action was not so likely to happen at a time when senators were still being elected by state legislatures. Still, a senator could not have totally disregarded mass public opinion without jeopardizing his party's chances at the polls and, indirectly, his own political future.

Most interpretations of the American-colonial experience have relied heavily upon the few studies that have attempted to establish the relationship between public opinion and the implementation of an imperial foreign policy in 1898. These studies generally used the newspaper and periodical press as their primary source of information, and most concluded that there was a growing public sentiment for expansion during the 1890s. This study shows, however, that there is other evidence which provides us with a more accurate measurement of the public's attitude toward expansion in the 1890s, but this evidence has been largely ignored by historians. An analysis of it puts to rest the historical myth that the decision to annex Hawaii, or the imperial policy which this action inaugurated, largely reflected a groundswell of favorable expansionist opinion within the nation.

---

[64] *Cong. Rec.*, 55 Cong., 2 sess. (1898), 6712. Sullivan, Money, and McLaurin did not participate in the debate, and no evidence has surfaced that explains their support of the resolution. Pettus, like Morgan, advocated annexation on strategic grounds. Control of the islands would strengthen the navy's position in the Pacific, he argued, and "whatever the cost may be, we ought to have a strong navy." *Ibid.*, 6574. From the beginning of the debate in 1893, Gorman and Morgan had advocated annexation. Annexation was compatible with Morgan's pet project of an isthmian canal. Morgan was a member of the Senate Foreign Relations Committee, but he seldom received a letter concerning foreign policy. Moreover, the senator claimed that the few letters he did receive on foreign affairs were from citizens of other states rather than from his own constituents. May, *American Imperialism*, 25.

[65] Four days after the vote on annexation, the *New York Times* commented: "it is worth while to recall how curiously lacking is any evidence of a strong and intelligent popular opinion in its favor." The editorial pointed out that "so far as the voice of the people can be said to have been heard at all it was through the members of Congress, and there is not a single one of these who can be said to have consulted his own constituents on the matter." *New York Times*, July 10, 1898, p. 16.

11

The American Remission of the
Boxer Indemnity: A Reappraisal

Michael H. Hunt

S TUDENTS of American foreign relations, particularly those interested in China
policy, have in recent years begun to examine critically the conventional wisdoms of their field.[1] Many of the old historical generalizations have fallen; some
still stand. One of the most vigorous of the vestiges concerns the remission by the
United States of a portion of the Boxer indemnity.[2] The story offers in cameo what
Americans have traditionally liked to believe relations with China were all about.
It goes as follows. Despite the outrages inflicted by the Boxers on Americans during the summer of 1900, the United States government made reasonable indemnity
demands. Moreover, it took China's part in the peace negotiations in Peking by
urging the other powers to scale down their total indemnity claims. Subsequently,
when American claims fell short of the amount China had agreed to pay, the admin-

Michael H. Hunt is an instructor in history at
Yale University.

[1] Recent works on American foreign relations in
the late nineteenth and early twentieth centuries
have sparked a stimulating controversy over the
nature of American expansionism. Unfortunately,
the participants have tended to emphasize the
American side of the story and to neglect the
"other side," whether Cuban, Spanish, Filipino or
Chinese. In the last case they have remained entranced with the appearance of American omni-
potence and Chinese frailty. As a result, the picture
of Sino-American relations is still one-sided. Heavy
reliance on American sources has caused historians
to perpetuate the turn of the century American
prejudices written into those sources, to down-
play some of the less attractive attitudes that
American policy makers have displayed in dealing
with the lesser breeds, and to all but ignore
Chinese policy and politics. I have tried to contribute to the debate by looking in this article
at American policy from the foreign perspective
during the Boxer indemnity remission episode. For
a more ambitious effort, see my unpublished Ph.D.
dissertation, "Frontier Defense and the Open Door:
Manchuria in Chinese-American Relations, 1895–
1911" (Yale University, 1971).

The general statements in the debate over
American expansionism are Walter LaFeber, *The
New Empire: An Interpretation of American Ex-
pansion, 1860–1898* (Cornell University Press,
1963); H. Wayne Morgan, *America's Road to
Empire: The War with Spain and Overseas Expansion* (New York, 1965); and Ernest R. May,
American Imperialism: A Speculative Essay (New
York, 1968). Works dealing specifically with China
policy are Marilyn B. Young, *Rhetoric of Empire:
America's China Policy, 1895–1901* (Harvard University Press, 1968); Thomas J. McCormick, *China
Market: America's Quest for Informal Empire,
1893–1901* (Chicago, 1967); Paul A. Varg, *The
Making of a Myth: The United States and China,
1897–1912* (Michigan State University Press, 1968);
and a review article on Varg by McCormick,
"American Expansion in China," *American Historical Review*, LXXV (June 1970), 1393–1396.

[2] The indemnity remission referred to in this
article is the first one, accomplished by executive
order on December 28, 1908. The returned funds,
representing indemnity in excess of the settled and
disputed claims of American citizens, business firms
and the federal government arising from the Boxer
affair, amounted to nearly $11,000,000, slightly
more than two-fifths of China's total Boxer obligation to the United States. The Chinese government used this money to educate Chinese in the
United States and to establish in Peking a pre-
paratory school, Tsing Hua University. Carroll B.
Malone, "The First Remission of the Boxer Indemnity," *American Historical Review*, XXXII
(October 1926), 64–68, has long been the standard
secondary account.

After the settlement of disputed claims the
United States Government made a second remission in May 1924. Because of the regional political
division in China at that time, the funds were
entrusted not to the Chinese government as was
done in the first remission but instead to the China
Foundation, a joint Chinese-American committee
to promote education and culture.

istration of Theodore Roosevelt spontaneously and unconditionally returned the surplus. For its part the Chinese government freely determined to devote the returned funds to educating Chinese youths in the United States as an expression of its gratitude. This version of the indemnity remission was meant to illustrate not only the fairness and far-sightedness of the American policy of promoting basic progressive changes in Chinese life but also to make clear that the decision to return the funds contributed to the reservoir of Chinese gratitude and good will toward the United States.

This act of generosity became almost at once the object of myth-making and of rhetorical excess. Sarah Pike Conger, wife of the American Minister to China and a survivor of the siege of the Peking legations, was one of the earliest enthusiasts. She wrote in 1910:

> The attitude of the United States . . . that caused her, without compulsion, to cancel the Boxer indemnity fund, is an attitude too deep, too broad, too high for word expression. Does not this attitude reveal a strong current of sisterly good will, when it is able to sweep away the heavy weights of financial gain? This attitude is not one of spontaneity; the seed was brought over in the *Mayflower;* it was planted in the virgin soil of liberty, where it rooted, and was watered. with treasured dewdrops; was nourished into being in Love's tenderness; was sustained in Truth's fortitude. This is the story of our country's attitude.[3]

Harley Farnsworth McNair's more moderate appraisal, written in 1924, is typical of the tone of later evaluations. "American nationals feel that their government has acted justly in returning excess funds to China. . . . It is pleasing to realize that the American sense of justice, friendship, and desire for fair play rises to the top each time. . . ."[4] McNair's view found its scholarly echo two years later in Carroll B. Malone's "The First Remission of the Boxer Indemnity." In this article, still the standard history of that event, Malone cautiously reached substantially the same conclusions as his predecessors. "There are no records to show that the United States imposed any specific conditions as to the use of these funds. . . . The published documents show that China expressed her deep gratitude, left the time and manner of the remission entirely to the American government, and apparently quite voluntarily stated her intention of using the money for the education of Chinese students in the United States. This was done as an expression of her appreciation of the friendliness of the American government."[5] Standard textbooks[6] and even one of the most recent general studies of American-Chinese relations,[7] following Malone

---

[3] *Letters from China* (Chicago, 1910), pp. 372–373.

[4] "The Return of the Indemnity Funds to China," in his *China's New Nationalism and Other Essays* (Shanghai, 1925), p. 206. For other similar comments, see Bishop James W. Bashford, *China: An Interpretation* (New York, 1916), p. 429; Lawrence F. Abbott, *Impressions of Theodore Roosevelt* (New York, 1919), p. 146; Edward Thomas Williams, *China Yesterday and Today* (New York, 1932), p. 252; Westel W. Willoughby, *Foreign Rights and Interests in China* (Baltimore, 1927), II, 1014; and Thomas F. Millard, *America and the Far Eastern Question* (New York, 1909), p. 319. Harold Isaacs, *Scratches on Our Mind* (New York, 1958), pp.

144–145, is one of the few accounts in English to deal critically with the remission.

[5] Carroll B. Malone, "The First Remission of the Boxer Indemnity," p. 68.

[6] Samuel Flagg Bemis, *A Diplomatic History of the United States* (4th ed.; New York, 1955), p. 488; Thomas A. Bailey, *A Diplomatic History of the American People* (6th ed.; New York, 1958), p. 482; and George E. Taylor and Franz Michels, *The Far East in the Modern World* (London, 1956), p. 621.

[7] Akira Iriye, *Across the Far Pacific: An Inner History of American-East Asian Relations* (New York, 1967), p. 124.

and the conventional wisdom, still praise this "generous" act. One of the hardiest vestiges of the old, optimistic view of America's relations with China, the indemnity remission in this familiar interpretation still retains its aura.

Not surprisingly, writers on the Chinese mainland view their country's dealings with the United States in a perspective at odds on many points with the interpretations advanced by "imperialist" scholars. This divergent general perspective finds its reflection in their treatment of the American indemnity refund. The best statement on it is by T'ao Chü-yin, a specialist in modern Chinese history:

> As everyone knows, regardless of what Americans do, it always revolves around money; only the remission of the Boxer indemnity . . . is considered a matter of 'chivalry and generosity.' But [in reality] their 'cultural investment' was used to open up a 'cultural leasehold' and an 'educational factory,' to spread the poison of enslaving thought, to overthrow and destroy the Chinese people's culture, and to injure the spirit of China's youth. Its motivation then was not chivalrous but was entirely cruel. Indeed Americans have called cultural investments 'fertilizer for America's trade with China,' and in substance it is completely like economic investment.[8]

In this view, the indemnity remission, rather than an act of benevolence, was instead merely an aspect of the cynical American scheme to subject China to commercial exploitation.

Predictably, the facts fail to give full comfort to either view. Between 1905 and 1909 the Chinese and American governments carried on a complex set of negotiations. During these negotiations the American President and Secretary of State decided that in the interest of both countries China should devote the money to education. They were in a good position to have their way because they enjoyed a virtual veto over whether to return the funds, in what amounts, and for what purposes. On the other hand, the Chinese government wished to use the funds in ways of its own choosing. At the same time it was in desperate need of financial relief. Thus, the Chinese found their preference to use the funds in their own way in conflict with the essential goal of having the funds speedily and fully returned. Consequently, they were vulnerable to threats that the remission might never take place unless they satisfied Washington's preconditions. In contrast to American strength, the weakness of China's position in the negotiations was apparent to all concerned. The final resolution of the issue, generally along the lines advocated by American leaders, reflected not so much American generosity and Chinese gratitude as this obvious disparity in bargaining strengths.

How did the United States decide on the size of its share of the Boxer indemnity? In January 1901 Secretary of State John Hay instructed the Minister to China, Edwin

---

[8] T'ao Chü-yin, "Wen-hua ch'in-lüeh ti tung-chi chi ch'i ying-hsiang," [Motivation behind cultural invasion and its influence] in his collection of essays, Mei-kuo ch'in-Hua shih-liao [Historical materials on American aggression against China] (Shanghai, 1951), p. 45. See also Liu Ta-nien, Mei-kuo ch'in-Hua chien-shih [A brief history of American aggression against China] (Peking, 1949), p. 29.

Many mainland historians who might be expected to deal with the remission question have stayed away and saved their heavy shot for more attractive "imperialist" targets in the late Ch'ing. Many of these historians, writing hurriedly in the heat of the Korean War, were limited because they drew heavily on sources in English, which suggested no clear line of attack on the remission question. Wang Shu-huai of the Institute of Modern History at the Academia Sinica on Taiwan has now in progress a general history of the Boxer indemnity.

H. Conger, to enter an American claim for $25,000,000 in damages. At the same time he warned that any sum over $150,000,000 in total indemnity to the powers might be "beyond the ability of China to pay" and advised his negotiators to try to scale down the overall claims of the powers while insisting on a fair proportion of the total for Americans.[9]

Hay's figure of $25,000,000 was immediately challenged by his representatives on the scene in Peking. Conger greeted with incredulity his superior's estimate that Americans were out of pocket by that amount on account of the Boxers. "It seems to me," he wrote back to Hay, "that in comparison with the reported expenditures of some of the governments which have had very much larger forces here than ours this amount must be too great."[10] William W. Rockhill, sent by Hay to assist Conger at the Peking talks, was also incredulous.[11]

Conger and Rockhill had put their fingers on a painful truth. American indemnity demands were excessive. (As later events were to prove conclusively, Hay's claim was nearly twice real American claims against China for damages done in the summer of 1900.) Although they had alerted Hay well before the signing of the indemnity protocol in June 1902, Hay apparently did not reconsider his demands. On the contrary, circumstantial evidence suggests that Hay stuck to his figure and rejected the opinions of his representatives because he had already purposely inflated American claims with the intention of using the excess as a bargaining counter in negotiations in Peking. One bargain Hay hoped to strike was for a reduction by the other powers of their indemnity demands. He feared that too great an overall indemnity might prove "disastrous to China" and thus upset China's foreign trade, in which American merchants had an important stake. Hay was also interested in securing from China new commercial privileges, an obvious benefit to United States exporters. To consummate either of these deals Hay was willing to reduce his indemnity demand by one-half or, in other words, to bring it down to a realistic level corresponding to actual American claims.[12] He set a course without risk to his country. By making his demand, which he described as "already reasonable,"[13] twice real claims, Hay created for himself a token to use in bargaining with the other powers over the Boxer settlement. But when he failed to effect a bargain, this avowed friend of China left the Chinese holding the debt.

While Hay's bargaining tactics were unfair to the Chinese, American participation in the Boxer indemnity negotiations is vulnerable to criticism for larger, practical reasons. The total indemnity of $330,000,000 was an incubus on China's program of reform and development in the last decade of the Ch'ing dynasty and later during the Republican period. The indemnity nearly doubled the size of the govern-

---

[9] Hay, telegraphic instructions to E. H. Conger, January 29, 1901 (enclosed in Conger to Hay, February 5, 1901), Minister to China: Despatches, U. S. National Archives microfilm.

[10] Conger to Hay, February 11, 1901, Minister to China: Despatches.

[11] Rockhill to Hay, February 4, 1901, Hay Papers, Library of Congress. The London *Times* correspondent in Peking recorded in his diary contemporary criticism of the over-large American claim. Cyril Pearl, *Morrison of Peking* (Sydney, 1967), p. 133.

[12] Hay's intentions must be surmised, for lack of any clear evidence elsewhere, from his instructions to his negotiators in Peking. In addition to his telegram to Conger of January 29, 1901, noted above, see in Diplomatic Instructions: China, U. S. National Archives microfilm, Hay's telegrams to Conger, December 29, 1900, and to W. W. Rockhill, April 29, May 10 and 28, and August 5, 1901.

[13] Hay to Rockhill, May 10, 1901, Diplomatic Instructions: China.

ment's annual payment on foreign debts and reduced the central government's uncommitted tax revenue from 65,500,000 taels a year to less than 40,000,000 taels. After 1901, more than half of its revenue, which might otherwise have benefited Chinese, was going into the hands of foreigners.[14] Because of this obligation, important programs sponsored by the central and provincial governments never got off the drawing board or else struggled along insufficiently funded.

Beyond the financial burden the indemnity left on China, there is the broader consideration of its justice. The Boxers had in part been stirred by the Western intruders. The foreigners, having walked unwelcomed into a hornets' nest, should have been neither surprised nor outraged when they were stung. In this broad perspective, differences between the general policy of the United States and that of the other powers in the Boxer negotiations pale to a common color. Whatever the United States did for China during those negotiations dims by comparison with the fact that the United States helped to formulate the terms of the settlement and to impose them on an unwilling China by threat of force, and that she ultimately benefited from her actions at China's expense.

Neither of Hay's bargains worked out and he was left with an indemnity surplus which would become publicly visible as the final claims were paid out.[15] He and President William McKinley privately resolved even before the United States signed the indemnity agreement to return the excess to China. Both Elihu Root, Hay's successor as Secretary of State, and Rockhill, now back in Washington serving as the State Department's expert on China, were aware of and shared this resolve.[16] None the less for several years neither government gave serious consideration to this surplus. Until 1905 the State Department and the Wai-wu Pu, the Chinese foreign office, were preoccupied with other questions, particularly with the major crisis provoked by the Russian occupation of Manchuria and the ensuing Russo-Japanese war conducted on Chinese soil.

Early in 1905 the Chinese Minister to the United States, Liang Ch'eng, initiated the effort to have the excess indemnity returned to China.[17] Liang, a native of Kwangtung like nearly all of his predecessors, had studied in the United States in

[14] Hsü T'ung-hsin, *Chang Wen-hsiang-kung nien-p'u* [*A chronological biography of Chang Chih-tung*] (Taipei reprint, 1969), p. 147; and H. B. Morse, *International Relations of the Chinese Empire* (New York, 1910–1918), III, appendix A. The financial situation was much the same in 1906. See the report by E. T. Williams, enclosed in Rockhill to the Secretary of State, September 26, 1906, State Department Numerical File 2112/-1, U. S. National Archives. (This collection is hereafter abbreviated "NF.")

[15] The indemnity protocol set China's debt to the United States, including the $25,000,000 principal and the interest on it through the final installment of 1939, at about $46,000,000. The protocol is reproduced in John V. A. MacMurray, *Treaties and Agreements with and concerning China, 1894–1919, Vol. I: Manchu Period (1894–1911)* (New York, 1921), p. 311.

[16] Hay to Rockhill, telegram, August 26, 1901,

Diplomatic Instructions: China; and Rockhill to Theodore Roosevelt, July 12, 1905, Rockhill Papers, Houghton Library, Harvard University. President Roosevelt made clear in an interview with the Chinese Minister that Secretary of State Elihu Root shared John Hay's wish that the excess indemnity be returned. Chinese Minister to the United States Liang Ch'eng to the Wai-wu Pu, received November 1, 1905, File on the indemnity remitted by the United States (Mei-kuo mieh-shou p'ei-k'uan), records of the Wai-wu Pu in the Diplomatic Archives of the Institute of Modern History, Academia Sinica, Taiwan. (This file is hereafter referred to as "WWP Indemnity File.") Root's recollections on the decision to return the indemnity, recorded in the biography by Philip C. Jessup, are not reliable. *Elihu Root* (New York, 1938), I, 385–387.

[17] Liang Ch'eng to the Wai-wu Pu, received May 13, 1905, WWP Indemnity File.

the 1870's as a member of the Yung Wing mission and returned in 1902, well prepared by Chinese standards, to head the Washington legation. Still, although Hay and McKinley had already informally determined to return the surplus indemnity to China, it was to take Liang over two years of prodding before the Roosevelt administration would make its intentions a matter of formal record.

The Chinese Minister had no sooner set discussions in motion than he found himself confronted by a hostile American government. Chinese resentment over mistreatment of their fellow countrymen visiting and living in the United States resulted in an anti-American boycott, which markedly cooled the atmosphere for talks. The Chinese government's repurchase of the American China Development Company's contract to finance and build the Canton–Hankow Railway and the massacre of American missionaries at Lienchow in Kwangtung in the same year left relations too strained for talks on the indemnity to proceed. Theodore Roosevelt's temper, always sensitive to what he regarded as questions of justice, rose while relations with China cooled.

> I intend to do the Chinese justice and am taking a far stiffer tone with my own people than any President has ever yet taken, both about immigration, about this indemnity, and so forth. . . . Unless I misread them entirely they despise weakness even more than they prize justice, and we must make it evident both that we intend to do what is right and that we do not intend for a moment to suffer what is wrong.[18]

Roosevelt was angry and refused to move ahead on the negotiations with the Chinese. Practical politics, however, as well as his feeling of outrage contributed to his decision. "The chance of my getting favorable action by Congress [on the remission] will be greatly interfered with by the failure of the Chinese to do justice themselves on such important matters as the boycott and the Hankow [railway] concession."[19] The administration made it clear to the Chinese Minister that for the moment talks on the remission were impossible.[20]

The thaw was not long in coming. Conditions in China, in Washington's opinion, began to improve. The boycott, against which the central government had finally set itself, began to lose steam in the late summer and early fall of 1905. Repurchase of the railway contract seemed more justified when details of the American company's mismanagement and contract violation came to light. And the Chinese government's swift and satisfactory action in the aftermath of the missionary massacre assured Washington it did not condone the attack. Tempers in Washington consequently began to cool, bringing hope of renewed contacts on the indemnity. Nevertheless, Liang Ch'eng, encountering a residue of hostility, found it necessary to move cautiously. He correctly guessed that the remission would not be quickly concluded.[21]

Through the following year and the early months of 1907 his efforts proved nearly as fruitless as in 1905. Although the Roosevelt administration had by mid-

---

[18] Roosevelt to Rockhill, August 22, 1905, in Elting E. Morison et al. (eds.), *The Letters of Theodore Roosevelt* (Harvard University Press, 1951–1954), IV, 1310. The administration's disapproval is also reflected in another letter by the President to Rockhill, August 29, 1905, in Morison et al., IV, 1326–1327, as well as in W. A. P. Martin, *The Awakening of China* (New York,

1907), p. 251; in Cyril Pearl, p. 156; and in Hay to Jeremiah Jenks, February 13, 1905, Hay Papers.
[19] Roosevelt to Rockhill, August 22, 1905, in Morison et al., IV, 1310.
[20] Liang Ch'eng to the Wai-wu Pu, received November 1, 1905, WWP Indemnity File.
[21] *Ibid.*, as well as W. A. P. Martin, p. 252.

THE BOXER INDEMNITY 545

1906 resumed its own leisurely pace toward settlement, the Chinese Minister's impatience to settle the matter mounted.[22] His successor, Wu T'ing-fang, who was to arrive later in the year, would be handicapped by entering the negotiations in midcourse. In addition, the administration was not disposed to cooperate with Wu. The State Department had a low opinion of his honesty and resented his appointment to the Washington post for the second time. And Roosevelt much preferred Liang Ch'eng to the "bad old Chink," as he liked to call the new appointee.[23] Liang's desire to win for himself the plaudits for negotiating the issue to a successful conclusion, rather than let them fall to his successor, no doubt fed his impatience with American procrastination. But above all, the Chinese government, always financially pressed, looked forward to getting the money back. With the hope of pressuring the administration into action, Liang tried to influence public opinion. He obliged newsmen with off-the-record interviews, gave speeches on China's claim, and sought out friendly Congressmen to support the cause.[24]

Root was annoyed. Under pressure his back stiffened. Reacting against the public clamor over the country's obligation to return the excess to China, he bristled that it is not "any less our money than any other money in the Treasury" and that when it is returned "it should be given as our money and not as China's money, or as money to which we have a doubtful title." The cry to return the excess, particularly loud from missionaries, ran against the lawyer's sense of orderliness and deliberation; he refused to be rushed. He was still committed to remission but "it will be quite a number of years," he cautioned the editor of a mid-Western church paper, "before that point is reached."[25] Liang realized that Root stood in his way and at first tried to tempt him to trade the return of the money for Chinese concessions on a new immigration treaty.[26] When that failed to interest Root, Liang reached beyond the Secretary of State to test the intentions of the President.

The intervention at the White House by the Secretary of the Interior and the Secretary of Commerce and Labor on the Minister's behalf turned the President's attention momentarily back to the surplus indemnity. Liang seized his opportunity, and in an interview with Roosevelt in late April outflanked Root by winning the President's personal promise that the administration would work for a swift settlement. In addition, Liang pressed Roosevelt to have the indemnity claims of the armed services audited. He was "absolutely" convinced that they had overstated their expenses during the Peking expedition and that "an examination will show the real expenses were only a fraction" of their claims.[27] Roosevelt, after a conference with both Liang and Root about May 2, also agreed to the audit.[28] Liang could now cate-

[22] Liang Ch'eng to the Wai-wu Pu, received October 3, 1906, WWP Indemnity File.

[23] Roosevelt to Root, September 26, 1907, in Morison et al., V, 809. On the State Department's hostility toward Wu, see the documents in NF 5971/9-14, 18.

[24] Liang Ch'eng to the Wai-wu Pu, received July 16, 1907, Supplementary indemnity file (p'ei-k'uan an pu-tsu), records of the Wai-wu Pu. (This file is hereafter abbreviated "Supplementary WWP Indemnity File.")

[25] Root to David S. Thompson, March 2, 1907, NF 2413/21.

[26] Charles Denby, Jr., to Root, memo, March 28, 1907, NF 2413/51.

[27] Liang Ch'eng to the Wai-wu Pu, received July 16, 1907, Supplementary WWP Indemnity File.

[28] Liang Ch'eng to the Wai-wu Pu, received July 16, 1907, WWP Indemnity File, and July 25, 1907, Supplementary WWP Indemnity File.

gorically assure his superiors that "it will not happen that they [the Americans] will eat their words to the amusement of all."[29]

With the President's interest aroused, his administration began to move with some of the speed so notably lacking earlier. On his instructions the War and Navy Departments reexamined their accounts. The results confirmed Liang's doubts and proved a source of embarrassment to Root. While the Navy found its claims were short of actual expenditures by about $400,000, the Army discovered its claims, compiled when Root was Secretary of War, overran real outlays by more than $2,000,000. The revised figures for the Army and Navy, when added to approximately $2,000,000 in private claims, put the total legitimate American claims at $11,655,000.[30] With the exact amount of the indemnity clear to all, Liang duly received in June 1907 the formal announcement for which he had worked for over two years.[31] Consequently, the President in his annual address to Congress the following December recommended the remission of the excess indemnity, and in January 1908 the House and Senate took up the question. With one part of the negotiations completed, Liang left the United States; it was up to his successor, Wu T'ing-fang, who reached Washington in the early fall of 1907, to see the issue through to a settlement.

Wu's role was, however, to be more restricted. He could do little to protect China's interest in the ensuing scuffle in Congress. As it threatened in the months ahead to reduce the size of the remission, thus in effect wiping out the savings Liang's audit had made for China, Wu responded as best he could. He not only kept in touch with friendly Congressmen, as Liang had done, but also went a step farther by secretly hiring a lobbyist to help him fight these new "excessive demands."[32] But he could do little publicly without inviting charges of interference in domestic affairs. This further debate and delay may have recalled to Wu's mind the grousing of Westerners over the unwieldy organization of the Chinese government. Another year would pass before the American government, having resolved the issue, could announce itself of one mind.

The controversy in Congress arose when the publicity given the possibility of remission revived the memory of unrecompensed damages done by the Boxers seven years earlier. The most important of the unsettled claims was that of the China and Japan Trading Company. The company had made a claim of $500,000, but the State Department refused to accept any more than a fraction of it. When the Roosevelt administration submitted to Congress a resolution to remit the excess indemnity reflecting the State Department's judgement on this and other claims, Henry Cabot Lodge guided the resolution smoothly through committee and on to easy Senate approval.[33] However in the House the resolution ran into trouble. A subcommittee of the Committee on Foreign Affairs, created to consider the Senate

---

[29] Liang Ch'eng to the Wai-wu Pu, received August 3, 1907, Supplementary WWP Indemnity File.

[30] Root to the Secretaries of War and the Navy, May 11, 1907, NF 2413/44a, 44b. The revised claims appear in NF 2413/56–57. The original claims are itemized in a memo of February 16,

1907, NF 2413/15.

[31] Root to Liang Ch'eng, NF 2413/58a.

[32] Wu to the Wai-wu Pu, received April 17, 1908, WWP Indemnity File.

[33] U. S., *Congressional Record*, 60th Cong., 1st Sess., 1908, XLII, Part 1, 563, 673, 720–722.

THE BOXER INDEMNITY   547

resolution and chaired by Edwin Denby, particularly took to heart the interests of this major exporter of American cotton goods to north China and Manchuria.[34]

The subcommittee proceeded to amend the Senate's resolution in favor of the trading company's claims despite Root's objection to this unwarranted Congressional interference in an affair of the Executive.[35] The subcommittee's amendments gave unsatisfied claimants, old and new, another chance to press for compensation and accordingly took from the amount to be returned to China $2,000,000 to meet these unsettled claims. In late February the Committee on Foreign Affairs approved the amendments unanimously and sent them along with the Senate resolution to the floor of the House.[36] The amendments came up for debate on May 23, 1908. In contrast to the perfunctory consideration the Senate had given the issue some months earlier, the House dealt with the substance of the disputed amendments in a spirited discussion. The members of the House went directly to the basic question of who had the preferred claim on the money—Chinese or Americans. To pose the question was for Denby to answer it. The Chinese, he declared, "have absolutely no standing in this matter, except that we desire to show them that our civilization means justice as well as battle ships. But it's better to be just and even generous to our own people whose markets and establishments were ruined in China before we begin to be generous to a foreign power. . . ."[37] The House voted its approval of the changes and sent them to the Senate. On Lodge's advice it accepted the revisions without debate, and the President signed the resolution on May 25.[38] Finally, the American government could announce its readiness to settle with the Chinese government the precise terms of the remission.

The debate over the use to which the funds would be put began long before the United States had formally announced its decision to return them. From the outset of the talks initiated by Liang Ch'eng, the American government made a prolonged and determined effort to have the Chinese government set the funds aside for education. The Chinese, preoccupied with more pressing problems, particularly in the outlying Manchurian provinces, developed their own plans and consistently resisted pressure to link the funds explicitly and formally to education. The discussions over this question, begun in 1905, carried on well into 1909.

In his first documented interview on the remission, the Chinese Minister learned from William W. Rockhill, the Minister-designate to China, that the President wanted from the Chinese an explicit report, ostensibly to satisfy congressional curiosity, on how the remission would be used before he would authorize its return.[39] Rockhill left Liang convinced that the Roosevelt administration expected China to finance education with the money. Reflecting on the interview, Liang wrote that "whether or not this is what the President has recently said, there is the

---

[34] Details of the company's claim and the subcommittee's treatment of it emerge from the documents in NF 2413/71, 91, 112, 125.

[35] Root to Denby, February 20 and 28, 1908, and Denby to Root, February 28, 1908, NF 2413/122, 124.

[36] *Congressional Record*, XLII, Part 1, 809, and Part 3, 2627.

[37] *Congressional Record*, XLII, Part 7, 6844.

[38] *Congressional Record*, XLII, Part 7, 6815, 6871, 6908, 6954. The House debate is on pp. 6841-6845. The resolution appears in John V. A. MacMurray, I, 311–312.

[39] Liang Ch'eng to the Wai-wu Pu, received May 13, 1905, WWP Indemnity File. The quotes in this and the following paragraph come from this despatch.

intention to interfere." The funds were not rightly America's in the first place. "The money should be returned and there is nothing exceptional in the act." Liang resented, as he knew his government also would, this attempt at interference and therefore rejected having strings attached to the return of the funds. "The use to which the remitted funds are put," he pointedly told Rockhill, "is a matter of domestic concern and cannot be announced in advance."[40]

In Liang's calculations, however, resentment was balanced by fear that the money might "in the end return to someone else's grasp." And this point must have impressed the Wai-wu Pu. Liang made amply clear that American expectations would in some way have to be satisfied if the negotiations on which he was embarking were to succeed in the face of the suspicions of the Roosevelt administration and Congress. Liang's idea of a suitable compromise was to give the Americans their educational program but without making explicit assurances linking the remitted funds irrevocably to this specific project. While meeting the substance of the American demand it would also save for China the form of self-determination as well as the excess funds themselves. Liang's formulation prefigured the ultimate settlement of the controversy.

In May 1905 the Wai-wu Pu received Liang Ch'eng's first report on his efforts in Washington and immediately forwarded a copy to Yüan Shih-k'ai, the politically influential official serving in Tientsin as the Commissioner of Northern Ports. Like other high provincial officials, he was perennially short of funds to meet the financial needs of his administration and welcomed the prospect of uncommitted money coming available. He suggested that the funds be devoted to mining and railway affairs, items high on the agenda of his government. In all probability a substantial portion of these funds would have under Yüan's guidance found their way to Manchuria, a crisis area in which he had shown a steady pattern of responsibility and concern since his rise to prominence.[41] Yüan's proposal was tempered by expediency. The report from Liang which Yüan had before him made clear the American preference for education. To make his proposal palatable to the Americans, whose decision it was, after all, whether the funds would be returned at all, Yüan suggested devoting the profits from his proposed enterprises to education. Further, by using the funds "to take up one or two self-strengthening projects of administrative importance," China would also be promoting education by building a foundation for training new skills. His proposal, Yüan suggested in an attempt to sway the foreign office, "still corresponds to Minister Liang's view."[42]

The Chinese foreign office greeted Yüan's suggestion with its accustomed caution.[43] It well knew most foreigners were hypersensitive to hints that an awakened China might take up for itself the very mining and railway projects normally left to foreign exploitation. The rights-recovery movement provoked suspicion among Americans like other foreigners in China, and the State Department fully shared their emotion. Even worse, Yüan's proposal, coming on the heels of the controversy

---

[40] Liang reiterated in a despatch later in the year this view that the funds were to be used as China itself decided. Liang Ch'eng to the Wai-wu Pu, received November 1, 1905, WWP Indemnity File.

[41] Yüan had participated in negotiations concerning Russian occupation of the region. With the outbreak of war between Japan and Russia, he was made responsible for military preparedness and helped shape his country's policy of neutrality.

[42] Yüan to the Wai-wu Pu, received May 23, 1905, WWP Indemnity File.

[43] The Wai-wu Pu to Yüan and to Liang Ch'eng, June 1, 1905, WWP Indemnity File.

THE BOXER INDEMNITY 549

with the United States over the Hankow-Canton railway, was ill-timed. The foreign office found itself in substantial agreement with Liang's analysis of the situation and was willing for the moment to give him free rein in his discussions. It side-tracked Yüan's proposal for fear it would hinder the talks before they were even well begun. Yüan did not quarrel with the foreign office's decision and for the moment did nothing else to influence the terms of the remission.

William W. Rockhill assumed the responsibility for promoting within the United States government and in Peking the idea that the indemnity should be used for education. He hoped to secure from the Chinese government a formal commitment, obtained without appearing to interfere, to devote the remitted funds to sending Chinese students to the United States.[44] Rockhill feared that without this commitment the Chinese might quietly shunt his project aside and find other uses for the money. Rockhill felt his program would benefit both China and the United States. In his view, China needed nothing less than reform from the bottom up if she were to survive as an independent state. Education "on modern lines" was an instrument well suited to the task. The United States stood to gain too. Education would promote political stability and commercial progress, thus making China a sounder and richer trading partner. At the same time the rise of American educated leaders in Peking would give the United States unprecedented influence. Rockhill, convinced that much hinged on the success of his proposal, promoted it with tenacity in both capitals.

He found his colleagues in Washington receptive to his ideas and to his suspicions about China's ability to otherwise use the indemnity constructively. Huntington Wilson, the Third Assistant Secretary of State, commented, "The return of the indemnity should be used to make China do some of the things we want. Otherwise I fear her gratitude will be quite empty."[45] William Phillips, who along with Wilson kept an eye on China, shared Rockhill's hopes. At the top of Rockhill's list of supporters was Root's name. In February 1908 the Secretary of State assured Rockhill, on home leave from his post in Peking, of his backing.[46]

Outside the American government the idea of linking the remission to education strongly appealed to Protestant missionaries in China and to educators. The dean of American missionary educators and one of the few American China experts of the day, Arthur H. Smith, became next to Rockhill its most influential supporter. In March 1906 during a visit to the United States, he arranged an interview with Theodore Roosevelt to press the idea. The specifics of Smith's proposal were much like Rockhill's: the returned funds were to finance study for some Chinese students in the United States and for others in American colleges in China (which, incidentally, were for the most part Protestant missionary institutions). Smith hoped

[44] Rockhill to Roosevelt, July 12, 1905, Rockhill Papers, and to Root, August 6, 1907, NF 2413/79.

In addition to Rockhill's and Yüan's proposals, one other was advanced. Professor Jeremiah Jenks of Cornell University urged that the excess indemnity be devoted to currency reform in China. His proposal, a revival of an earlier recommendation to the Chinese government, failed to win support either in the United States or in China.

Chang Chih-tung's opposition had already proven more than enough to kill the idea. Rockhill too disparaged the plan. Jenks to John Hay, February 10, 1905, Hay Papers.

[45] Huntington Wilson, memo, November 22, 1907, NF 2413/79.

[46] Root to Rockhill, May 27, 1908, NF 2413/138a.

this act would at once recoup for the United States some of the good will dissipated in the immigration controversy and strengthen the bonds between the two countries by creating an influential body of Chinese leaders of American education.[47] As another educator put the matter in a memo set before the president, the educational project would achieve in China nothing less than "the intellectual and spiritual domination of its leaders."[48]

The efforts of the apostles of education found fertile ground in the President's conventional view of China. Roosevelt saw an uncivilized country, prey to the more vigorous countries of the West because of its weakness and lack of patriotism. Prepared by missionary propaganda to view educational work as a civilizing force among this backward race, Roosevelt quickly assented in April 1906 to the wisdom of Smith's proposal and the following year took up the theme in his annual address. Roosevelt suggested to Congress the importance of having Chinese students come to the United States to study as a means of helping China adapt to modern conditions. His suggestion, following in the text of the address his recommendation in favor of indemnity remission, could leave little doubt that the educators and Rockhill had managed to link the two together in his mind.[49]

There are good reasons why the idea should have had such wide and strong appeal in the United States. It was not novel; on the contrary, it drew its inspiration from the common wisdoms of the culture. Americans of all persuasions shared a common faith in education as a progressive force and as a cure for social and political ills. China's antipathy to Western ideals, at least as Washington hoped to introduce them, made education a necessary first step toward repealing the old order and introducing all the elements of civilization American style. Behind education would come such long sought reforms as the introduction of the gold standard, greater freedom for commerce, and increased reliance by the Chinese on foreign specialists, especially in finance, railway and mining affairs. Rockhill and Smith drew on this belief in the efficacy of education and, despite their years of experience in China, applied the ideals of their cultural world to the problems of another. The ease and speed with which they won support indicated the strength of this essential tenet of American faith.

The education proposal also drew on precedents in America's relations with China. Its antecedent was a proposal made by an old China hand of an earlier generation, S. Wells Williams, for the disposal of a different indemnity surplus. The popular idea also drew its inspiration from another memory, the Yung Wing mission. Had conservative mandarins not sabotaged this educational enterprise it might have ultimately boosted American influence to a level about which American China hands of all persuasions and degrees of expertness could only dream. The new proposal was indeed an attempt at reviving that prematurely terminated experiment

---

[47] Lawrence F. Abbott, pp. 143–145, and Arthur H. Smith, *China and America Today: A Study of Conditions and Relations* (New York, 1907), p. 220.

[48] Edmund J. James (President, University of Illinois), "Memorandum concerning the sending of an Educational Commission to China," quoted *in extenso* in Arthur H. Smith, pp. 213–218.

[49] Roosevelt's view of China appears in his let-

ters to George Ferdinand Becker, July 8, 1901, to John Hay, September 2, 1904, and to W. W. Rockhill, August 22, 1905. These letters are reproduced in Morison et al., III, 112; IV, 917; and IV, 1310, respectively. Roosevelt's letter to Smith of April 3, 1906, is in Morison et al., V, 206. The address is in *Papers Relating to the Foreign Relations of the United States, 1907* (Washington, D. C., 1910), p. lxvii.

THE BOXER INDEMNITY   551

and securing, albeit belatedly, the benefits that had been expected of Yung Wing's mission. The education plan offered a helping hand to the United States as well as China and appealed to the instincts of self-interest and altruism on which American relations with China most firmly rested.[50]

But in Peking Rockhill found himself not only confronted with Chinese resistance but challenged as well by a revived and revised version of Yüan Shih-k'ai's earlier tentative self-strengthening proposal. In 1907 associates of Yüan took up his proposal—it seems likely at the suggestion of Yüan himself—and depended on his support in the capital for getting approval for it. The authors of this new Manchurian self-strengthening proposal were the newly appointed Governor-General of Manchuria, Hsü Shih-ch'ang, and his subordinate, T'ang Shao-i, Governor of Fengtien. The two carried with them to their posts in the northeast a mandate from the Empress Dowager to strengthen China's position there against Russia and Japan.

Hsü had become alarmed during a tour of Manchuria in the winter of 1906–1907 by the threat from Russia and Japan. The economic and political backwardness of the region made it easy for them to penetrate but difficult for Chinese authorities there to defend. The urgent tasks, Hsü had reported to the throne, were to develop a Chinese-controlled system of transport, to encourage colonization, to develop natural resources, and to reform and extend the Chinese political administration. Clearly, he had concluded, a foreign loan would be needed to carry out this ambitious program.[51] Although Hsü had not yet specifically linked the loan to the Boxer remission, he watched for an opportunity, to come later in the year, to do so.

After his appointment as Governor-General in April 1907, Hsü in team with T'ang Shao-i began to consider the best means of carrying out this program. Their answer was to organize a bank under official control to allocate funds, oversee their use, and collect the profits. They began, moreover, to think of the bank as an instrument of foreign policy as well as of internal development. Manchuria was imperilled by two powers. China's best hope of maintaining its hold on the area was to neutralize Japan's and Russia's influence by encouraging other powers to take a concrete interest. The bank could be used to create this interest by getting its operating capital from third powers. T'ang saw in the bank an instrument for creating a balance of power within Manchuria while at the same time strengthening China's hand there.[52] In June 1907 Hsü formally presented the idea to the throne. In the following month he received permission to begin his search for the 20,000,000 to 30,000,000 taels (equivalent in 1908 to about $13,000,000 to $20,000,000) necessary to organize the bank.[53]

---

[50] A convenient factual summary of the earlier indemnity resulting from damage done in 1856 around Canton and its remission is Hoh Yam Tong, "The Boxer Indemnity Remissions and Education in China" (unpublished Ph.D. dissertation, Columbia University, 1933), pp. 44–50. On the Yung Wing mission see Thomas LaFargue, *China's First Hundred* (State College of Washington, 1942), and Y. C. Wang, *Chinese Intellectuals and the West 1872–1942* (University of North Carolina Press, 1966), pp. 42–45, 74–75, 84–85.

[51] Hsü Shih-ch'ang, *T'ui-keng-t'ang cheng-shu*

[*Collected official papers of Hsü Shih-ch'ang*] (Taipei reprint, 1968), I, 363–376.

[52] This is the line of reasoning pursued in a memorial of June 1907 contained in Hsü Shih-ch'ang, I, 480–487, which I believe to have been written by T'ang.

[53] Hsü's memorial is in his collected papers, I, 471–475. The edict of approval is summarized in *Te-tsung shih-lu* [*Veritable records for the reign of the Kuang-hsü Emperor*] (Taipei reprint, 1964), 593.10–11. Hsü had begun to consider the development bank idea shortly after his return to

In October the Manchurian administration began to press the bank scheme and through the remainder of 1907 and the first half of 1908 kept the proposal alive and before the attention of the central government. In mid-October Hsü set off for Peking to discuss the bank in detail.[54] In January 1908 he memorialized again on the matter,[55] and in mid-March convened a meeting in Mukden of the Manchurian Governors to finalize the proposal. The secret conference determined that the bank loan was to be floated in the United States. The loan was to receive an Imperial guarantee and to be paid off from Manchurian revenue and the uncollected part of the American Boxer indemnity.[56] With the decision made, T'ang carried the plan to Peking for further discussions with the central government.[57]

Late in 1907 Hsü and T'ang had encouraged the American consul general in Mukden, Willard Straight, to begin sounding out the opinions of his influential countrymen on the bank scheme. Straight was in an ideal position to act as intermediary between the two sides. He had established a confidential relationship with both T'ang and E. H. Harriman, the American railway magnate interested in Manchurian enterprises, and his official status permitted him to carry the Chinese proposal directly to the State Department. Straight was eager to make a reality of the bank proposal, which, if the Boxer indemnity financed it, would enhance American interests in Manchuria and strike a blow for China and the United States against Japan. In his enthusiasm Straight adopted the bank proposal and pushed it forward as if it were his own. Straight's first opportunity for advocacy came with the visit to China of Secretary of War William Howard Taft in the fall of 1907. Known to share along with Root the President's confidence, Taft would make a convert of importance. As his party, which Straight had joined in Vladivostok, sped along the Russian railway, Straight briefed the Secretary on Manchurian affairs and on the bank proposal. He played with apparent success on the theme that the United States should return the excess indemnity without strings and that the Chinese proposal for its use put within the grasp of the United States a rare opportunity to further its own and China's interests in Manchuria. When Straight got off the train in Harbin, he carried Taft's approval of the plan and his assurances that Root and Roosevelt would give it "favorable consideration."[58]

Straight hoped to use Taft's approval as a lever to nudge the State Department toward consideration of the bank-indemnity proposal. "The Secretary of War, while wishing it clearly understood that the American government could not presume to dictate the purpose for which the released portion of the Indemnity should be employed, nevertheless thought that the suggestion . . . , should it emanate from China herself, might be favorably received."[59] However, Taft, instead of promoting Straight's proposal, retreated from his brief foray into the world of foreign policy

Peking from his inspection tour of Manchuria. His memo on it is in his collected works, III, 1755–1776.

[54] Hsü Shih-ch'ang, I, 550–557, for the memorial of October 21, 1907; and Willard Straight to the Assistant Secretary of State, November 9, 1907, NF 2321/16.

[55] Hsü Shih-ch'ang, II, 661–663, for the memorial of January 3, 1908.

[56] Straight to Henry Fletcher, March 11 and 12, 1908, found in Fletcher Papers, Library of Congress, and NF 2413/129, respectively.

[57] Rockhill to Root, April 28, 1908, NF 2112/27.

[58] Straight, memo, November 23, 1907, NF 2413/93. See also the memo which he presented to Taft during the interview and his progress report to Taft, both dated December 2, 1907, NF 2413/98–99.

[59] Straight to the Assistant Secretary of State, December 9, 1908, NF 2413/91. See also Straight to Fletcher, March 12, 1908, NF 2413/129.

THE BOXER INDEMNITY   553

making back to the safety of administering the War Department and to the pressing obligations assumed by his quest for the presidential nomination. Straight was left isolated in his unpopular position. The chief of the consular bureau curtly informed him he was not to meddle further.[60]

T'ang Shao-i, with whom Straight was to remain in contact, now took up the task of actively promoting the bank scheme on the American side. While in Peking during the summer of 1908 consulting with the central government on Manchurian affairs, T'ang paid a visit to Rockhill to explain his plan. He hoped to neutralize the well known objections of the American Minister with the assurance that the bank would promote education. Rockhill, already familiar with the plan from Straight, was not to be won to it and told his visitor so.[61]

T'ang at the same time continued his efforts, begun the previous year, to draw E. H. Harriman into a loan agreement. Now, however, T'ang wished to interest him in a bank rather than in a railway. He worked through Straight to break down the American financier's insistence on investing only in railways. T'ang tantalized him with the prospect that participation in the Manchurian bank would not only get Harriman his Manchurian railway but also win for him a major role in national railway enterprise. "The prospect of directing the railways of a nation," which T'ang offered, was powerful bait.[62] Although T'ang could not have seriously meant what he said, his proposition—serious or not—won Harriman. Harriman replied that he would begin discussions as soon as the Chinese had "an immediate, clear, offer" to make on the railway, even if it were tied to the bank.[63]

Hsü and T'ang thereupon decided that the next logical step was to confront the State Department with China's wishes on the disposal of the excess indemnity and to negotiate a loan agreement, using the indemnity as security, with Harriman in New York. They could bypass Rockhill by sending a special representative. Yüan Shih-k'ai supported the idea and accordingly slipped into a Wai-wu Pu memorial on the remission of the Boxer indemnity a seemingly innocuous request that a special minister travel to the United States to offer thanks for the generous deed. Several days later the requested imperial edict was issued naming T'ang for the job.[64]

When T'ang in the spring of 1908 revealed the details of his project to use the indemnity for a Manchurian bank, Rockhill was astounded. He wrote back to Root, "I do not anticipate the T'ang memorial [on the bank loan] will be acted upon; it seems to me perfectly impracticable. I am only astonished that such an able man as T'ang could have evolved it."[65] Rockhill, however, wisely did not take the Chinese project's failure for granted. He began to press his views on the Wai-wu Pu with new

[60] Wilbur J. Carr to Straight, February 10, 1908, NF 2413/92–94.

[61] Rockhill to Root, April 28, 1908, NF 2112/27.

[62] The quote is from Straight to Harriman, October 7, 1907. See also Straight to Harriman, February 16, 1908. Both are in Straight Papers, John M. Olin Library, Cornell University. Straight to Fletcher, March 17, 1908, Fletcher Papers, describes T'ang's views on the role Harriman might play.

[63] Alex Millar (Harriman's secretary) to Straight, June 12, 1908, Straight Papers. See also Harriman

to Straight, June 5, 1908, Straight Papers.

[64] Wai-wu Pu, memorial, misfiled under July 23, 1908, WWP Indemnity File. The Imperial edict of July 18, 1908, appears in Wang Yen-wei and Wang Liang (compilers), Ch'ing-chi wai-chiao shih-liao: Kuang-hsü ch'ao [Historical materials on late Ch'ing diplomacy: the Kuang-hsü reign] (Peking, 1935), 215.14. See also Rockhill to Root, July 30, 1908, NF 2413/157.

[65] Rockhill to Root, April 28, 1908, NF 2112/27.

energy. As early as 1905 Rockhill had let the Chinese know that the American government favored using the indemnity for education. He genuinely believed that he had secured Yüan Shih-k'ai's tentative assent to the education project. Rockhill clearly preferred to discount whatever reservation Yüan might have expressed; Yüan in turn had every reason to treat the Minister's pet project agreeably if doing so would speed up the indemnity remission.[66]

Rockhill began in the spring of 1908 to seek formal Chinese approval of his education scheme. He bluntly informed representatives of the Wai-wu Pu that "any action on the part of China which might indicate a disposition to ignore the assurances heretofore given us . . . might indefinitely delay final action in the matter."[67] On May 27, 1908, he received notice from Root that Congress had approved remission and that he could begin formal consultations with the Chinese foreign office.[68] On June 10 Liang Tun-yen, an envoy from Yüan Shih-k'ai, the new president of the Wai-wu Pu, obtained from Rockhill a draft note stating the American terms. Liang returned to see Rockhill on June 30 and announced that the Wai-wu Pu's senior officials had agreed to accept the note substantially as Rockhill had drafted it. It appeared that the Chinese by taking up the educational proposal on Rockhill's terms had bowed to his hard line. But in fact their formal reply did not make the link between the indemnity money and education explicit. Rockhill discovered this and again warned that having failed "clearly and formally" to accept the American proposal *in toto*, the Chinese government might for the moment lose the excess indemnity. On July 9 Rockhill threatened for the third time, once again to T'ang, that the return of the indemnity was conditional.

The persistent refusal of the Wai-wu Pu unequivocally to tie the remission to the educational mission brought to the Minister's mind a new fear, that his project might founder at the last on Chinese intransigeance. When T'ang proposed that a supplementary note giving details of the educational scheme could accompany the Wai-wu Pu's note of thanks for the remission and serve as a substitute for the explicit and formal pledge that the United States had been working for, Rockhill seized on the suggestion to break the deadlock and save his hopes. The Chinese regained the indemnity without losing the appearance of autonomy on its use.

However, no sooner had Rockhill agreed to the bargain than he discovered the Chinese foreign office looking for loopholes. On July 11 Liang Tun-yen presented for Rockhill's inspection the supplementary note. In it Rockhill found omitted—quite inadvertently, Liang smoothly informed him—the number of years the educational project was to run. With that "error" corrected, Rockhill on July 14 formally informed the foreign office of the indemnity remission; the Wai-wu Pu at the same time, as prearranged, replied with its thanks and informed Rockhill of its desire to meet the wishes of the President that Chinese students come to the United States to study. In the supplementary note, crucial to the compromise, the Wai-wu Pu spelled out the details of the arrangement: the first four years China

---

[66] *Ibid.*, and Rockhill to Roosevelt, July 12, 1905, Rockhill Papers, contain references to these informal assurances.

[67] Rockhill thus summarized his comments to T'ang in his despatch to Root of April 28, 1908, NF 2112/27.

[68] Root to Rockhill, May 27, 1908, NF 2413/138a.

THE BOXER INDEMNITY   555

would send one hundred students annually; thereafter, throughout the period of the remission, at least fifty students would go annually. The Wai-wu Pu nowhere acknowledged the connection between the remission and the educational project. On that fine point the agreement rested.[69]

Rockhill's discovery later in the month that T'ang was to go to the United States revealed to him that the Chinese had not yet given up on the bank plan. Rockhill immediately set to work to bolster his position in Washington. He warned William Phillips that the Chinese, hard pressed for funds, were sending T'ang in search of relief and that the State Department must not allow Chinese wishes to upset a plan designed for their own good. "The carrying out of the educational mission is, in the long run, an infinitely more valuable return for the money than the wildcat schemes it would be employed in by the 'Manchurian Bank.' "[70]

Phillips prepared the defenses in Washington against marauding Chinese. He alerted his superiors to the danger and suggested that they deter T'ang by publicizing the indemnity compromise which Rockhill had just reached in Peking. "This having been done, T'ang will hesitate to request us to let China make use of the money for Manchurian purposes, which he really has a right to do, strictly speaking. . . ."[71] Rockhill also took the precaution of warning Root to be on his guard. Rockhill cautioned that T'ang, despite his incapacity ("densely ignorant on all financial questions, and of political economy I doubt if he . . . know[s] even the name"), was nevertheless "extremely ambitious and so long as his patron, Yüan Shih-k'ai, remains in power, T'ang will have to be counted with."[72] Duly warned, Root joined in the preparations for T'ang's arrival by approving the publicity plan. Phillips confidentially assured Rockhill that "every one here [is] absolutely in sympathy with your idea."[73]

T'ang left China publicly commanded to give thanks for the return of the indemnity and secretly authorized to negotiate a loan. He reached Washington on November 30, 1908, but Rockhill's warnings, freely circulated by Phillips, had had the intended effect. T'ang made no progress with the unfriendly State Department. He found it difficult even to get to see the Secretary of State to discuss the proposal to use the indemnity remission as security for a loan.[74] Frustrated, T'ang left for Europe in January 1909.

The Roosevelt administration was not interested in creating complications in the Far East. Phillips told Rockhill as much: "I do not think the Department intends to have trouble in Manchuria, either with Russia or Japan. The Secretary

---

[69] The account of Rockhill's negotiations are drawn primarily from his detailed report to Root, July 16, 1908, and his letter to Phillips, August 1, 1908, NF 2413/146 and 148 respectively. Also see Rockhill to Root, telegram, July 15, 1908, NF 2413/140, and the formal notes exchanged by Rockhill and the Wai-wu Pu, WWP Indemnity File.

[70] Rockhill to Phillips, August 1, 1908, NF 2413/148.

[71] Phillips to Alvey A. Adee, memo, September 9, 1908, NF 2413/148.

[72] Rockhill to Root, July 30, 1908, NF 2413/

157.

[73] Phillips to Rockhill, September 19, 1908, Rockhill Papers.

[74] Huntington Wilson to Root, memo, December 5, 1908, and undated Straight memo, both in NF 2413/220. The record of T'ang's unproductive interview with Root on December 9, 1908, is in NF 2413/218.

For greater detail on the ambitious Chinese plans for Manchuria, including the unsuccessful effort to enlist American support in 1907 and 1908, see my dissertation, "Frontier Defense and the Open Door," pp. 147–218.

is especially anxious not to become embroiled in little incidents with either of those two powers...."[75] T'ang, who was playing for high stakes in Manchuria, had come to the United States looking for a backer but found the American government suspicious of him and unwilling to accept the risks even at second hand. The Root-Takahira agreement, concluded shortly before T'ang's arrival and guaranteeing the *status quo* in the Pacific, was a concrete expression of the administration's cautiousness.

Yet another obstacle to the success of T'ang's mission was the death of the Empress Dowager and its unsettling effect on Peking politics. T'ang had to move cautiously on the Harriman loan until certain of his own standing at home and that of Yüan Shih-k'ai, on whose support his mission depended. At the same time, Washington's open opposition to T'ang's plan for use of the indemnity in support of China's position in Manchuria and the unexpected conclusion of the Root–Takahira agreement mocked Yüan's hopes for a policy of limited cooperation with the United States. The double failure made Yüan vulnerable to attack by his political opponents, and as the attacks, justified on more grounds than one, made headway, T'ang grew even more cautious. Thus, as the setback to T'ang's mission and to misplaced hopes for American assistance provided a handy pretext for toppling Yüan, so also did Yüan's fall further diminish the prospect of T'ang's salvaging anything for Manchuria.

The State Department and Rockhill were determined to protect the indemnity's ties to education and refused to give serious consideration to this opportunity to defend American interests in Manchuria by helping China to strengthen its position there. They altogether ignored the desperate need of the Chinese for funds to carry on their program of frontier defense and their clear preference to "strengthen their country a bit before distributing dynamics and moral philosophy in prize packages."[76] They could not recognize China's determined and intelligent attempt to cope with crisis in Manchuria.

The old version of the remission does not stand up under examination. American indemnity claims were excessive, and Secretary of State John Hay knew it from the start. The administration of Theodore Roosevelt ignored Chinese claims on the surplus as long as possible and finally under pressure returned the funds—but only on the condition that they be used not as China but as the United States wished. The only reservoir of good will the remission helped to fill was in the imagination of Americans.

The decision to press the education scheme arose in part from a feeling of cultural superiority and a desire to help a backward ward along the path of progress. Americans pressed that scheme to prevent the Chinese government from squandering the money and to insure for the Chinese people some benefit from the remission. American policy makers, ever suspicious, found in China's plans for Manchuria

---

[75] Phillips to Rockhill, September 19, 1908, Rockhill Papers. Two recent works on Roosevelt's Far Eastern policy make quite clear that he was concerned that China questions not trouble his relations with Japan. See Charles E. Neu, *An Uncertain Friendship: Theodore Roosevelt and Japan,* *1906–1909* (Harvard University Press, 1967); and Raymond A. Esthus, *Theodore Roosevelt and Japan* (University of Washington Press, 1966).

[76] Straight (paraphrasing T'ang) to Fletcher, March 17, 1908, Fletcher Papers.

the kind of "wildcat" project they had grown to expect from the Chinese. For its part the Chinese government was quick to see the American attitude as a form of interference. The United States had unfairly taken the money and now refused to return it for the use its rightful owners considered most urgent. The conditions the United States attached to the remission violated the integrity of China's financial administration, and the Chinese foreign office, intent on maintaining at least the semblance of administrative autonomy, adamantly refused formally to accept the American demand. The Chinese had no wish to set a precedent for other conditional remissions and most of all desired to give no cause for alarm by appearing to lose to the Americans another stitch of financial independence.

Some Chinese recognized in America's education project not just interference but an even more dangerous frontal assault on Chinese values. Chang Chih-tung, whose popular formulation, "Western studies for practical affairs; Chinese studies for the essentials," guided China's educational reform in the late Ch'ing, predictably resisted this attempt to reverse priorities by putting Western values at the center of Chinese education. He began his battle, waged through the Board of Education, in late 1907 and carried it to a successful conclusion in September 1909. His stubborn opposition forced the State Department to abandon its hopes of having an American appointed by the Chinese government to superintend students in the United States. Chang insured a modicum of Chinese control by putting in the safe hands of the Board of Education the responsibility for selecting students to go to the United States. The American legation, excluded from shaping the regulations for the educational mission closer to its heart's desire, could only complain that these "conservatives" were eliminating many of the candidates well prepared in Western subjects by unreasonably severe examinations in Chinese studies.[77]

Americans in their fervor to educate the Chinese acted on an ethnocentric conviction that China's salvation could only come through conversion to Western moral, economic and political values. "Education will sweep away the incrustations that hamper progress, and as each improvement in the ranks of the official class occurs, such addition will hasten the advance and spread of education. Thus the downfall of one will go hand in hand with the rise of the other."[78] Americans in dealing with China clung to familiar verities with as much ardor as the notoriously culture-bound Chinese, and the Chinese defended their values with as much determination as the zealous promoters of the education project advanced their scheme.

While the American government used the indemnity remission to promote values considered essential to China's survival, it did not forget its own self-interest. Americans argued that the indemnity education program would benefit China, but they did not try to hide the benefits they hoped to derive from a corps of American-educated Chinese leaders.

They will be studying American institutions, making American friends, and coming back here to favor America for China in its foreign relations. Talk about a Chinese

---

[77] Wai-wu Pu to the Board of Education, December 14, 1907, and to the Board of Revenue, December 3, 1907, both in Supplementary WWP Indemnity File; Board of Education to the Wai-wu Pu, September 13, 1908, WWP Indemnity File; and Wai-wu Pu and Board of Education, joint memorial, June 20, 1909, reproduced in Shu Hsin-

ch'eng, *Chin-tai Chung-kuo liu-hsüeh shih* [*A modern history of Chinese students abroad*] (Shanghai, 1927), pp. 75–78. The relevant State Department documents are in NF 2413/243, 256, 274, and in NF 5315/349.

[78] William B. Parsons, *An American Engineer in China* (New York, 1900), pp. 311–312.

alliance! The return of that indemnity was the most profitable work Uncle Sam ever did. . . . They will form a force in our favor so strong that no other government or trade element of Europe can compete with it.[79]

The education enthusiasts would have seen their self-interested hopes dissolve before their eyes if they had ever given the education-leadership proposition serious thought. Entranced by the illusion of education as an easy route to greater influence in China, they never realized the irony in the active opposition of three notable alumni of the Yung Wing mission—T'ang Shao-i, Liang Ch'eng and Liang Tun-yen—to this plan to train a generation of pro-American leaders in China. In addition, the State Department, which knew that Chinese students suffered from discrimination in American colleges, managed to smother the obvious thought that resentment over American insults might outweigh gratitude for access to American education.[80] The charge that the indemnity remission was a "cultural investment" made with the hope of economic dividends seems altogether fair and consistent with the arguments used by the American proponents of the education scheme.

In serving its self-interest the American government also found the indemnity a valuable hostage to guarantee Chinese good behavior. The Roosevelt administration did not hesitate to threaten withholding the surplus to bring the Chinese government to heel during the controversies and incidents plaguing relations during 1905. The administration of William Howard Taft proved equally adept at using it to coerce China. During the Hukuang railway controversy, which arose in the spring of 1909, the new American administration found its patience strained by Peking's opposition to Americans' sharing in the loan and instructed the Peking legation to feel free to use the unreturned money to force compliance with United States demands. "If the Government of China should now fail scrupulously to respect its engagements the President might well deem it just to recoup the injury to America involved in such a breach of faith by exercising his authority to discontinue our remission of [the] indemnity."[81] Taft and Knox, like Roosevelt and Root, employed the indemnity to insure China's good behavior in trying times.

American leaders in the early twentieth century were convinced that their Chinese counterparts, relics of the discredited past, lacked the intelligence and will to protect themselves or America's vital stake in China. Even the handful of American "China experts" seldom clearly or sympathetically considered the divergences in the values and interests of the two countries. The room for confusion, misunderstanding and recrimination in this unequal and distant relationship was naturally great. The American government, which acted on assumptions it never seriously questioned and made decisions which took no serious account of China's views, gave good cause for proud and patriotic Chinese to resent its attitude and feel frustrated by its policy. Like the host who finds himself supplanted in his own home by his dinner guest, the Chinese had reason to complain, as one Chinese editor did in

---

[79] Frank G. Carpenter quoted in "The Awakening of China," *Daily Consular and Trade Reports*, no. 3636 (Nov. 15, 1909), pp. 8–9.

[80] Phillips to E. C. Baker, memo, September 3, 1909, NF 2413/268–270.

[81] Huntington Wilson to Peking legation, telegram, June 19, 1909, NF 5315/259.

THE BOXER INDEMNITY   559

1908, "It is truly as if our country were a guest whose affairs were to be managed by these nations which make arrangements together."[82] Those who perpetuate the old fable of magnanimity and gratitude are finding comfort in a false image of themselves and of the Chinese.

---

[82] *Chung-yang ta-t'ung jih-pao* [*Central daily news*], edition in December 1908, translated in NF 16533/59.

12

The Panama Canal and Sea Power in the Pacific

Alfred Thayer Mahan

UNLESS present expectation be greatly deceived, within two decades two events will have altered very materially the territorial conditions which underlie the capacity of the United States to exert power at sea. Such changes on land influence materially the subsequent dispositions of the navy, enabling it to be more effectively utilized. One of these events will be the opening of the Panama Canal. The other, already past, has been the war with Spain, issuing in the independence of Cuba from European control and in the territorial acquisitions of the United States resulting from the war.

From a military point of view, these acquisitions have advanced the southern maritime frontier of this country from the Gulf coast to a line coincident with the south shore of Cuba, prolonged to Porto Rico; throwing into the second line the Gulf harbors, from Key West to the Mississippi. These are reduced thus to the order of purely defensive ports, instead of the primary rank of naval bases for offensive operations held by them twenty years ago—a change to which have contributed also the hydrographic

ARMAMENTS AND ARBITRATION

difficulties of entrance and exit consequent upon the greatly increased size of battle-ships. This new condition is summarized in, and effected by, the cession of Guantanamo as a naval base; provided, of course, that due measures are taken for the security of the base, so that ships may not be tied to the defense of a position the one value of which will be that the fleet can depend upon it for supplies and repairs, yet leave it for a measurable time to its own protection, sure of finding it and its resources safe upon return.

The occupation of the Canal Zone under conditions of complete sovereignty (with qualified exceptions in the cities of Colon and Panama) may be regarded accurately, from the military point of view, as a most helpful modification of our proper coast-line, making it, by the interposition of Guantanamo, practically continuous for a fleet from the Atlantic to the Pacific. It will be continuous because possessing throughout adequate points of support— the one service which, from the military point of view, the land renders to the sea. To secure this condition, however, the Canal, like Guantanamo, must be fortified. There is, unhappily, much exaggerated talk on one side and the other as to the relative advantages of navies and fortifications for purposes of defense. Neither is secure without the other. As I have said, a fleet must be able to go away for a calculated time, with a reasonable prospect of finding its ports unsurprised, still its own, when it

PANAMA CANAL AND SEA POWER

returns. The port must be able to spare the fleet for a similar period, confident that it can look out for itself till reinforced or supplied. The analogy is that of an army in campaign, which is crippled in movement if it has to cover its bases as well as to carry on other necessary operations.

A number of eminent citizens, more actuated by a commendable desire for peace than instructed in military considerations, not long ago put their names to a paper directed against the fortification of the Canal. In this they say, among other things, "With all the fortifications possible it is still apparent that . . . in time of war a guard of battle-ships at each of its entrances would be an absolute necessity, and equally apparent that with such a guard the fortifications would be unnecessary." I fear some naval officers, at home and abroad, dubbed in England the Blue Water School, are partly responsible for this popular impression of the need of the constant presence of battle-ships. It is precisely in order that a constant guard of battle-ships may not be necessary that fortifications are requisite. Fortifications liberate a fleet for action whenever elsewhere required; and, by preserving the Canal for use as a bridge between the two oceans, render less imperative the maintenance of a big fleet in both.

The maintenance of the Canal in effective operation is one of the large elements in the future development of sea power in the Pacific. No other nation has in the Canal the same interest of self-preserva-

ARMAMENTS AND ARBITRATION

tion that the United States has. Not only is this true as regards the Panama Canal, but no similar condition of dependence upon a canal exists anywhere else to near the same degree. The closest parallel is Suez, as compared with the Cape of Good Hope. Suez offers Great Britain an inside route to her great Australasian colonies, as well as to India; but the existence of the British Empire does not depend upon that route as vitally as the ability of our thickly settled Atlantic coast to come to the aid of the Pacific depends upon Panama, as compared with Magellan. This necessity is so urgent as to make the Canal, as before said, essentially a part of the coast-line of the United States.

The primary object of the Canal may have been commercial, or it may have been military. I doubt whether many of those conspicuous in its advocacy and inception analyzed to themselves which of these two obvious features was chief in their individual estimation. From either point of view, and from both, the opening of the Canal will conduce decisively to influence the development of sea power upon the Pacific. Its effect will be much the same as that of the construction of a new railroad judiciously planned, which opens out the new country through which it passes, or to which it leads, and thus not only renders it available to commerce, but by perpetual interaction of population and production increases both. More people, more wants; more

PANAMA CANAL AND SEA POWER

people, more production. Both wants and production mean increased transportation.

This effect of the Panama Canal upon sea power will have two principal aspects—one civil, one military. The civil effect will be the more rapid peopling of the Pacific coasts of North and South America, with consequent necessary increase of commerce. The military effect will be the facility with which the navy of the United States, and that of the government controlling Canada, can pass from one side to the other, in support of either coast as needed. I say somewhat generally, but advisedly, the government controlling Canada; for, while Canada is a part of the British Empire, and therefore will receive the support of the British navy where its interests are concerned, and while Canada also, taken as a whole, is for the time present attached to the British connection, as the Thirteen Colonies were from 1732 to 1770, it is difficult, in view of current political discussions in Canada, especially those touching the question of support to the empire, not to feel that the preponderant tone there does not in this respect reflect that of Australia, New Zealand, or even of South Africa. The strong opposition in the French provinces to the government proposals for the development of a Canadian navy, the apologetic defense of the measure by the then premier, Sir Wilfrid Laurier, himself a French Canadian, in which the assertion of Canadian independence of action is more conspicuous than that of devotion to imperial in-

ARMAMENTS AND ARBITRATION

terests, tend to prove a looseness of allegiance, which already simulates the independence of separation and may issue in it. After these words were written, the inference contained in them received support from the reported effect produced upon imperialistic sentiment in Great Britain by the Reciprocity agreement with the United States framed by Sir Wilfrid Laurier's government. In short, there does not appear to be between Canada and Great Britain that strong dependence of mutual interest in defense, of which the British navy is the symbol and the instrument, and which binds together the other self-governing communities. I regret this, because I believe it the advantage of the United States that Great Britain, by her relations to Canada, should be strongly committed to the naval support of the north Pacific coasts. The ultimate issue will manifestly affect the question of sea power in the Pacific, according as it involves the British navy or only a Canadian. Meantime, under present conditions, the opening of the Canal will bring the British navy six thousand miles nearer the Pacific coast of Canada.

The greatest factor of sea power in any region is the distribution and numbers of the populations, and their characteristics, as permitting the formation and maintenance of stable and efficient governments. Such stability and efficiency depend upon racial traits, the distinguishing element of which is not so much the economical efficiency of the individual citizen as his political capacity for sustained

PANAMA CANAL AND SEA POWER

corporate action—action which, however marked by internal contentions, is in the main result homogeneous and organic. As a matter of modern history, so far, this capacity has been confined to nations of European civilization, with the recent exception of Japan. At times, it is true, great masses of men have for a period moved in unison, as by instinct, with an impetus that nothing for the moment could resist. The Huns, the Arabs, the Turks, are instances in point; but none would cite either the peoples or their governments as instances of political efficiency. At other times great personages have built up an immense sway upon their own personality alone; but the transiency of such is too proverbial for indication. The political aptitudes of the average citizen, steadied by tried political institutions, are the sole ground of ultimate national effectiveness.

The most immediate, the foremost, question of the Pacific, as affecting sea power, therefore, is the filling-up of the now partly vacant regions, our own Pacific coast, with that of the British Empire in Canada and in Australasia, by a population of European derivation. It is most desirable that such immigration should be from northern Europe, because there is found the stock temperamentally most consonant to the local institutions; but, from whencesoever coming, immigrants to all the regions named will find awaiting them settled forms of government, differing from one another much in details and somewhat in views, but all derived ultimately

ARMAMENTS AND ARBITRATION

from the traditional ideals which we call Anglo-Saxon, to which we who have inherited them are apt to attach peculiar value and virtue. Let us not forget that the roots can be traced to the old days when the Angles and the Saxons really dwelt on the east side of the North Sea, before they found a new home in England. Thus long continuity of existence, power of development, faculty to adapt themselves to many differing circumstances of environment, as well as to absorb and to assimilate alien elements, have given a proof of their excellence more decisive than the perhaps too partial estimate of those who live under them.

That the Panama Canal can affect the rapid peopling of the American Pacific coasts is as evident as it is to be desired. That a ship-load of immigrants can be carried through relatively quiet seas direct to the Pacific ports, without the tiresome and expensive transcontinental journey by rail, will be an inestimable contribution toward overcoming the problems of distribution and of labor. It will disperse also the threatening question of Asiatic immigration to the northern Pacific coasts by filling up the ground—the only perfectly sound provision for the future. No European labor element thinks of emigrating to Asia, for the land there is already overcrowded. Were conditions reversed, Asiatic governments and working-men would feel the same objection as is now felt throughout the American Pacific to an abundant influx of laborers of wholly

PANAMA CANAL AND SEA POWER

different traditions, who do not assimilate socially and cannot be assimilated politically. Here is no question of superiority or inferiority of race, the intrusion of which simply draws a misleading trail across the decisive reason, which is the fundamental distinctions of origin and of historical development. Already, scarcely a month after the new treaty with Japan was confirmed, the attempt has been again made thus to confuse the issue, if the quotation from a Japanese periodical is to be accepted.[1] The question is one of age-long differences, proceeding from age-long separations, producing variations of ideas which do not allow intermingling, and consequently, if admitted, are ominous of national weakness through flaws in homogeneity. The radical difference between the Oriental and the Occidental, which is constantly insisted upon, occasions incompatibility of close association in large numbers for the present, and for any near future.

The existing tendency of immigration to seek our Pacific coast is seen from the recent census, which shows that those States have progressed in population to a greater extent, proportionately, than most other parts of the country. While, however, such

---

[1] The *Japanese American Commercial Weekly*, quoted in the New York *Tribune*, March 27, 1911. " The present understanding with regard to Japanese immigration will be adhered to by the Japanese government with all its sincerity. Yet there is no denying the fact that the Japanese people in general are not satisfied with the arrangement. They cannot help feeling that they are not receiving fair treatment from the American government; *that the exclusion agreement stamps upon them the stigma of inferiority.*" (My Italics.)

ARMAMENTS AND ARBITRATION

result is indicative of tendency, it must be remembered that ratio of increase does not prove corresponding absolute gain; fifty per cent. on one thousand only equals twenty-five on two thousand. The Pacific coast States are still scantily peopled. Thus Washington contains 17 persons to the square mile, Oregon 7, California 15; whereas New York has 191 and Ohio 117.[1] The result of such conditions, where no artificial obstacle intervenes, is seen in Hawaii. These islands geographically belong to the American continent, being distant from it only 2,100 miles, whereas they are 3,400 from Japan, the nearest part of Asia; yet a plurality of the population is Japanese, from an immigration which began only forty years ago. The political—international—result may not improbably be traced in the well-known intimation of the Japanese government to that of the United States in 1897 that it could not see without concern the annexation of the islands. If the local needs which caused this condition had occurred after the opening of the Canal, the required labor could have been introduced from southern Europe,[2] which is now furnishing an excellent element to Cuba. In such case Hawaii as a naval base would have received a reinforcement of military strength, in a domiciled population of European derivation and traditions.

The Hawaiian group is an outpost of the United

[1] Census of 1910.
[2] As it is, there are over 15,000 Portuguese in the islands.

164

PANAMA CANAL AND SEA POWER

States of first importance to the security of the Pacific coast; but its situation is one of peculiar exposure. During the eighteenth century Great Britain at Gibraltar held the entrance of the Mediterranean successfully against all comers; but in the same period she twice lost Minorca, an outpost like Hawaii, because the navy was too heavily engaged in the Atlantic, and the land forces elsewhere, to afford relief. In case of the fall of Pearl Harbor, where the defense of Hawaii is concentrated, an enemy temporarily superior to the United States in local naval force would become possessed of a fortified permanent base of operations within half-steaming distance of the Pacific shore. On that shore, in furtherance of his designs, he could establish temporary depots for coaling and repairs; as Japan in the recent war did at the Elliott Islands, sixty miles from Port Arthur, then the decisive objective of her military and naval operations. Such advanced temporary positions need a permanent base not too far distant, such as the Japanese home ports Sasebo and Kure afforded the Elliott Islands, and as Pearl Harbor in the instance considered would to a navy resting upon it.

But if Pearl Harbor should hold out successfully, a superior American fleet on arrival finds there a secure base of operations, which with its own command of the water, due to its superior strength, enables it to neutralize and ultimately to overthrow any system of operations or attack resting on

ARMAMENTS AND ARBITRATION

improvised bases and inferior fleet force. One has only to imagine the effect upon the Japanese land operations in Manchuria if Rozhestvensky had destroyed Togo's fleet and so established control of the water between Japan and Manchuria. The same line of reasoning applies to Corregidor Island, in Manila Bay, qualified by the greater distance of the Philippines from America.

The Pacific coast of America is less thickly populated, less extensively developed, than the Atlantic. Labor there is dearer, and the local coal as yet distinctly inferior for naval purposes to Eastern coal, necessitating sending fuel there. All upon which a fleet depends for vitality is less abundant, less cheap, and therefore more remote. These economical reasons, until qualified by military urgency, render expedient the maintenance of the fleet in the Atlantic. Division of it is forbidden by military considerations, in that it is too small; the half is weaker than any probable enemy. At present, not less than four months would be required for the battle-fleet to reach Pearl Harbor in effective condition. With the Canal, less than four weeks would be necessary.

These considerations affect the time that Pearl Harbor needs to hold out, and illustrate the military gain from the Canal; but they do not affect in any sense the necessity for a superior navy. Canal or no canal, if a fleet be distinctly inferior, it can protect the coast committed to its charge only to a limited degree and for a limited time, unless it can

PANAMA CANAL AND SEA POWER

reverse the balance by professional skill. The professional skill may be forthcoming—it is the affair of the commander-in-chief—but real naval security is original superiority of force, and that is the affair of the nation represented in Congress.

The great English-speaking colonies of Australia and New Zealand will be less immediately and directly affected as to populating by the Panama Canal; but its influence upon Pacific America, including Hawaii, cannot be a matter of small importance to communities which share with equal fervor the determination that their land shall be peopled by men of European antecedents. This identity of feeling on the subject of Asiatic immigration between Australia and the North American Pacific, both inheritors of the same political tradition, is certain to create political sympathies, and may drag into a common action the nations of which each forms a part. This particular determination, in the midst of that recent prevalent unrest which is called the Awakening of the East, is probably the very largest factor in the future of the Pacific, and one which eventually will draw in most of the West-European nations in support of their present possessions in the East. Immediately north of Australia, barricading it, as it were, from west to east, is a veritable Caribbean of European tropical possessions—Sumatra, Java, to New Guinea—distributed between Germany, Great Britain, and Holland; while immediately north of them again come the

ARMAMENTS AND ARBITRATION

Philippines under American administration. It is needless to say that support to such distant dependencies means military sea power; but it is less obvious, until heeded, that the tendency will impart a common object—a solidarity of interest—which may go far toward composing present rivalries and jealousies in Europe. To none, however, can this interest be so vital as to Great Britain, because Australasia is not to her a dominion over alien races, as India is, and as are most European possessions in the East. The Australians and New-Zealanders are her own flesh and blood; and, should the question of support to them arise, the Panama Canal offers an alternative route not greatly longer to eastern Australia, and shorter by over twelve hundred miles to New Zealand. It is, however, in the developed power of Pacific America, including Canada, that Australia in the future will find the great significance of the Panama Canal.

The question of immigration is now engaging the aroused attention of the new "Labor" government in Australia. Equally with our own Pacific slope, peopling will be there a large influence in the sea power of the Pacific. The question is felt to be urgent, because much of the vast territory of Australia is empty. Excluding aborigines, the population is less than two to the square mile. In New Zealand the proportion is only nine. The huge tropical district in Australia known as the Northern Territory, with an area of 523,620 square miles, con-

PANAMA CANAL AND SEA POWER

tains but one thousand whites. After a seeming attempt to coddle the labor question, to sustain high wages by discouraging immigration, Australia is awaking to the untenable and perilous situation in which a people is placed when seeking to hold a great inheritance which they neither occupy nor by numbers can develop. It matters not for the moment whence the danger may come. From some quarter it will, soon or late—probably soon. Overcrowded millions not far off will not look indefinitely upon open pastures denied them only by a claim of pre-emption. An abundant population in possession is at once a reason and a force.

To those who do not follow passing events which seem remote from ourselves, it should be of interest to recall—for it is cognate to our subject—that the still recent year 1910 witnessed the visit to Australia and New Zealand of Lord Kitchener, the greatest military organizer and most distinguished British soldier now in active service. The object desired by the colonial governments was that a scheme of defense based upon territory, population, and resources should be devised, after personal examination, by the man who, as commander-in-chief in India, had recast comprehensively the military system upon which rests the defense of three hundred millions of people, and of a territory which in area is a continent. The broad details of his recommendations have been made known through the press, but are not here material. It is sufficient to

ARMAMENTS AND ARBITRATION

say that, since his departure, a new "Labor" government of the commonwealth has come into power, and in all decisive particulars has adopted his plan. The nature of the popular preponderance behind this government is sufficiently indicated by the name—Labor. It is the first since the organization of the Commonwealth—the union of the several states—that has possessed a homogeneous working majority; and it is significant of the future that the first care of a labor ministry has been to provide an efficient military organization, and to entertain measures for the development of a railway system which shall minister not only to economical development, but to national military security.

In introducing the necessary legislation the Minister of Defense, after fully adopting Lord Kitchener's scheme, "attacked those who placed faith in arbitration." He declared "that Australia would refuse to arbitrate about Asiatic exclusion, and must be prepared to maintain its own laws against attack. If any one asked why the Labor party was especially keen on military matters, the answer was that the proposed social and industrial reforms of the party required freedom from disturbance, which they must effectively secure."[1] In the Australian press of the following day, quoted in telegrams to the London *Times*, no dissent from this speech is noted. "The reception accorded to the bill indicates a complete severance of the question from party

[1] *The Mail* (tri-weekly London *Times*), August 19, 1910.

PANAMA CANAL AND SEA POWER

politics. It is assured of an untroubled passage through both houses."[1]

It is not difficult here to note the identity of tone with that of the Pacific slope of the United States and of Canada, to the frequent embarrassment of both central governments. It is increasing in imperativeness in British Columbia, is extending thence eastward to Alberta and Saskatchewan, and is felt even as far as Winnipeg. Use the phrase "national honor," "vital interests," or what you will, there are popular sentiments and determinations which defy every argument but force. It is the failure to note these which vitiates much of the argument for arbitration. Such sentiments, on both sides, are large factors to be taken into account in the forecast of the future of sea power in an ocean one of whose shores is Asiatic, the other European in derivation.

The Panama Canal will tend to link the several English-speaking communities affected by these feelings, and to emphasize their solidarity; not least by the greater nearness which it will give the North American districts to the more thickly settled, and consequently more powerful, Atlantic regions with which they are politically united. Debatable ground, undeveloped occupation, such as exists in them all, is from this particular point of view an especial source of weakness. In none of them, and especially in Australia and New Zealand, is the population proportionate to the soil. The garrison is not

[1] *The Mail*, August 22, 1910.

ARMAMENTS AND ARBITRATION

commensurate to the extent of the walls. Hence immigration becomes a pressing question; and in Australia radical land legislation to break up huge unimproved holdings, and so to facilitate agricultural immigration, is a prominent feature in prospective legislation.

This state of things is a matter of consummate moment, and will compel the sympathy of American Pacific communities with peoples who discern a common danger, and who share a common political tradition. This weakness explains also the evident closer attachment of Australasia than of Canada to the mother-country. Not only is there no alien element, like the French Canadian, but there is far greater exposure and sense of dependence, such as our own ancestors felt when Canada was French. Here enters the sea power of Great Britain into the Pacific with an urgency even greater than that of commercial gain. It is there a question of keeping her own. So far as Australia is weak in numbers, she is proportionately dependent upon power at sea to prevent those numbers from having to encounter overwhelming odds on shore. In this, her case resembles that of the British Islands themselves. She has shown sense of that dependence by the adoption of naval measures much more virile than those which in Canada are meeting opposition; but at best her resources are not sufficient, and dependence on the mother-country will be for a long time inevitable.

PANAMA CANAL AND SEA POWER

The appositeness of these preparations of Australia—and of New Zealand—has been emphasized recently by the resolute persistence of Germany in augmenting materially her naval programme. The latest measures voted, May, 1912, add three heavy battle-ships to the projected total, making forty-one in all; raise the number in active commission from sixteen to twenty-five; and increase the personnel by over fifteen thousand men, which when realized will give a total of over seventy-five thousand.

Lord Kitchener is quoted[1] as saying: "It is an axiom of the British government that the existence of the empire depends primarily upon the maintenance of adequate and efficient naval forces. As long as this condition is fulfilled, and as long as British superiority at sea is assured, then it is an accepted principle that no British dominion can be successfully and permanently conquered by an organized invasion from oversea." The remark was addressed to Australia specifically, and accompanied with the admonition that a navy has many preoccupations; that it may not be able immediately to repair to a distant scene of action; and that therefore the provision of local defense, both by forts and mobile troops, is the correlative of naval defense. This impedes and delays an invader, lessens his advance and the injury possible, and so expedites and diminishes the task of the navy, when this, having established preponderance elsewhere, is able

[1] *The Mail*, April 18, 1910.

ARMAMENTS AND ARBITRATION

to appear in force upon the distant waters of a remote dependency.

It will be recognized that the result here stated is that predicated from the arrival of a superior American fleet at Hawaii. What is true of a territory so distant from Great Britain as Australia is doubly true of the relations of the American navy to its two coasts, the Pacific and the Atlantic, of which the Gulf coast in this connection may be regarded accurately as an extension. In the eye of the navy the three are parts of one whole, of which the link, the neck of the body, will be the Canal—as Australia is not merely a remote dependency, but a living member of the British Empire. There is, however, a vital difference between a member and the trunk. Amputation of the one may consist with continued life, as Great Britain survived the loss of her Amercan colonies; but the mutilation of the trunk means, at the best, life thenceforward on a lower plane of vigor.

The military, or strategic, significance of the Panama Canal, therefore, is that it will be the most vital chord in that system of transference by which the navy of the United States can come promptly to the support on either coast of the local defenses; which it is to be presumed will be organized as Australia contemplates, even though the presumption be over-sanguine, in view of our national ignorant self-complacency. With a competent navy, and with the Panama Canal secured, not merely as to tenure, but with guns of such range as to insure

174

PANAMA CANAL AND SEA POWER

deployment in the open sea at either end—a necessary condition of all sea-coast fortification—invasion will not be attempted, for it can lead to no adequate results.

It is continually asserted that no invasion of the United States will ever be attempted, because conquest is not possible. Conquest of a fully populated territory is not probable; but dismemberment, such as the instance of France deprived of Alsace and Lorraine by Germany, or more recently of Bosnia and Herzegovina taken from Turkey by Austria, is possible. In the latter case, Turkey, Russia, and all Europe were silenced by arms two years ago. What is more within the scope of possibility is the exaction from defeat of terms well-nigh unendurable. An Australian[1] has recently said, "We recognize well that, if the British navy be once overthrown, a condition of peace will be that its present power shall not be restored." *Vae victis.* Defeat of the American navy, followed by a prolonged tenure of parts of American territory, which would then be feasible, might be followed by a demand to give up the Monroe Doctrine, to abandon Panama, to admit immigration to which either our government or a large part of our population objects, and on no account to attempt the re-establishment of a military or naval force which could redeem such consequences. So Rome forever disabled Carthage in the conflict between those two alien and rival civilizations.

[1] Sir George Reid, the High Commissioner for Australia in Great Britain. *The Mail,* July 8, 1910.

ARMAMENTS AND ARBITRATION

So much for national defense, the first of military objects because it is the foundation on which national action securely depends. But in actual warfare the defensive in itself is ineffectual, and useful only as the basis from which the offensive, technically so styled, is exerted. So in a general scheme of national policy, assured security at home is above all valuable by enabling a government to be effectively firm and influential in its support of its external commercial interests, of its necessary policies, and of its citizens abroad. The frequent impatient disclaimer of such interests, of such policies, and of the necessity of power—not necessarily the use of force—to insure them, simply ignores, not the past only, but current contemporary history. The French Minister for Foreign Affairs has spoken recently, in a public utterance, of "the ever-increasing part which diplomacy is called upon to play in the commercial activity of nations." American enterprise and American capital are seeking everywhere lawful outlets and employments. There are many competitors from many other nations; and all governments make it now part of their business to insist on the lawful admission of their own people, and in many cases to obstruct the intrusion of rivals. The Pacific in its broad extent and upon its coasts contains some of the most critical, because least settled, of these questions. Besides the ancient Asiatic peoples on its western shores, all the principal European states possess therein colonies and naval

PANAMA CANAL AND SEA POWER

stations; consequently are possible parties to the as yet remote final adjustments. America in the Philippines has in the Pacific that which she may not call her own possession, but has recognized as her especial charge.

The Panama Canal will be the gateway to the Eastern Pacific, as Suez is to the Western. It will lie in territory over which the United States has jurisdiction as complete, except in the cities of Colon and Panama, as over its other national domains. It is entitled to protection equally with all others; and far more than most, not on its own account chiefly, but because of its vital consequence to all three coasts, and to their communications. This consequence rests upon its being the only link between them, enabling the United States to concentrate the fleet with the greatest rapidity upon any threatened or desired point. In nothing is general importance, national importance, as contrasted with local, more signally illustrated than it is in the Canal and in the navy. Nowhere are considerations of local advantage more out of place and discreditable than in dealing with these two great factors of national security and dignity. Their combined effect, so essential to defense, is no less important to the influence of the country throughout the Pacific Ocean. I say, influence; not supremacy, a word which my whole tone of thought rejects. How large a part China, for instance, has played in our international policy of the last decade is easy to recall; nor is there

ARMAMENTS AND ARBITRATION

room to deny our interest in her, or her look toward us and toward others at the present moment. Even in Great Britain, by formal treaty the ally of Japan, and now in *entente* with Russia, anxiety concerning the future in Korea and Manchuria is shown, and not without cause.

In brief conclusion, Sea Power, like other elements of national strength, depends ultimately upon population—upon its numbers and its characteristics. The great effect of the Panama Canal will be the indefinite strengthening of Anglo-Saxon institutions upon the northeast shores of the Pacific, from Alaska to Mexico, by increase of inhabitants and consequent increases of shipping and commerce. To this will contribute that portion of present and future local production in the North American continent which will find cheaper access to the Atlantic by the Canal than by the existing transcontinental or Great Lakes routes. An official of the Canadian Pacific Railway has stated recently, before the London Chamber of Commerce, that even now British manufactures find their way to British Columbia by the Suez Canal; how much more by Panama, when that canal becomes available! If manufactures, then immigrants; and equally, for it is facility of transportation which determines both. The effect, he estimated, would extend inland to the middle of Saskatchewan, seven or eight hundred miles from the Pacific coast; and his plea was for British immigration as well as for British trade, to offset the known inrush

PANAMA CANAL AND SEA POWER

from the western part of the United States. Whether American or English, there will be increase of European population. This development of the northeast Pacific will have its correlative in the distant southwest, in the kindred commonwealths of Australia and New Zealand; the effect of the Canal upon these being not direct, but reflected from the increased political force and military potentiality of communities in sympathy with them on the decisive question of immigration. The result will be to Europeanize these great districts; in the broad sense which recognizes the European derivation of American populations. The Western Pacific will remain Asiatic, as it should.

The question awaiting and approaching solution is the line of demarcation between the Asiatic and European elements in the Pacific. The considerations advanced appear to indicate that it will be that joining Puget Sound and Vancouver with Australia. It is traced roughly through intervening points, of which Hawaii and Samoa are the most conspicuous; but there are outposts of the European and American tenure in positions like the Marshall and Caroline Islands, Guam, Hongkong, Kiao Chau, and others, just as there are now European possessions in the Caribbean Sea, in Bermuda, in Halifax, remains of past conditions. The extensive district north of Australia, the islands of Sumatra, Java, Borneo, New Guinea, and others, while Asiatic in population, are, like India, European in political control.

179

ARMAMENTS AND ARBITRATION

During the period of adjustment, needed for the development of Pacific America and Australasia, naval power, the military representative of sea power, will be determinative. The interests herein of Great Britain and of the United States are preponderant and coincident. By force of past history and present possessions the final decision of this momentous question will depend chiefly upon them, if concurring. Meantime, and because of this, the American navy should be second to none but the British. To this the American may properly cede superiority, because to the British Islands naval power is vital in a sense in which it is not to the United States.

13

Protestant Missionaries and American Colonialism in the Philippines, 1899–1916: Attitudes, Perceptions, Involvement

Kenton J. Clymer

When the United States wrested the Philippines from Spain, sizeable numbers of Americans found their way to the Islands. Some, such as Dean C. Worcester, found fulfillment there as high-ranking government officials. Others made money, or attempted to, as cowboys in Mindanao or as merchants in Manila. And some came to bring the True Religion and make the society pure. They shared much. All saw themselves as pioneers on an exciting, but dangerous, frontier. To some degree they all tried to be "civilizers." They supported the American decision to take the Islands and resisted nationalist designs to weaken American control. The missionaries alone tried to serve as the conscience of the American experiment.

In one sense, the missionaries who went to the Philippines were part of a crusade that had begun some years before to "evangelize the world in a single generation." Their activities in the Islands are part of a nearly global phenomenon. But the Philippines was *American* overseas territory, and newly acquired territory at that. Thus, the missionaries' activities became equally a part of American nationalism and imperial history. A study of their thought helps define the colonial mentality. In this essay, Professor Kenton J. Clymer of the University of Texas at El Paso explores the attitudes and perceptions of the first generation of Protestant missionaries as they related to the American colonial government. He finds that the missionary community was not monolithic, that on some matters it was deeply divided. On balance, however, the missionaries supported the general direction of American policy, while not hesitating to criticize the government vigorously, particularly on moral issues. Their criticism was seldom anti-imperialist in nature, however, for they sought to purify American rule, not end it.

A modified version of this essay will appear in Clymer's forthcoming book, *Protestant Missionaries in the Philippines, 1898–1916* (Urbana, University of Illinois Press).

Among the Americans who ventured to the Philippine Islands in the early years of the American occupation were Protestant missionaries. By 1905 several main-line denominations—Presbyterian (U.S.A.), Methodist-Episcopal, American Baptist, Christian and Missionary Alliance, Christian (Disciples of Christ), Episcopalian, and United Brethren—had established missions. In addition, a small holiness group, the Peniel mission, operated in Zamboanga, staffed by an Apache Indian and a Swede; the Seventh-day Adventists arrived in 1905 and established a permanent mission in 1908. The Free Methodists had one unofficial missionary couple in the islands for a few years, and there were perhaps some Mormons and Christian Scientists working unofficially.[1] Allied organizations, such as the American Bible Society and its British counterpart, were also active, as was the Young Men's Christian Association. Initially the "Y" worked mostly among American servicemen and civilians.

Studies of the missionaries can help elucidate the Phil-American experience from various perspectives. Many of them left extensive records which cast light not only on theological matters but on Phil-American society and government.[2] Nor were the missionaries without influence on the American government and Philippine society. At a time in American history when the missionary movement attracted considerable support and enthusiasm, even from Presidents like William McKinley and Woodrow Wilson, colonial administrators could not well afford to ignore religious opinion. Governor William Howard Taft, in fact, cultivated missionary leaders in the Philippines. The impact of the missionaries on the Philippines directly is less easy to assess. Only about 3 percent of the present-day population traces its religious roots to the Protestant missionaries, but it is a commonplace belief that Protestants have had considerably more influence at many levels of society than their numbers would suggest.[3] Some observers credit Protestantism with raising the moral tenor of Philippine society, fostering a respect for law and education, and inculcating such "Protestant" values as frugality and social equality. It has even been claimed that Protestantism increased respect for women, the family, and the elderly. But objective studies are scarce.[4]

Just how much lasting influence the missionaries had deserves further investigation. What can be said with some assurance now, however, is that most missionaries of the first generation welcomed the American occupation; supported the American purpose (or at least what they perceived that purpose to be); attempted to influence governmental decisions in order to purify, but not to reduce, America's paternalism; used their influence to infuse American ideals; and tried to reconcile Filipinos to American oversight. They were, in a real sense, allies of the government in what both perceived as a "civilizing" mission.

PROVIDENTIAL EXPANSION

Missionary expansion to the Philippines was part of the larger missionary outburst in the late nineteenth century which, in turn, had its roots in the evangelical revivals of Dwight Moody, John R. Mott, and others. Its objective was to evangelize the world in a single generation. A missionary who embarked for Manila or the provinces was not, therefore, ipso facto, an agent of the national purpose. At least one described himself as an anti-imperialist, and others were indifferent to the secular authorities.[5] Applicants for a missionary position who were ultimately sent to the Philippines often listed the Islands as only one of several preferences.

But, ever since the Civil War, most Protestants had identified the survival and expansion of the United States with the divine plan. "God cannot afford to do without America," a Methodist

Episcopal bishop told a large crowd in 1864.[6] Increasingly, Protestants believed that American-style democracy required an evangelical base. "The August Ruler of all the nations," said the president of Wesleyan University in 1876, "designed the United States of America as the grand repository and evangelist of civil liberty and of pure religious faith. And," he added, "the two are one."[7] Such sentiments were commonplace. As a group of Methodists advised President McKinley a quarter of a century later, "Civil liberty is really found only under the shadow of the evangelistic gospel."[8]

Ideological compatibility between church and state found practical expression in missionary efforts to further the national purpose and in the close relations that many of the missions enjoyed with the government. As early as the 1830s, missionaries in the Oregon country served the nation as well as the church, a fact that caused William A. Slacum, an official emissary from the President, to do what he could to fortify the Oregon missions.[9] Perhaps the closest ties between the missions and the state occurred in 1872 when President Ulysses S. Grant, in a move designed to eliminate corruption and provide more efficient management, entrusted administration of the Indian reservations to the various mission boards.[10] Later in the same decade, Mrs. Rutherford B. Hayes, wife of the President, accepted the presidency of the Methodist Women's Home Missionary Society.[11]

Given the strong belief in the godliness of American institutions, most evangelical Protestant clergymen and many laypersons viewed American territorial expansion in 1898 as divinely inspired. "God has given into our hands, that is, into the hands of American Christians, the Philippine Islands," the Presbyterian General Assembly affirmed only two weeks after Commodore Dewey's victory at Manila Bay. "By the very guns of our battleships," the statement continued, God "summoned us to go up and possess the land."[12]

Though there were dissenters, the large majority of first-generation missionaries in the Philippines accepted the providential viewpoint and rejoiced in America's new imperial destiny. If some missionary applicants listed the Philippines as only one of several preferences for their assignment, others chose to go to the Islands because they were now in American hands. Several missionaries already established in foreign stations when the Philippines were acquired requested transfers to the Islands,[13] for here was a chance for the purest religion (evangelical Protestantism) to join hands with the most Christian of states (the United States) in carrying out the plan of Providence. One woman missionary, for example, was "thrilled" when her ship dropped anchor in Manila Bay, "not because it was my first touch with eastern life, for I had been in many other eastern cities, but because it was my first experience of this kind of life under the Stars and Stripes. I had lived many years in Burma under the British flag," she explained, "and now I was to learn what American rule would do for this branch of the Malaysian race in the Philippines."[14]

So strongly did most missionaries support the American purpose that, like their counterparts in the United States, there was an almost incestuous quality to their thought. Presbyterian James B. Rodgers joined Methodist Missionary Bishop William F. Oldham in appealing for funds "to serve God and the fatherland."[15] Episcopalian Bishop Charles Henry Brent advised Governor Taft that his only motive in going to the Philippines was "to serve the nation and the kingdom of righteousness."[16] Brent even insisted that Episcopalians build dignified edifices and use good equipment because Filipinos "estimated the value of the State through the Church."[17] Homer C. Stuntz, a prominent Methodist, thought that the interdenominational college he was attempting to found would "be a desirable ally of the Government,"[18] while Bruce Kershner cautioned his fellow Disciples missionaries to measure carefully the ramifications before criticizing the government, lest they foster revolution.[19] From such perspectives, not only was the national role to be a Christian one, but the mission's role was to be national in orientation. Few would have contested the chairman of the Presbyterian church's standing committee on foreign missions, when he reminded missionaries in the Philippines that "patriotic loyalty is a cardinal tenet of American Protestantism."[20]

In any event, most missionaries in the Philippines assumed, as a Baptist expressed it, that "the purpose and attitude of our country is absolutely altruistic." They also expected the government to be paternalistic, for, like most Americans of the age, including the most respected social scientists, the missionaries by and large believed that Filipinos and most other non-Anglo-Saxon peoples were culturally, and perhaps racially, deficient and incapable of governing themselves. [21]

One reason for the backwardness of Philippine society, according to the missionaries, was that Spain had done little in her occupation of three centuries to uplift her wards. The brightness and quickness of Filipino children faded as they became older, observed a Presbyterian missionary physician, a fact he ascribed not so much to inherent racial incapacities as to poor Spanish tutelage. "Let them learn under proper conditions and teachers that they are men," he wrote, "and they will in time come to be a nation as capable of self government as the Japanese." [22]

Not only had Spain failed to introduce modern educational, political, and social systems, the missionaries felt, but she had supported a venal, degraded, and politically grasping ecclesiastical establishment that had Christianized the populace in only the most nominal sense. As Methodist Bishop James M. Thoburn wrote several years *before* the American occupation, "These [Philippine] islands present as needy a field for [Protestant] missionary effort as any of those farther south, where Christianity is wholly unknown." [23] Extreme denunciations of Spain's shortcomings may well betray a certain defensiveness about Protestant missionary activity in an already Christian land, and in their more reflective moments thoughtful missionaries credited Spain with introducing important religious truths. But even the most balanced assessments agreed that Spanish Catholicism had weaknesses sufficiently profound to justify a Protestant presence in Spain's former colony. [24]

THE GOVERNMENT AND THE WHITE MAN'S BURDEN: MILITARY CONQUEST

Given the deficiencies of Philippine society, the missionaries believed it was America's obligation to bear what Rudyard Kipling termed "the white man's burden." Just precisely what they expected the government to do was variously, and often vaguely, expressed. But, in general, Philippine culture was to be upgraded by infusing American material and spiritual values and by bringing to the islanders American political and economic concepts and arrangements.

There was a surprisingly strong cautionary note, however. Though not opposed to American rule, some missionaries feared that an unselective and rapid infusion of Western influences might overwhelm and demoralize Philippine society, particularly the mountain people who had had the least contact with the outside world. The popular view that civilization had a regenerating effect on culturally underdeveloped people was illusory, thought the *Philippine Presbyterian.* [25] The Episcopalians, who carried on a significant ministry in the mountains of Luzon and Mindanao, were the most sensitive to the dangers that "civilization" posed. A trip across Mindanao in 1904 led Bishop Brent to comment, "One fears for them [the pagan groups of Mindanao] if, or when, they come under the influence of 'civilization.'" More than most missionaries, the Episcopalians distinguished between Christianity, on the one hand, and American (or Western) civilization, on the other. There was no need to interfere with most Igorot customs, wrote Walter C. Clapp. "Clothes are not the essence of Christianity." [26]

But, with the partial exception of those who were apprehensive about the threat civilization posed to indigenous cultures (and the exception *was* only partial), [27] most missionaries welcomed the government's efforts to change Philippine culture and values. Like other humanitarian imperialists, missionaries were sometimes overly sanguine about the possibilities of effecting meaningful societal transformation and blind to the consequences. But, like Kipling, few expected the effort to be easy or appreciated. The United States, wrote a Methodist missionary, should not expect "to enjoy the sweets of appreciated service"; instead it should "courageously bear the 'white man's burden.'" [28]

One of the difficulties the United States encountered from "unappreciative" Filipinos was armed resistance. Believers in the white man's burden were thus confronted with an immediate and bloody challenge. Yet, those missionaries who welcomed America's assumption of sovereignty, particularly those who believed that it was part of a providential design, could not logically object to the use of force, if necessary, to confirm that sovereignty.

There was, in fact, virtually no missionary opposition to the military purpose. A few extremists thought that God himself directed American operations during the conflict; others argued that America's wars had always been humanely inspired and the Philippine campaign was no different.[29] It was also comforting to think, as most missionaries did, that the resistance was composed of disorganized, marauding bands of common bandits.[30] Insurgent leaders, it was commonly said, were motivated chiefly by "personal ambitions for place and power" and did not enjoy much popular support.[31] Emilio Aguinaldo might be intelligent, wrote the secretary of the Presbyterian board after an extended visit to the Islands in 1901, but he was an "Oriental despot" whose rule, if allowed, would be as bloody as that of the Sultan of Turkey.[32]

Some missionaries, along with some civil and military officials, acknowledged that the resistance had widespread support and that the Filipino forces fought bravely and capably.[33] This view revealed that missionaries were not of one mind and embarrassed the government, which took great pains to deny the popular base of resistance. But varying assessments of the nature of the resistance did not produce differing recommendations, for the missionaries spoke with virtually one voice in saying that the resistance was misguided and must be crushed, regardless of the degree of popular support it enjoyed, so that American beneficence could proceed. "All that the governor, the commission, the school master, the civil judge, and the missionary are attempting," wrote Homer Stuntz in a widely read account, "would have been impossible without the work of the soldier."[34]

The propensity of most Americans (including missionaries) to characterize the armed conflict as an "insurrection" served further to disguise the nature of the Filipino resistance. The term "insurrection" implied an uprising against an already established American regime, which was correct, if at all, only in the Manila area. For the most part, the conflict was objectively an American war of conquest. Whether most missionaries who

used the term "insurrection" consciously intended to misconstrue the nature of the resistance may be doubted. But Bishop
Brent, at least, understood that "insurrection" had certain important connotations favorable to the American cause, for he
once chastised the English writer John Foreman for referring to
the "war" in the Philippines rather than to the "insurrection."[35]

The issue of American atrocities during the war troubled the
missionaries. Early in 1902, a Baptist in Panay complained, without results, to military authorities that American soldiers had
killed a number of innocent people.[36] But that was exceptional.
The more common view was that isolated acts of cruelty were
unfortunate but inevitable and should not distract attention
from the generally praiseworthy conduct of the military. Few
missionaries criticized the American version of the Spanish
tactic of *reconcentracion,* the herding of civilians into secure
enclosures in order to make the elimination of guerrillas easier;[37]
and Zerah C. Collins of the Y.M.C.A. even defended the infa-
mous General Jacob Smith, who ordered Samar turned into a
"howling wilderness." When President Roosevelt retired the
General, Collins surmised he had been punished for political
reasons.[38]

Missionary refusal to take seriously the atrocity issue resulted, in part, from the fact that anti-imperialists, whom the
missionaries cordially distrusted, made the atrocity question a
central one in their critique of American imperialism. The missionaries were reluctant to give credence to anti-imperialist
charges.[39]

What criticism there was of military policy tended to be that
the army was not aggressive enough. Even those who rejected
the optimistic picture painted by American authorities urged
new and "vigorous measures."[40] All looked forward to the election of 1900, assuming that McKinley's Administration had
restrained the military to benefit his candidacy. Once William
Jennings Bryan, the anti-imperialist candidate, was defeated,
reasoned Presbyterian J. Andrew Hall, "we look forward for all
this to change." The authorities, Hall wrote approvingly, would
no longer "be so lenient with those they catch as heretofore."[41]
When in fact the President ordered a more vigorous policy after
the election, the missionaries were pleased. The new policy

"seems to be working like a charm," wrote one, "and the country is coming to its right mind."[42]

For similar reasons, the earliest missionaries deplored the so-
called Bates Agreement (or Treaty) of 1899. That agreement,
negotiated by General John C. Bates on behalf of the United
States with the Sultan of Sulu, was irregular, but apparently
legal. Though the agreement served the immediate purpose of
neutralizing Muslim areas during the Philippine-American war,[43]
it was widely condemned. James B. Rodgers found it "irritating
to see the Sultan treated with so much deference for he is a villain," and he considered the agreement another example of the
doubtful policy of conciliation. Even more opposed was John
McKee of the Christian and Missionary Alliance who, ignoring
provisions of the agreement that restricted the movement of
Americans and, by implication, forbade proselytizing among
the Muslims, preached in Sulu and other Muslim areas in 1900
and again in 1902. "God has laughed at such diplomacy,"
McKee concluded.[44]

Though the military must have considered missionaries like
McKee a nuisance, good relations more normally prevailed.[45]
Missionary reports and letters, for example, regularly included
accounts of assistance from the military in such matters as
housing, transportation, and communication. The Y.M.C.A. enjoyed the closest of relationships with military personnel, since
it was a semi-official arm of the government. If "Y" materials
are to be credited, in fact, military officers were unanimous in
their enthusiastic support for the organization. But the missionaries of other agencies also received encouragement, as well as
favors, from the military and in some instances accepted military
advice on when and where to begin work. Some missionaries, in
turn, offered advice on ways to increase the army's efficiency.
In 1899, for example, Bishop James M. Thoburn, who was in
Manila when the war commenced, urged the United States to
follow the English colonial practice of enlisting indigenous people into the ranks.[46] James B. Rodgers, who arrived a few weeks
later, interviewed and evaluated prisoners of war. It is difficult
to disagree with a recent scholarly assessment, that "Rodgers
was clearly working with the United States occupation forces;

he would have been termed by Marxists an instrument of imperialism."[47]

Just as the missionaries supported the military during the Philippine-American War, those with responsibilities in Mindanao applauded initial attempts to exert military control over the Muslims. For centuries, the various Muslim groups of the south had fiercely maintained a practical independence from Spain, and they were no more inclined to acknowledge American hegemony without a struggle. But, as the fighting became protracted and brutal (it lasted for more than a decade after the official end of the Philippine-American War),[48] Bishop Brent, who had admired the repressive policy of Military Governor Leonard Wood, at first demurred, and then openly attacked the American use of arms. "The Moro is still unsubdued," he said in October 1913, "and I say more honor to the Moro! We can go on with our oppressive measures to the end of time," he added, "but all we can effect is annihilation."[49] Brent's opposition, which was late in developing, was the only significant exception to missionary support of the military's combatant role.

THE GOVERNMENT AND THE WHITE MAN'S BURDEN: IMPROVING SOCIETY

Outside of Muslim areas, overt resistance to American arms had largely ended by the time President Roosevelt declared the "insurrection" at an end on 4 July 1902, and the civil government took over the bulk of the white man's burden. The missionaries applauded much that the government undertook. Improvement in public health and in public works attracted especially widespread favorable comment. The missionaries repeatedly remarked on the transformation of Manila under American rule. Under the Spanish, wrote a Seventh-day Adventist, the capital city "was indescribably filthy."[50] The change was apparent by 1904. When Fred Jansen, a Presbyterian, returned to the city that year after an extended absence, he could scarcely recognize it.[51] By 1909, one missionary insisted, Manila "was fast becoming one of the most attractive cities of the Orient," and two years later another claimed it was "one of the nicest and cleanest cities of the East."[52] Perhaps Methodist Bishop Henry Warren summed it up most colorfully. The Americans, the bishop wrote, found Manila "a pesthole, and made it a health resort."[53]

There were occasional discordant notes. A Y.M.C.A. official admitted that, "in a city where scores of thousands live in wretched nipa shacks on low, undrained land," there was too much truth in the observation that "many if not most of the splendid improvements that are being made in the Islands, are chiefly for the pleasure or advantage of the Americans and foreigners generally." But such criticisms were rare and confined to an occasional private letter—especially in the case of "Y" officials.[54] Most would unhesitatingly have agreed with a United Brethren spokesman that "the American Government is here doing a real missionary work on a very large scale."[55]

Although the missionaries thought the government's purpose deserved support, they sometimes encountered indifference, even hostility, from government officials who did not share their view that the interests of church and state were intermingled. Homer Stuntz recalled that American officials in Dagupan initially "cursed us, and expressed the wish that we would go away and never return."[56] A Presbyterian found that civil employees feared to identify themselves with Protestant causes for fear it would "hurt their prospects of promotion,"[57] while, as late as 1913, the leading Baptist missionary felt that government officials still considered missionaries "a pernicious element in the Philippines."[58] And there were numerous complaints that officials catered too much to the Roman Catholic hierarchy which was, by definition, opposed to Protestant missions.[59]

Among the important officials whom the Protestants viewed with suspicion was James F. Smith, a Catholic who served on the Philippine Commission from 1903 to 1909, including over two years as Governor General (1906–1909). They also found W. Cameron Forbes, who succeeded Smith as Governor General (1909–1913), less than cordial. Though Forbes respected Bishop Brent, served on the boards of some Episcopalian organizations, and contributed to the Y.M.C.A., he was contemptuous of most clergymen. Missionaries, he once wrote, were "usually the most grossly incompetent people that live."[60]

The official against whom the missionaries voiced their

strongest objections was the outspoken and arrogant Secretary of the Interior, Dean C. Worcester. When the Commissioner attempted to block Episcopalian efforts to purchase land in Bontoc for a mission station, missionary Walter C. Clapp could not contain his anger. Worcester, he wrote, was "a despot as merciless and malicious as one would expect to find in the Middle Ages," while Bishop Brent, agreeing with his subordinate, prepared a letter (left unsent) to his friend Theodore Roosevelt asking that the official be deposed.[61] If the missionaries disliked Worcester passionately, they could take comfort in the fact that they were not alone. The Secretary, wrote an official of the Manila Y.M.C.A., was "most cordially hated by his subordinates and Americans generally and . . . is almost universally execrated by Filipinos."[62]

On the other hand, government officials who encouraged mission work more than counterbalanced those who were critical. Expressions of encouragement ranged all the way from polite but meaningless gestures (Governor General Luke Wright once granted an interview to Seventh-day Adventists and flattered them by suggesting that, inasmuch as they took seriously the Biblical admonition to labor six days and rest on the seventh, they could do good service by teaching the Filipinos how to work),[63] to monetary contributions and active involvement in mission work. Especially in Mindanao were government officials solicitous. Peter G. Gowing's statement, that, "beyond the extension of a few courtesies, American governmental officials [in Mindanao] did not actively aid any Christian missionary activities,"[64] underestimates the encouragement and assistance rendered by the officials. Robert F. Black, the first Congregationalist to venture to the Islands, found officials in Mindanao eager to assist him. Black was permitted, for example, to travel on government ships after that privilege had been withdrawn from other civilians. "I hardly think I am going to compromise myself by accepting these favors," he wrote uneasily to his board. "What do you think?"[65]

Government assistance to Black was not merely a matter of courtesy, for officials saw value in his missionary activity. They encouraged Black and other American Board missionaries to expand their work. In 1911, Governor Henry Gilheuser of the

Davao district stated publicly that "the church is one of the strongest governmental agents that we have." The new Congregational chapel that the Governor was helping to dedicate constituted, he said floridly, "another stone in the wall of Americanism which is slowly but surely being built up around these Islands."[66] In 1915, Frank Carpenter, the popular Governor of the Department of Mindanao and Sulu (1914–1920), urged the Congregational missionaries to take charge of a government school in Mumungan (now Baloi), and a few days later he asked Frank C. Laubach to introduce athletics—"base-ball evangelism" Laubach termed it—to the Moros.[67]

Episcopalians, too, found officials on Mindanao eager for them to begin work. Both Leonard Wood, the Provincial Governor, and General George W. Davis, the supreme military commander in the Philippines, agreed that there was "great opportunity" for the Episcopalians on the island. From Zamboanga, a little later, the Episcopalian missionary in charge reported that Wood was "in thorough accord with & will back us in every way." Brent, in fact, was concerned that criticism would develop if it were generally known how candid governmental officials had been in their expressions of support. "This is not for publication or notice at all in print," he once cautioned his mission board, while relaying Wood's words of encouragement.[68]

Those officials who encouraged the establishment of Protestant missions were surely shrewder than those who were indifferent or hostile, for the missionaries were, at least in the short run, a force for reconciliation and conservatism.[69] No one understood better the value of the missions to the government than William Howard Taft.[70] As the first civil Governor of the Islands (1901–1903), Taft established lasting relationships with several Protestant missions. He traveled to the Islands in 1902 with Bishop Brent and later that year sought the Bishop's counsel when President Roosevelt offered him a seat on the Supreme Court.[71] The following year, shortly before he returned to the United States to become Secretary of War, Taft spent an hour with the Methodist leader Homer Stuntz, who had admired the Governor ever since his inaugural address,[72] and hammered out an agreement whereby missionaries could submit names to fill vacancies in the Phil-American government.[73] In future years the missionaries did not hesitate to communicate with Taft, and some became his staunch political supporters as well.[74]

If it is true that in India the British government did its best to inhibit the spread of Christianity and that "never at any time or in any way" did it "identify itself with the missionary cause,"[75] the same was demonstrably not so with the American government in the Philippines.

CREATING THE NEW FILIPINO

Of all of the government's undertakings, none was so "missionary-like" as the massive educational effort. In other lands, in fact, a major portion of the missionary's time and resources was devoted to establishing and operating schools. Because, in the Philippines, the government assumed the task of education, the missionaries were left free to engage in other pursuits. This alone predisposed them to praise the schools. But to the missionaries the schools had important cultural advantages as well. To the evangelical Protestant mind of that age, the American public school held a significance far beyond its obvious educational and patriotic functions. Protestants might quarrel among themselves on a variety of issues, but they joined in support of the public school. Support of the public school was, in fact, an integral part of the Protestants' "strategy for a Christian American." Though the American school was officially secular, in practice Protestant values pervaded it. Nationalism and Protestantism were joined in the public school to produce, it was hoped, the highest form of Christian civilization.[76]

The missionaries had great hope, therefore, that the new public schools in the Philippines, modeled after the American school, would help create a new Philippine society free from superstition and outmoded styles of life. The New Filipino, like the American, would be democratic in inclination, questioning in mind, strong in body, and in general capable of contributing to the new society. His value structure would be American and, by implication, Protestant. The schools, wrote a Presbyterian, inculcated "American ideas" and created "a practical American spirit." Finally, he would be pro-American and would reject emotional calls for independence. "By the time they are really ready for independence," wrote Charles N. Magill, "they will not want it. I believe that they will then realize what an honor it is to be a part of the greatest nation in the world."[77]

One very important result of the school's effort to recast Philippine society, to the missionary mind, would be the liberation of the people from Roman Catholic authority, a goal of both religious and national importance, in their view. Frank C. Laubach stood quite literally alone in arguing that the public schools provided no opening at all for the Protestant message.[78] The rest insisted, fervently and often openly, that, as a Baptist missionary expressed it, "every public school can be counted an evangelical force in a Roman Catholic country."[79] By 1911, Methodist missionary Marvin Rader insisted that the public schools had "broken the hold Romanism has upon these students."[80] So frank were the missionaries about the value of the schools in the fight with Rome that government officials, had they read the missionary press, would have been sorely discomforted.

At the same time, the missionaries always feared that Catholics had, or threatened to have, too much influence in the educational system at all levels. As early as March 1899, James B. Rodgers observed that the Catholic church would "make desperate efforts to hold the schools in their power and try to perpetuate the old system,"[81] and throughout the period the missionaries remained ever vigilant. They often found evidence of Catholic efforts to influence educational policy; too often, they felt, the "Romanists" were succeeding. In 1903, Presbyterian missionaries noted the arrival of two Catholic teachers in Dumaguete and assumed that their appointment indicated increasing Catholic influence in high places.[82] The following year, a Baptist missionary in Panay felt that the government was pandering to the "Romanist party," while Methodist Harry Farmer, in Pangasinan province, reported that Catholic teachers and principals taught Catholic doctrines in the schoolroom, required students to attend Mass, and warned them not to listen to the Protestants.[83] In 1907, Homer Stuntz complained directly to President Roosevelt about the "rapid promotion of Roman Catholic teachers."[84] In 1908, a Disciples missionary felt that the Department of Education exhibited "a spirit of fear and subserviency to Roman Catholic opinion," while the following year an Alliance missionary reported that Jesuits had infiltrated the schools of Zamboanga.[85] Complaints of this sort never outweighed the positive aspects of the educational system, in the missionary mind, but, as late as 1915, when Frank Laubach dismissed the schools as essentially without value to the Protestant cause, he pointed to Catholic influence to support his argument.[86]

Some missionaries considered the efforts of educational administrators to remain absolutely neutral in religious affairs as evidence of hostility and/or Catholic influence. Protests of this nature were especially evident during 1901–1903 when Fred W. Atkinson was Secretary of Education. During the Atkinson period, missionaries complained, Protestant teachers and administrators were flatly forbidden to express their religious views, even outside the classroom;[87] if one Presbyterian report is to be credited, teachers could not even entertain a missionary in their homes, "even when there was no other place in the village where he might obtain boiled water and food free from cholera germs."[88] Reports of this sort led one missionary to refer to the "terrors of the Atkinson period" in one of his annual reports.[89]

The missionaries were gratified when David Prescott Barrows, a devout Protestant, succeeded Atkinson as Superintendent in 1903. But, in 1904, James F. Smith, a Catholic, became Secretary of Public Instruction. As Barrows's superior, Smith had ultimate responsibility for the Islands' educational system. A report that the Catholic church in the United States had condemned the unfortunate Smith's supervision of the Department of Education did little to lessen Protestant suspicions. "When dealing with tricky people it is well to be cautious," advised a Baptist publication, adding that few Protestants in the Philippines took the denunciation seriously.[90]

In any event, the basic policy requiring teachers to remain neutral in religious matters and to refrain from influencing the religious views of their students remained unchanged, and some missionaries continued to feel that the policy represented an unconstitutional infringement; furthermore, they complained, the policy was enforced only on Protestant teachers.[91] Observing cases of drunkenness among some teachers, one missionary mused that it would be better for the government to order "its employees to abstain from alcohol rather than from religion."[92]

Complaints about governmental school policy reflected the missionaries' deep concern that a school system that excluded moral instruction would produce a generation of skeptics instead of morally responsible, committed Christians. As early as 1902, Arthur J. Brown observed that, by calling into question the old verities, the schools would be preparing the soil for the "noisome seeds of infidelity and atheism."[93] To the missionaries, this presented grave dangers, for it was from the schools that the leaders of the new society would come. "Educated pagans," to use Laubach's phrase, in leadership positions presented a spectacle too horrible to contemplate.[94] In short, there was a danger that the public school in the Philippines, for all of its good points, would lack the crucial moral component found in the American school. Without that moral dimension, the value of the school as the bearer of Christian civilization diminished.

Nevertheless, many missionaries defended the government's policy as the best possible under Philippine conditions. Arthur J. Brown, who was well aware of the dangerous potential of a secular school, argued with indisputable realism that any other policy would increase Catholic influence. If religious influences were permitted in the schools in a land that was overwhelmingly Catholic, he pointed out, Catholics would benefit more than Protestants. Though the missionaries continued to be sharply divided on the issue,[95] probably a majority eventually accepted Brown's reasoning and supported the authorities. In 1910, for example, the Presbyterian committee on religious liberty concluded that the policy was reasonable, and the mission as a whole concurred.[96]

The religiously neutral school presented an exciting, and generally welcome, challenge to the missions to provide the moral dimension the public school allegedly lacked. The establishment of parochial schools was, in part, a response to the perceived shortcomings of the public school.[97] But, instead of erecting competing institutions, the missionaries more usually attempted to create a Protestant presence near the schools in the form of kindergartens, dispensaries, social clubs, and, above all, dormitories. A portion, at least, of the future leaders might be saved from free thinking, and they in turn would help ensure the success of the American-created, new, Christian society.[98]

Protestant worry about the direction of public education was connected with the larger issue of religious liberty. The freedom of religious expression, in fact, was to the missionaries the most important advantage of American rule. But, especially in the early years, the missionaries questioned whether the government took seriously enough its role as the guarantor of religious freedom. Time after time, the missionaries complained, local officials (usually Filipinos) failed to investigate instances of interference with their religious meetings and of persecution of their adherents. If a case was brought before a justice of the peace, it was too often dismissed on a pretext or technicality.[99] Though appeals to higher authorities (often Americans) might achieve better results, the situation would never be truly satisfactory, the missionaries believed, as long as the government at the highest levels remained inordinately sensitive to Catholic interests.

The Philippine Commission's decision in 1904 to proclaim a holiday in honor of Nuestra Señora de Rosario, the Virgin of Antipolo, was an early example, the missionaries thought, of the government caving in to "Romish pressure," as Homer Stuntz put it in a long letter to Theodore Roosevelt.[100] Three years later, Protestant sensitivities were even more deeply bruised when the Commission deigned to be present while Nuestra Señora was crowned patron saint of the Philippines.[101]

Significantly, the latter action occurred when James F. Smith was Governor General, a period when complaints alleging religious persecution and government unconcern seem to have multiplied. Baptist Charles W. Briggs wrote that "all who have been watching the course of events have noted the decided increase in religious preferment and in persecutions since our present Catholic Governor-General came into office," while a Presbyterian in Cebu went so far as to claim that "religious liberty is a myth."[102] The most celebrated allegations of religious persecution during Smith's tenure, and of the government's ineffectual response, were brought to public attention by the Reverend Harry Farmer, a prominent Methodist missionary. Convinced that affairs in the islands were "very much in the hands of the

Roman Catholics, and to all indications and purposes, Church and State are one,"[103] Farmer filed at least four complaints with the authorities in 1908 alleging persecution in Navotas, Meycauayan, and Vigan. When Farmer concluded that government officials had failed to investigate his complaints adequately, he published the details in a Methodist publication, after which religious magazines in the United States picked up the story. It created a minor sensation for a time and threatened to embarrass William Howard Taft, the Republican candidate for the presidency.[104]

Complaints of religious persecution diminished notably under Smith's successor, W. Cameron Forbes—an irony, given Forbes's contempt for missionaries. The Presbyterian Committee on Religious Liberty received no complaints at all in 1909 and only one the following year.[105] In 1911, missionaries in Bohol reported "a good deal of persecution," but they added that it occurred in "a quiet way." The same year, mission personnel in Camarines observed that persecution occurred "only in outoftheway [sic] places."[106]

THE GOVERNMENT AND MORAL ISSUES

Just as the missionaries were willing to criticize the government for allegedly failing to uphold religious freedom, so too they were not silent when the government pursued policies or sanctioned activities that departed from American Protestant moral norms. They were, in this sense, the conscience of the American experiment.

Even while the Philippine-American War was in progress, some missionaries engaged in sustained attacks on the Army's policy that permitted soldiers to purchase intoxicants on military bases. The missionaries also insisted, especially in the early years, that public officials set a good example by regular attendance at religious services. So vocal did criticism become of members of the Taft Commission for alleged non-attendance that each commissioner felt obligated to file a written statement denying that there was a government policy discouraging church attendance.[107] Bishop Brent dismissed most of these allegations (some brought by his own Episcopalian missionaries) as unjustified.[108] (Taft did not attend at first, apparently because no chair could comfortably accommodate his ample frame, whereupon Brent ordered a suitable chair constructed.)[109] But, like other missionaries, the Bishop believed that public officials had an obligation to maintain high standards of conduct, including church attendance. When Judge Adolph Wislizenus objected to being treated as "a potted palm that can be carried around to decorate a religious festival," Brent shot back, "Attendance on public worship is a public duty."[110]

Another moral issue that attracted missionary attention in the early years was the sale of opium. In particular, the Protestants were outraged when in 1903 the Philippine Commission proposed to regulate the sale of the drug by granting a monopolistic franchise to the highest bidder. The missionaries regarded this proposal as unbecoming to an American government and feared that under the plan the opium concessionaire would not, as he was supposed to do, limit his sales to persons already addicted. Because of strong missionary pressure (Methodist Bishop James M. Thoburn told Secretary of War Elihu Root to his face that the monopoly idea was "bad, and only bad, and bad continually"),[111] the government backed down. President Roosevelt personally ordered Governor Taft not to pass an opium bill until he, Roosevelt, had approved it.[112] In the end, Taft shelved the plan and appointed a three-man commission, which included Bishop Brent (at Brent's own request), to review the entire matter. After a serious investigation, the special commission suggested a solution, involving the gradual phasing out of the opium trade and no government-sponsored franchise, that met with the approval of all concerned. "Our gratitude to God for this termination of the opium debate should be very real and very great," concluded the Methodist Committee on Public Morals.[113]

The missionaries regularly urged the elimination of a host of other evils (including obscene postcards). But the moral issue that most persistently attracted their attention was gambling, something they fervently tried to eliminate or at least place under the most stringent regulation. In 1906, the Methodists took the lead in forming the Moral Progress League, whose primary concern was to suppress "the extensive public gambling that has developed *unchecked under the American administration.*"[114] The League acquired a substantial boost when Bishop Brent endorsed its purpose in a biting sermon that received front-page coverage in the *Manila Times,* in which he accused the Philippine Commission of moral timidity for failing to come to grips with the problem of gambling.[115]

The Moral Progress League had some immediate success,[116] yet, less than two years after the organization was founded, the municipal government of Manila raised missionary hackles by letting a concession for a cockpit, where gambling would be permitted, at the semi-official annual carnival. Although the concession was a local matter, the missionaries suspected that Governor General Smith was really responsible, and they berated him and the Philippine Commission as much, if not more, than the Manila authorities.[117] The Evangelical Union, which represented most Protestant groups, protested to President Roosevelt, and the Reverend Mercer G. Johnston, rector of the Episcopal cathedral in Manila, condemned the authorities in a colorful sermon entitled "A Covenant with Death, An Agreement with Hell."[118] One consequence of Mercer's diatribe was that he gained the lasting enmity of Commissioner Forbes, who rejoiced when a sizeable number of parishioners withdrew from the cathedral in protest.[119]

In fact, the missionaries' anger seems misdirected. Far from instigating or approving of the action of the Manila government, members of the Philippine Commission considered it ill-advised. Forbes thought the municipal board consisted of "fools," and he fancifully suggested that the board be abolished.[120] Forbes and Governor General Smith each offered 1,000 pesos, as did the Evangelical Union, to buy up the concessionaire's permit, without success.[121] But the Commission had no authority to overrule the decision, and the missionaries' inability or unwillingness to understand the Commission's predicament irked Forbes. "If these propositions of the ministers [to cancel the concession] were made to me as a business man at home," he wrote, "the least that could happen to them would be to be taken by the seat of the breeches and back of the neck to the top of the stairs and then to be kicked down."[122]

This time, Protestant objections proved unavailing. The authorities in Washington upheld the Philippine Commission's refusal to intervene, and those attending the carnival that year found the cockpit operating as planned.

THE GOVERNMENT'S FAILURE TO LEAD

A common thread runs through missionary criticism of the government. Whether they chastised it for pursuing a too lenient military policy, for being too susceptible to Catholic pressure, for not encouraging church attendance, or for failing to deal effectively with moral issues, the government stood charged with lacking in leadership ability, with suffering from a failure of nerve. This was even more apparent to the missionaries when they evaluated the government's overall performance as upholder of the white man's burden, of its moral obligations to the Filipinos. For example, the Baptists, more than any other mission group, wanted to eliminate the system of *caciquismo,* which they perceived as exploitative and degrading, something that sapped the very personhood from the peasants. The American regime, they were sure, would root out prevailing practices: "The conditions . . . exist today in an atmosphere where they can no longer thrive. The government system . . . is going to undermine the whole social structure that has so long been dominant."[123] But, within a few years, doubts developed about whether the government really wanted to carry through the kind of social revolution required to dislodge an institution as deep-seated as *caciquismo.*[124]

The government's failure to lead manifested itself even more clearly, most missionaries believed, in the granting of too many concessions to Filipinos, who were as yet ill-suited, they felt, to carry out important responsibilities, especially if these involved the making of policy. This attitude was evident in the skepticism with which the missionary community greeted the establishment of the Philippine Assembly in 1907.[125]

When Secretary of War Taft arrived in Manila to open the assembly, the Reverend Stealy B. Rossiter, pastor of the English-speaking Presbyterian church in Manila, engaged the former Governor in an unseemly debate over the appropriateness of Taft's policy of "The Philippines for the Filipinos," with which Rossiter vehemently disagreed.[126] Similarly, many missionaries threw themselves fervently into the effort to prevent an even worse policy from being enacted under the Democrats, who won the election of 1912. Several of the leading missionaries, including Presbyterian Rodgers, Methodist Oldham, and Episcopalian Brent, involved themselves in the strongly retentionist Philippine Society, an involvement that led to serious repercussions on the mission field.[127]

By this time, missionary opinion was not monolithic. Disciples missionaries Bruce Kershner and C. L. Pickett, for example, were not worried by the prospect of a change in policy and almost welcomed it.[128] In addition, just as the Jones Bill promising independence was being debated, a second generation of missionaries began to arrive, a generation influenced by the almost revolutionary changes just then beginning to take place in missionary thought. The outbreak of World War I added to the growing challenge to missionary optimism and certainty. Representatives of this new group in the Philippines, men like Congregationalist Frank C. Laubach and Disciple Leslie C. Wolfe, had no objection to independence. Even within the retentionist majority there were divisions. Bishop Oldham, for example, advocated setting a specific date sometime in the future for a vote on the political future of the Islands, whereas Bishop Brent opposed the idea.[129] But a majority still felt that the time was not ripe for Filipinos to look after their own destiny and that the American government had been entirely too prone to accede to Filipino and anti-imperialist demands.

In the opinion of these missionaries, the government needed to rule with a steady hand. The government must have "the whip over the door," as one Episcopalian missionary put it bluntly, "for the Malay Willie will not be a good boy nor learn his lessons unless it is in sight."[130] Missionaries of this persuasion were "running scared," genuinely fearful that the American experiment would fail. The Filipinos would "never be able to govern themselves if the government continues its present policy," Brent stated publicly in 1907, much to the chagrin of President Roosevelt.[131] To educate and elevate the Filipinos to the desired level was not the work of a day or even of a few years. It required a dedicated, imaginative, career-oriented colonial civil service working for at least a generation. "If a man like General [Leonard] Wood could be undisturbed as governor for twenty years and be surrounded by men of the same type," wrote another Episcopalian, "the thing to all appearances would be done."[132]

Unfortunately, the missionaries felt, the American colonial service did not measure up. Politics infested it. Administrators, including the Governor General, were replaced all too often. Too many colonial officials despised their surroundings and longed to return home. Too often they remained aloof from Filipino society, exploited the people, and addressed them contemptuously. American *policy* in the Philippines would "never be accused of a lack of imagination," wrote a Baptist medical missionary in a sensitive essay, "but I fear that many who endeavor to execute that policy may be accussed [*sic*] of a lack of *heart*." He explained:

The building of roads, the opening up of the interior, the establishing of new avenues of communication, new and better governmental methods and the maintaining of a splendid school system all accomplished by determination and indomitable energy, will not avail to win the hearts of the people and lead them to a higher life, so long as it is done in a deliberate, calculating way with none or very little heart-felt sympathy. . . . The Islands need men and women who are willing to admit that the spiritual and temporal welfare of the humblest peasant is worth as much as ours or mine. How unfortunate it is to find that the majority of minor governmental officials and some other Americans find it impossible to speak a good word for the Filipino people.[133]

In their efforts to save the government from its own mistakes, a number of missionaries, though by no means all, held out the example of European colonial administrations, notably the British experience in India. Methodist Bishop Thoburn, who had lived for many years in India, alluded to the British model on occasion, as did Bishop Brent, who read and traveled widely in an effort to familiarize himself with non-American colonialism. Though Brent did not entirely approve of British administration, sensing that British colonialists were too self-serving and overly pessimistic about the prospects of eventual native rule, at least the British experience was not characterized by the "instability, superficiality, feverish haste, and unreality" that, he felt, infected the American effort.[134] On the contrary, the

English, Brent thought, possessed a steadfastness of purpose, good government, a sense of duty, a dedicated colonial civil service, and policy-makers who, through long experience, had acquired perceptive insights into the "oriental mind."

This is not to say that the missionaries were completely disillusioned. Few of the first generation, after all, supported Filipino demands for independence, though that was beginning to change. Most would have insisted that the government had pursued an enlightened colonial policy, all things considered, that deserved support. Much as some of them admired the British, they contended that the American vision was more humane, more democratic, perhaps even more Christian. If only America would slow down a bit and professionalize its colonial service, if it would pursue its goals at a "steady jog trot" instead of a "gallop," as Brent put it, American colonialism might yet become the best in the world.[135]

Were the missionaries, then, agents of American imperialism? They defined their task in theological terms: To carry the Protestant Gospel to a land that had hitherto excluded it. Those who could clearly differentiate between Protestantism and Americanism cannot properly be called imperial agents. But an important segment of the missionary community—including the leading missionaries of most churches—consciously sought to infuse American concepts and values along with Protestantism, just as they often did in other lands.[136] And probably most missionaries could not escape, did not even want to attempt to escape, the bounds of their culture. They too served the interests of the state. They viewed the American occupation as providential, or at least as an expression of American benevolence that deserved their support. They accepted the necessity for the military conquest of the Islands. During the war, they deferred to military opinion, and a few gave advice and even direct support to the authorities. In the main, they applauded the civil government's attempts to remake Philippine society, physically and culturally, along American lines. They served as a force to reconcile Filipinos to their new fate. Their sometimes heated, sometimes telling criticisms of the government were intended to purify and make more effective American colonialism; almost none of them questioned the American presence.

Whether the missionaries were effective colonial agents cannot yet be determined in a definitive fashion, but there are some indications that they were. Throughout the colonial period, the churches were organically tied to their American counterparts. American churchmen visited the islands regularly. The most promising Filipino pastors and educators studied at institutions of higher learning in the United States. Only after national independence arrived did the major Protestant churches achieve an independent status, notably with the merger of several missionary-founded churches to establish the United Church of Christ in the Philippines (UCCP) in 1948. Even today, however, the UCCP retains close ties with American church-related organizations, while the United Methodist Church in the Philippines, whose membership equals that of the UCCP, is still officially connected with the American branch. As late as 1973–1974, in fact, an American United Methodist bishop exercised temporary ecclesiastical authority over the crisis-torn Philippine church.

Nationalistic resentments did sometimes erupt against American missionaries, resulting in important schisms.[137] But the bulk of the congregations remained loyal, and a fascination with America was a notable attribute of prominent Filipino Protestant clergymen.[138] Some have even expressed themselves in language resembling that of the early missionaries. Three United Methodist bishops, for example, all active in the 1970s, have written that the American occupation of the Philippines was providential. President McKinley, writes the distinguished clergyman D. D. Alejandro, brought "a new day for religious liberty and freedom of conscience in the Philippine Islands, a country long enslaved by a so-called Christian church, utterly selfish, intolerant and unscriptural in its practices."[139] If Filipino Protestants can accept missionary-inspired notions of providential history, is it not reasonable to assume that they also absorbed important American values?

To be sure, there are today strong nationalistic currents in the Filipino churches. Methodists are seriously considering severing their ties with the American church, and, in all communions, there is a heightened awareness, and rejection, of a "colonial mentality." But is it too much to speculate that the public condemnation of the martial-law rule of President Ferdinand Marcos by the UCCP and other Protestant bodies resulted from the profound attachment of its members to democratic principles, principles that may well spring from the recesses of the Filipino soul or even from aspirations common to all people, but which were most obviously inculcated jointly by the American regime and the missionaries?[140] Perhaps the missionaries were more effective agents of American ideas than either they or the government ever imagined.

Chapter 6. Protestant Missionaries and American Colonialism in the Philippines, 1899–1916: Attitudes, Perceptions, Involvement, by Kenton J. Clymer

Reference Abbreviations
BIA Bureau of Insular Affairs

1. Charles W. Briggs, *The Progressing Philippines* (Philadelphia, Griffith and Rowland, 1913), p. 135.
2. An investigation of the Protestant missions in the Philippines is perhaps best begun by perusing the relevant portion of Kenneth Scott Latourette, *A History of the Expansion of Christianity*, Vol. V, *The Great Century in the Americas, Australia, Asia and Africa A.D. 1800–A.D. 1914* (New York and London, Harper, 1943). A more complete introduction is Peter G. Gowing, *Islands Under the Cross: The Story of the Church in the Philippines* (Manila, National Council of Churches in the Philippines, 1967). Arthur Leonard Tuggy, *The Philippine Church: Growth in a Changing Society* (Grand Rapids, Eerdmans, 1971) is a brief account. Camilo Osias and Avelina Lorenzana, *Evangelical Christianity in the Philippines* (Dayton, United Brethren Publishing House, 1931) is an older account by two important Filipino converts.

   More specialized accounts not written by participants include Mariano C. Apilado, "Revolution, Colonialism, and Mission: A Study of the Role of the Protestant Churches in the United States' Rule of the Philippines, 1898–1928" (PhD dissertation, Vanderbilt University, 1976), one of the few studies based on extensive archival investigation; Donald Dean Parker, "Church and State in the Philippines 1896–1906" (PhD dissertation, Divinity School, University of Chicago, 1936), which is weak on analysis but which contains much valuable information; some of the contributions to Gerald H. Anderson's fine edited collection of essays, *Studies in Philippine Church History* (Ithaca and London, Cornell University Press, 1969); Richard L. Deats, *Nationalism and Christianity in the Philippines* (Dallas, Southern Methodist University Press, 1967). I have written several articles on various aspects of the early Protestant mission experience: "The Methodist Response to Philippine Nationalism, 1899–1916," *Church History*, 47:421–434 (December 1978); "Methodist Missionaries and American Colonialism in the Philippines, 1899–1913, *Pacific Historical Review*, 49:29–60 (February 1980); "The Limits of Comity: Presbyterian-Baptist Relations in the Philippines, 1900–1925," *Kabar Seberang*, 10–11:76–84 (December 1982); "Methodist Missionaries and Roman Catholicism in the Philippines, 1899–1916," *Methodist History*, 18:171–178 (April 1980); and "The Episcopalian Encounter with Roman Catholicism in the Philippines, 1910–1916," *Philippine Studies* 28:86–97 (1980).

   There are also some important studies of individual missions, including David L. Rambo, "The Christian and Missionary Alliance in the Philippines, 1901–70" (PhD dissertation, New York University School of Education, 1974); Elmer A. Fridell, *Baptists in Thailand and the Philippines* (Philadelphia, Judson [1956]); F.V. Stipp, "The

Disciples of Christ in the Philippines" (DD Thesis, Yale Divinity School, 1927); Lee Donald Warren's account of the Seventh-day Adventist mission, *Isles of Opportunity: Progress and Possibilities in the Philippines* (Washington, D.C., Review and Herald Publishing Association, 1928); Walter N. Roberts, *The Filipino Church: The Story of the Development of an Indigenous Evangelical Church in the Philippine Islands as revealed in the work of The Church in the United Brethren in Christ* (Dayton, The Foreign Missionary Society and the Women's Missionary Association, United Brethren in Christ, 1936). Methodist work is examined in Richard L. Deats, *The Story of Methodism in the Philippines* (Manila, Published for Union Theological Seminary by the National Council of Churches in the Philippines, 1964); Dionisio D. Alejandro, *From Darkness to Light: A Brief Chronicle of the Beginnings and Spread of Methodism in the Philippines* ([Manila?] Philippine Central Conference, Board of Communications and Publications, United Methodist Church, 1974); and J. Tremayne Copplestone, *History of Methodist Missions,* Vol. IV, *Twentieth-Century Perspectives (The Methodist Episcopal Church, 1896–1939)* (New York, Board of Missions of the United Methodist Church, 1973), pp. 170-239. On the Episcopalian undertaking, see William Henry Scott, "Staunton of Sagada: Christian Civilizer," *Historical Magazine of the Protestant Episcopal Church,* 31:305-339 (December 1962); and Alexander C. Zabriskie, *Bishop Brent: Crusader for Christian Unity* (Philadelphia, Westminster, 1948).

Among the general accounts by the missionaries themselves (or their close associates), the most valuable is Frank C. Laubach, *The People of the Philippines: Their Religious Progress and Preparation for Spiritual Leadership in the Far East* (New York, Doran, 1925). Other accounts include John B. Devins, *An Observer in the Philippines* (Boston, American Tract Society, 1905); Briggs, *The Progressing Philippines;* Homer C. Stuntz, *The Philippines and the Far East* (Cincinnati, Jennings and Pye, 1904); William F. Oldham, *India, Malaysia, and the Philippines: A Practical Study in Missions* (New York, Eaton & Mains, 1914); Arthur J. Brown, *The New Era in the Philippines* (New York, Fleming H. Revell, 1903). The best account of the Baptist mission is by an early missionary, H.W. Munger, *Christ and the Filipino Soul: A History of the Philippine Baptists* (n.p., 1967). James B. Rodgers, *Forty Years in the Philippines: A History of the Philippine Mission of the Presbyterian Church in the United States of America, 1899–1939* (New York, Board of Foreign Missions of the Presbyterian Church in the United States of America, 1940) is a good account. Elmer K. Higdon and I.W. Higdon, *From Carabao to Clipper* (New York, Friendship Press, 1941) is a very fine account of the Disciples mission, though the book concentrates on the period after 1916.

3. See, for example, Gerald H. Anderson and Peter G. Gowing, "The Philippines," in Gerald H. Anderson, ed., *Christ and Crisis in Southeast Asia* (New York, Friendship Press, 1968), p. 153. It should also be noted that some Protestant influences were at work in the formation of the Philippine Independent Church (Iglesia Filipina Indepen-

diente), which at its height claimed the allegiance of as many as one-third of the population. Today the church has 3 or 4 percent; it maintains a connection with the Episcopal church.

4. Hermogenes Cera, "The Impact of Evangelical Faith Upon Philippine Culture" (BD Thesis, Union Theological Seminary, Dasmarinas, Cavite, Philippines), especially pp. 58–61. Anthropological studies of the effects of Protestantism in specific areas of the Philippines include F. Landa Jocano, "Conversion and the Patterning of Christian Experience In Malitbog, Central Panay, Philippines," in Peter G. Gowing and William Henry Scott, eds., *Acculturation in the Philippines: Essays on Changing Societies (A Selection of Papers Presented at the Baguio Religious Acculturation Conference from 1958 to 1968)* (Quezon City, New Day Publishers, 1971), pp. 43–72; and John J. Carroll, "Magic and Religion," in John J. Carroll et al., eds., *Philippine Institutions* (Manila, Solidaridad Publishing House, 1970), pp. 40–74.

5. "Biography of H.W. Widdoes" (unpublished typescript), United Brethren in Christ records, United Methodist Archives, Lake Junaluska, N.C. (hereafter cited as United Brethren records), p. 25; Clymer, "Methodist Missionaries and American Colonialism in the Philippines, 1899–1913."

6. Bishop Matthew Simpson, quoted in Philip D. Jordan, "Immigrants, Methodists, and a 'Conservative' Social Gospel, 1865–1908," *Methodist History*, 17:16 (October 1978).

7. Cyrus Foss, quoted in ibid., p. 17.

8. Gerald H. Anderson, "Providence and Politics behind Protestant Missionary Beginnings in the Philippines," in Anderson, ed., *Studies in Philippine Church History*, p. 289.

9. Ray Allen Billington, *The Far Western Frontier 1830–1860* (New York and Evanston, Harper & Row, 1956), p. 83.

10. R. Pierce Beaver, *Church, State, and the American Indians: Two and a Half Centuries of Partnership Between Protestant Churches and Government* (St. Louis, Concordia Publishing House, 1966), pp. 122–176; Sydney F. Ahlstrom, *A Religous History of the American People* (New Haven and London, Yale University Press, 1972), p. 861.

11. Jordan, "Immigrants, Methodists, and a 'Conservative' Social Gospel," p. 37. In 1882, the Society declared that the "work of the missionary and the patriot is one."

12. Quoted in *The Report of the Philippines Mission of the Presbyterian Mission of the Presbyterian Church in the U.S.A. 1904; Together with Short Sketches of the Work of its Several Stations from the Inception of the Mission in 1899* (Manila, Methodist Publishing House, 1905), p. 5.

13. Arthur J. Brown, *Report of a Visitation of the Philippine Mission of the Presbyterian Church in the United States of America* (New York, Board of Foreign Missions of the Presbyterian Church in the United States of America, 1902), p. 10.

14. Quoted in Cornelia Moots, *Pioneer 'Americanas' or first Methodist Missionaries in the Philippines* (n.p., 1903), p. 13.

15. William F. Oldham and James B. Rodgers for the Evangelical Union, 25 March 1905, Presbyterian Church in the U.S.A. Board of Foreign Missions. Missions Correspondence and Reports, microfilm reel 288,

Presbyterian Historical Society, Philadelphia. (References to the Presbyterian Mission Correspondence and Reports available on microfilm will hereafter be cited as Presbyterian Mission Correspondence, reel ---).

16. Charles Henry Brent to William Howard Taft, 14 April 1902, William Howard Taft Papers, Manuscript Division, Library of Congress, microfilm reel 35.

17. Brent to W.A. Leonard, 26 October 1901, Charles Henry Brent Papers, Manuscript Division, Library of Congress. The following year Brent wrote, "For God and Country is the watchword of this outpost of the Church's work." Brent to John W. Wood, 20 September 1902, Philippine Mission Correspondence, Archives and Historical Collections of the Episcopal Church, Episcopal Theological Seminary of the Southwest, Austin, Texas (hereafter cited as Episcopal Mission Correspondence).

18. Homer C. Stuntz to Taft, 27 July 1906, Taft Papers, reel 602.

19. [Bruce L. Kershner], "The Mission and the Government" (unpublished manuscript), read 31 December 1907, at the seventh annual conference of the Philippine Mission of the Disciples of Christ. Bruce L. Kershner Papers, Disciples of Christ Historical Society, Nashville.

20. George F. Pentecost, "Protestantism in the Philippines," Preached at Manila, P.I., December 21, 1902 (printed sermon), p. 14. Copy in the Presbyterian Historical Society.

21. H.H. Steinmetz, "Vacation Ramblings," *Pearl of the Orient,* 11:5–6 (July 1914). Missionary communications emphasized the possibilities of improvement under American and Protestant tutelage, suggesting that the perceived deficiencies were cultural ones. But it is sometimes difficult to distinguish between deficiencies perceived as purely cultural and those deemed to derive, in part, from inherent racial incapacities. In 1928, the prominent missionary spokesman Sherwood Eddy reflected on the attitude of optimistic certainty that pervaded the turn-of-the-century missionary outburst and assumed that racial superiority commonly entered into that attitude. "Then," he recalled, "we felt called to take up 'the white man's burden' and go out from our 'superior' race to the backward peoples of the world." G. Sherwood Eddy, "Can We Still Believe in Foreign Missions?" in Gordon Poteat, ed., *Students and the Future of Christian Missions* (New York, Student Volunteer Movement for Foreign Missions, 1928), p. 78.

22. J. Andrew Hall, "Philippine Life and Character" (unpublished manuscript), pp. 1, 3–4, Presbyterian Historical Society.

23. J[ames] H. Thoburn, *India and Malaysia* (Cincinnati, Cranston & Curts, 1892), p. 504.

24. See, for example, Stuntz, *The Philippines and the Far East,* p. 86; and Ernest J. Pace to Samuel S. Hough, 12 September 1909, United Brethren Records. The Episcopalian mission represents something of an exception to these generalizations, for it was more sympathetic to Roman Catholic theology and therefore generally refused to establish work among the Catholic population. Nevertheless, Episcopalian correspondence contains numerous denunciations of Roman Catholic corruption in the Philippines and indicates a strong resentment of Catholic methods.

25. "Civilization Dangers to Backward Peoples," *Philippine Presbyterian,* 11:2 (August 1911).

26. Brent to John W. Wood, 15 July 1904, Episcopal Mission Correspondence. Walter C. Clapp, *Bontoc Bulletin,* #3, Epiphanytide, 1905, ibid.

27. One Episcopalian missionary, for example, while aware of "the vices of the civilized West," wrote that it was not until the "Americans appeared on the scene as the great civilizing, elevating power" that there had "been a semblance of safety or a lessening of the profound suspicion of the savage." Irving Spencer, "Bagobo Land," *Spirit of Missions,* 70:387 (May 1905).

28. "Liberties Unappreciated," *Philippine Christian Advocate,* 8:[3] (November, 1908).

29. John McKee, "Alliance Missions," *Christian and Missionary Alliance,* 31:303 (31 October 1903); Paul Doltz, "The American Volunteer" (unpublished manuscript), Paul Doltz Correspondence, Presbyterian Historical Society.

30. This theme was a common one. See, for example, "Bishop Thoburn's Instructive Words," *Christian Advocate,* 76:1056 (29 August 1905); Eric Lund to Henry C. Mabie, 4 October 1900, American Baptist Mission Correspondence, Baptist Historical Society, Rochester, microfilm reel 80 (hereafter cited as Baptist Mission Correspondence) Bessie White, "God's Providence in the Entering of the Philippines," *Christian and Missionary Alliance,* 25:119 (1 September 1900); and Charles W. Briggs to E.R. Merriam, 11 April 1901, Baptist Mission Correspondence, reel 181.

31. Homer C. Stuntz, *The Philippine Mission of the Methodist Episcopal Church* (New York, Missionary Society of the Methodist Episcopal Church, n.d.), p. 16. See also, *"A Missionary for the Philippines," Christian and Missionary Alliance,* 22:145 (April 1899).

32. Brown, *Report of a Visitation,* p. 85.

33. Presbyterian David S. Hibbard, for example, wrote, "If things are as 'eminently satisfactory'" as General Otis claimed, "it does not require much to satisfy the General." In Panay, Hibbard added, the Filipino soldiers were disciplined and had "the sympathy of almost all the natives." Hibbard to F.F. Ellinwood, 24 July 1900, Presbyterian Mission Correspondence, reel 287. See also Bessie White, "The Philippines from a Missionary Standpoint," *Christian and Missionary Alliance,* 24:1 (24 March 1900).

34. Stuntz, *The Philippines and the Far East,* p. 135.

35. Charles Henry Brent, "American Democracy in the Orient" (manuscript article), enclosed in Brent to Taft, 6 April 1905, Records of the Bureau of Insular Affairs Relating to the Philippine Islands, National Archives, Washington, D.C., file 12848. (Hereafter cited as BIA file - - - -). At least one missionary, Presbyterian Leonard P. Davidson, did use the term "American-Filipino war." Quoted in Alice Byram Condict, *Old Glory and the Gospel in the Philippines: Notes Gathered during Professional and Missionary Work* (Chicago, New York, and Toronto, Fleming H. Revell, 1902), p. 65.

36. Charles W. Briggs to - - - -, 7 March 1902, Baptist Mission Correspondence, reel 181.

37. Bishop Brent and an Episcopalian nurse, Ellen T. Hicks, were invited to inspect the reconcentration camp at Bacoor. They found nothing amiss. See Charles Henry Brent, "Various Notes on Matters Philippine" (manuscript article), 24 October 1905, Episcopal Mission Correspondence; Ellen T. Hicks, "An Experiment in Nursing: A Belated Story," *Spirit of Missions,* 71:320–321 (April 1905); and Journal of W. Cameron Forbes (5 vols., unpublished), I, 272–273 (entry for 4 August 1905), W. Cameron Forbes Papers, Houghton Library, Harvard University.

38. Z[erah] C. Collins, "With the Y.M.C.A. in the Spanish-American War in the Philippines" (unpublished manuscript), Collins biographical file, Y.M.C.A. Historical Library, New York.

39. James B. Rodgers to Ellinwood, 28 August 1899, Presbyterian Mission Correspondence, reel 287. Stuntz, *The Philippines and the Far East,* p. 136. Anti-imperialist critics who publicized atrocities, wrote Stuntz, possessed minds that "forever miss currents, and get caught in eddies."

40. David S. Hibbard to Ellinwood, 24 July 1900, Presbyterian Mission Correspondence, reel 287.

41. J. Andrew Hall to Ellinwood, 1 November 1900, ibid. Hibbard had complained that the Army had been "carefully feeding and housing the prisoners and making them as comfortable as they are in their own homes." Hibbard to Ellinwood, 23 October 1900, ibid.

42. Rodgers to Ellinwood, 21 January 1901, ibid., reel 288.

43. Peter G. Gowing, *Mandate in Moroland: The American Government of Muslim Filipinos 1899–1920* (Quezon City, Philippine Center of Advanced Studies, 1977), pp. 35, 36.

44. Rodgers to Ellinwood, 11 January 1900, Presbyterian Mission Correspondence, reel 287; Jonathan McKee, "Alliance Missions," *Christian and Missionary Alliance* 31:303–304 (31 October 1903). The Alliance supported its missionary, and urged that the agreement, "which, instead of bringing peace, can only bring more bitter misunderstanding and evil," be overturned. Ibid., 29:106 (23 August 1902). When the Bates agreement was abrogated unilaterally in 1904, the missionaries were presumably gratified.

45. For a contrary view contending that the military viewed Protestant Missions as an unsettling factor and preferred to cultivate relations with the Catholics, see Donald Dean Parker, "Church and State in the Philippines 1898–1906" (PhD dissertation, University of Chicago, 1936), pp. 195, 262–263; and John Marvin Dean, *The Cross of Christ in Bolo-land* (Chicago and New York, Fleming H. Revell, 1902), pp. 49–50.

46. "Bishop Thoburn's Instructive Words," *Christian Advocate,* 74:1056 (6 July 1899).

47. Apilado, "Revolution, Colonialism, and Mission," p. 129.

48. Gowing, *Mandate in Moroland,* pp. 141–225 passim.

49. Newspaper clipping, "Sees Pagans in Fifth Avenue as in Luzon," penciled *New York Tribune,* 18 October 1913, BIA file 12848. All

that the Moro had learned from Western nations, Brent wrote shortly thereafter, was "that we are able to kill him." Copy, Brent to Henry L. Higginson, 3 February 1914, Brent Papers. Brent attempted, apparently without success, to get Congressional support for better medical services for the Moros. So devoted did he become in later years to humanitarian work among the Muslim Filipinos that he directed that any memorial gifts received upon his death be used to assist such efforts. Copy, Brent to Mabel T. Boardman, 26 March 1914, Brent Papers; copy, Senator G.H. Hitchcock to Boardman, 13 May 1914, ibid.; Zabriskie, *Brent*, p. 73.

50. E.H. Gates, in the *Advent Review and Sabbath Herald,* 83:11 (10 May 1906).

51. Cited in Rodgers to F.M. Bond, 16 March 1904, Presbyterian Mission Correspondence, reel 288.

52. Stealy B. Rossiter, "The Philippines Before and After the Occupation, May 1, 1898" (unpublished manuscript) ibid., reel 289; L.V. Finster to A.G. Daniells, 23 August 1911, Record Group 11 (Presidential), Incoming Letters 1911-F, Seventh-day Adventist Archives, Washington, D.C.

53. Henry W. Warren, "The United States in the Philippines," *Christian Advocate,* 79:2032 (15 December 1904). For other comments lauding American efforts to improve public health, see Rodgers to Ellinwood, 26 March 1902, Presbyterian Mission Correspondence, and Robert W. Carter to Arthur J. Brown, 27 October 1907, ibid., reel 289.

54. J.M. Groves to W.D. Murray, 30 June 1909, Y.M.C.A. Historical Library. "Publish nothing which may compromise the administration or officials," a Y.M.C.A. official admonished John R. Mott. [W.A. Tener] to John R. Mott, 1 September 1908, ibid.

55. Samuel S. Hough, quoted in "Biography of H.W. Widdoes," p. 249.

56. *Eighty-Sixth Annual Report of the Missionary Society of the Methodist Episcopal Church for the Year 1904* (New York, Board of Foreign Missions of the Methodist Episcopal Church, 1905), p. 273.

57. Alex A. Pieters to Ellinwood, 29 April 1903, Presbyterian Mission Correspondence, reel 288.

58. Charles W. Briggs, "The Pulahanes in Panay," *Missionary Review of the World,* 34:515 (July 1911).

59. For example, Arthur W. Prautch, "A Crime, Not a Blunder" (unpublished manuscript), Record Group 74-11, Philippine Islands Correspondence (Prautch folder), Records of the Methodist Episcopal Missionary Society, United Methodist Archives (hereafter cited as R.G. 74-11, United Methodist Archives). Arthur W. Prautch, "Marriage Question in the Philippines" (unpublished manuscript), 28 December 1899, ibid. David S. Hibbard to F.F. Ellinwood, 29 December 1899, Presbyterian Mission Correspondence, reel 287. Dean, *Cross of Christ in Bolo-land,* pp. 49-50. On the questionable validity of the criticism, see Rodgers to Ellinwood, 6 February 1900, Presbyterian Mission Correspondence, and Donald Dean Parker, "Church and State in the Philippines, 1896-1906," *Philippine Social Science Review,* 10:381-382 (1938).

60. Journal of W. Cameron Forbes, V, 174 (entry for 14 January 1913).
61. Walter C. Clapp to John W. Wood, 9 July 1908, Episcopal Mission Correspondence; Brent to John W. Wood, 21 November 1908, ibid.
62. J.H. Groves to Sherwood Eddy, 29 June 1914, Y.M.C.A. Historical Library. Worcester's reputation changed, however, at least in some important Protestant circles. No one doubted his intellectual abilities, and, by 1912, even Brent felt that the Commissioner had "a genuine and self sacrificing love for the primitive folk." Brent to W.C. Rivers, 21 October 1912, Brent Papers. See also Frank C. Laubach to J.L. Barton, 27 March 1916, Philippine Mission Records, American Board of Commissioners for Foreign Missions, Houghton Library, Harvard University (hereafter cited as American Board Mission Correspondence).

   Worcester, for his part, counted Brent among his friends, and in 1914 he endorsed the Bishop's efforts to organize a non-denominational "Christian peace work" among the Moros. Dean C. Worcester, *The Philippines Past and Present* (2 vols., New York, Macmillan, 1914), II, 643. Worcester's endorsement is referred to in Edward H. Fallows to Hamilton Holt, 18 August 1914, a copy of which is in the Brent Papers. When the Commissioner resigned in 1913, the publication of the Disciples mission observed, surely incorrectly, that Americans reacted with "almost universal regret." "This and That," *Philippine Christian*, 13:1 (10 September 1913).
63. G.A. Irwin, "Malay Peninsula and the Philippines," *Advent Review and Sabbath Herald*, 82:14 (15 June 1905).
64. Peter G. Gowing, "The White Man and the Moro: A Comparison of Spanish and American Policies Toward Muslim Filipinos," *Solidarity*, 6:40 (March 1971).
65. Robert F. Black to Judson Smith, 14 May 1903, American Board Mission Correspondence. A favor that must have been especially meaningful to the missionary involved Colonel Harbord's decision to order a Constabulary physician to remain in Davao to assist with the birth of Black's child. The physician may well have saved Mrs. Black's life. Black to Smith, 3 July 1905, ibid.
66. "Address by Major Henry Gilheuser, Governor of the District of Davao, October 13, 1911" (unpublished manuscript), ibid.
67. Laubach to James L. Barton, 28 December 1915, ibid.; Laubach to Enoch F. Bell, 6 January 1916, ibid.
68. Brent to John W. Wood, 8 August 1903, Episcopal Mission Correspondence; Irving Spencer to Wood, 15 May 1904, ibid.; Brent to Wood, 8 August 1903, ibid.
69. Perhaps Bruce Kershner of the Disciples mission expressed most persuasively the advantages missions brought to the government. At a time "when the premonition of Oriental power and invasion" was "creeping like a chill up the spine of the West," he wrote in a reflective paper, it behooved the missionary community to foster conservative change only. As the promoters of carefully controlled change, Kershner thought, the missionary and the government were surely allies. For, like the government, the missionary was "holding back the billows which may break with desolating power upon his own

people . . . . He feels that he is the one whose hand is upon the balance wheel of a nation and his influence is the same as kings, emperors or presidents." Bruce L. Kershner, "Missionary Inspiration" (unpublished manuscript), n.d. [1911?], given to Stephen J. Cory, Kershner Papers.

70. See, for example, James B. Rodgers to Taft, 22 March 1905, and Taft to Rodgers, 10 February 1906, BIA file 12662.

71. Charles Henry Brent, "The Church in the Philippine Islands: A Trip through Northern Luzon," *Spirit of Missions,* 68:792 (November 1903).

72. Homer C. Stuntz, "Governor William Howard Taft, of the Philippines," *Christian Advocate,* 76:1380 (29 August 1901).

73. Stuntz to Adna B. Leonard, 24 December 1903, R.G. 74-11 (Stuntz folder), United Methodist Archives.

74. Clymer, "Methodist Missionaries and American Colonialism."

75. Stephen Neill, *Colonialism and Christian Missions* (New York, McGraw-Hill, 1966), p. 93.

76. Robert T. Handy, *A Christian America: Protestant Hopes and Historical Realities* (New York, Oxford University Press, 1971), pp. 38–40, 101-105, The quotation is on p. 101.

77. George W. Wright to Arthur J. Brown, 13 April 1905, Presbyterian Mission Correspondence, reel 288. Charles N. Magill to Brown, 7 July 1910, ibid., reel 289.

78. Laubach to J.L. Barton, 6 May 1915, American Board Mission Correspondence.

79. Report of Charles W. Briggs (unpublished), 16 January 1907, Baptist Mission Correspondence, reel 181.

80. Marvin Rader to Adna B. Leonard, 17 March 1911, R.G. 43, file 66-12 (Rader folder), United Methodist Archives.

81. Rodgers to F.F. Ellinwood, 5 March 1899, Presbyterian Mission Correspondence, reel 287.

82. Walter O. McIntyre to Arthur J. Brown, 21 October 1903, ibid., reel 288.

83. Charles L. Maxfield to Miss MacLaurin, 27 December 1904, Baptist Mission Correspondence, reel 194. "Private Journal of Harry Farmer: Beginnings of Methodism in the Agno Valley Area, the Philippines, 1904-1907" (unpublished), 8 May 1904; 9 December 1905; 26 August 1905, pp. 21-22, 95-96, 143; United Methodist Church national office, Manila.

84. Stuntz to Roosevelt, 2 February 1907, BIA file 4213-1. The BIA, which investigated Stuntz's "rather bitter complaint," found it to be without substance. Unsigned BIA memorandum, ibid.

85. W.H. Hanna, "Religious Liberty in the Philippines," *Christian Evangelist,* 45:1161 (10 September 1908). David O. Lund, quoted in Elizabeth White Jansen, "A Visit to Zamboanga, Philippines," *Christian and Missionary Alliance,* 8 May 1909, p. 90.

86. Laubach to J.L. Barton, 6 May 1915, American Board Mission Correspondence.

87. See, for example, Leon C. Hills to F.F. Ellinwood, 13 January 1902,

Presbyterian Mission Correspondence, reel 288.

88. Copy, L.B. Hilles to Dr. Sauber, 20 August 1903, ibid. If such a policy ever existed, it was quickly rescinded or ignored, for, during their travels, missionaries regularly lodged with American schoolteachers. See, for example, "The Journal of Harry Farmer," passim.

89. *Eighty-Sixth Annual Report of the Missionary Society of the Methodist Episcopal Church for the Year 1904*, p. 273. It seems likely that Atkinson was not very sympathetic with Protestant missionary work, for he once wrote that "The prospects as to Protestant work . . . are not very encouraging." Fred W. Atkinson, *The Philippine Islands* (Boston, Ginn, 1905), p. 225.

90. *Pearl of the Orient*, 3:38 (October 1906).

91. H.W. Langheim to Arthur J. Brown, 26 May 1909, Presbyterian Mission Correspondence, reel 289.

92. Robert W. Carter to Dr. Halsey, 5 October 1909, ibid.

93. Brown, *Report of a Visitation*, p. 54.

94. Laubach to James L. Barton, 6 May 1915, American Board Mission Correspondence. For similar expressions, see Rader to A.B. Leonard, 17 March 1911, R.G. 43, file 66-12 (Rader file), United Methodist Archives; Charles Maxfield to "Dear Friends," 2 February 1912, Baptist Mission Correspondence, reel 198; and Eric Lund, "Schools in the Philippines" (unpublished manuscript) enclosed in Lund to Thomas S. Barbour, 28 March 1906, Baptist Mission Correspondence, reel 197.

95. George W. Wright strongly defended the government's school policy and claimed that relationships with the teachers were "most cordial and happy" (Wright to Brown, 18 May 1909, Presbyterian Mission Correspondence, reel 289), whereas H.W. Langheim and Charles Hamilton disagreed. They felt that the policy was enforced only in cases involving Protestant teachers and, in any event, raised serious constitutional problems (Langheim to Brown, 26 May 1909, ibid.; Hamilton to Brown, 20 August 1909, ibid).

96. "Philippine [Mission] Minutes, 1910," (unpublished) ibid., reel 290.

97. For example, Laubach, *People of the Philippines*, pp. 333–334.

98. Charles Maxfield to "Dear Friends," 2 February 1912, Baptist Mission Correspondence, reel 198; galley proofs of J.L. McLaughlin's report of April 1907, to the American Bible Society, enclosed in William I. Haven to Taft, 3 April 1907, BIA file 1158.

99. For example, "Journal of Harry Farmer," 7 February 1906, pp. 176-177; Robert W. Carter to Arthur J. Brown, 27 October 1907, Presbyterian Mission Correspondence, reel 289. Carter noted the "active opposition" to Protestant work "from government officials."

100. Stuntz to Roosevelt, 4 December 1904, BIA file 11980.

101. Copy, Bruce L. Kershner to W.H. Hanna, 9 October 1907, Kershner Papers, J.L. McElhany, in *Advent Review and Sabbath Herald*, 84:19-20 (12 December 1907). The missions were also angered a few years later when the government helped reconstruct the town of Antipolo. See "This and That," *Philippine Christian*, 8:[1] (10 October 1913).

102. Clipping, Charles W. Briggs to the editor, 21 May 1908, "Unjust and

Perilous Favoritism," *The Examiner,* 9 July [1908], BIA file 2396. James A. Graham to Arthur J. Brown, 18 December 1907, Presbyterian Mission Correspondence, reel 289.

103. Harry Farmer to William F. Oldham, 5 October 1908, file 43, box 339 (Mrs. Harry Farmer), United Methodist Archives.

104. I have dealt with this matter in more detail in "Methodist Missionaries and American Colonialism."

105. "Philippine [Mission] Minutes," January 1910 and December 1910, Presbyterian Mission Correspondence, reel 290.

106. Report of Bohol Station, Presbyterian Philippine Mission, received 29 December 1911; and Report of Camarines Station, Presbyterian Philippine Mission, received 29 December 1911; both in United Presbyterian Church in the United States of America, Philippine Mission Correspondence, 1911–1921, Record Group 85, box 1, file 2, Presbyterian Historical Society.

107. Statements on file in BIA file 2396. The statements were made in August and September 1902.

108. Walter C. Clapp to Arthur S. Lloyd, 12 August 1902, Episcopal Mission Correspondence; Brent to E.F. Baldwin, 24 July 1903, Brent Papers.

109. Zabriskie, *Brent,* pp. 54–55.

110. Adolph Wislizenus to Brent, 31 January 1910, Brent Papers; Brent to Wislizenus, 21 February 1910, ibid.

111. Memorandum, James M. Thoburn, "Opium Monopoly in the Philippines," (memorandum of a hearing of 9 July 1903, before Elihu Root), BIA file 1023–44. For other protests, see Methodist Episcopal Mission of the Philippine Islands to Wilbur Crafts, 2 May 1903, BIA file 1023–17, and Report of the American Church in Manila of the [Presbyterian] Philippine Mission, 1903, Presbyterian Mission Correspondence, reel 290.

112. Telegram, Roosevelt to Taft, 9 June 1903, BIA file 1023–24.

113. *Official Journal of the Second Annual Session of the Philippine Islands Mission Conference of the Methodist Episcopal Church* [1906] (Manila, Methodist Publishing House, 1906), p. 48. See also Parker, "Church and State," (dissertation) pp. 271–272.

114. "The Moral Progress League in Manila," *Christian Advocate,* 80:1319 (30 August 1906).

115. Brent's endorsement of the Moral Progress League was not unqualified. It tended to be overly emotional, he thought, and did not provide constructive alternatives. Still, the Bishop concluded, "The Spirit of God is in it." *Manila Times,* 16 July 1906, pp. 1–2. Although Forbes was a good friend of Brent, he resented the Bishop's position in this instance. See Journal of W. Cameron Forbes, II, 60, 62 (entries for 3 July and 2 August 1906).

116. Unidentified clipping, "The Government and Gambling in the Philippines," enclosed in Mrs. Stephen L. Baldwin to Roosevelt, 31 July 1908, BIA file 6633.

117. Ibid.; Journal of W. Cameron Forbes, II, 402 (entry for 21 February 1908).

118. Telegram, Evangelical Union to Roosevelt, 15 February 1908, BIA file 6633; Mercer G. Johnston, "A Covenant with Death, An Agreement with Hell" (printed sermon), preached in the Cathedral of St. Mary and St. John, Manila, 23 February 1908, copy in BIA file 6633. Johnston also cabled Roosevelt directly; see Johnston to Roosevelt, received 24 February 1908, BIA file 6633.
119. Journal of W. Cameron Forbes, II, 408 (entry for 3 March 1908).
120. Ibid., II, 396 (entry for 5 February 1908).
121. Clarence Edwards, "Memorandum for the Secretary of War: In Re: Concession for a Cockpit During a Carnival at Manila," 24 February 1908, BIA file 6633.
122. Journal of W. Cameron Forbes, II, 403 (entry for 21 February 1908).
123. *Missions in the Philippines* (Boston, American Baptist Missionary Union, [1906]), p. 40.
124. H.H. Steinmetz, "A Social Gospel for the Philippines," *Pearl of the Orient*, 10:3–8 (July 1913). Methodist Harry Farmer also surmised that the government had lost interest in helping the poor. See Harry Farmer, "Contending for Religious Liberty," *Philippine Christian Advocate*, 7:6–8 (July 1908).
125. For example, copy, Brent to W.C. Rivers, 25 November 1907, Brent Papers.
126. The debate can be followed in the *Manila Times* during October and November 1907, and in Rossiter's correspondence with the mission board during the same period. Presbyterian Mission Correspondence, reel 289.
127. For missionary involvement in the Philippine Society, see BIA file 16654; issues of the *Philippine Bulletin* (published by the Philippine Society), copies in ibid.; Apilado, "Revolution, Colonialism, and Mission," pp. 269–274; and Clymer, "The Methodist Response to Philippine Nationalism," pp. 431–432.
128. Copy, C.L. Pickett to Bruce Kershner, 12 March 1914, Kershner Papers; Kershner to D.O. Cunningham, 12 September 1914, ibid.
129. W.F. Oldham, "The Profits and Peril of Philippine Autonomy—At This Time," *Report of the Thirty-first Annual Lake Mohonk Conference of Friends of the Indian and Other Dependent Peoples, October 22d, 23d, and 24th, 1913*, p. 129; "Philippine Society Banquet," *The Philippine Bulletin*, 1:3 (July, 1913). For the changes in missionary thought, see Valentin H. Rabe, *The Home Base of American China Missions, 1880–1920* (Cambridge, Council on East Asian Studies, Harvard University, 1978), pp. 173–191, and Paul A. Varg, *Missionaries, Chinese, and Diplomats: The American Protestant Missionary Movement in China, 1890–1958* (Princeton, Princeton University Press, 1958), pp. 99–104, and Chapter 9.
130. Walter C. Clapp to John W. Wood, 22 May 1904, Episcopal Mission Correspondence.
131. Brent, quoted in the *Manila Times*, 16 November 1907, p. 3, col. 3, citing the *Washington Post* of 9 October 1907. President Roosevelt

352 *Notes to Pages 166–170*

was so disturbed by the Bishop's criticism that in private he questioned Brent's veracity, suggested that his knowledge of history was sadly deficient, and complained that his analogies were inept, his arguments absurd, and that he had given aid and comfort to the anti-imperialists. "Surely he must be suffering from some great mental strain," the President conjectured. Roosevelt to Silas McBee, 27 August 1907, in Elting E. Morison, ed., *The Letters of Theodore Roosevelt* (8 vols., Cambridge, Harvard University Press, 1951–1954), V, 772–775. In spite of this temporary falling out, the two men remained good friends.

132. [Arthur Seldon] Lloyd, "To Bontoc and Back Again," *Spirit of Missions*, 72:367 (May 1907).
133. Steinmetz, "A Social Gospel for the Philippines," pp. 3–8.
134. Copy, Brent to Mrs. George Monks, 27 April 1907, Brent Papers.
135. Quoted in Daniel R. Williams, *The Odyssey of the Philippine Commission* (Chicago, A.C. McClurg, 1913), p. 350.
136. See, for example, Michael V. Metallo, "American Missionaries, Sun Yat-sen, and the Chinese Revolution," *Pacific Historical Review*, 47:266 (May 1978).
137. Apilado, "Revolution, Colonialism, and Mission," pp. 254–286; Clymer, "The Methodist Response to Philippine Nationalism," pp. 424–427; Richard L. Deats, "Nicolas Zamora: Religious Nationalist," in Anderson, ed., *Studies in Philippine Church History*, pp. 325–336.
138. Cornelio M. Ferrer, "How to Survive in the Ministry" (typescript), p. 63, Cornelio M. Ferrer Papers, United Methodist Archives.
139. Alejandro, *From Darkness to Light,* p. 16; Cornelio M. Ferrer and Paul Locke A. Granadosin, "The Episcopal Address: Philippine Central Conference, The United Methodist Church, November 29, 1972" (mimeographed), Ferrer Papers.
140. Robert L. Youngblood, "The Protestant Church in the Philippines' New Society," *Bulletin of Concerned Asian Scholars*, 12:19–29 (July-September 1980). Youngblood discusses Roman Catholic attitudes toward martial law in "Church Opposition to Martial Law in the Philippines," *Asian Survey*, 58:505–520 (May 1978).

14

Wilsonian Idealism and Japanese Claims at the Paris Peace Conference

Noriko Kawamura

According to Ray Stannard Baker, head of the Press Bureau of the American Committee to Negotiate the Peace, the Paris Peace Conference in 1919 was a battlefield of two ideas: the "Old Diplomacy," practiced by imperialists of the Old World, and the "New Diplomacy," advocated by idealistic internationalists under the leadership of President Woodrow Wilson.[1] This dichotomy, however, does not fully explain the antagonism between Japan and the United States at the end of World War I. This study explores further possible explanations of President Wilson's failure to fend off the Japanese challenge to the principles of Wilsonian internationalism as set forth in his Fourteen Points. It argues that Japanese-American differences were more than either simple disagreements over diplomatic principles or particular disputes over economic, territorial, or political concessions. Hidden behind the conflict was another dichotomy— between America's universalism and unilateralism, on the one hand, and, on the other, an incipient particularistic regionalism and pluralism derived from Japanese leaders' assessment of

The author would like to thank Robert J. C. Butow, Wilton B. Fowler, Jonathan G. Utley, and the *PHR* referees for their helpful comments and advice.

1. Ray Stannard Baker, *Woodrow Wilson and World Settlement* (3 vols., Garden City, N.Y., 1923), passim.

power relations in East Asia and their strong sense of nationalism and racial identity.

As the United States became engulfed in the Great War in Europe, President Wilson embraced an idealistic internationalism centered around principles of open diplomacy, freedom, self-determination, and international justice. He was convinced that these were universal principles, and he sought to make them the basis upon which every nation conducted foreign relations. Wilson's universalistic idealism stemmed from his unwavering faith in Christianity and in the superior moral values, political sophistication, cultural traditions, and racial characteristics of Western civilization.[2]

Wilson's failure to resolve his disagreements with Japan stemmed to no small extent from his firm belief in the universality of his internationalist ideals: Nations that failed to adhere to his ideals he considered morally wrong. He unilaterally applied his ideals to the East Asian situation without a full comprehension of regional realities. His knowledge of East Asia was limited and colored by reports from diplomats and "experts" who shared his zeal for America's mission in East Asia. By treating Japan as a morally inferior state and turning America's rivalry with Japan in East Asia into a crusade against an uncivilized force, Wilson made it impossible to find a workable compromise. Wilson's inflexible unilateralism was one of the limitations of his idealism.

As a late developer by Western standards, Japan strove to attain equality with the West and join the ranks of the great powers. It emulated rivals by adopting their expansionist and imperialist practices. Because of geographical proximity, Japan was eager to benefit from the treaty port system the Western powers had established in China. Japanese leaders quickly learned to use alliances, secret treaties, and, if necessary, mili-

---

2. This interpretation of Wilson's idealism is based on the following sources: Lloyd E. Ambrosius, *Wilsonian Statecraft: Theory and Practice of Liberal Internationalism during World War I* (Wilmington, Del., 1991); Lloyd E. Ambrosius, *Woodrow Wilson and the American Diplomatic Tradition: The Treaty Fight in Perspective* (Cambridge, Eng., 1987); Michael H. Hunt, *Ideology and U.S. Foreign Policy* (New Haven, Conn., 1987); Arthur S. Link, *Woodrow Wilson: Revolution, War, and Peace* (Arlington Heights, Ill., 1979); Thomas J. Knock, *To End All Wars: Woodrow Wilson and the Quest for a New World Order* (New York, 1992); David Steigerwald, *Wilsonian Idealism in America* (Ithaca, N.Y., 1994).

tary force to further their national interests. They paid due respect to the existing rules and precedents in the imperialist game established by the Western powers. Japan did not take any drastic actions without reaching prior understandings with other major powers, especially its ally, Great Britain. In these ways, Japanese leaders considered their country to be a fair player in the arena of international competition.

Nevertheless, the view of the world that Japanese leaders embraced at the time of World War I was provincial. It focused narrowly on the protection of Japan's security and the enhancement of national interests and prestige. Having established a foothold on the northeastern edge of the Asian continent through wars with China (1894–1895) and Russia (1904–1905), Japanese leaders searched for a more self-assertive foreign policy appropriate for an emerging great power in Asia. The outbreak of hostilities in Europe provided the opportunity to launch a vigorous program of continental expansion, and throughout the war Japanese foreign policy was built upon the selfish purpose of national aggrandizement. However, the diplomatic blunder of the Twenty-one Demands on China—the 1915 treaties in which China agreed to abide by Japanese-German agreements over the disposition of German rights, interests, and concessions in Shandong at the close of the war—triggered a serious debate in Tokyo over the rationale and the method of Japanese continental expansion.

In the course of searching for a comprehensive new policy toward the Asian continent, senior leaders in Japan gradually developed a pluralistic and regionalistic approach to justify Japanese hegemony in East Asia. By focusing on both the geopolitical separation of Asia from the West and the differences between the racial and cultural heritage of Asian and Western states, they moved toward a pluralistic stance, arguing that a nation's conduct could be based on different principles from those laid out by the Western great powers.

Similarly, from the outset of the modernization efforts, many political and intellectual leaders in Japan claimed that a "special relationship" existed between Japan and China. They pointed to obvious geopolitical, economic, and strategic commonalities, and, particularly among powerful senior statesmen known as "genro," to the idea of a "common culture and com-

506   Pacific Historical Review

mon race" (*dobun doshu*) that the peoples of the two countries shared. Genro Masayoshi Matsukata argued in favor of a special position for Japan in China by using the idea of Japanese "tutelage" over China. Another genro, Shigenobu Okuma, who served as premier from 1914 to 1916, espoused the idea of the "yellow man's burden."[3]

During World War I, Aritomo Yamagata, the most influential genro, emerged as the leading advocate of Sino-Japanese cooperation and articulated a series of famous policy slogans, such as Sino-Japanese "accord" (*teikei*) and "coexistence and co-prosperity" (*kyoson kyoei*). Yamagata believed that the Great War was part of an international trend toward "an increasing intensity in racial rivalry." Pointing to racial discrimination against Asians, such as the anti-Japanese movement in California, he argued that if the colored races of Asia hoped to compete with the culturally advanced white races, "China and Japan, which are culturally and racially alike, must become friendly and promote each other's interests."[4] Although he admitted that Japan had specific national interests in Manchuria, he emphasized that Japan must also set its sights on "the self-protection of Asians and for the coexistence and co-prosperity of China and Japan."[5] Japan's wartime leaders saw in these arguments the ideological foundation for an Asian Monroe Doctrine, a Japanese version of imperialism that was regionalistic and even anti-Western in motivation.

Yamagata and other Japanese leaders exhibited curiously ambivalent attitudes toward China. On the one hand, they believed that their country's national survival dictated that they secure Japan's "life-line" to the continent by any means possible, including exploitation of their weak neighbor through intimidation and coercion, so far as the great powers would permit. Simultaneously, as the only non-Western imperial power in East Asia, the Japanese also felt justified in claiming a special pater-

---

3. Peter Duus, Ramon H. Myers, and Mark R. Peattie, eds., *The Japanese Informal Empire in China, 1898–1937* (Princeton, N.J., 1989), xxvi.

4. Aritomo Yamagata, "Written Opinion Concerning China Policy," August 1914, in Azusa Oyama, ed., *Yamagata Aritomo ikensho* [Collection of memoranda by Aritomo Yamagata] (Tokyo, 1966), 339–345.

5. William G. Beasley, *Japanese Imperialism, 1894–1945* (Oxford, Eng., 1987), 118.

nalistic position in the region on the grounds of geographical propinquity as well as common racial and cultural background. They naively believed that China would accept Japan's tutelage if it understood Japan's true intentions. For example, when Yamagata proposed a Sino-Japanese entente pledging "union and cooperation," his foremost goal was to encourage China's confidence in Japan through persuasion and guidance. In doing so, he took it for granted that China would follow Japan's leadership and consult with Tokyo in its dealings with other foreign countries.

In these respects, the United States and Japan stood far apart in their views of the world when hostilities in Europe came to an end in November 1918. By the time President Wilson and the Japanese delegation assembled for the first meeting of the Supreme Council of the Peace Conference, both sides had diametrically opposite objectives based on incompatible visions of the postwar world.

* * *

The American delegation to the peace conference had as its objective a new world order as envisioned in President Wilson's Fourteen Points. So far as Wilson was concerned, the Fourteen Points were the only possible program for world peace. The realization of such principles as open diplomacy, freedom of the seas, free trade, and the self-determination of states, he declared to Congress in January 1918, hinged on the creation of a league of nations. He reiterated this position in his address on September 27, 1918, at the Metropolitan Opera House in New York, stating that "the constitution of that League of Nations and the clear definition of its objective must be . . . the most essential part of the peace settlement itself." Here and elsewhere, he insisted that "no special or separate interest of any single nation or any groups of nations can be made the basis of any part of the settlement which is not consistent with the common interest of all."[6] Having secured from

---

6. U.S. Department of State, *Foreign Relations of the United States, 1918*, Supplement 1 (2 vols., Washington, D.C., 1933) I, 12–17; hereafter cited as *Foreign Relations, 1918*. Arthur S. Link, ed., *The Papers of Woodrow Wilson* (69 vols., Princeton, N.J., 1967–1994), XLV, 534–539; LI, 129–130; hereafter cited as *Papers of Woodrow Wilson*.

508   Pacific Historical Review

both Germany and the European Allies a pre-armistice agreement that they would, as a matter of principle, embrace the Fourteen Points as the basis of peace, Wilson presumed that the Fourteen Points would shape the peace conference and, in turn, the postwar world.

Wilson gave the lowest priority to questions concerning the disposition of the German colonies. On the way to Paris, he revealed to chief members of the Inquiry (a special commission directed by Colonel Edward M. House to prepare the U.S. government's program for peace) his belief that the mandate system through the League of Nations would provide a satisfactory solution to the matter. His plan was to make the German colonies "the common property of the League of Nations" to be "given to one of the smaller states to administer as the mandatory" of the League primarily in the interest of the natives. Wilson stressed that the peace conference would not tolerate "arrangements" made in "the old style" and that "only the adoption of a cleansing process would recreate or regenerate the world."[7] George L. Beer, an expert on colonial questions for the Inquiry, was disturbed by the President's suggestion, commenting in his diary that Wilson's mandatory idea was "a very dangerous and academic type of thinking."[8] Beer knew that colonial administration required skill and experience in both the governing state and the colony.

Prior to the peace conference, there is little evidence of Wilson's thinking about German rights and concessions in Shandong. This had been an extremely delicate subject between the Japanese and American governments since the crisis over the Twenty-one Demands in 1915. The crisis aroused Wilson's suspicion of Japan's territorial ambition in China. The American government had refused to recognize the treaties signed between the Chinese and Japanese governments on May 25, 1915. In the summer of 1918, Wilson was again upset by the way Japan took advantage of his proposal for a joint military expedition to Vladivostok by dispatching a far larger number of troops than he had expected. Wilson therefore had no intention

7. Diary of William C. Bullitt, Dec. 9 [10], 1918, *Papers of Woodrow Wilson*, LIII, 351; memorandum by Isaiah Bowman, Dec. 10, 1918, *ibid.*, 355.

8. George L. Beer's Diary, Dec. 10, 1918, quoted in James T. Shotwell, *At the Paris Peace Conference* (New York, 1937), 75.

of accommodating Japanese interests at the expense of China. In November 1918, when the President had a brief interview with Chinese Minister V. K. Wellington Koo (one of the five Chinese plenipotentiaries at Paris), he expressed his willingness to support China's case at the coming peace conference.[9]

Prior to the Paris conference, the Inquiry offered little advice about the Shandong question because the organization lacked "qualified, trained scholars" capable of dealing with Asian problems. Lawrence E. Gelfand has suggested that the Inquiry's reports on East Asian issues, which were unsympathetic toward Japanese aspirations in Asia, were produced by nonexperts. Some thirty years after the conference, Charles Seymour recalled that even Stanley K. Hornbeck, Chief of the Far Eastern Division of the Inquiry since September 1918, was inadequately prepared, saying that "Hornbeck knew something about the Far East but he learned most of it from 1919 on."[10]

While the American Embassy in Tokyo offered little insight into the thinking of the Japanese leadership to the end of formulating American policy, alarming reports from the American minister to Beijing, Paul S. Reinsch, had a significant influence on Hornbeck and other East Asian advisers just before the opening of the conference. Reinsch, who had been Hornbeck's mentor at the University of Wisconsin, was the embodiment of Wilsonian universal idealism and unilateralist internationalism. After alerting the State Department to Tokyo's attempts to silence Chinese opposition to the Japanese claims at Paris, Reinsch made an unusual request to Washington, asking the State Department to transmit his telegram directly to President Wilson in Paris. In his message, Reinsch indicted Japan's wartime actions in China and appealed for Wilson's personal intervention, because the President had become "to the people of China the embodiment of their best hopes and aspirations." Reinsch said, "I have been forced through the experience of five years to the conclusion that the methods applied by the Japanese military masters can lead only to evil and destruction." He argued that "only the refusal to accept the result of

---

9. Arthur Walworth, *Wilson and His Peacemakers: American Diplomacy at the Paris Peace Conference, 1919* (New York, 1986), 360–361.

10. Lawrence E. Gelfand, *The Inquiry: American Preparation for Peace, 1917–1919* (New Haven, Conn., 1963), 63–66, 227, 260–265, 315.

510   Pacific Historical Review

Japanese secret manipulation in China during the last four years, particularly the establishment of Japanese political influence and privileged position in Shantung" could prevent China from becoming a dependent of Japan. He said that German rights in Shandong "lapsed together with all Sino-German treaties upon the declaration of war" and that a succession of treaty rights from Germany to Japan was therefore impossible.[11]

Hornbeck gave unqualified support to Reinsch's plea from Beijing. He believed that his mentor's observations on the East Asian situation were "uniformly and absolutely accurate" and "worthy of the most careful consideration of the Peace Commissioners." Edward T. Williams, the other Far Eastern technical expert of the American Mission, concurred. He commented that "the spirit of Japan is that of Prussia, whom [sic] Japanese leaders openly admire and whose government they deliberately chose for a model." Throughout its history, he continued, Japan's objective had been to dominate Asia, and the present cabinet of Takashi Hara was no exception. Employing Wilsonian rhetoric, Williams concluded that "Japan must be restrained if justice is to prevail or liberty survive in the Far East."[12]

The recommendations President Wilson received in the early stage of the peace conference clearly reflected the anti-Japanese sentiments of the East Asian "experts" of the Inquiry. Their reports insisted that Japan should be prohibited from control over the port of Qingdao and that the entire German-leased territory in Jiaozhou and the Shandong Railway should be restored to China. With a view to freeing China from obligations under the Twenty-one Demands, the Inquiry recommended that all Sino-Japanese agreements concluded during the war involving the transfer or allocation of territory, special rights, or privileges should "be subject to screening for ap-

---

11. Frank L. Polk to the Commission to Negotiate Peace, undated [received Jan. 5, 1919]; Paul S. Reinsch to Polk, Jan. 6, 1919, U.S. Department of State, *Foreign Relations of the United States 1919: The Paris Peace Conference* (13 vols., Washington, D.C, 1942–1947), I, 151–158; hereafter cited as *Paris Peace Conference*. *Papers of Woodrow Wilson*, LIV, 77–82.

12. Stanley K. Hornbeck to the Commission to Negotiate Peace, undated, *Paris Peace Conference*, II, 525–526. Edward M. House papers cited in Roy W. Curry, *Woodrow Wilson and Far Eastern Policy, 1913–1921* (New York, 1957), 253. Burton F. Beers, *Vain Endeavor: Robert Lansing's Attempt to End the American-Japanese Rivalry* (Durham, N.C., 1962), 154.

proval, revision, or rejection by the peace conference." The Inquiry went so far as to suggest that the peace conference review the Sino-Japanese treaties with regard to Japan's sphere of influence in South Manchuria and Eastern Inner Mongolia. The recommendation also included a rather unrealistic proposal to internationalize all railroads in Manchuria. In order to pacify Japanese expansionist zeal but, apparently, without careful consideration, the Inquiry simply proposed that Japan be allowed to have the Russian maritime provinces.[13]

There is no evidence to suggest that Wilson and his advisers, prior to their arrival in Europe, knew that Tokyo had secretly secured British and French agreement to support Japanese claims to German rights in Shandong and the German islands in the Pacific north of the equator. In the spring of 1917, British Foreign Secretary Arthur J. Balfour had provided Colonel House with the text of various secret treaties that Great Britain had concluded with the Allies, but he had not enclosed the agreement with Japan over Shandong and the German islands in the Pacific. In the fall of 1917, Japan's special envoy, Kikujiro Ishii, had told Secretary of State Robert Lansing that England had practically agreed that Japan would retain the German Pacific islands north of the equator and that England would keep those south of the equator.[14] When Wilson had met with British Prime Minister David Lloyd George on December 30, 1918, for "an informal interchange of views" on the issues to be discussed at the peace conference, the prime minister revealed that his government "had definitely promised to Japan the Islands in the Northern Pacific." Wilson responded that "he was by no means prepared to accept the Japanese Treaty" and hinted that he meant to act "as a buffer to prevent" the Japanese from retaining those islands. Curiously, Lloyd George made no mention of his support for Japan's claims to the German concessions in Shandong. Several months earlier,

---

13. "Black Book 2: Outline of Tentative Report and Recommendations Prepared by the Intelligence Section in accordance with Instructions, for the President and the Plenipotentiaries," Feb.13, 1919, Woodrow Wilson Papers, Library of Congress (microfilm copy). Gelfand, *The Inquiry,* 265–269, 322, 325.

14. *Papers of Woodrow Wilson,* XLII, 156–157. U.S. Department of State, *Foreign Relations of the United States: The Lansing Papers, 1914–1920* (2 vols., Washington, D.C., 1940), II, 433; hereafter cited as *Lansing Papers.*

in late October 1918, after the Japanese and Chinese governments had concluded an agreement regarding joint operation of the Shandong Railway, the Japanese embassy had informed the State Department of the substance of the agreement, but the question of the postwar disposition of Shandong was never discussed between Tokyo and Washington until the two countries' delegates met at Paris in 1919.[15]

In contrast to America's global peace program, Japan was concerned with the issues that affected its interests in East Asia and the Pacific. Japan's objectives at the peace conference concentrated narrowly on three areas: 1) succession to the German rights and concessions in Shandong, 2) acquisition of the German islands in the Pacific north of the equator (the Carolines, Marshalls, and Marianas), and 3) securing safeguards against racial discrimination in the event that the conference decided to establish the League of Nations.

In September 1918, a few days before his resignation, Premier Masatake Terauchi, protégé of Genro Yamagata, had further fortified Japan's claims to the Shandong Railway by concluding three new agreements with the Beijing government under Duan Qirui. Terauchi, who shared his mentor's vision of Sino-Japanese cooperation (*teikei*) and "the coexistence and co-prosperity of China and Japan," had worked during the war to instill in Chinese leaders a reliance on the Japanese Empire through financial assistance known as the Nishihara Loans. Terauchi had used part of these loans to strike a deal with the Duan government on the Shandong Railway. In the Sino-Japanese agreement signed on September 24, 1918, the two countries agreed to place the Shandong Railway (between Jiaozhou and Jinan) under their joint management and to share police duty along the railway. One of the provisions, which later became controversial at the peace conference, stipulated that the "Japanese are to be employed at the headquarters of this police force, at the main stations, and at the police training school." In two other agreements (signed on September 28), the Duan government accepted a loan of 40 million

---

15. Minutes of the British War Cabinet, Dec. 30, 1918, *Papers of Woodrow Wilson*, LIII, 562–563; Japanese Embassy to the Department of State, Oct. 30, 1918, *Foreign Relations, 1918*, 205.

yen from the Japanese government: 20 million yen for military purposes and 20 million yen for the construction of four new railroads in Shandong, Manchuria, and Mongolia.[16]

On the following day, September 29, 1918, a moderate, Takashi Hara, became the first party politician to assume the premiership. While Hara modified Japan's China policy somewhat, the new government did not alter Japanese objectives at the peace table. Hara opposed the aggressive military-oriented policy toward the Asian continent followed by the Terauchi government in collaboration with the army, Japanese financiers, and the Duan government in Beijing. He also opposed the Siberian expedition and advocated cordial relations with the United States. However, as an astute political survivor, Premier Hara was fully aware that giving up Japan's foothold in Shandong would cost him his political career. Japan's policy throughout the war had focused on the acquisition of the German concessions in Shandong. For senior statesmen, the military, and the civilian bureaucracy, a reversal in that policy on the eve of the peace conference was unthinkable. Hara ultimately swam with the current, embracing the policy of the two preceding cabinets.

When the Japanese government learned that President Wilson's Fourteen Points were to become the basis of the peace settlement, the Advisory Council on Foreign Relations (*gaikochosakai*, the highest level foreign policy body during the war) convened to discuss Japan's response. Members of the Advisory Council were concerned mainly with two issues. First, Wilson's principle of self-determination seemed to pose a serious problem for the disposal of the German colonies. Although the council members had no idea of Wilson's specific views on Shandong and the Pacific islands, they were determined to press Japan's claim regardless of the American position.[17] By December 2, 1918, both the Advisory Council and the Hara

16. Foreign Ministry of Japan, *Nihon gaiko nenpyo narabini shuyo bunsho* [A Chronology and Major Documents on Japanese Foreign Policy] (2 vols., Tokyo, 1966), I, 464–468. English translation in *Foreign Relations of the United States, 1919,* I, 571–572.

17. Tatsuo Kobayashi, ed., *Suiuso nikki: Rinji gaiko chosa iinkai kaigi hikki to* [Diary of the Green Rain Villa: Records of the Advisory Council on Foreign Relations, etc.] (Tokyo, 1966), 284–293.

cabinet formally decided that the Japanese government would return the territorial rights of Jiaozhou Bay to China only after Germany ceded the leased territory to Japan unconditionally. This would avoid the possibility of a direct restitution of the territory from Germany to China. The council and Hara also decided to insist on Japan's authority to settle the issue of retrocession directly with China without outside interference.[18]

What the Japanese really wanted to acquire, through the two-step procedure described above, were the railway and the coal mines in Shandong Province. War Minister Giichi Tanaka bluntly reminded Advisory Council members that, should Japan fail to obtain the Shandong Railway, it would lose control of Shandong Province as a whole, thereby losing "the artery that extends the power" of the Japanese Empire to the Asian continent. The council overwhelmingly supported specific instructions to Japanese delegates at Paris, directing them to do their "very best" to secure the railway and the mines. In demanding the cession of these economic interests from Germany, the Japanese delegates were to set forth "a plain and straightforward political argument based on the rights of a victor."[19]

Senior Japanese statesmen shared a self-indulgent belief that China would accept Japan's tutelage if they could make China understand Japan's true intentions. When the Japanese foreign minister learned from Beijing that Chinese Foreign Minister Lu Zhengxiang intended to visit Tokyo on the way to Paris and make careful "preliminary arrangements" on the matter of Chinese peace terms with the Japanese authorities, he interpreted the report as the Chinese foreign minister's willingness to reach an understanding with Tokyo on the Shandong issue. Accordingly, the Advisory Council on Foreign Relations adopted a resolution to the effect that, upon the Chinese foreign minister's arrival in Tokyo, "we will explain our decision [on the retrocession of Jiaozhou] and make him understand our just attitude and clear away misunderstandings;

---

18. Cabinet decision, Nov. 22, 1918, Foreign Ministry of Japan, *Nihon gaiko bunsho, 1918* [Documents on Japanese Foreign Policy] (Tokyo, 1969), III, 635; Kobayashi, ed., *Suiuso nikki*, 316–317.

19. Kobayashi, ed., *Suiuso nikki*, 318–324; Kosai Uchida to Sutemi Chinda, Dec. 26, 1918, *Nihon gaiko bunsho*, III, 667–669.

and we must take measures so that Japan and China can keep in step with each other in the coming peace conference."[20]

Leaders in Tokyo believed that Japan and China should take care of matters by themselves and were not prepared to tolerate Western intervention in Sino-Japanese affairs, which they saw as a threat to Japan's prestige in the eyes of the Chinese. The Shandong controversy at Paris turned out to be one of those occasions that the Japanese feared most. At the close of the Advisory Council's December 1918 meeting that forged Japan's official position on Shandong, Miyoji Ito concluded uneasily: "Our national prestige will be impaired should we demand permanent retention of Qingdao and later be forced to withdraw that demand because of America's protest."[21]

The second and equally important question that the Advisory Council considered was President Wilson's proposed League of Nations. Documents from the Foreign Ministry and from the Advisory Council indicate that Japanese leaders were genuinely concerned about the possibility that racial prejudice might jeopardize Japan's position in the League of Nations. Draft guidelines prepared by the Foreign Office for the Japanese delegation at Paris urged indefinite postponement of plans to create a League of Nations, on the grounds that "racial prejudice among nations" was widespread and that Western powers' control of the League threatened grave disadvantages to Japan. At the same time, the Foreign Office also concluded that, "in case the League of Nations is to be established, the Empire cannot remain isolated outside the organization." Therefore, should the establishment of the League become unavoidable at the peace conference, the Foreign Office proposed "appropriate safeguard[s] against disadvantages which the Empire may suffer because of the racial prejudice."[22]

The Advisory Council, too, expressed deep apprehension about the League of Nations. Council members were afraid that unless the principle of equality were absolutely guaranteed by the League, "the United States and the top-ranking nations in Europe" might use the League "to freeze the status quo and

---

20. Kobayashi, ed., *Suiuso nikki*, 316.
21. *Ibid.*, 317.
22. *Ibid.*, 286.

516 **Pacific Historical Review**

hold in check the development of second-rate and lower-ranked nations." Accordingly, the council unanimously supported a resolution that at the peace conference 1) Japan would try to postpone the creation of the League of Nations; and 2) in case the peace conference decided to organize the League, the Japanese delegation must seek a safeguard against racial discrimination.[23]

In this way, Japanese objectives at the Paris Peace Conference challenged Wilsonian principles at two levels. Japan's territorial claims tested the Wilsonian ideal of self-determination and its unilateral application to German concessions and colonies. Japan's efforts to secure safeguards against racial discrimination in the League of Nations questioned the effectiveness and fairness of the principle of international federalism embodied in the League of Nations. Japanese regional and racial identities questioned the universality of the Western-oriented solution to international conflicts.

Once the peace conference began, the Japanese delegation discovered that the disposition of the German islands in the Pacific was the least divisive issue separating them from President Wilson. After Australia, New Zealand, and South Africa demanded annexation of the German colonies under their occupation, the Japanese simply asked for equal treatment in the Pacific north of the equator. While British and American negotiators tried to work out a compromise, Japan's delegates remained silent. President Wilson, who was determined to approve nothing less than a system of mandates under the supervision of the League of Nations, clashed with Prime Minister William Hughes of Australia. Eventually Wilson prevailed, and Hughes agreed to accept the provisions of the "C-Mandate," which stipulated that the German islands were to be "administered under the laws of the mandatory states as integral portions [of the mandatory states] . . . in the interests of the indigenous population."[24]

The Hara government in Tokyo did not have much difficulty in accepting the provisions for mandatory status, including regulations for nonfortification and the open door in the

---

23. *Ibid.*, 308–310.
24. Council of Ten, Jan. 30, 1919, *Paris Peace Conference*, III, 795–796, 799–800.

islands. Indeed, Nobuaki Makino, the leading member of the Japanese delegation at Paris, strongly urged his government to approve the mandatory proposal. After learning from Lloyd George that Australia and New Zealand were expected to accept the mandatory principle, Makino advised Tokyo that it would be unwise for Japan alone to oppose. He explained that the mandatory idea appeared to be intended as a face-saving gesture to Wilson by upholding the mandatory principle and at the same time guaranteeing the virtual annexation of the German islands by the British Dominions.[25] To Makino, the deal was a realistic compromise.

Wilson expressed some uneasiness about granting the northern islands to Japan. On January 30, 1919, the day the decision was reached on the mandate system, he told David H. Miller that "these islands lie athwart the path from Hawaii to the Philippines and . . . they could be fortified and made naval bases by Japan." Referring to the Japanese government's breach of faith with regard to the Siberian intervention, the President confided that he would not trust the Japanese again. He had also written to Colonel House earlier that "a line of islands in her [Japan's] possession would be very dangerous to the U.S." However, his concern was mitigated later when Tokyo accepted the provisions for a "C-Mandate," which prohibited the construction of naval bases or fortifications on these islands.[26]

More problematic for Japan was the issue of race and the League of Nations, for Japan's attempt to include a racial equality clause in the League of Nations covenant was thwarted by unforeseen circumstances. Some contemporaries (and some later historians) have held that Japan used the racial equality proposal as a bargaining chip to obtain the German concessions in Shandong.[27] The Japanese concern about racial discrimination, however, was genuine; Tokyo's instructions on this issue were explicit from the very beginning. Certainly, Tokyo may have weighed the racial issue against Japanese interests in

---

25. Kobayashi, ed., *Suiuso nikki*, 386–400; Uchida to Keishiro Matsui, Feb. 3, 1919, *Nihon gaiko bunsho, 1919*, III, 382.

26. Diary of David Hunter Miller, Jan. 30, 1919, *Papers of Woodrow Wilson*, LIV, 379; *ibid.*, 347, note 2.

27. Robert Lansing, *The Peace Negotiations: A Personal Narrative* (New York, 1921), 243; Baker, *Woodrow Wilson and World Settlement*, II, 239. Curry, *Woodrow Wilson and Far Eastern Policy*, 257.

Shandong when both claims met with strong opposition at Paris. But Japan's decision to withdraw the proposal for racial equality was a result, primarily, of adamant objection from the British Dominions.

At the outset of the conference, the Japanese delegation worried that the United States might be the major obstacle to Japan's racial equality proposal. Makino knew how politically troublesome the racial issues could be for President Wilson on the West Coast of the United States. In 1913, Makino, as foreign minister, had negotiated in vain for the repeal of alien land legislation in California. However, when Makino and Sutemi Chinda opened informal negotiations with Colonel House, they found him surprisingly supportive of the Japanese proposal and learned from him that even Wilson might approve a milder declaration on racial equality.[28]

The true stumbling block turned out to be staunch opposition from Australia's Prime Minister Hughes. By mid-February Japanese delegates realized that the British would not agree to the proposal unless the Dominions changed their minds. In light of the British attitude, Tokyo was told, "evidently, it is going to be difficult to fulfill our wish." After negotiations with Colonel House and Lord Robert Cecil of Britain, Japanese delegates proposed a compromise that included in the preamble of the Covenant an endorsement of the principle of racial equality. When the prime ministers of the British Dominions deliberated on this proposal on March 25, 1919, all but Hughes agreed to accept it. Hughes rejected repeated requests by the Japanese to discuss the proposal. Jan C. Smuts of South Africa, who tried to mediate between Hughes and the other Dominion representatives, told Makino that, if Japan insisted upon bringing up the race question at the plenary session and if Hughes opposed it, "I shall have to fall in line and vote with the Dominions, like a

28. Matsui to Uchida, Feb. 15, 1919, *Nihon gaiko bunsho, 1919*, III, 443–444. House Diary, Feb. 4, 5, 1919, *Papers of Woodrow Wilson*, LIV, 485, 500. President Wilson considered the following compromise proposal to be acceptable: "The equality of nations being a basic principle of the League, the H.C.P. agree that concerning the aliens in their territories, they will accord them, so soon and so far as practicable, equal treatment and rights in law and in fact, without making any distinction on account of their race or nationality" (*Papers of Woodrow Wilson*, LIV, 500).

'good Indian.'" Thus, by the end of March, Japan's efforts to negotiate with the British Dominions had proved futile.[29]

In Tokyo, the Advisory Council on Foreign Relations met on March 30 to discuss how Japan could withdraw the racial equality proposal without losing its dignity. The foreign minister insisted that the delegates keep the record straight as to Japan's position on the race issue. Premier Hara thought that some nominal manifestation of the principle would suffice as a face-saving gesture. He did not think the issue warranted Japan's withdrawal from the League of Nations.[30]

Following Tokyo's instructions, with a view to leaving Japan's position in a written record, Makino and Chinda asked the League of Nations Commission to vote on their amendment to the preamble. Eleven out of seventeen present voted in favor of the amendment. The United States abstained. President Wilson ruled that the amendment was not adopted since it had not received the unanimous approval of the commission. Makino asked to record in the minutes the number of votes cast in favor of the Japanese amendment.[31]

Although the reasons why President Wilson abstained from voting on the racial question are not entirely clear, it is obvious that he did not fight for the principle of equality. At the meeting on April 11, he simply suggested that the wisest course for the United States would be not to press the matter. There are at least two possible explanations for Wilson's inaction and silence on this matter.

First, Wilson was well aware of strong opposition to the principle of racial equality in his own country. He feared that its adoption by the League might allow Asians to demand the repeal of laws banning or restricting Asian immigration. Wilson's opponents at home might claim that the League was in-

---

29. House Diary, Feb. 13, 1919, *ibid.*, LV, 155; Matsui to Uchida, March 25, 30, 1919, *Nihon gaiko bunsho, 1919*, III, 483–485, 487–490; Stephen Bonsal, *Unfinished Business* (Garden City, N.Y., 1944), 169–170; Nobuaki Makino, *Kaikoroku* [Memoirs] (Tokyo, 1978), II, 205–206.

30. Keiichiro Hara, ed., *Hara Kei nikki* [Diary of Takashi Hara] (Tokyo, 1965), V, 81.

31. Matsui to Uchida, April 13, 1919, *Nihon gaiko bunsho, 1919*, III, 496–497; minutes of a meeting of the League of Nations Commission, April 11, 1919, *Papers of Woodrow Wilson*, LVII, 259–265.

terfering in America's domestic affairs.[32] The truth is that the American commissioners were reluctant to accept even the modified Japanese proposal for racial equality. As Dr. Cary T. Grayson put it, "it was not necessary for the United States openly to oppose the suggested amendment because Australia and New Zealand through the British representatives had taken the position of positive opposition." Because of the outright objection of the British Dominions, the Japanese even felt grateful to Colonel House, on whom they called almost every day to work out a compromise. House wrote in his diary: "It has taken considerable finesse to lift the load from our shoulders and place it upon the British, but happily, it has been done."[33]

Second, caught in the crossfire between Japan's proposal and the opposition of the British Dominions, Wilson did not want a heated debate or publicity on this sensitive issue outside the conference room. He was so preoccupied with the establishment of the League of Nations that he did not want the question of race to become a divisive issue. "My own interest," Wilson said to the commission, "is to quiet discussion that raises national differences and racial prejudices. I would wish them, particularly at this juncture in the history of the relations with one another, to be forced as much as possible into the background." One of the limitations of Wilson's idealist approach to the League of Nations seems to have been his decision to let racial prejudices "play no part in the discussions connected with the establishment of this League."[34] To achieve his noble goal, he chose to close his eyes to one of the most serious factors contributing to political fragmentation in the world.

The settlement of the German rights and concessions in Shandong, Japan's primary objective at Paris, turned out to be one of the most controversial issues at the peace conference. It surprised and frustrated all the parties involved, especially the Japanese and Americans. As the conference unfolded, Japanese delegates who had not anticipated much difficulty in securing their claims to Shandong met with formidable oppo-

---

32. Diary of Cary T. Grayson, April 11, 1919, *Papers of Woodrow Wilson*, LVII, 239–240.

33. *Ibid.*, LVII, 240; House Diary, Feb. 13, 1919, *ibid.*, LV, 155.

34. Remarks upon the Clause for Racial Equality, April 11, 1919, *ibid.*, LVII, 268–269.

sition from both the Chinese and Americans. At the Council of Ten on January 27, Makino presented Japan's case for the unconditional cession to Japan of all German rights and concessions in Shandong, with the understanding that Japan would eventually return the territorial rights to China. Makino declared that Japan intended to keep Sino-Japanese negotiations strictly between the two countries and outside the peace conference. The Japanese were caught by surprise the following day when Chinese Minister Koo demanded the direct restoration to China of the leased territory of Jiaozhou, the Shandong Railway, and all other rights Germany had possessed in Shandong Province prior to the war. Following Reinsch's earlier proposal to President Wilson, Koo argued that China considered the agreements concluded during the war as provisional and subject to revision by the peace conference.[35] The Japanese felt betrayed by the Chinese, for they had relied on Chinese Foreign Minister Lu's promise that the Chinese delegation would act in concert with the Japanese.

The question of Shandong deeply troubled President Wilson. According to Ray Stannard Baker, "the Japanese crisis, while shorter and sharper, troubled the President more than any other—and the result of none, finally, satisfied him less." On one occasion Wilson told Baker that "he had been unable to sleep on the previous night for thinking of it."[36] He had great sympathy for China's plight and considered the Shandong question to be a prime case for self-determination. Moreover, his own experience with the Japanese government during the war had convinced him not to trust it easily. His American advisers on East Asia, as well as Secretary of State Lansing, were united in opposition to the Japanese claims. The other American commissioners, except Colonel House whom the Japanese considered their "friend," also had little sympathy for Japan.

While the Council of Ten was making arrangements to deliberate the Sino-Japanese treaty and agreements of 1915 and 1918 concerning Shandong, China's anti-Japanese press campaign further aroused Wilson's suspicion of Japan and caused

35. Council of Ten, Jan. 27, 28, 1919, *Paris Peace Conference*, III, 737–740, 749–757.
36. Baker, *Woodrow Wilson and World Settlement*, II, 223.

much bitter feelings on the part of the Japanese. When the Japanese foreign minister instructed his country's minister in Beijing to warn the Chinese government not to publish the secret agreements without consulting with Japan, the anti-Japanese faction within the Beijing government seized the opportunity to spread negative charges against Japan. On February 4, Wilson received a report that the Japanese intended to retain "the whole of Shang-Tung permanently" and were threatening "military intervention" and "the immediate withdrawal of all financial support" from China. Wilson ordered Reinsch to advise the Chinese government to stand firm; at the same time he instructed the American ambassador in Tokyo to express "our distress that there should be these indications that the Japanese government is not willing to trust to the fairness and justness of the Peace Conference."[37]

Diplomatic exchanges between Tokyo and Beijing reveal the surprise and indignation felt by Japanese officials over the Chinese accusations. While the acting Chinese foreign minister later corrected the press reports, his action received little attention. In the end, China's anti-Japanese press campaign and its attempt to enlist the help of the United States in forcing Japan to abandon its claims served only to harden Japanese determination. In Beijing Minister Yukichi Obata told the Chinese Foreign Office that to succumb to the Chinese demands because of Western pressure would undermine Japan's international prestige and national self-respect; furthermore, the Japanese people could not bear such a "humiliation."[38]

On this point, Edward T. Williams mistakenly commented that the publicity given to the activities of Obata in Beijing "did lots of good" and that "there's nothing like public criticism to control the Japanese."[39] The American experts at Paris did not fully grasp the psychology of Japan's relations with China. Fac-

37. Uchida to Yukichi Obata, Jan. 31, 1919, *Nihon gaiko bunsho, 1919*, III, 119–121; Polk to Wilson and Robert Lansing, Feb. 4, 1919, *Papers of Woodrow Wilson*, LIV, 474–476; Wilson to Lansing, Feb. 7, 1919, *ibid.*, LIV, 548.

38. Obata to Uchida, Feb. 3, 4, 13; Uchida to Obata, Feb. 5, 1919, *Nihon gaiko bunsho, 1919*, III, 124–125, 127–130, 151–156.

39. Letter from Edward T. Williams to Breckinridge Long, March 6, 1919, Breckinridge Long Papers, Library of Congress, cited in Russell H. Fifield, *Woodrow Wilson and the Far East: The Diplomacy of the Shantung Question* (New York, 1952), 154.

ing a hostile challenge from China and the United States, the Japanese no longer saw the Shandong settlement merely as a matter of expanding national interests; they regarded it as a matter of national prestige in the broader context of East Asian politics.

When the Council of Four began the final deliberation of the Shandong question in mid-April 1919, Japanese delegates realized that President Wilson was the major obstacle to the fulfillment of their goal. Wilson clearly stated his position in the council: "My sympathies are on the side of China, and we must not forget that, in the future, the greatest dangers for the world can arise in the Pacific." Not knowing the specifics of the Sino-Japanese treaty and agreements, Wilson insisted that the council must first study them because, in his own words, "I know by experience that they [the Japanese] are very clever in the interpretation of treaties."[40] Makino and Chinda met privately with Wilson on April 21 and explained that some of the provisions of the treaty and the agreements in question were already in effect and that the Shandong problem was only a matter of implementing them. They told Wilson that, "if the already existing and clearly stated treaty was disregarded and the problem was decided by a completely different mechanism for settlement, it was difficult to say whether in the end the plenipotentiaries would be able to sign the preliminary treaty or not." They also pointed out that, because of a breach of faith on the part of China and its hostile propaganda against Japan, the Shandong problem was no longer just a matter of leased territory but had become "a grave issue in the general political situation in the Far East."[41]

On the same day in Tokyo, the Advisory Council on Foreign Relations reached a crucial decision. Calling China's actions at Paris a "betrayal," Miyoji Ito argued that, should Japan's claim be defeated at the conference, "China would treat Japan with contempt" and Japan would totally lose its prestige in the East. Ito, therefore, proposed that the government should be prepared to withdraw from the League of Nations. The rest of the council members fell in line with his opinion, including

---

40. Council of Four, April 15, 1919, *Papers of Woodrow Wilson*, LVII, 358–359.
41. Matsui to Uchida, April 22, 1919, *Nihon gaiko bunsho, 1919*, III, 244–247 (English translation in *Papers of Woodrow Wilson*, LVII, 581–585).

Premier Hara, who stated that his government could put up with neither direct restitution to China nor trusteeship by the League of Nations.[42] That same day, Foreign Minister Kosai Uchida cabled to the Japanese delegation at Paris not to sign the Covenant of the League of Nations should Japan's Shandong claims be repudiated. He added: "in order to maintain our government's dignity there shall be no room for conciliatory adjustment."[43] Tokyo's firm instruction gave the Japanese delegates no way out.

The following day, April 22, after having heard the Japanese and Chinese cases separately, the Council of Four was leaning toward a decision in favor of Japan. First, both Lloyd George and Georges Clemenceau made it clear that they had definite wartime agreements with Japan. Second, Japanese delegates declared that they were under an explicit order from their government not to sign the treaty "unless they were placed in a position to carry out Japan's obligation to China." Although the Chinese delegation urged the council to undo the Sino-Japanese treaty of 1915 and the agreements signed in 1918, not only the British and French prime ministers but also President Wilson defended the "sacredness of treaties." Wilson had serious reservations about the Sino-Japanese treaty of 1915, but he could not question the validity of the British and French commitment to Japan's claim. Lloyd George stated that his country's engagement with Japan was "a solemn treaty" and that "Great Britain could not turn round to Japan now and say 'All right, thank you very much. We wanted your help, you gave it, but now we think that the treaty was a bad one and should not be carried out.'" Ironically, Wilson had to tell the Chinese delegation that "sacredness of treaties had been one of the motives of the war" and that "it had been necessary to show that treaties were not mere scraps of paper."[44]

Convinced that Japan's threat to withdraw from the peace conference was not a bluff, Wilson chose to compromise. This, he hoped, would provide an "outlet to permit the Japanese to save their face and let the League of Nations decide the matter

42. Kobayashi, ed., *Suiuso nikki*, 464–467.
43. Uchida to Matsui, April 21, 1919, *Nihon gaiko bunsho, 1919*, III, 242.
44. Council of Four, April 22, 1919, *Paris Peace Conference*, V, 139–148.

later." As he put it to Lloyd George and Clemenceau, he believed "it is necessary to do everything to assure that she [Japan] joins the Leag.ie of Nations." He was afraid that "if she stands aside, she would do all that she could want to do in the Far East."[45] He apparently believed that the League of Nations would police Japan's behavior in East Asia once it became a member, so that Japan would not violate China's territorial integrity and political independence.

The gist of the compromise the Japanese and President Wilson agreed upon was that, after the German rights had been ceded to Japan, it would return the Shandong Peninsula in full sovereignty to China, retaining only the economic privileges granted to Germany and the right to establish a settlement in Qingdao. Being jealous of protecting Japan's power and prestige in East Asia, the Japanese delegation asserted that this declaration must be "a voluntary expression of the Japanese delegates' interpretation" of the restitution of Shandong stipulated by the treaty of 1915 and that no impression should be given that this decision had been forced upon Japan.

The Shandong compromise was a means to keep the influence of Wilsonian idealism alive in East Asia. It demonstrated Wilson's firm faith in the League of Nations and the universality of the international system and morality that his League represented. When he said, "I am above all concerned not to create a chasm between the East and the West,"[46] he did not mean to create a federalism that would accommodate the hegemony of a regional power in the East. He was thinking, instead, of an international mechanism that would unilaterally enforce his universal values as League members saw fit. The problem was that Japan was apprehensive about, indeed repelled by, an international body dominated by Western powers.[47]

---

45. *Papers of Woodrow Wilson*, LVIII, 113; Council of Four, April 22, 1919, *ibid.*, LVII, 622–626; *Paris Peace Conference*, V, 145.

46. Council of Four, April 22, 1919, *Papers of Woodrow Wilson*, LVII, 626.

47. Obviously, the Chinese government had a considerably different perspective on these events; see Stephen G. Craft, "John Bassett Moore, Robert Lansing, and the Shandong Question," *Pacific Historical Review*, LXVI (1997), 231–249. Interestingly, President Wilson managed to antagonize both Japan and China in this controversy, leaving both sides feeling betrayed and suspicious of American motives.

526   Pacific Historical Review

* * *

In the end, the Shandong compromise at Paris did no; settle the differences between Wilson and the Japanese with regard to details of the future disposition of Shandong. Both sides simply shelved the problem for the moment and signed the Treaty of Versailles on June 28, 1919. Thus, the picture that emerges from Wilson's response to the Japanese claims at the Paris Peace Conference reveals the inadequacy of his idealistic policy toward East Asia. Wilson's absolute faith in the universality of his ideals, and his unyielding determination to turn his vision of a new world order into a reality, prevented him from understanding what was driving an emerging non-Western country like Japan to expand at the expense of weaker neighbors. His unilateral attempt to impose a new order, however righteous his intentions, was doomed to a disappointing outcome.

Japanese leaders, who took advantage of the European war to the end of expanding Japan's foothold in East Asia, considered Wilsonian opposition to Japanese claims at Paris as another attempt by Western powers to block the growth of an Asian regional power. Forgetting the blemishes in their conduct on the Asian continent, the Japanese felt that President Wilson's interference in Sino-Japanese negotiations over Shandong was humiliating and that his failure to support the principle of racial equality unjust. They viewed Wilsonian universal internationalism simply as hypocritical rhetoric that hindered the advancement of their country. Baron Makino, who later served Emperor Hirohito as Lord Keeper of the Privy Seal, commented in his memoirs about Wilson's unilateral approach at the peace conference. According to Makino, it was hard to associate Wilson's personality with democracy. The President seemed to him to be "a politician best suited to a dictatorship."[48]

48. Makino, *Kaikoroku*, II, 226.

15

American Intervention in Russia: The North Russian Expedition, 1918–1919

John W. Long

During the past sixty years, particularly in the recent era of the intensified Cold War, the tangled question of American participation in the Allied military intervention in Russia following the Bolshevik Revolution of 1917 has attracted much attention from scholars, both Soviet and Western. After some initial restraint on their part, Soviet historians have arrived at the more or less unanimous conclusion that the United States not only enthusiastically joined the other Allied powers in the intervention but also actually assumed leadership over a conscious and deliberate attempt to destroy the infant Soviet state at its inception.[1] On the other side, Western scholars have proposed a wide variety of putative explanations for American intervention, ranging from considerations of contemporary power politics through an entire catalogue of sophisticated political and psychological analyses to outright accusations of malevolent ideological intent on the part of American decision makers.[2]

---

[1] The most recent full-length Soviet studies of American intervention are A. V. Berezkin, *Oktiabr'skaia revoliutsiia i SShA, 1917–1922 gg.* [The October Revolution and the USA, 1917–1922] (Moscow, 1967); and L. A. Gvishiani, *Sovetskaia Rossiia i SShA, 1917–1920* [Soviet Russia and the USA, 1917–1920] (Moscow, 1970). See also R. Sh. Ganelin, *Sovetsko-amerikanskie otnosheniia v kontse 1917–nachale 1918 g.* [Soviet-American Relations from late 1917 to early 1918] (Leningrad, 1975). For an excellent account of the tortured evolution of Soviet historiography on intervention see John M. Thompson, "Allied and American Intervention in Russia, 1918–1921," in C. E. Black, ed., *Rewriting Russian History* (2d ed., New York, 1962), pp. 319–80; and George F. Kennan, "Soviet Historiography and America's Role in the Intervention," *American Historical Review* 65 (January 1960): 302–22.

[2] Chief among those who have interpreted American intervention in essentially political terms are Betty M. Unterberger ("President Wilson and the Decision to Send American Troops to Siberia," *Pacific Historical Review* 24 [February 1955]: 63–74; and *America's Siberian Adventure, 1918–1920* [Durham, NC, 1956]) and John A. White (*The Siberian Intervention* [Princeton, 1950]), both of whom argue a basically anti-Japanese motivation; Christopher Lasch ("American Intervention in Siberia: A Reinterpretation," *Political Science Quarterly* 76 [June 1962]: 205–23; and *American Liberals and the Russian Revolution* [New York, 1962]), who sees the policy as a function of wartime military strategy; and George F. Kennan (*Soviet-American Relations, 1917–1920*, vol. 2, *The*

In spite of the considerable attention devoted to the problem, however, a comprehensive picture of American intervention in Russia still has not entirely emerged. It would seem that this situation derives first of all from the fact that American involvement in Russia unfolded in two distinct stages that have received unequal treatment from historians. The first of these stages—the period of the formulation of American interventionist policy—began shortly after the Bolshevik seizure of power in November 1917 and continued until the issuance on 17 July 1918 of President Woodrow Wilson's aide-mémoire, which effectively initiated American activity in Russia. This preliminary period of American engagement, which culminated in the "decision to intervene" in Russia, has been studied and restudied by historians.[3]

The second stage of American intervention in Russia was the period of the actual implementation of the policy, which lasted from mid-1918 to early 1920 and also has attracted the attention of scholars, but this attention has been very unevenly distributed. The apparent reason for this disproportion is that American involvement in Russia was effected in two distinct operations: the one to Vladivostok and Siberia, an undertaking that has been thoroughly researched by historians, and the other to Archangel and North Russia, which by comparison has been virtually neglected by Western scholars.[4]

Decision to Intervene [Princeton, 1958]; and *Russia and the West Under Lenin and Stalin* [Boston, 1961], pp. 65–116), who cites the impact on Washington of Allied diplomatic pressure with emphasis on the need to assist the so-called Czech legion (see note 15). Among those who emphasize ideological motivations, the New Left contention that intervention was essentially anti-Bolshevik is represented preeminently by William A. Williams in "American Intervention in Russia, 1917–1920," *Studies on the Left* 3–4 (1963–1964): 24–68; and *American-Russian Relations, 1781–1947* (New York, 1952), pp. 105–75). A similar argument, which sees intervention as the consequence of the personal ideological predilections of President Woodrow Wilson, is made by Robert J. Maddox in "Woodrow Wilson, the Russian Embassy and Siberian Intervention," *Pacific Historical Review* 36 (November 1967): 435–48; and *The Unknown War with Russia: Wilson's Siberian Adventure* (San Rafael, CA, 1977). Finally, N. Gordon Levin, Jr., in *Woodrow Wilson and World Politics* (New York, 1968), has advanced the view that intervention was motivated primarily by an American desire to create in Russia a liberal-capitalist bulwark against both German militarism and revolutionary Bolshevism. For additional data, as well as a useful overview of the entire historiographical problem, see Betty M. Unterberger, ed., *American Intervention in the Russian Civil War* (Lexington, MA, 1969).

[3]See above, note 2. Focus on the initial period of American involvement in Russia, with emphasis on the possible motivations for the policy, is characteristic of almost all of the existing studies of intervention. Recently this existing research has been thoroughly reviewed and reevaluated in an excellent article by Eugene P. Trani, "Woodrow Wilson and the Decision to Intervene in Russia: A Reconsideration," *The Journal of Modern History* 48 (September 1976): 440–61, which brings to bear virtually all of the presently available sources on the subject.

[4]On American intervention in Siberia see the studies of Unterberger, White, Lasch, and Maddox (see note 2); Clarence A. Manning, *The Siberian Fiasco* (New York, 1952); and Sophia R. Pelzel, *American Intervention in Siberia, 1918–1920* (Philadelphia, 1946). By contrast, the only full-length study of American intervention in North Russia is E. M. Halliday, *The Ignorant Armies* (New York, 1958), which, however, emphasizes military

AMERICAN INTERVENTION IN RUSSIA 47

Whatever its causes the practical consequence of the prevailing disparity in the treatment of the two American expeditions to Russia has been the creation of an incomplete, if not actually distorted, picture of American intervention in which the history of the North Russian expedition has been largely eclipsed by that of the better known Siberian operation.[5] This unsatisfactory situation is the more unfortunate in that the experiences of the two expeditions to Russia were, in fact, widely dissimilar and permit quite different, though not necessarily conflicting, interpretations of American policy. Thus, in Siberia the implementation of American strategy was from the outset greatly influenced by the specter of Japan, whose imperialist aspirations in the area were of acute concern to the United States and profoundly affected the nature and duration of the entire American expedition. In the north, by contrast, although there were certainly some difficult problems, American policy was basically free of the particular extraneous political complications that obtained in Eastern Siberia. It is the thesis of this analysis that the history of the North Russian expedition is, in fact, more representative of Washington's real attitude toward involvement in Russia than is the more complex expedition to Siberia and therefore must be fully integrated into any final assessment of American interventionist policy.

Current Soviet and New Left historiography to the contrary, the discussion of American intervention in Russia after 1917 must begin with the unequivocal assertion that any such policy on the part of the United States was from the start extremely reluctant and severely restrained. This fact, apparent in the history of the Siberian expedition, is even clearer in the case of North Russia and places American policy in marked and highly significant contrast to the much more aggressively interventionist positions of the U.S. principal European allies, Great Britain and France.

The origins of the widely divergent concepts of intervention that came to be held by the United States and its European associates can be traced back to the immediate aftermath of the Bolshevik Revolution. For a variety of reasons, especially the Bolsheviks' immediate withdrawal from World War I and prompt initiation of peace talks with the Central Powers, the European allies, by the end of 1917, had developed a hostile

---

history and lacks a full scholarly apparatus. A second work, Leonid I. Strakhovsky, *The Origins of American Intervention in North Russia, 1918* (Princeton, 1937), is confined to the preliminary period of American activity in the north as is the unfinished study by Kennan, *The Decision to Intervene,* pp. 15–57, 245–76, 363–80, 417–29. Significantly, the same disparity does not obtain in Soviet scholarship, which has studied both locales of American intervention in roughly equal proportion. See the historiographical review of S. F. Naida and V. P. Naumov, *Sovetskaia istoriografiia grazhdanskoi voiny i inostrannoi voennoi interventsii v SSSR* [Soviet Historiography of the Civil War and Foreign Military Intervention in the USSR] (Moscow, 1966).

[5]See Unterberger, *American Intervention in the Russian Civil War,* in which, although North Russia is mentioned in passing, virtually all of the assembled documents and interpretive selections deal basically with Siberia.

attitude toward the new Soviet government.[6] Accordingly, although they did not immediately give up all hope of accommodation with the new regime, the Entente powers soon commenced the machinations that led eventually to armed intervention in Russia.

From the outset the United States did not share its allies' negative reaction to the Bolshevik regime. On the contrary, the American attitude toward the new government, though not enthusiastic, was characterized by a far greater degree of detachment and a much less marked proclivity for precipitate action than was manifested by the Entente powers. To some extent this restraint was probably a function of the less intense relationship of the United States to the World War, deriving perhaps from its late entry into the fray and corresponding lack of sacrifice as compared with the European powers. Much more important than this psychological factor, however, were the personal predilections of President Wilson, who throughout this period was the real voice of authority in American foreign policy.[7] In his approach to the Russian problem, as in all the areas of his endeavor, the president's views were conditioned above all by his steadfast adherence to certain moral and ethical principles, among which two of the most sacred, at least in the foreign sphere, were noninterference and self-determination. Although in his Russian policy the president was temporarily induced in the summer of 1918 to relax these principles somewhat, his continued devotion and eventual return to them in the subsequent period was the decisive factor in American intervention.[8]

In accord with Wilson's cherished beliefs, the unofficial American attitude toward the new Soviet government was announced publicly in

[6]For a summary of Allied reaction to the Bolsheviks see Robert D. Warth, *The Allies and the Russian Revolution* (Durham, NC, 1954), pp. 158 ff; and Arno J. Mayer, *Political Origins of the New Diplomacy, 1917–1918* (New Haven, 1959), pp. 267–90. The antipathy of the Allies for the Bolsheviks was intensified by the latter's publication of the Entente's secret treaties (22 November) and still further aggravated by the Soviets' repudiation of all foreign state debts (3 February).

[7]The following discussion of Wilson's foreign policy role and conceptions is based on Arthur S. Link, *Wilson the Diplomatist* (2d ed.; Baltimore, 1963), pp. 3–29, which was refined and updated in his *Woodrow Wilson: Revolution, War, and Peace* (Arlington Heights, IL, 1979), pp. 1–20. As Link points out, in all important matters of foreign policy Wilson was his own master and exercised "almost absolute personal control" over American decision making. On the other hand, as Trani has demonstrated, Secretary of State Robert Lansing and his subordinates, who were consistently more anti-Bolshevik than Wilson, occasionally succeeded in circumscribing certain of the president's options on Russia. Trani, "Wilson and the Decision," pp. 449–52. Aside from this kind of limited interference, however, no other persons or agencies exercised any significant effect on Wilson's Russian policy.

[8]To date, there has been surprisingly little published research on Wilson and Russia. See Brenda K. Shelton, "President Wilson and the Russian Revolution," *The University of Buffalo Studies* 23 (March 1957): 111–55, a rather elementary master's thesis; and Lloyd C. Gardner, *Wilson and Revolutions, 1913–1921* (Philadelphia, 1976), a New Left analysis which also covers Mexico. A new study by Betty M. Unterberger, "Woodrow Wilson and the Russian Revolution," has not yet been published.

AMERICAN INTERVENTION IN RUSSIA 49

December 1917 as "non-recognition" combined with the strict avoidance of any interference in the internal affairs of Russia.[9] This position, privately described as "do nothing," was based upon the president's conviction, repeatedly expressed in his personal correspondence, that outside interference would not only not help the situation in Russia but might even be harmful.[10]

The mere unofficial declaration of American noninterference in Russia, however, was not sufficient for President Wilson, who desired to make even more explicit his commitment to Russian self-determination. Accordingly, when he delivered his Fourteen Points address on 8 January 1918, which, in fact, was largely prompted by the Bolsheviks' recent propaganda at Brest-Litvosk, the president devoted Point VI of his text to a ringing reaffirmation of American dedication to the principle of noninterference in Russia: "The nations of the world [should seek for Russia] an unhampered and unembarrassed opportunity for the independent determination of her own political development and national policy. . . ." Indeed, concluded the president, "the treatment accorded Russia by her sister nations in the months to come will be the acid test of their good will . . . and their intelligent and unselfish sympathy."[11] However idealistic, this formulation expressed President Wilson's strong attachment in the Russian situation to the tenets of self-determination and noninterference.[12] Nevertheless, in "the months to come" not even the president

---

[9]*New York Times,* 7 December 1917, p. 3. Significantly this position, which was the result of "several conferences" between Wilson and Lansing, was only adopted after Wilson resisted a much harsher line favored by the secretary of state with which, according to Lansing, the president was "not in entire" accord. See the unpublished typescript of Lansing's *War Memoirs* from which this comment was deleted in the published version. Selected Papers of Robert Lansing, Mudd Library, Princeton University, Princeton, NJ, Box 1, Envelope D (hereafter cited as Lansing Papers).

[10]The phrase "do nothing" was used in a memorandum by Lansing of 7 December 1917, Lansing Papers. But as Trani has observed, it is really "a much more accurate description of Wilson's policy than Lansing's." Trani, "Wilson and the Decision," p. 447, n. 20. For examples of the president's repeated assertions that it was essential not to become embroiled in Russia, see his letters to Lincoln Colcord, 6 December 1917, Dr. Charles W. Eliot, 21 January 1918, and Joseph P. Tumulty, 23 February 1918, Woodrow Wilson Papers, Manuscripts Division, Library of Congress (hereafter cited as Wilson Papers, LC). In this regard, mention should be made of the great impact on Wilson of his recent difficult experience of intervention in Mexico, which had left him with a keen awareness of the limitations of interference in the domestic affairs of other nations. Arthur S. Link, *Woodrow Wilson and the Progressive Era, 1900–1917* (New York, 1954), pp. 107–44.

[11]Ray Stannard Baker and William E. Dodd, eds., *The Public Papers of Woodrow Wilson,* 3 vols. (New York, 1927), 3:155–62. That "the Russian situation" constituted "the chief *raison d'être*" of the speech is attested to in Charles Seymour, *The Intimate Papers of Colonel House,* 4 vols. (Boston and New York, 1928), 3:330.

[12]In this spirit the president even flirted at this time with the idea of recognition of the de facto Bolshevik government. Wilson to Lansing, 20 January 1918, and Wilson to Senator Robert L. Owen, 29 January 1918, Wilson Papers, LC. This idea, however, was vigorously opposed by the State Department. Trani, "Wilson and the Decision," pp. 450–51.

himself was able wholly to withstand "the acid test" to which the Russian problem was destined to subject his high ideals.

As President Wilson was engaged in spelling out his determination not to become involved in Russia, his principal European allies were busy doing precisely that. Building on their initial distrust of the Bolsheviks, in the early months of 1918 the British and French sought in every way possible to gain some kind of independent foothold in Russia. Among the major points of Allied interest in this regard were Archangel and Murmansk, the two chief seaports of the Russian north. Indeed, in early March, utilizing an alleged German threat in neighboring Finland, the British engineered the military occupation of Murmansk by a small contingent of Royal Marines.[13] Thereupon, in a series of decisions beginning in mid-April, the British War Cabinet decided to send a general military mission to Murmansk under the command of Major General Frederick C. Poole for the express purpose of "cooperation in any Allied intervention" in Russia.[14]

Having thus embarked on intervention, the British quickly became conscious of their own critical inability to provide the necessary manpower to carry out this policy. To meet this need the War Cabinet on 17 April approved a plan for the employment in the north of at least a part of the Czechoslovak legion, which had been formed in Russia during the war and was then en route out of the country via the Trans-Siberian Railroad and Vladivostok.[15] This plan, which involved the diversion of some 20,000 Czechs to Archangel and Murmansk, encountered some resistance in Paris but was nevertheless adopted at a meeting of the Allied Supreme War Council on 2 May.[16] Even the prospective addition of the Czechs, however, was not sufficient to satisfy the British War Office, which during May became convinced that more troops were needed in the

---

[13]Richard H. Ullman, *Anglo-Soviet Relations, 1917–1921*, vol. 1, *Intervention and the War* (Princeton, 1961), p. 118. Ostensibly carried out for the protection of local Allied interests, the landing at Murmansk was initially invited by Moscow in the person of Commissar of Foreign Affairs L. D. Trotsky. This spirit of cooperation, however, was soon altered in the aftermath of the Brest-Litovsk peace. See also ibid., pp. 113ff; and Kennan, *The Decision to Intervene*, pp. 43ff.

[14]War Office, "Instructions and Scope of British Military Mission Under Major-General F. Poole," W. O. 32/5643, no. 4A, Public Record Office, London (hereafter cited as PRO). This important file on the initial phase of Allied activity in the north was not utilized in Ullman's standard account.

[15]War Cabinet minutes, W. C. 393, 17 April 1918, Cab. 23/6, PRO. On the Czech legion see J. F. N. Bradley, *La Légion tchécoslovaque en Russie, 1914–1920* (Paris, 1965).

[16]Minutes, Supreme War Council, 5th session, 2d meeting, Abbeville, 2 May 1918, Modern Military Records Division (MMRD), RG 120, Records of the Supreme War Council (RSWC), Box 23, Department of State, National Archives (hereafter cited as DSNA). Based on Joint Note No. 25, "Transportation of Czech Troops from Russia," Annexure, Minutes, Permanent Military Representatives (PMR), 27th meeting, Versailles, 27 April 1918, MMRD, RG 120, RSWC, Box 21, DSNA. See also David F. Trask, *The United States in the Supreme War Council* (Middletown, CT, 1961), pp. 115–16.

AMERICAN INTERVENTION IN RUSSIA   51

north.[17] In these circumstances, Allied attention was increasingly drawn to the United States, which alone among the Western powers possessed the available manpower to carry through the proposed intervention.

Commencing in early 1918 the Allied campaign to persuade the United States to participate in intervention dragged out for more than six months. The story of how the Allies during this period relentlessly and systematically pushed, pressured, and otherwise coerced President Wilson into his eventual agreement to take part in their Russian under-taking often has been told and requires no elaborate repetition.[18] Instead, it will suffice to review only those developments during this formative period of American engagement in Russia that bear primarily on North Russia. Although this separation of what ultimately became the two locales of American intervention is not always meaningful, it will nevertheless serve to demonstrate how North Russia was, at least at first, a tactical element in the strategic considerations of both the Allies and the Americans.[19]

The long interval leading up to the final extraction of American agreement to participate in intervention can be divided into two unequal periods. During the first, which lasted from January to early May 1918, American opposition to intervention was founded primarily on principle. Perhaps the high point of U.S. resistance in this regard was reached in early March when President Wilson dispatched a personal message to the Fourth Congress of Soviets then convening in Moscow to ratify the treaty at Brest-Litovsk. In this message, which evoked some alarm in the State Department, the president extended to the Russian people "the sincere sympathy" of the United States and assured the delegates of his continued determination to secure for Russia "complete sovereignty and inde-pendence in her own affairs."[20]

---

[17]Commander of the Imperial General Staff [CIGS], War Office, "Situation at Murmansk," 0.1/162/465, Secret, 18 May 1918, W. O. 32/5643, no. 13, PRO.

[18]See notes 2 and 3. Also W. B. Fowler, *British-American Relations, 1917–1918: The Role of Sir William Wiseman* (Princeton, 1969). Significantly, the most recent study of the problem concludes that American intervention was motivated primarily by Allied pressure on Wilson. Trani, "Wilson and the Decision," pp. 445–49.

[19]In his recent perceptive study, Trani cautioned against separating the two sites of American intervention in Russia. Trani, "Wilson and the Decision," p. 441, note 2. While I believe that his point is well taken as regards the final decision to intervene reached in July, I am convinced that separation of the two locales is useful to the analysis of American and Allied strategy in the period leading up to the decision and absolutely essential thereafter since, as I have indicated, the actual experiences of the two American expeditions to Russia were quite different. Indeed, it is precisely the failure to treat the implementation of the North Russian operation separately from the Siberian that has led to the present incomplete comprehension of American policy.

[20]Baker and Dodd, eds., *Public Papers of Wilson,* 3:191. On the State Department's consternation and consequent revision of Wilson's initial draft of this message, see Trani, "Wilson and the Decision," p. 451. For his part, Lansing felt that the message should have been followed by "a definite announcement of policy toward Bolshevism" but found the president "unwilling . . . to make such a declaration." Unpublished typescript of *War Memoirs,* Lansing Papers.

Nor during this early period was American opposition to intervention confined merely to verbiage. For example, in early April, having failed in repeated direct approaches to the Americans, the Allies attempted to exert pressure on Washington indirectly by means of the Supreme War Council. On 8 April the British government presented a draft note to the permanent military representatives of the council, calling for joint intervention in Russia as an urgent function of the war against Germany. As regards the north, this argument, often employed in efforts to enlist American assistance, was predicated on the need to protect Murmansk against an alleged German threat and also to prevent any transfer into enemy hands of the substantial Allied military stores located at Archangel.[21] Notwithstanding these contentions, which continued to be used as justifications for Allied action in the north, the British effort was promptly scotched by the American military representative, General Tasker H. Bliss, who simply refused to sign the proposed note, which as a result could not be implemented.[22]

In spite of this stubborn American opposition, the pressure of Entente supplication in favor of intervention continued relentlessly. Nevertheless, it was not until early May that the first crack in the wall of American resistance to intervention appeared. This break centered on North Russia. On 11 May, in a conversation with British Ambassador to Washington Lord Reading, Secretary of State Robert Lansing remarked that the intervention problem "had really become two problems" in that action at Murmansk and Archangel would receive "far more favorable consideration" on the part of the United States than intervention in Siberia, which was complicated by "the racial [i.e., Japanese] problem."[23] This distinction between intervention in Siberia and North Russia, which Wilson himself had drawn in an earlier note to Lansing, seems now to have suggested the germ of an idea to the president.[24] Thus, while by no

---

[21]Joint Note No. 20, "The Situation in the Eastern Theatre," Annexure, Minutes, PMR, 25th meeting, Versailles, 8 April 1918, MMRD, RG 120, RSWC, Box 21, DSNA. In truth, neither of the arguments in favor of action in the north had much basis in fact. No serious German effort to attack Murmansk was ever planned, and the Allied war stores at Archangel were already in process of removal to the interior by the Bolsheviks. Kennan, *Intervention,* pp. 20–21, 40–41, 245–47, 250–51. Among other reasons advanced for intervention, the British note included "assistance" to the Czech legion with which Wilson was known to be sympathetic.

[22]Report of General Tasker H. Bliss, military representative of the United States on the Supreme War Council, 6 February 1920, U.S., Department of State, *Foreign Relations of the United States: The Lansing Papers, 1914–1920,* 2 vols. (Washington, 1940), 2:272–73) (hereafter cited as *FRUS,* followed by appropriate year). On other efforts to enlist the Supreme War Council on behalf of intervention see Trask, *United States in Supreme War Council,* pp. 103ff.

[23]Secretary of state to the president, 11 May 1918, *FRUS, 1918: Russia,* 2:160. Lansing repeated the point at a second interview with Reading five days later. Secretary of state to the president, 16 May 1918, *FRUS: Lansing Papers,* 2:360–61.

[24]Wilson to Lansing, 8 March 1918, Wilson Papers, LC.

AMERICAN INTERVENTION IN RUSSIA   53

means abandoning his previous viewpoint on intervention, which he informed Lansing on 20 May he still considered "most unwise," the chief executive accepted the distinction made between the two prospective sites of intervention and began to manifest a more receptive attitude toward the possibility of action in the north.[25] In fact, there is every reason to believe that this change in Wilson's position was merely tactical, a concession intended to ward off any future Allied pressure for intervention by agreeing to a strictly limited operation in a remote, confined geographical area. If this was the president's strategy, it was bound for disappointment.

Predictably, the newly altered American position was quickly picked up in London, where the British War Cabinet immediately sensed the opportunity to use the north as an opening wedge to initiate American action in Russia. Accordingly, on 27 May, British Foreign Secretary Arthur James Balfour dispatched a powerful appeal to President Wilson. Calling attention to the "vital" importance of Murmansk, the foreign secretary emphasized the "essential" need for American assistance at that port, which, he noted in an aside carefully calculated to play upon Wilson's delicate sense of loyalty, was also important to demonstrate the fact of inter-Allied unity.[26] The impact of this message was communicated to the president on 31 May, effectively bringing to an end American opposition in principle to intervention. Thus, on the afternoon of 1 June the chief executive summoned the secretary of state to the White House for a special conference. The result of this meeting was a decision that the United States would agree to send troops to Murmansk provided such a diversion were approved by Allied Supreme Commander General Ferdinand Foch.[27] This approval was soon forthcoming.[28] In the meantime, the president's decision, as communicated by the Chief of Staff, was announced by General Bliss to his colleagues on the Supreme War Council.[29]

---

[25]Wilson to the secretary of state, 20 May 1918, *FRUS, Lansing Papers,* 2:361–62. The president's decision in this regard was undoubtedly facilitated by the fact that he had consented during the previous month to a British request for the dispatch to Murmansk of an American warship. In doing so, however, Wilson gave strict orders to the commander of this vessel, the U.S.S. *Olympia,* "not to be drawn in further . . . there without first seeking and obtaining instructions from home." Wilson to Lansing, 4 April 1918, Wilson Papers, LC.

[26]Foreign Office, Balfour to Lord Reading (Washington), no. 3239, 27 May 1918, F. O. 371/3285, 85326/6/38, PRO. Paraphrased in the British ambassador to the secretary of state, 29 May 1918, *FRUS, 1918: Russia,* 2:476. Forwarded to Wilson "without comment" in the secretary of state to the president, 31 May 1918, Foreign Affairs Branch (FAB), RG 59, 861.00/1907 1/2, DSNA.

[27]Memorandum of the secretary of state, 3 June 1918, *FRUS, 1918: Russia,* 2:484–85.

[28]See Bliss to March, 22 June 1918, MMRD, RG 120, RSWC, Box 21, DSNA; and *The Memoirs of Marshal Foch,* trans. T. B. Mott (Garden City, NY, 1931), pp. 346–47.

[29]Minutes, PMR, 34th meeting, Versailles, 3 June 1918, MMRD, RG 120, RSWC, Box 21, DSNA. Bliss's announcement is reprinted in Trask, *United States in Supreme War Council,* p. 118. It is interesting that this version, which is cited from the Bliss Papers, Library of Congress, omits from the original message the word "heartily" in describing the president's

The military experts of the Supreme War Council lost no time in seizing the opportunity at last extended by Wilson's concession. Meeting at Versailles on 3 June, they produced Joint Note No. 31 calling formally for intervention in North Russia.[30] By the terms of this document the Allies were to send from four to six battalions of infantry to the north in order to retain Murmansk and, if possible, to occupy Archangel. With the adoption of this resolution, Allied intervention in North Russia, still ostensibly anti-German, became official.

Notwithstanding its approval of Joint Note No. 31, the opposition of Washington to intervention did not come to an end, although it was reduced to practical considerations, particularly to arguments about the policy's dubious military efficacy. In this regard the major American disputants became the highest ranking officials of the War Department, with Secretary Newton D. Baker and Chief of Staff General Peyton C. March both adamantly opposed to intervention.[31] In fact, this opposition was never really overcome, and to the end the War Department remained the most obstinate opponent of American intervention in Russia.

On 11 June, not long after the adoption of Joint Note No. 31, the British government cabled Washington requesting the allocation for the northern expedition of three battalions of American infantry plus the requisite ordnance and auxiliary forces.[32] This request, though modest, was considerably in excess of what had just been authorized by the Supreme War Council. Incensed, the War Department commenced a lengthy exchange with London regarding the prospective size of the American contingent, which dragged into the last days of June. Finally, at the beginning of July the British decided to remand the whole question to Versailles for the joint consideration of the full membership of the Supreme War Council.

The Seventh Session of the Supreme War Council, which met 2–4

sympathy with intervention. March to Bliss, no. 59, 28 May 1918, MMRD, RG 120, RSWC, Box 20, DSNA. It is possible that this omission was a subtle expression of the general's personal distaste for the project. See note 31 below.

[30] Joint Note No. 31, "Allied Intervention at Russian Allied Ports," Annexure, Minutes, PMR, 34th meeting, Versailles, 3 June 1918, MMRD, RG 120, RSWC, Box 21, DSNA. Approved on the same day. See Minutes, Supreme War Council, 6th session, 3rd meeting, Versailles, 3 June 1918, MMRD, RG 120, RSWC, Box 23, DSNA.

[31] General Peyton C. March, *The Nation at War* (Garden City, NY, 1932), p. 134. For his part, Baker later wrote: "The only real disagreement I ever had with President Wilson was about the sending of American troops to North Russia. I was opposed to it. . . . The expedition was nonsense from the beginning." Ray Stannard Baker, *Woodrow Wilson: Life and Letters*, 8 vols. (New York, 1939), 8:284n. At Versailles, Bliss was also opposed to the policy. Bliss to March, 24 June 1918, MMRD, RG 120, RSWC, Box 22, DSNA. In fact, Wilson agreed with his military experts but felt bound to support intervention, as he told Baker, because the Allies had "so much set their hearts" on the policy. Baker to March, 7 September 1927, Papers of Newton D. Baker, Library of Congress, Box 150 (hereafter cited as Baker Papers).

[32] Balfour to Lord Reading (Washington), no. 3599, 11 June 1918, F. O. 371/3786, 98963/6/38, PRO.

AMERICAN INTERVENTION IN RUSSIA   55

July 1918, made the final decisions on intervention in Russia, both in the north and in the far east. On 2 July the council decided to intervene in Siberia.[33] On the next day a similar decision was reached regarding North Russia. Following a convincing appreciation of the situation by a British official just returned from Murmansk, the council resolved that:

> ... the British, French and Italian Governments should expedite the dispatch [to North Russia] of those forces agreed on to carry out Joint Note 31 of the Military Representatives, and that the American Government should be asked to send a force of three American battalions and other units already asked for by the British Government in their telegram dated 11th June.[34]

The text of this resolution, which constituted a complete endorsement of the British position, was telegraphed to Washington by each of the Allied governments individually "for the information of President Wilson."[35]

The concerted pressure of the members of the Supreme War Council was apparently sufficient to force the president's hand once and for all. Thus, during the first half of July, although privately he still expressed misgivings about the policy, the chief executive at last agreed to American participation in severely restricted expeditions to both Siberia and North Russia.[36] However, Wilson's continued distaste for intervention was clearly reflected in the very document by which it was finally authorized— the highly ambiguous aide-mémoire of 17 July 1918.[37] This statement, which was drafted personally by the president was, at least to some extent, a blunt rejection of the whole policy of intervention. According to the aide-mémoire, the American government could see "no advantage" to military intervention in Russia and could not, "therefore, take part in such intervention or sanction it in principle." Having taken this strong stand, the president then thoroughly clouded the issue by yielding to "the judgment

---

[33]Minutes (and Annexure), Supreme War Council, 7th session, 1st meeting, Versailles, 2 July 1918, MMRD, RG 120, RSWC, Box 23, DSNA.

[34]Minutes, Supreme War Council, 7th session, 2nd meeting, Versailles, 3 July 1918, MMRD, RG 120, RSWC, Box 23, DSNA. The British official in question was First Lord of the Admiralty Sir Eric Geddes. His report is cited in full in Lord Derby (Paris) to Balfour, no. 817(D), 3 July 1918, F. O. 371/3286, 117420/6/38, PRO.

[35]Diplomatic liaison officer, Supreme War Council, to the secretary of state, no. 100, 2 and 3 July 1918, *FRUS, 1918: Russia*, 2:241–46.

[36]Wilson's decision (with specific reference to Siberia) was first announced at a joint meeting of his chief advisers at the White House on 6 July. Memorandum of the secretary of state, 6 July 1918, *FRUS, 1918: Russia, 2:* 262–63. Two days later, in a letter to House, the president wrote that he had been "sweating blood" over what to do about Russia but found that "it goes to pieces like quicksilver under my touch." Wilson to House, 8 July 1918, Wilson Papers, LC. On 12 July, British agent Sir William Wiseman reported that he found the president "still opposed to intervention and somewhat apprehensive lest the step . . . should lead him into a much more extended policy." Fowler, *British-American Relations*, p. 191.

[37]The text of the aide-mémoire (which appeared over the signature of Secretary of State Lansing) is in *FRUS, 1918: Russia*, 2:287–90.

of the Supreme [War] Council" and agreeing to American action in Russia in order "to help the Czecho-Slovaks" and, more equivocally, "to steady any efforts at self-government or self-defense in which the Russians themselves may be willing to accept assistance."[38]

Seen in retrospect there is little doubt that President Wilson sincerely believed that his aide-mémoire had expressed an essentially limited conception of intervention in Russia, a policy he fully intended to sustain.[39] For their part, the Allied powers either misunderstood the document, which is possible given its ambiguity, or else deliberately chose to ignore it. In either case what followed in Russia, at least in the north, bore little relation to the president's expectations.

Whatever its real intent the immediate consequence of the aide-mémoire was to remove the last obstacle in the way of full-scale intervention in Russia, which proceeded according to the plans of its most enthusiastic proponents. On 30 July, General John J. Pershing detached from his command in France the necessary American troops for service in North Russia: the 339th Infantry Regiment (three battalions) and its auxiliaries, the 1st Battalion 310th Engineers, the 337th Field Hospital, and the 337th Ambulance Company.[40] Under the overall command of Colonel George E. Stewart, these units became the nucleus of the future American Expeditionary Force, North Russia (AEFNR).[41] After preparation in England the Americans set sail for North Russia on 27 August.

Even before the embarkation of the troops, however, the northern

---

[38]The president's ambiguity was apparently deliberate and stemmed from his plan, as related to Secretary of War Baker, "to limit the American contribution [to intervention] as much as possible but still play the game with our allies." Baker to March, 7 September 1927, Baker Papers, LC.

[39]From the outset, however, the president felt uneasy about the policy laid down in the aide-mémoire and, within a month of its issuance, was already expressing "no confidence" in his judgment about "the complicated situation in Russia." See his letters to Thomas G. Masaryk and Victor Lawson, 7 August 1918, Wilson Papers, LC.

[40]See John J. Pershing, *My Experiences in the World War*, 2 vols. (New York, 1931), 2:175–76; and United States, Army War College, Historical Section, *Order of Battle of the United States Land Forces in the World War. American Expeditionary Forces*, vol. 1, *General Headquarters, Armies, Army Corps, Services of Supply and Separate Forces* (Washington, 1937), pp. 380–89. According to this authoritative source, the approximate number of American troops sent to Russia was as follows: North Russia—5,710, Siberia—8,388. These totals are not nearly so unequal as is often assumed.

[41]Available information on the AEFNR is voluminous but widely dispersed. The official records of the expedition are in Organization Records AEFNR (OR AEFNR), MMRD, RG 120, 17 Boxes, DSNA. The papers of the expedition's commander, Colonel Stewart, are in the United States Military Academy Archives, USMA Library, West Point, New York. Finally, various personal papers and materials of subordinate officers and men of the expedition are preserved in the Michigan Historical Collections (MHC), The University of Michigan, Ann Arbor. In addition, there are several published accounts of participants in the expedition of which the most valuable are Joel R. Moore, Harry H. Mead, and Lewis E. Jahns, *The History of the American Expedition Fighting the Bolsheviki* (Detroit, 1920); and A Chronicler (John Cudahy), *Archangel: The American War with Russia* (Chicago, 1924).

AMERICAN INTERVENTION IN RUSSIA   57

expedition already had taken a turn sharply at variance with American intentions. To a great extent this situation was attributable to the personality and approach of the British commander-in-chief in the north, General Poole. From the moment of his arrival at Murmansk in late May, Poole, an extremely ambitious and enthusiastic interventionist, had displayed an increasingly belligerent activity in the area.[42] In late June, he crowned his efforts by unfolding an almost unbelievably aggressive plan of future operations in the north. It called for the virtual invasion of central Russia with an army of 5,000 Allied troops, which he predicted would be quickly joined by some 100,000 anti-Bolshevik Russians.[43] However fanciful, this scheme, which was apparently Poole's inspiration, received the prompt approval of the Supreme War Council, and by 2 August the general had completed the first stage of his plan, the occupation of Archangel.[44] This action was carried out by a polyglot Allied force including some fifty sailors from the U.S.S. *Olympia*, who were used for this purpose in direct violation of President Wilson's strict orders.[45] In spite of the paucity of his reserves, the British commander immediately commenced an energetic offensive to the south with the cities of Kotlas and Vologda, deep in the interior, as his ultimate objectives.

Such were the circumstances in North Russia when the transports bearing the AEFNR at last dropped anchor in Archangel harbor on 4 September. Almost at once General Poole ordered two of the three American infantry battalions to the fighting fronts, with the one down the Northern Dvina River toward Kotlas and the other on the railroad to Vologda.[46] These orders, which were contrary to both the spirit and the letter of President Wilson's aide-mémoire, placed the American commander, Colonel Stewart, on the horns of a dilemma. Although he inexplicably still had not been entrusted with a copy of the president's directive, Stewart was vaguely aware that his commander in chief had given instructions for nothing more than the defense of the northern ports and the rendering of assistance to the local Russian population.[47] These orders, however, for all intents and purposes were being violated now by

---

[42]Dispatch of Major-General F. Poole to the War Office, 5 October 1918, *The London Gazette,* 2 April 1920 (Supplement, 6 April, no. 31850), pp. 4107–11 (hereafter cited as Poole Dispatch). The original of this document, from which the published version differs in some significant particulars, is in W. O. 32/5703, PRO.

[43]Poole (Murmansk) to War Office, no. E. 81, 27 June 1918, W. O. 33/962, no. 28, PRO.

[44]Minutes, Supreme War Council, 7th session, 2d meeting, Versailles, 3 July 1918, MMRD, RG 120, RSWC, Box 23, DSNA.

[45]Poole Dispatch, pp. 4109–10. For Wilson's strict proscription on the usage of the American sailors without express permission from Washington, see above, note 25.

[46]"339th Operations, Organization and Reports, Jan. 12, 1918 [*sic*] to Dec. 18, 1918," Stewart Papers, USMA, Folder 1.

[47]"Orders and Instructions for Usage of American Troops, August–October 1918," ibid.

his immediate superior. In confronting this problem, the American commander could take little comfort from the attitude of his political counterpart in the north, Ambassador David R. Francis, who with the rest of the Allied diplomatic corps recently had taken refuge at Archangel after fleeing from Bolshevik Russia. Although Francis, an ardent interventionist, had received a paraphrase of the aide-mémoire as early as mid-August, he had decided that it pertained only to Siberia, and he was, as he reported to the State Department, encouraging American troops "to obey the commands of General Poole."[48] In this confusing situation the baffled Colonel Stewart, who was later the object of much largely undeserved criticism, retired to his headquarters, where he finally received a copy of the aide-mémoire on 5 October.[49] By that time it was already too late for him to alter the situation, which had gone completely beyond his control.

From the moment of their arrival at the various fronts in the north, American troops were regularly engaged in numerous small-scale combats with Bolshevik forces.[50] Whether this misuse of American soldiers in the north was brought to the attention of President Wilson, who was increasingly engrossed in other more pressing problems, is not certain. That the president would have deplored the fact, however, is clear from the one element of the northern situation that came to his notice at that time, namely, a request for more Allied troops in the area. On 2 September the military representatives of the Supreme War Council received an appeal from General Poole for the dispatch of additional reinforcements to North Russia.[51] This request, which flew directly in the face of an earlier stipulation by the council that no further reserves would be sent to the north, particularly enraged General Bliss, who by no means was enamored with the northern expedition. "I think," wrote Bliss to Chief of Staff March on 7 September, that "the British possibly feel that they may have 'bitten off more than they can chew' [in North Russia] and want to throw the responsibility elsewhere. This they cannot do if I have anything to say about it."[52]

For his part, having been informed of the situation by General March, President Wilson readily concurred. "I think you know already,"

─────────────────────────────────────

[48]Francis (Archangel) to Bliss (Paris), 19 August 1918, FAB, RG 84, Petrograd Embassy File (PEF), Correspondence, 1918, DSNA; and the ambassador in Russia to the secretary of state, no. 1207, 27 August 1918, *FRUS, 1918, Russia,* 2:515–16.

[49]"Orders and Instructions for Usage of American Troops," Stewart Papers, USMA, Folder 1. The operative sections of this copy of the aide-mémoire have been heavily underscored, apparently by Stewart.

[50]The best account of the military history of the northern expedition is in Halliday, *The Ignorant Armies.* See also the memoir-history of A. A. Samoilo and M. I. Sboichakov, *Pouchitel'nyi urok* [A Salutary Lesson] (Moscow, 1962). The former author was the Soviet commander in the north.

[51]Minutes, PMR, 44th meeting, Versailles, 2 September 1918, MMRD, RG 120, RSWC, Box 21, DSNA.

[52]Bliss to March, no. 19, 7 September 1918, MMRD, RG 120, RSWC, Box 22, DSNA.

AMERICAN INTERVENTION IN RUSSIA   59

he wrote to March, "that the judgments expressed [by Bliss] are my own also."[53] Accordingly, at a subsequent meeting of the military representatives on 14 September, General Bliss attacked the request for more troops in the north and insisted that General Poole be directed to adhere strictly to his original instructions. Surprisingly, the other military representatives agreed with their American colleague, and Poole's request was denied.[54] Although subsequent efforts to alter this decision were made, especially by the French, the American resolve held firm.[55] Finally, to put an end to further speculation on the subject the American position was bluntly announced in a general circular addressed to all the major Allied governments on 26 September. "So far as our cooperation is concerned," read this statement, the government of the United States shall insist that "all military effort in northern Russia be given up except the guarding of the ports themselves and as much of the country round about them as may develop threatening conditions. . . . No more American troops will be sent to the northern ports."[56] In spite of its categorical tone, there is no indication that this message had any effect whatsoever on the actual military situation in North Russia. On the contrary, American troops remained prominent on all the fronts in the north and continued to engage in sporadic clashes with units of the fledgling Red Army.

As if their military misuse were not sufficient violation of President Wilson's orders, American troops in the north also were drawn into the trammels of local Russian domestic politics. Thus, on the night of 5/6 September, a coup d'état was engineered at Archangel by a clique of high-ranking Russian military officers, who abducted the members of the regional anti-Bolshevik government and shipped them off under guard to an island in the White Sea.[57] Since this event coincided exactly with the first appearance of American soldiers in Archangel, the local populace, as Ambassador Francis reported, "naturally concluded that we had encouraged and supported the kidnapping, if . . . not planned it."[58] Even worse, when the coup was followed by a general protest strike of the city's

---

[53]Wilson to March, 18 September 1918, MMRD, RG 120, RSWC, Box 22, DSNA.

[54]Minutes, PMR, 46th meeting, Versailles, 14 September 1918, MMRD, RG 120, RSWC, Box 21, DSNA.

[55]On the French effort to get American reinforcements for the north and the stout resistance of Bliss, see Bliss to Baker, no. 25, 3 October 1918, and Bliss to March, nos. 26 and 27, 5 and 9 October 1918, MMRD, RG 120, RSWC, Box 22, DSNA.

[56]The secretary of state to the ambassador in Great Britain, 26 September 1918, *FRUS, 1918, Russia*, 2:394–95. Repeated to the ambassadors in France and Italy and the chargé in Japan.

[57]The inspiration for the coup was primarily political. The officers involved were strongly conservative and resented the socialist orientation of the local government. See Professor A. C. Coolidge (Special State Department Agent, Archangel) to the secretary of state, 28 September 1918, FAB, RG 59, 861.00/2899 1/2, DSNA; and Leonid I. Strakhovsky, *Intervention at Archangel* (Princeton, 1944), pp. 42–59.

[58]Francis to Captain B. B. Bierer (U.S.S. *Olympia*, Murmansk), 26 September 1918, FAB, RG 84, PEF 800, Correspondence, 1918, DSNA.

workers, American troops were used, without the knowledge of Colonel Stewart, to operate the local streetcars, in effect as strikebreakers.[59]

The coup at Archangel evoked the first open American protest against the situation in North Russia. In mid-September, when Washington was informed that General Poole probably had been implicated in the coup, Secretary of State Lansing dispatched a vigorous message to London decrying Poole's conduct, which the secretary pointed out was "entirely at variance" with the policy set forth in President Wilson's aide-mémoire. If this behavior were not at once terminated, warned Lansing, the president "will be compelled to consider the withdrawal of the American troops from the superior command of General Poole . . . in accord with the announced policy of this Government."[60]

The American protest elicited important changes in the north. After some reorganization the kidnapped government was returned to Archangel and hastily reinstated. More importantly, on 14 October, General Poole was recalled from North Russia and replaced by a new commanding officer, General W. Edmund Ironside.[61] The new commander, who was distinctly apolitical, soon reorganized and greatly improved the Allied situation in the north. However, Ironside could do nothing to clarify the confused status of his American troops, who continued to constitute the majority of the Allied combat forces in the north.

At that juncture the ultimate anomaly not only of the American but also of the entire Allied situation in Russia was abruptly laid bare by the sudden conclusion of the World War. In fact, the unexpected termination of hostilities on 11 November found the victorious powers virtually without any definitive policies regarding Russia. The Allies were compelled perforce to fall back on the *status quo ante* until such time as the Russian problem could be clarified by joint consultation of the nations engaged in intervention.[62] Meanwhile, in anticipation of the public outcry that seemed certain to greet the decision to remain in Russia even temporarily, Allied spokesmen quickly devised several mitigating justifications for the policy, including such arguments as the moral obligation of the Allies to protect the

---

[59]Ambassador in Russia to the secretary of state, no. 391, 10 September 1918, *FRUS, 1918, Russia,* 2:532–33; and David R. Francis, *Russia from the American Embassy* (New York, 1921), pp. 261ff.

[60]The secretary of state to the ambassador in Great Britain, no. 1313, 12 September 1918, *FRUS, 1918, Russia,* 2:533–34. Even before the coup the president had complained bitterly to Lansing about "the utter disregard of General Poole and of all the Allied governments" of the policies outlined in his aide-mémoire. Wilson to Lansing, 5 September 1918, Wilson Papers, LC.

[61]See Field Marshal Lord Ironside, *Archangel 1918–1919* (London, 1953), pp. 25ff; and Ironside (Archangel) to War Office, no. E 671/G., 18 October 1918, W. O. 33/962, no. 433, PRO.

[62]On the postarmistice disarray prevailing among the Allies regarding Russia see John M. Thompson, *Russia, Bolshevism and the Versailles Peace* (Princeton, 1966), pp. 10–61; and Arno J. Mayer, *Politics and Diplomacy of Peacemaking* (New York, 1967), pp. 284–343.

AMERICAN INTERVENTION IN RUSSIA 61

so-called "loyal" Russians against the vengeful Bolsheviks and, in the north, the physical impossibility of leaving the area because of the freezing of the White Sea.[63]

Curiously, although Washington avoided participating in any of this postarmistice rationalizing about intervention, the United States conspicuously failed to take any decisive action with respect to Russia in the immediate aftermath of the war. In spite of a plaintive cable from an unhappy Colonel Stewart requesting the immediate withdrawal of his troops from the north, no official statement on American policy in Russia was at once forthcoming.[64] This failure to take an unequivocal stand on Russia, a source of continuing frustration to President Wilson, was clearly the consequence of more pressing demands on his attention and of his frequently expressed belief that any final resolution of the Russian problem would have to await the joint decision of the Allies at the impending peace conference.[65] That the chief executive was not comfortable with this position, however, is clear from his private response at that time to still another recommendation that American troops should be immediately withdrawn from Russia. In replying to this suggestion, the president frankly acknowledged his indecision about "the immediate proper course in Russia" and complained ruefully that he was already finding it "harder to get out [of Russia] than it was to go in."[66] The result of Wilson's decision to defer action on Russia was that no statement on American policy was received at Archangel until early December, when a message from the State Department blandly announced that there would be "no change in the situation until the question of how to further assist Russia . . . is determined by discussion with the Allied Governments at Paris."[67]

This indecisive American response to the postarmistice situation at Archangel, the only brief lapse in American resolve during the entire period of the northern intervention, had unfortunate repercussions. While Washington dallied, hostilities continued in North Russia. Indeed, on the day the war ended in western Europe, Allied troops, including two companies of Americans, were heavily engaged in a savage battle at

---

[63]"Memorandum on Our Present and Future Military Policy in Russia" by General Henry Wilson, CIGS, 13 November 1918, W. O. 33/1004, Section B. Précis A, PRO. For a withering critique of the pro-interventionist arguments see W. P. and Zelda Coates, *Armed Intervention in Russia, 1918–1922* (London, 1935), pp. 135–38.

[64]Stewart to Americally Sowest (American Headquarters, London), no. CO68, 14 November 1918, Stewart Papers, USMA, Folder 1.

[65]British agent Wiseman's "Notes of an Interview with the President at the White House, October 16th, 1918" cited in Fowler, *British-American Relations*, p. 196. As early as late September the president had expressed to Wiseman his frustration that "control of the Russian situation" was "slipping from his grasp." Ibid., p. 194.

[66]Wilson to Grenville MacFarland, 27 November 1918, Wilson Papers, LC. A similar strong recommendation advocating withdrawal was also received from Secretary of War Baker. Baker to Wilson, 27 November 1918, ibid.

[67]The acting secretary of state to the chargé in Russia [DeWitt C. Poole], no. 386, 4 December 1918, *FRUS, 1918, Russia*, 2:574.

Tulgas, a village on the Northern Dvina River.[68] This clash, which the soldiers ironically dubbed "the Battle of Armistice Day," marked the beginning of a precipitate decline of Allied morale that lasted until the end of the northern intervention.[69]

Coincident with the decline in morale, Allied military fortunes in North Russia took a turn for the worse. In mid-January 1919 the Soviet Sixth Army, recently strengthened and reorganized, staged its first significant offensive of the northern campaign against the exposed Allied salient around Shenkursk, an important outpost some two hundred miles south of Archangel.[70] The outcome of this overwhelming assault, the brunt of which was borne by American troops, was a near disaster. On 25 January, heavily outnumbered and invested from three directions, the besieged Allied garrison hastily evacuated Shenkursk under cover of darkness. Three days later a new front was stabilized some fifty miles to the rear.

The attack on Shenkursk may have been intended by Soviet leaders to remind the Allied peacemakers, who were then assembling at Versailles, of the continuing urgency of the Russian problem. If so, it was unnecessary. The fact that at least President Wilson had neither forgotten about nor essentially altered his ideas on Russia became apparent from the moment of his arrival at the peace conference. Accordingly, when British Prime Minister David Lloyd George, just before the official opening of the conference, proposed that the Allies invite all the contending factions in Russia to come together and discuss "conditions of a permanent settlement," his initiative was eagerly seized upon by the president, who had been searching for just such a peaceful way out of the Russian imbroglio.[71] Drawn up by Wilson personally, the result was the so-called Prinkipo

---

[68]The official report on the battle of Tulgas is in "Extracts from Correspondence Files of Allied GHQ Archangel," Stewart Papers, USMA, unfiled. For the analogous Soviet report see A. G. Gorlenko and N. R. Prokopenko, eds., *Severnyi front 1918–1920: Dokumenty* [The Northern Front 1918–1920: Documents] (Moscow, 1961), doc. no. 112, pp. 144–46.

[69]The best published account of Allied morale problems at Archangel is in Ralph Albertson, *Fighting Without a War* (New York, 1920). For a Soviet interpretation see G. G. Alakhverdov, "Razlozhenie v voiskakh interventov i belogvardeitsev na severe Rossii v 1918–1919 godakh" [Demoralization Among the Troops of the Interventionists and the White Guards in North Russia in 1918–1919], *Voprosy istorii* [Problems of History], no. 7 (1960): 121–34.

[70]See Halliday, *The Ignorant Armies*, pp. 123–46; and M. Angarskii, "Shenkurskaia operatsiia (ianvar' 1919 goda)" [The Shenkursk Operation (January 1919)], *Voenno-istoricheskii zhurnal* [The Military-Historical Journal], no. 2 (1959): 48–62.

[71]David Lloyd George, *The Truth About the Peace Treaties*, 2 vols. (London, 1939), 1:199–200, 320–23. In fact, in his efforts to achieve a peaceful resolution of the Russian problem, the president had already dispatched an unofficial envoy, W. H. Buckler, to Stockholm for informal discussions with Bolshevik troubleshooter Maxim Litvinov. Wilson to Lansing, 10 January 1919, Wilson Papers, LC. The result of these talks, just reported to Versailles, was apparently decisive in winning Allied approval of Lloyd George's proposal. *FRUS: The Paris Peace Conference [PRC], 1919,* 3:643–53.

proposal, whereby all the "organized groups" in Russia were invited to send representatives to the Prinkipo Islands, Sea of Marmora, in order to discuss the details of a peace settlement.[72] Nothwithstanding the president's good intentions, the Prinkipo proposal was not crowned with success. Only the Bolsheviks agreed to the proposed meeting, which therefore collapsed.

The failure of the Prinkipo plan, however, did not put an end to Allied discussion of the Russian problem. On the contrary, on 14 February, Winston S. Churchill, newly appointed British secretary of war and a vigorous proponent of intervention in Russia, appeared in Paris and raised the issue again at a meeting of the Supreme War Council. The British government, announced Churchill, wanted to know whether "the Allied policy which had led to . . . Prinkipo was to be pursued or, if not, what policy was to be substituted for it." The war secretary declared that he was opposed to the evacuation of Russia and urged the Allies to send "volunteers" and every kind of military assistance to the anti-Bolsheviks. In response, President Wilson, who was about to leave Paris for the United States, stated flatly that Allied intervention was doing "no sort of good" in Russia since there were not enough troops there to defeat the Bolsheviks and no one was prepared to send more. It was clear, added Wilson, that the Allies would have to leave Russia "some day or other." His inclination, he plainly implied, was to do so at once.[73]

On the next day, discussion of Russia was resumed at a meeting of the influential Council of Ten. In the absence of President Wilson, the forceful Churchill quickly took charge of the proceedings and presented a shrewdly conceived proposal, the upshot of which amounted to the initiation of an Allied military crusade in Russia.[74] Predictably, this *démarche* evoked a sharp reaction from the United States. From the mid-Atlantic President Wilson wired that he was "greatly surprised by Churchill's Russian suggestion. . . . It would be fatal to be led further into the Russian chaos."[75] On the next day in a statement clearly revealing his ignorance of the real state of affairs in North Russia, the president sternly enjoined the American delegation in Paris to make "very plain" to the British "that we are not at war with Russia and will in no circumstances . . . take part in military operations there."[76] On 17 February the Churchill proposal was

---

[72] The full text of the Prinkipo message is in *FRUS, 1919, Russia*, pp. 30–31. The best account of the Prinkipo effort is Thompson, *Russia and Versailles*, pp. 82–130.

[73] See Minutes, Supreme War Council, 14th session, Paris, 14 February 1919, *FRUS, PPC, 1919*, 3:1041–44; and Winston S. Churchill, *The World Crisis*, vol. 4, *The Aftermath, 1918–1928* (New York, 1929), pp. 170–73. In addition to ending intervention, Wilson also expressed American willingness to meet informally with "representatives of the Bolsheviks."

[74] See Minutes, Council of Ten, Paris, 15 February 1919, *FRUS, PPC, 1919*, 4:10–21; and Churchill, *The Aftermath*, pp. 174–78.

[75] Wilson (U.S.S. *George Washington*) to the Commission to Negotiate Peace, no. W-6, 19 February 1919, *FRUS, 1919, Russia*, pp. 71–72.

[76] Wilson to House (Paris), 20 February 1919, Wilson Papers, LC.

the subject of a final heated debate within the Council of Ten.[77] In the face of stubborn American opposition, the plan was finally shelved. The future of intervention, in spite of Washington's hopes for its satisfactory termination, remained without any general inter-Allied resolution.

It was apparently the inability of the Allies to agree unanimously on a common course of action in Russia that finally decided President Wilson to act on the unilateral evacuation of the north. There is strong evidence that the chief executive also was prompted by a rapidly mounting tide of domestic opposition to any further intervention in Russia. As far as the north was concerned, this opposition had had its origins in the period immediately following the armistice and was initially centered in those midwestern states from which the majority of the American troops in North Russia hailed. This regional opposition to intervention, which was motivated primarily by the simple desire to "bring the boys home" from Russia, was essentially apolitical.[78] However, it was not long before this regional campaign was taken up in the halls of Congress, where it soon brought together an incongruous band of political allies, including Republican isolationists led by Senator Hiram Johnson (CA), President Wilson's political enemies headed by Senator Henry Cabot Lodge (R.-MA), and various legislators from both parties who felt that the United States should either do more in Russia or get out of the country altogether.[79] As a result, by early 1919 the intervention question, according to Secretary of War Baker, had become "the most delicate" issue in domestic politics. It culminated on 14 February in the near passage of Senator Johnson's Resolution No. 411, which declared that "in the opinion of the Senate the soldiers of the United States as soon as practicable should be withdrawn from Russia."[80]

It was against this turbulent background that President Wilson at last made his decision to leave North Russia. On 5 February, General Sir Henry Wilson, British Chief of Staff, wrote to General Bliss in Paris requesting the dispatch of two companies of American railroad troops to

---

[77]So acrimonious was this debate that its substance was deleted from the public record. Minutes, Supreme War Council, Paris, 17 February 1919, *FRUS, PPC, 1919,* 4:28. The essence of the meeting, however, has been reconstructed from memoir and archival sources in Thompson, *Russia and Versailles,* pp. 143–45.

[78]Governor Albert E. Sleeper (Michigan) to Wilson, 7 January 1919, Wilson Papers, LC. The regional campaign to end intervention was greatly stimulated by disparaging reports from North Russia by correspondents Paul Scott Mowrer and Frazier Hunt of the *Detroit News* and *Chicago Tribune,* respectively. For the description of a typical "bring the boys home" meeting, see Mrs. J. M. Crissman to John S. Crissman, 10 February 1919, John S. Crissman Papers, MHC.

[79]On the congressional opposition to intervention see Mayer, *Politics and Diplomacy,* pp. 331–39, 447–49.

[80]Baker to Wilson, 1 January 1919, Wilson Papers, LC. Senate Resolution No. 411 was originally proposed on 13 January. U.S., Congress, Senate, *Congressional Record,* 65th Cong., 3rd sess., 13 January 1919, p. 1313. The final vote on the resolution was a tie, and Vice President Thomas Marshall was forced to cast his ballot in order to have the motion tabled. Ibid., 14 February 1919, pp. 3334–42.

AMERICAN INTERVENTION IN RUSSIA   65

Murmansk.[81] Basing himself on Bliss's memorandum on this subject, President Wilson on 18 February authorized the secretary of war to make public his agreement to the British request on strict condition of "the prompt withdrawal of American and Allied troops in North Russia at the earliest possible moment that weather conditions will permit in the spring."[82] In fact, this vague and rather presumptuous statement was the American government's only formal announcement of its intention to withdraw from North Russia. As far as President Wilson was concerned, however, the decision was final.

Although the president's decision was relayed to Archangel as early as 20 February, its purport was only indifferently made known to the Allied and American military forces on the ground.[83] As in the post-armistice situation, the failure to make clear American policy in the north had unfortunate consequences. On the one hand, no strong discouragement was given to local Allied, especially British, military authorities, who, prompted by Churchill, already were planning further offensive action in the north.[84] Subsequently, this created resentment on both sides and left a residue of recrimination that sharply divided the Allies in North Russia. By the same token, the failure to communicate clearly the president's decision had a decidedly debilitating effect on the declining morale of the American troops in the north and undoubtedly contributed to the wave of unrest that swept through their ranks in the late winter and spring of 1919.[85] Although this discontent had no serious consequences, it caused undue bitterness and a still further depression of American élan in the north.

The decline in American morale in North Russia was soon arrested

---

[81]March, *The Nation at War*, p. 148.

[82]*FRUS, 1919, Russia*, pp. 617–18. Based upon Bliss to Wilson, 12 February 1919, Wilson Papers, LC. The Bliss memorandum is partially reprinted in March, *The Nation at War*, pp. 148–49.

[83]According to Chargé d'Affaires DeWitt C. Poole, the president's decision was immediately publicized in Archangel and vastly improved American morale in the north. Chargé in Russia to the acting secretary of state, 20 February 1919, *FRUS, 1919: Russia*, pp. 617–18. On the other hand, as late as the end of March, the chief American military authorities in the north complained that they were still without any official confirmation of the decision. See military attaché, Archangel (Colonel J. A. Ruggles) to Colonel B. H. Warburton (military attaché, Paris), no. 21, 29 March 1919, MMRD, RG 120, GHQ AEF, Military Attaché Reports, Box 5827, DSNA; and Stewart Papers, USMA, Folder 2.

[84]On the so-called Churchill plan, see the War Office compilation "North Russia, 1919," W. O. 33/950, pp. 17–20, PRO; and Thompson, *Russia and Versailles*, pp. 213ff.

[85]The best published account of the unrest at Archangel, which was rife among all the Allied troops in the north, is Strakhovsky, *Intervention at Archangel*, pp. 161–63. For additional fascinating data on specifically American discontent see the Lt. Charles B. Ryan and Sgt. Silver K. Parrish Papers, MHC. In at least one instance of American disaffection, an appeal addressed "To the Bolsheviki soldiers" and signed by "Soldiers boys of the U.S.," there is specific reference to the latter's belief that American troops had been "ordered out of Russia by our President" and the consequent promise that "if you wait 2½ months we will be out of Russia." This appeal in both English and Russian translation is appended to the Pvt. Kenneth A. Skellenger Diary, MHC.

once and for all. On 17 April the rumors of impending American withdrawal from the north were dramatically confirmed by the arrival at Archangel of Brigadier General Wilds P. Richardson, who had been briefed personally by President Wilson to take charge of American evacuation.[86] Richardson, who immediately relieved Colonel Stewart in command of the AEFNR, carried out his orders to the letter. In spite of persistent British efforts to delay their departure, with the opening of navigation in June the first contingents of American troops were shipped out of Archangel.[87] In regular sequence all the remaining American units at the port, as well as the two companies of railroad troops at Murmansk, were similarly dispatched.[88] By 23 July 1919 American intervention in North Russia formally had come to an end.

The history of the North Russian expedition does not so much revise as clarify and supplement existing political interpretations of American intervention. While it is undoubtedly true that American engagement in Russia was motivated by such considerations as wartime military strategy, assistance to the Czech legion, and suspicion of Japan, these factors apply primarily to the initial formative stage of American involvement in Russia and thereafter are relevant, for the most part, only to the Siberian expedition. In order to obtain an integrated and comprehensive view of American intervention, it is necessary to enlarge the existing picture to include the expedition to North Russia, with particular emphasis on the actual implementation of that operation.

In addition, to reach a full evaluation of American intervention it is essential to begin by stressing that Washington's basic attitude toward involvement in Russia was from the outset extremely reluctant. Indeed, throughout the early period U.S. interest in intervention was sustained only by constant and unremitting Allied pressure. During this initial stage of intervention it is perhaps not crucial to draw a sharp distinction between the future sites of American activity in Russia. While the north was briefly utilized as a tactical element in the calculations of both the Allies and the Americans, the ultimate decision announced in President Wilson's aide-mémoire, which it cannot be sufficiently overemphasized, called for severely limited intervention, was explicitly applied to both areas of subsequent American engagement in Russia.

It is not until analysis passes to the actual implementation of the policy outlined in the aide-mémoire that the distinction between the two

---

[86]Report of Brig. Gen. Wilds P. Richardson, commanding American E. F. N. R., 27 June 1919, MMRD, RG 120, GHQ, AEF, G-3 (Operations), Folder 707, DSNA.

[87]"Troops and Civilians Evacuated from North Russia from 1st June, 1919 to 12th October, 1919," *The Evacuation of North Russia, 1919* (London, 1920), p. 44. On British efforts to defer evacuation and the American response, see Bliss to Wilson, 29 May and 26 June 1919, and Wilson to Bliss, 10 and 28 June 1919, Wilson Papers, LC.

[88]See "Troops and Civilians Evacuated," p. 44; and the supplemental report of Richardson, commanding American E. F. N. R., 23 July 1919, MMRD, RG 120, GHQ AEF, G-3 (Operations), Folder 707, DSNA.

AMERICAN INTERVENTION IN RUSSIA   67

locales of American intervention becomes critical. In Siberia, the presence of such elements as the Czech legion, German and Austrian prisoners of war, and especially the Japanese quickly combined to make difficult the full realization of the president's concept of limited intervention. Although serious problems attended the placing of the expedition under British command, by contrast in North Russia the intended policy of President Wilson was much more in evidence. In every instance in which his attention was drawn to the north, the president insisted upon strict adherence to his stated concept of intervention and vigorously objected to any violations of it, although the full extent of those violations apparently was never made clear to him. Most significantly, when his postarmistice efforts to achieve a general resolution of the Russian problem finally collapsed, the chief executive moved unhesitatingly toward the unilateral evacuation of North Russia (though not notably of Siberia) in full accord with his announced principles.

The history of the northern expedition emphatically belies charges of malevolent ideological motivation on the part of the United States. In the case of North Russia, there is simply no evidence to support the contention that President Wilson was motivated by an ideological desire to crush Bolshevism and convert the Russians to his own political convictions. In short, using the north as its true measure, American intervention in Russia cannot justifiably be interpreted as merely an early manifestation of the Cold War.

16

Look Back in Anger: The Western Powers and the Washington Conference of 1921–1922

Malcolm H. Murfett

By the time the principal delegates had assembled at Washington in November 1921 to begin tackling the emotive issues of comparative naval strength and relative power in the Pacific, they were well aware that the political imperative for disarmament matched the popular mood of the time in the West. It was a situation that had emerged in the wake of the "Great War" and the eclipse of the German and Russian surface fleets when it became almost impossible for even the most sentimental, or insecure, of military enthusiasts on either side of the Atlantic to defend the maintenance of a huge naval establishment at vast cost to the state when there appeared to be no obvious European enemy in sight. From the time that the British War Cabinet recognized this fact and decided on 15 August 1919 to implement its so-called Ten-Year Rule, the days of the large Grand Fleet were numbered. Apart from its economic role in keeping scores of servicemen and those in the ancillary industries in gainful employment, the Royal Navy, in particular, had become so grossly inflated as a result of the war that a policy of rationalization was long overdue. Naturally, the question was one of degree. How deep would the cuts go? While some might talk mistily of the prestige that naval prowess and "showing the flag" in various corners of the globe was still supposed to create, it was patently obvious that Britain did not need seventy capital ships for this purpose.[1]

Although the heyday of imperialism may have definitely passed, there were still service chiefs on both sides of the Atlantic and also in Japan who thought that disarmament was a dirty word. In Japan the announcement of the 8:8 naval building program and the launching of the latest post-Jutland battleship, *Mutsu*—33,800 tons, armed with eight 16-inch guns—appeared to indicate that the elimination of potential rivals did nothing to lessen the desire for a formidable capital ship fleet.[2] By the same token, Josephus Daniels, the U.S. secretary of the navy, had gone on record in 1916 as stating that the Americans were committed to building a navy "second to none." That pledge, which had been subsequently endorsed by President Woodrow Wilson, had not changed by November 1921 despite the election of a Republican administration under Warren Gamaliel Harding in the previous autumn.[3]

Undoubtedly the key element in this strikingly bipartisan approach to U.S. naval policy lay in the considerable reservoir of suspicion and resentment built up against the Japanese in recent years. Apart from their rapacious activities in China, which threatened both the freedom of trade and the "Open Door" principle, the Japanese had alarmed many Americans with their wartime seizure and administration of the former German colonial possessions in the Pacific. Once the Versailles treaty in 1919 had officially conferred upon the Japanese the mandated control of much of Micronesia for the foreseeable future, the U.S. Navy Department found itself in a most undesirable strategic dilemma with Guam surrounded and communication lines to the Philippines compromised beyond belief. Calls for a strident U.S. response to Japanese encroachment in this sensitive area of the ocean had not gone unanswered by the government in Washington. While schemes to offset this perceived threat to American interests in the region were being formulated by U.S. military planners, the unease felt by leading congressional and administration figures for the Japanese intensified and coalesced into outright hostility toward any continuation of the Anglo-Japanese alliance.[4]

This unlikely diplomatic compact, fashioned initially in a low-key way in 1902 for want of anything better, had steadily become a source of real strength to each Power. Naval cooperation between the Allies in World War I, for example, had proved especially valuable to the British and, although strains and a sense of irritation with the alliance had grown in later years, overall, the feeling in government circles in London and Tokyo remained reasonably positive about maintaining this surprisingly durable international arrangement.[5] Despite the negative aspects of this friendship, one is tempted to say that if left to themselves, the two Powers would have probably renegotiated an extension of their alliance. They were not accorded that privilege.

As the day of renewal approached—and it was a moot point whether the alliance was supposed to lapse in 1921 or a year later—the British government was made fully aware that it risked alienating not only the Americans but also the Canadians if its accord with the Japanese was given a further lease of life. David Lloyd George's coalition government, already conscious of its parlous financial position after the war and its degree of indebtedness to the United States, was not prepared in the final analysis either to ignore or resist the calls for an end to the alliance made from both within and without the Commonwealth.

Nonetheless, rather than tamely surrendering, it fought a dogged rearguard action for some months before accepting the inevitable. Its strategy was to try and convince the Harding administration that the Anglo-Japanese alliance posed no military threat to the United States. By describing it as a harmless instrument of diplomatic cooperation and a useful way of influencing the inscrutable Japanese, the alliance was actually portrayed by the British as a far more positive than negative factor in international relations.[6]

Such a self-serving commentary—even if it was not entirely incorrect—did nothing to allay the fears expressed in U.S. government circles that the mere existence of the alliance, by emboldening the Japanese in the Far East, constituted a real source of danger to U.S. economic and commercial interests in China and the Pacific. Moreover, if a serious clash of interests were to occur between the Americans and the Japanese over, say, trading rights in China, the U.S. Navy Department was inclined to assume that the crisis might develop into a military confrontation between the two sides. If this were the case, it reasoned that the British might be dragged into the affair on the side of their Eastern ally. Conversely, an Anglo-American commercial dispute in this region might easily result in the Japanese siding with their British ally against the United States. Assumptions of this nature had been made by the navy war planners in Washington from 1919 onward. Their strategic and tactical plans to deal with the menace posed by a hostile Anglo-Japanese military alliance can be seen in the *Red-Orange* war plans that they devised at this time and maintained throughout the 1920s.[7]

It did not seem to matter what the British government said in its defense— the impossibility of war with the United States notwithstanding—the fact remained that the Republican administration was adamantly opposed to the Anglo-Japanese alliance and sought its official demise. After a last-ditch effort to hold onto the alliance was spoiled by resolute Canadian opposition at the 1921 Imperial Conference, held in London between June and August, the British government was forced to stall for time. Neither Lloyd George nor his foreign secretary, Lord Curzon, wished to see the alliance officially interred unless an effective international agreement covering Far Eastern and Pacific issues had been devised to take its place. In their eyes and those of the principal delegates to the Imperial Conference, the only effective alternative to the existing alliance would be some form of treaty or series of resolutions that the United States would be prepared to sign and ratify. Few doubted, given the failure of Congress to ratify the Treaty of Versailles, however, that such a scheme was far easier to propose than to implement. Nonetheless, the British felt that something had to be done. From this idea sprang the necessity for the convening of an international conference on the Pacific which Lloyd George's government was anxious, for political reasons, to host.

Again it was thwarted. President Harding had no desire to be upstaged on this issue by either the Welsh wizard or his ennobled colleague from the House of Lords. By proposing a conference that would link the drive for naval disarmament with the outstanding problems of the Pacific and the Far East, the Americans could seize the initiative and metaphorically cut the ground from underneath the British prime minister's feet. As a result, when Harding's secretary of state, Charles Evans Hughes, sent out invitations for this joint conference on 11 August 1921, both the British and the Japanese wondered just what the U.S. administration had in mind. Their relatively poor relations with the United States ensured that they remained none the wiser as the weeks passed and the conference, which was to be held in November at Washington, drew ever closer.

Smarting under this blow, Curzon conveniently discovered an excuse not to attend a conference that many on the eastern side of the Atlantic thought might turn into a diplomatic nightmare. Fortunately, Lloyd George could call upon a fine replacement in Arthur Balfour—a former prime minister with a wealth of ministerial experience—to lead the British delegation consisting of Lord Lee, the first lord of the Admiralty, and Sir Auckland Geddes, the British ambassador at Washington. Although there were to be technical support staff in attendance, most notably, Admiral Sir David Beatty, the first sea lord and chief of naval staff, the Americans had asked that to facilitate progress in these talks the service experts should be kept on a tight rein.

Despite this virtual injunction against the use of high-ranking service personnel on the delegations, the Japanese prime minister, Hara Kei, had selected Admiral Katō Tomosaburō, the navy minister since 1915, as his chief delegate. He would be flanked by Ambassador Shidehara Kijūrō and Prince Tokugawa Iesato, the president of the Japanese upper house. Katō was destined to play a prominent part in the discussions at Washington. In fact, throughout the conference, Balfour, Hughes, and he came to wield power in much the way plenipotentiaries had done in the past.[8]

Of the three, only Hughes, of course, knew what lay in store for the others when the conference opened in the Continental Hall on 12 November 1921. His memorable opening speech on that day—proposing massive cuts in all existing surface fleets and detailing which individual units were destined for the breakers yard—left his audience in a state of shock and captured news headlines around the world. None of the delegations expected the Americans to advocate such a dramatic scale of disarmament as the one Hughes had put forward on this occasion. Its sheer audacity became an inspiration to many people who wished to see an end to competitive naval building. While not all shared in the chorus of praise, the overwhelming response from journalists, politicians, and members of the public was remarkably favorable. Thereafter, the British, Japanese, French, and Italian delegations were left with little option but to debate the Hughes plan for disarmament rather than to propose any schemes of their own. It is tempting to say that for all of them after this explosive start, the Washington conference became an exercise in damage limitation and one in which success was not guaranteed.[9]

Hughes's bold plan was formulated in response to political necessity. Arms limitation had become an increasingly attractive option to pursue in establishing a viable foreign and defense policy for the United States in the postwar period. Senator William Borah's campaign for an end to competitive naval building, which he had waged incessantly in the public domain since the ending of World War I, had done much to popularize the issue both in Congress and throughout the country. Widespread newspaper support for arms control and the successful passage of the Borah resolution in Congress had ensured that a considerable amount of momentum for orchestrating some form of naval disarmament program had been built up by summer 1921.[10] Undoubtedly alive to the political possibilities of championing this cause, Harding may have wished to put himself and his administration at the head of this drive for economy, common sense, and peace. Naturally enough, a unilateral decision to disarm, especially when other Powers and potential enemies were not doing so, was dismissed as posing too many unacceptable risks for the country advocating such a revolutionary policy. Therefore, if the Americans wished to take the lead in arms control, which they did, their brief was to procure an international agreement on disarmament which all the major countries would be prepared to sign and adhere to in the future. This considerable undertaking is what inspired the Harding administration to issue formal invitations to the British, Japanese, French, and Italians to attend the naval limitations talks at Washington in autumn 1921.

It can be safely assumed that it was tacitly understood by all parties to the Washington conference that the Anglo-Japanese alliance would become a casualty of this diplomatic gathering. Britain suspected that if it yielded to U.S. demands on this issue, it might be in a better position to negotiate with the United States on the total size of the fleet. Clearly, the British government already had accepted as inevitable a one-Power standard of naval strength, that is, equality with the U.S. Navy (USN) as far as capital ships were concerned, but it had other ideas about smaller types of warship, particularly the cruiser and the destroyer. (Capital ships were those displacing more than 10,000 tons—in effect, battleships, battle cruisers, and aircraft carriers. Auxiliary ships were smaller types of warships.) While the Lloyd George government had envisaged the establishment of comparative ratios between the five naval Powers, they had not expected the sharp quantitative reductions that Hughes had revealed in his opening address. Their position on the relative size of the capital ship fleets was simple; they would only be prepared to accept a situation of equality with the USN providing they maintained a two-Power standard against all other combinations of Powers. In other words, the total number of Royal Navy (RN) battleships and battle cruisers would have to exceed those of the Japanese and French (or Italian) capital ship fleets combined.[11]

In truth, of course, the British were really in no economic position to drive a hard bargain with the world's richest and most powerful nation on naval affairs, or much else besides, if they wished to forge a new and more positive era in Anglo-American relations. If they did not like the U.S. proposals and refused to agree to them, what alternative was there to embarking upon a prohibitively expensive naval race against a Power that had the economic capability and industrial infrastructure to outbuild the RN from the outset? By November 1921, the Admiralty had long since come to the conclusion that this was ultimately a hopeless task. It neither had the funds nor the political will to replace adequately those of its vessels which were old, slow, and poorly armored in comparison with the USN, let alone become committed to increasing the size of its fleet with the aid of a vastly expensive, new construction program. Balfour and his delegation, therefore, did not have a particularly good hand to play at Washington, and the Americans realized that as much as the British did.

Depending upon one's assessment of the Washington conference, Hughes was either the hero of the hour or the villain of the piece. His plan for naval disarmament was far more radical than anything envisaged by those who had been advocating a "stop now" policy to arms control. Using comparative data on existing and projected capital ship fleet strength provided by the USN General Board, and recognizing the overriding need to contain the anticipated growth in the world's battle fleets, Hughes became convinced that the cause of global peace was worth no small sacrifice on behalf of each of the major naval Powers. Rejecting the cautious approach of his naval advisers, his plan called for the immediate cancellation of all existing capital shipbuilding programs; a naval holiday of ten years duration in which no capital ship construction would be allowed and the scrapping of thirty ships from the USN (fifteen new and fifteen old), twenty-three from the RN (four new and nineteen old), and seventeen from the Imperial Japanese Navy (IJN) (seven new and ten old). Should the Hughes plan be adopted without amendments, the Americans would have at their disposal eighteen capital ships (500,650 tons), the British twenty-two (604,450 tons), and the Japanese would be left with ten (299,700 tons).[12]

In Hughes's scheme, a fairly generous allowance was made for the fact that much of the British fleet was older, slower, and more inefficient than those capital ships of the other two navies. Nonetheless, by not achieving the immediate equality in naval strength that many Americans desired, Hughes proposal was bound to be subject to a good deal of carping criticism from those who were unsympathetic to the plight of the RN·and did not see why it deserved special treatment. In Hughes's defense, the secretary of state had no intention of preserving this position of British numerical superiority in capital ship strength and tonnage for the foreseeable future. In fact, both he and Colonel Theodore Roosevelt, Jr., the assistant secretary of the navy, had taken steps to address this question directly by compiling a sophisticated naval replacement program, under conditions of the strictest secrecy, before the conference began. In essence, they had drawn up a detailed schedule of vessels from all three navies that were to be scrapped and replaced in the course of the next twenty years. After the stipulated ten-year naval building holiday, Hughes's replacement program for capital ships of more than twenty years of age would be implemented. Under the terms of the scheme, the individual replacement vessels were not to exceed 35,000 tons. In addition, there was to be a total upper limit for replacement vessels fixed at 500,000 tons for both the USN and RN and 300,000 tons for the IJN. This would ensure that once the replacement program had been completed in 1942, a ratio of 5:5:3 between the fleets would have been achieved with fifteen capital ships each for the Americans and British, and nine for the Japanese.[13]

Hughes's plan was not solely confined to the battleship or battle cruiser, let alone the three naval Powers referred to above. Apart from dealing with aircraft carriers as well as other forms of auxiliary warships on the basis of the same 5:5:3 tonnage ratio, a modification of this scheme was presumably designed to be extended at a later stage to the French and Italian fleets. While declining to deal with this aspect of the overall problem in his speech, the U.S. secretary of state delegated the matter to the naval subcommittee of the conference for its recommendations. Hughes's conduct in marginalizing the French and Italian delegations on this important issue managed to cause offense to both of them. Aristide Briand, the French premier, responded to this explicit commentary on his country's naval status, a fact reflected publicly in the seating arrangements at the conference sessions, by soon making a much publicized exit from the proceedings at Washington. Latin sensitivities also were ruffled by the conference proceedings. Of the two minor European naval Powers, however, the wounding of Gallic pride was always likely to have the greater consequences and so it was to prove in the coming weeks.[14]

Whatever the level of dissatisfaction reached in the French or Italian camps, of more immediate concern to the Americans was the reaction to be anticipated from both the British and Japanese delegations. While serving officers in both navies were bound to be aghast at the disarmament proposals, the crucial decision about acceptance or rejection of the Hughes plan would eventually lie with the politicians at home and their representatives at the Washington conference. Did they possess the nerve to grasp the initiative provided for them on this occasion by the U.S. secretary of state? It is clear from the tortuous negotiations that followed in the wake of Hughes's memorable opening salvo on 12 November, that although the various Powers felt compelled by public opinion to accept the broad outlines of the U.S. plan, they remained understandably anxious to limit the amount of damage done to their own naval positions. One method of reducing the individual impact of the disarmament scheme, of course, was to secure the successful passage of favorable amendments to its original terms. Diplomacy of this nature was far from easy, but both the British and Japanese delegations, by possessing the necessary patience, skill, and guile, showed that it could be done.

It would be a mistake to suggest, however, that they both achieved the same degree of success. On the contrary, there was little comparison between the few isolated diplomatic victories secured by the British and the important concessions given to the Japanese. An explanation for this substantial discrepancy in what the two delegations achieved at Washington appears to lie in the belief that the Japanese had more to offer the Americans in the realm of Far Eastern affairs than did the British. Japan's strategic position and the military strength it could exert along the western rim of the Pacific gave it a regional importance that transcended all other Powers at this conference. Consequently, Katō and Shidehara could use these singular advantages to ensure that the Japanese would be given special terms in return for their acceptance of the Washington treaties.

Once Hughes had announced his formidable agenda on the first day of the conference, the other delegations were left to scramble around in a furious quest for a reasoned response to it. Beatty, lamenting the fact that the British had not built any capital ships since 1916, looked askance on the prospect of a further 10-year naval holiday and the loss of the four super-*Hoods*, each of at least 45,000 tons, which his government had ordered only a month before on 21 October 1921. Moreover, while he agreed with the 5:5:3 ratio in principle for capital ships, he did not favor its retention for auxiliary classes of warship, especially the cruiser and destroyer, since this would redound to the disadvantage of the RN in the protection of British interests around the globe.[15] Katō was no happier. As things stood, the Japanese would lose their latest battleship, *Mutsu*, which had been partly financed from public subscriptions, and would be forced to accept a capital ship ratio of 60 percent, a figure which was 10 percent lower than they had projected and insisted upon in the preconference estimates of future comparative naval strength.[16]

As a result of these reservations, the conference would prove to be an exercise in limited obduracy and skillful compromise. For a month, British concerns largely took a back seat to the polite but firm demands of the Japanese for the retention of the *Mutsu* and an improvement in the capital ship ratio. It soon became clear to the Americans from deciphered intercepts of messages that passed between Katō's delegation and Tokyo that the latter had no intention of scrapping the *Mutsu* whatever the Americans said or did. Even so, there was a prospect that the Japanese might be prepared to yield on the 5:5:3 ratio providing the *Mutsu* was retained. This is essentially what happened. Responsible for creating an impasse in the conference proceedings, Katō exacted his price in mid-December for removing the obstacle; the *Mutsu* would be retained along with the *Nagato*, another superdreadnought, which had been on Hughes's original list for preservation. This decision pushed the tonnage limit for the Japanese well over the 300,000 limit, even if the Americans took up Tokyo's offer to scrap the ten-year-old battleship *Settsu*. If the Japanese were allowed to breach this tonnage limit, the British and the Americans themselves wished to do likewise and thereby maintain the 5:5:3 ratio.[17]

By cracking the Japanese diplomatic code, U.S. intelligence provided reliable information for the U.S. secretary of state about current thinking on the issues before the delegations at Washington. This was a very important asset, one that enabled Hughes and his confidant, Roosevelt, to remain one step ahead of the other delegations on most, if not all, issues. They had already worked out a compromise solution in order to resolve the *Mutsu* problem before Japanese intransigence on this issue actually threatened the success of the conference. In the amended scheme offered by Hughes in mid-December, the Japanese would be allowed to retain the *Mutsu* and have a revised ceiling of 315,000 tons for their capital ship fleet. In return, to preserve the capital ship ratio as 5:5:3, the United States would return the *Colorado* and *Washington*, both of which were nearing completion at 32,600 tons, and scrap *Delaware* and *North Dakota*, its two oldest dreadnoughts that had originally been on the retained list. This change would push the tonnage limit for the United States to 525,000 tons.[18]

British opinion about the retention of the *Mutsu* was well known in Washington. Balfour and his delegation were obviously aware of the mathematical computations of bowing to Japanese wishes on this issue. Put simply, if the 5:5:3 capital ship ratio was to be maintained intact, and the British believed that it should, the RN would be allowed to construct two more battleships of up to 35,000 tons each. Nonetheless, in order to conform with the new upper limit of 525,000 tons, these new vessels could only be added to the fleet at the expense of scrapping four more of the oldest British battleships. Appreciating this fact did not stop Balfour's delegation from pleading special case status and claiming, vainly as it turned out, that these vessels ought to be super-*Hoods* of roughly 45,000 tons each. A claim of this kind, excessive and alien to the nature of Hughes's original plan, was bound to incur the wrath of the Americans, which it did, and be opposed by the Japanese, which it was. In the end, Balfour sensibly decided that it was futile insisting upon something to which the other two major naval Powers were implacably opposed and scaled down his government's demands to the construction of two battleships each of 35,000 British tons (37,000 American tons). Once these vessels were built, the RN would consent to scrap four of its battleships of the *King George V* class. This belated British offer finally was accepted, along with the Japanese compromise, and on 15 December 1921 the world's press was duly informed about the achievements reached on disarmament thus far at the conference.[19]

In order to obtain a worthwhile agreement on naval limitations and disarmament, including acceptance of the 5:5:3 ratio, each of the major Powers had been forced to make some sacrifices. Although the physical loss of so many capital ship units may have been the most dramatic feature of the disarmament agreement, nagging doubts about their effectiveness under all circumstances had already begun to be expressed by the aircraft lobby in the United States. This particular Mahanian heresy was mainly attributed in the early postwar period to aviation enthusiast General William (Billy) Mitchell. His claims about the alleged vulnerability of the capital ship to aerial bombardment were largely discounted until, in a series of bombing trials organized by the U.S. Navy Department, his aircraft managed to sink the ex-German dreadnought *Ostfriesland* in July and the battleship USS *Alabama* in September 1921. Mitchell's spectacular success against these vessels must have disturbed even the most faithful disciples of Alfred Thayer Mahan and the "Blue Water" school of naval strategy. These doubts would surface again later in the conference over the question of the number of aircraft carriers each naval Power would be finally allowed to possess.[20]

Notwithstanding the long-term viability of the capital ship, if Katō's compromise over the 5:5:3 ratio had merely consisted of his insistence upon the retention of the *Mutsu*, one would have wondered what value to have put on it, especially since the other two naval Powers had each added two net battleships to their fleets in a bid to offset her future presence within the IJN. Baron Katō was far shrewder than that. From the beginning of December he had linked acceptance of the 5:5:3 ratio not only with the *Mutsu*, but also an agreement covering nonfortifications and naval bases in the Pacific. This scheme, with which he had been conversant for at least a year, had been proposed initially within his own department as a means of improving the prospects of home defense and providing a degree of monopoly power for the IJN in the western Pacific. Unearthing this idea on 1 December 1921, Katō suggested that acceptance of the 5:5:3 ratio might be somewhat easier to arrange if the other naval Powers were to agree not to fortify any of their island possessions in the Pacific and neither upgrade nor build any new naval bases in the region.[21]

This highly controversial proposal introduced a far more dangerous element to the talks at Washington than the dispute surrounding the retention of the *Mutsu*. If the other Powers agreed to the Japanese scheme, the Americans would not be able to improve their existing naval facilities in Hawaii or the Philippines, let alone construct advanced bases at either Guam or Midway. As for the British, their adoption of the status quo in the Pacific would forbid them from turning Hong Kong into a first-class naval base and was bewilderingly ambiguous on the future role of Singapore. Despite the baleful warnings of those in both American and British military circles who saw no virtue and merely sinister intent in Katō's plan, Hughes and Balfour realized that disarmament was sufficiently worthy and advantageous a cause that in order to secure agreement on its terms some element of sacrifice was needed from each of the Powers. Although a partial agreement had been cobbled together in time for the press communiqué on 15 December, none of the delegations could have doubted it was anything other than a temporary respite and that more animated discussion and further heart-searching would have to take place before a permanent and final settlement could be arranged. So it was to be.

Much of the ensuing trouble was to be caused by the British who attempted to foist their own exclusion zone upon the other Powers. Their projected zone— basically a large parallelogram covering the area from the equator to 30 degrees north latitude and from 110 degrees east longitude to the international dateline— would enable them to retain both Singapore and Papuan Bay in New Guinea, which Admiral Viscount Jellicoe had glimpsed as a possible site for another naval base. (Jellicoe had undertaken a tour of the white dominions of the British Empire in 1919 in order to make proposals for improving Imperial defense.) Whatever its merits from the British perspective, this zone had few positive features for either of the other two delegations. In the face of steadfast opposition, therefore, the British position eventually crumbled and the parallelogram disappeared to be replaced by a commitment not to build new bases or fortify their islands or possessions east of 110 degrees east longitude.[22]

By the time the naval limitation treaty was actually signed on 6 February 1922, Hughes had won a reprieve for Hawaii, but had agreed to Katō's plan as far as the Aleutians, the Philippines, and Guam were concerned. For his part, Balfour had surrendered the issues of Hong Kong and the contrived Pacific parallelogram, but had wrought concessions from the Japanese in respect to Australia, Canada, New Zealand, and Singapore. As for the Japanese, they were to observe the status quo in Amami-Oshima, the Bonin Islands, Formosa, the Kuriles, the Loochoo Islands, and the Pescadores.[23] What these concessions meant, of course, was that the Japanese had been provided with more than a minimal measure of security in their own waters. In fact, the nonfortification rule ensured that the IJN would be by far the most dominant naval power in the western Pacific. Neither the Americans, whose naval base at Pearl Harbor was 3,374 nautical miles distant from Tokyo, nor the British, whose Singapore base once completed would be 2,888 nautical miles from the Japanese capital, were in a position to do much to contest this degree of monopoly power that could be exerted by Katō's navy from this time onward. Indeed, the very fact that the upgrading of all forward bases in the central and western Pacific had been specifically ruled out by this agreement meant that, if relations with the Japanese turned sour at any stage in the future, both the USN and its British equivalent would find it extremely difficult to defend their own interests in the region, let alone put any direct pressure on the IJN to improve the overall situation.

Many serving naval officers on both sides of the Atlantic, and not only the xenophobes among them, found this aspect of the naval limitation agreement difficult to swallow. For them, political expediency had compromised the ability of the military services to perform their allotted tasks of hemispheric defense and the protection of American or British interests overseas including, the maintenance of the Open Door in China. Not only had their capital ship fleets been savagely mauled by the three plenipotentiaries but, more importantly, their capacity to wage war, if necessary, in the central or western Pacific had been seriously undermined by this naval agreement. It was also quite evident that the Americans and the British, without forward bases in the region from which their battle fleets could operate, would have to revise their war plans to take account of this material change in their circumstances in the region. As questions had already been raised about the future security of the Philippines and Guam from 1911 onward, this agreement ought to have reinforced fears expressed by early war planners at the USN War College at Newport. Curiously, the U.S. military managed to misinterpret those signals. Some remained aware of the weak state of Philippine defenses and their probably early loss to an enemy attack; others chose for their own political motives to pretend that these defenses would hold until a relief mission arrived from the United States. By the same token, the British recognized that Hong Kong's long-term security was as tenuous as that of the Philippines if

Anglo-Japanese relations deteriorated in the future to the point of war. Apart from any other strategic considerations, the British had not even started to build their naval base at Singapore in 1921. Until that base was completed and ready for active duty in the late 1930s, the nearest first-class naval base to the Far East that a British battle fleet could use stood at Malta, a mere 5,926 nautical miles distant from Singapore! Henceforth, therefore, it became difficult to disagree with the notion that both western Powers had become dependent to an almost unacceptable extent for the protection of their commercial and other interests in the region upon the maintenance of good relations with their Asiatic partner.[24]

Hopes of an improved relationship between these Powers had been increased somewhat by the much anticipated demise of the Anglo-Japanese alliance in the early days of the conference. American dislike of the latter and insistence upon its abolition—sentiments well known by all concerned long before the delegates had arrived in Washington—could hardly be ignored for long once the conference had actually convened. Naturally enough, the elimination of this twenty-year-old military alliance would be easier for its original signatories to accept if it could be replaced with something almost equally as effective. Unfortunately, the signing on 13 December 1921 of a four-Power treaty on the Pacific did not provide such advantages. This supposedly more consultative nonmilitary orientated agreement involved not only the so-called "Big Three" Powers but also, at U.S. insistence, France as well.

Why the French merited a place in the treaty was certainly not clear to either the British or the Japanese at the time and remains somewhat obscure to many historians even now. Although explanations have been provided—the most neutral being that it was an inexpensive sop to Gallic pride wounded at the failure of its delegation to be consulted on the major naval questions of the day—many cynics saw the inclusion of the French as a further means of ensuring that unanimity and cooperation among the Powers on the Far East would be made more difficult in the future. Whatever the real motive for bringing the French into the treaty, the Americans stand accused of having behaved in a Machiavellian manner, and it is difficult not to find against them on this charge. At a *prima facie* level, however, the invitation extended to France to join the "Big Three" on Pacific and Far Eastern questions might not be judged as being utterly futile. Apart from their colonial presence in the Pacific and Indochina, the French had a trading interest in China which they wished to defend. Nonetheless, for the most part they could do this with the aid of a few river gunboats and occasional sorties in the region by a number of their more impressive warships. Moreover, the French were seen by the Americans as a minor seapower and had been treated as such at the conference sessions. If their relative inferiority to the "Big Three" was not going to diminish—indeed, if anything, it was likely to worsen still further—their ability to pose a naval threat in the Far East was too small to worry about. If they were unlikely to be a potential enemy, therefore, could they be a useful ally? Again, the likelihood is that they would not be able to mount much of a defense force to assist in dealing with a sudden short-term crisis in the Pacific, much less provide one for long-term operations in that ocean. So, if they were not being absorbed for offensive or defensive purposes, one is entitled to ask why the Americans bothered to invite them to sign the treaty in the first place? Strategically, it made little constructive sense. One is left musing that their inclusion appears to undermine the Far Eastern and Pacific treaty from the outset and may have been, as the cynics suggested, merely a convenient device to end the hated Anglo-Japanese alliance.[25]

Although the terms of the four-Power treaty were plausible enough, the element of wishful thinking involved was considerable. Apart from respecting the various interests of the signatory Powers in the Pacific, the four-Power treaty sought to create an agreed formula for resolving any disputes that might arise between any or all of the four countries in this region. If any future dispute could not be resolved satisfactorily in the first instance by the interested parties themselves, the other signatories of the treaty were to be invited to participate in a four-party conference to settle the issue. This may all sound eminently satisfactory, but it did not take much intelligence to imagine a scenario that did not fit neatly into this well-ordered scheme. What, for instance, was likely to happen if such a conference failed to resolve the dispute? An interesting and revealing commentary on the failure of the Powers to address this question is shown by a close examination of the terms of the four-Power treaty. Nothing exists in any of the four articles to indicate that further steps might have to be taken in future to deal with a particularly intractable crisis between the signatory Powers in the Pacific. Silence on what the Powers should do in such an emergency was an intentional omission on the part of those who drafted the treaty. This was hardly a positive endorsement of the four-Power pact or its role as a viable, diplomatic grouping in the future. Yet, for all its shortcomings, what more could have been expected from a treaty that would require ratification by the United States Congress, a body that already had recorded its objection to furnishing any form of international guarantee to other Powers in the future? It is difficult to escape the conclusion, therefore, that both the British and the Japanese realized that the cost of bowing to U.S. pressure on this issue would be a much less effective four-Power pact than their original alliance had been. As a consequence, the former allies were prepared to drive a hard bargain with the Americans on other matters at the conference and derive as much satisfaction as possible from any future agreements on both naval disarmament and the thorny question of China.

If the British and Japanese were determined to secure a *quid pro quo* from the Americans for surrendering the advantages of their old alliance, so too were the French anxious to play a much more aggressive role in the conference than they had to date. They achieved their aim, but only at the expense of alienating the other delegations. Naval strength was quite naturally one of their primary concerns. Unfortunately, their assessment of what their navy required—ten capital ships of 350,000 tons—was based largely on outmoded historic considerations. It did not match the estimates of their current worth as a naval Power produced by the "Big Three." Moreover, the Americans found themselves in a quandary because the British had made it emphatically clear that they could only accept the 5:5:3 capital ship ratio if they could preserve a two-Power standard over any combination of the other naval Powers. In other words, since the British would have fifteen capital ships in the battle fleet and the Japanese had been awarded nine, neither the French nor Italian navies could be allowed to have any more than five each at their disposal. Hughes knew that the British were adamant on this point and were unlikely to back down or compromise further upon it. Therefore, he sought the acceptance of Briand on 16 December 1921 for a capital ship ratio of 1.75 for France as against 5 for both Britain and the United States and 3 for Japan.

Flattered by Hughes's direct appeal to him not to wreck the conference by refusing to agree to the capital ship ratio, Briand complied generously with the American secretary's request for a final settlement on this matter. What looked like a fine and noble gesture was accompanied, alas, by a stark announcement of the French government's total rejection of any extension of the 5:5:3:1.75 capital ship ratio to cover what he described as "defensive" classes of warship. This was a shorthand form for such units as light cruisers and submarines. As far as the latter category was concerned, the French soon made it clear that they demanded equality with the Americans and the British at a figure of 90,000 tons—a submarine fleet of 47,150 tons greater than their existing strength. French claims of this extravagant nature were positively unhelpful to the laborious process of consensus building that had been pursued by the "Big Three" at Washington. Naturally, none of the other delegations were enchanted by this proposal or keen to accept it even under duress.[26]

British annoyance with their neighbors across the English Channel was particularly fierce and demonstrative on this controversial subject. By this time it was well known in Washington that both Beatty and Lee shared a loathing for the submarine, which they evidently saw as a piratical craft that could be used for devious and unfair purposes in war. Their call for its total abolition, a curiously unrealistic stance—influenced, one suspects, as much by traditional class notions of unsporting and unworthy behavior as much as by any strategic or tactical considerations—could not have been further from the position adopted by Briand and his delegation in Washington. Albert Sarraut and Admiral de Bon, leading members of that French team in the United States, had no such reservations about the continued existence of the submarine; seeing it as a vessel that could be used for perfectly legitimate defensive purposes, including action against merchant shipping under certain circumstances. Their comments did nothing to rescue Anglo-French relations from the weak and febrile state into which they had sunk after the war. Lee, who is rarely described as anything other than inept in his role as first lord, actually made matters worse by quoting a portion of highly incriminating text from an article written by Capitaine de Frégate Castex that had appeared in *La Revue Maritime* in January 1920 on submarine campaigns conducted during the "Great War." Castex, a man of some influence within the French naval establishment and recently appointed principal lecturer on its senior officers' course for 1922, had appeared to understand and defend as justifiable the use of unrestricted submarine warfare by the Germans in the 1914–1918 war. Lee's use of the quote caused a furor, as did his embellishment that Castex was on record as stating that the submarine was the ideal vessel for undermining and overthrowing the power of the RN in the future. Castex's inflammatory prose, whether the result of mere wishful thinking or actual contingency planning, was as offensive as it was xenophobic. While the Admiralty could not accurately judge the degree of support for Castex's views within French naval circles, the prospect of a burgeoning submarine fleet planned by its former ally across the Channel was disquieting to say the least.[27]

By the end of December 1921, therefore, the British had become insistent upon the drawing up and rapid implementation of a systematic code of conduct for all future submarine operations. A member of the American delegation, Elihu Root, had duly obliged by introducing a series of rules on 28 December. Root was a much respected figure and vastly experienced in the ways of diplomacy, being a former senator and cabinet member under both President McKinley and President Roosevelt. Lee's use of the Castex article two days later was, therefore, a calculated attempt to pressurize the French into not only officially repudiating the Castex line but also adopting the Root resolutions on engagements with enemy shipping. These were intended to curtail some of the more nefarious activities of submarines vis-à-vis merchant shipping. Apart from outlawing a shoot-on-sight policy, Root required the adherence of all submarines to an agreed set of stop-and-search procedures for merchant vessels belonging to an enemy Power and demanded that provision be made for rescuing the crew of any such ship before it could be destroyed. If such conditions could not be met, the submarine was theoretically to break off the engagement and not press home an attack on the vessel. Despite their humanitarian values, these rules were not very well defined in cases where, say, a merchant ship might refuse to heed a hostile submarine's warning to stop and be searched. Could the submarine torpedo the vessel for failing to stop regardless of the fact that no arrangements could be agreed upon between them to rescue the crew of the merchant ship before its destruction might take place? Root did not elucidate further on this point, and the other Powers did not press the matter. If this appears strange, as it does, one suspects it stems from a prevailing belief that the most beneficial aspect of the Root resolutions was the outlawing of the submarine as a potent commerce destroyer and that universal agreement on this matter outweighed all other factors. Whether any of these rules of civilized behavior would be actually followed by submarines in a war was, of course, a moot point. Furthermore, unless these resolutions were adopted as an integral feature of other international naval treaties in the future, their legal authority would lapse if and when the Washington treaties came to an end on 31 December 1936.[28]

Lee's ploy achieved some success: Admiral de Bon unreservedly repudiated Castex's highly opinioned remarks and France adhered to the Root resolutions.

If the first lord hoped that the French would become any more accommodating on the size of their future submarine fleet, however, he was destined to be very disappointed. Neither Briand's administration in Paris nor his delegation in Washington showed any willingness to compromise on tonnage levels or ratios for either submarines or, indeed, for other so-called defensive classes of warship. Blame for the failure to reach agreement on auxiliary vessels should not just be laid at the door of the French, even though they were guilty of being obstructive at Washington. At least an equal share of the opprobrium must be meted out to the British who never shrank from requesting a much larger cruiser and destroyer fleet than the other Powers on the grounds that these vessels were required for trade protection and to service the disparate needs of the global empire that they had inherited and were charged with defending. For a combination of both historic and economic reasons, therefore, the British found themselves siding with the French in arguing against extending the 5:5:3 ratio concept to vessels displacing less than 10,000 tons. Once the Americans could see that the European Powers were not going to budge on these issues, they sensibly chose not to try and force through an agreement and, by so doing, risk ruining what had already been achieved on the subject of disarmament at Washington. As a result, the problem of what to do with these very important classes of warship was left unresolved by the delegates who, with some relief, passed the buck back to their respective governments for further discussion.

Although the Washington conference failed to solve the problems of the optimum size of auxiliary ship fleets for the major sea Powers, it was at least conspicuously successful in extending the capital ship ratio to cover the latest type of warship—the aircraft carrier—whose future was far from clear at this stage. Hughes had originally set carrier limits for the "Big Three" on the 5:5:3 principle at 80,000 tons for both the United States and Britain, with 48,000 set aside for the Japanese. This ceiling was considered far too low for each of the seapowers, who could see no effective way of building aircraft carriers below at least 25,000 tons each. This meant that while the Japanese might be able to have two carriers, the British would have to make do with three and the French and the Italians one each. As Admiral Acton of Italy pointed out with some relish, possession of a solitary carrier was wholly insufficient since every time it was in dock for any reason the fleet would be totally denuded of its aircraft cover. This type of argument, which was aired in the naval subcommittee meetings, spilled over to the plenary sessions where the main delegates were soon locked in animated debate over carrier displacement and fleet strength. In the end, the delegates agreed that the 5:5:3 ratio could be applied to this type of vessel, but Hughes's original limits on total tonnage were simply ignored as being too low for practical purposes. As a result, both the Americans and the British were to be allowed to build a carrier fleet of up to 135,000 tons; the Japanese were permitted to construct a fleet of 81,000 tons; and the French and Italians were each given approval for a carrier force of 60,000 tons. All carriers were seen as being experimental at this time—a ruling that was as accurate as it was useful—so replacement vessels could be ordered without reference to the age of the original craft that were to be scrapped.[29]

Although it was decided that the standard displacement of individual carriers was not to exceed 27,000 tons, the Americans found themselves in an ambivalent position both supporting limitation and, yet, arguing for exceptions to be made to it. Their dilemma stemmed from the fact that the U.S. Navy Department was determined to convert two of their battle cruisers, USS *Lexington* and USS *Saratoga*, into aircraft carriers of 33,000 tons each. Their unwillingness to yield on the conversion of these two ships embarrassed Hughes, who had slated them both for scrapping under the terms of his disarmament scheme. This situation complicated the diplomatic process and temporarily hijacked the disarmament movement. For instance, it did not take the British and the other Powers long to seize upon the value of the conversion process and insist upon receiving similar concessions. Admiral Sir Ernle Chatfield, the assistant chief of naval staff, who had been looking for some way of retaining two of the RN's super-*Hoods*, convinced Balfour that an important principle was at stake and could not be ignored. Largely as a result of British pressure, therefore, the Americans were obliged to support a modification of the general rule on displacement limitation so as to enable each of the signatory Powers to build at least one, and in the case of Britain and Japan, two, of their carriers at up to 33,000 tons each. Once this point had been agreed upon, Hughes persuaded the other delegates to accept an 8-inch maximum gun caliber for all carriers. Nonetheless, his negotiating efforts achieved precious little when it came to devising a limit to both the number of such guns that could be installed on board each vessel and the quantity and type of aircraft that were to be carried by these ships. So much for disarmament! Of these two omissions in the eventual treaty, the failure to put any restrictions on the aircraft component of the carrier fleets was by far the most important and must be seen as among the more notable shortcomings of the five-Power naval limitation agreement.[30]

While the principal delegates and naval experts were busily engaged in working out the details of the two main treaties referred to above, an even more tempestuous series of exchanges was taking place in Washington on the future of China and East Asia between the representatives of the nine Powers with interests in that troubled region. For much of the time, talks on the vexed questions of tariff autonomy, extraterritoriality, the size of the military forces in China, and the return from Japanese control to Chinese sovereignty of Manchuria and Shantung were acrimonious and inconclusive. Japan had no wish to withdraw from China and negotiated accordingly; China, incapable of expelling the Japanese from the disputed territory by force, was desperate for diplomatic support from the United States. Unfortunately the Americans, who felt nobly about the Open Door and the return of Shantung, failed to give much of a lead on anything else until quite late in the proceedings. Of the other Powers involved, the British, being exceedingly uncomfortable about their own gains at China's expense in the scramble for concessions in the late 1890s, were in no position to adopt a high moral tone at any stage in these tortuous negotiations. To make matters worse, the representatives of Belgium, France, Italy, the Netherlands, and Portugal contributed little of note to these proceedings and seemed to be at Washington merely to make up the numbers.[31]

Weeks of labored and vituperative discussions had taken place before these ailing and frustrating talks were rescued from further decline by the influential Democrat, Senator Thomas Walsh of Montana. His congressional resolution of 20 January 1922, asking for a progress report on the Shantung negotiations, touched off a spirited debate on the future of this territory that reverberated in Washington political circles and throughout the editorial columns of the major daily newspapers in the United States for the rest of the month. Those parts of Shantung, which had been seized by Germany in the "Scramble for China" and then acquired by Japan in the opening weeks of the war in 1914, had assumed a certain symbolic significance for the Americans. Over the years it had become difficult, if not impossible, to reconcile an explicit U.S. commitment to the Open Door with the retention of Japanese control over this troubled Chinese province. Therefore, when rumors began circulating on Capitol Hill that Congress would ratify neither the naval limitation treaty nor the four-Power pact unless a satisfactory solution was found to the Shantung question, Hughes and the rest of his delegation took the matter seriously. These fears grew in the wake of the starkly hostile American reaction to Japanese policy in China touched off by the Walsh initiative. Thereafter, the domestic U.S. political agenda demanded both the reaffirmation of the Open Door principle, as well as a new deal for Shantung. Hughes, Harding and the Republican party could not afford to ignore either of these popular goals if they wished to savor their moment of triumph at Washington.[32]

Once this fact had been recognized, the Americans, aided and abetted by Balfour, began to exert maximum diplomatic pressure upon the Japanese either to restore Shantung to Chinese sovereignty or risk losing everything they had gained thus far at the conference. This compelling argument was not lost on the astute Japanese delegates, Katō and Shidehara, who sensibly responded by eventually agreeing to yield on this and other Far Eastern questions. Apart from supporting a modest increase in the Chinese tariff rate and a new Open Door treaty for China, the Japanese offered to withdraw their troops from Siberia— so ending another long-standing grievance. No mention was made of any similar withdrawal from Manchuria, however, but this fact was glossed over by the Americans who had reached the conclusion that an inferior agreement was better than none on this subject. As a result, while the Japanese concessions on the Far East were basically limited, they still had political value in the short term by removing the last major obstacles on the path to a nine-Power pact on China. Whether this treaty was anything more than a face-saving agreement was doubtful from the very beginning—as the Chinese were acutely and painfully aware— but it did serve a purpose, namely, rescuing the naval disarmament proposals from the brink of what would have been a costly failure. Such a laudable aim may not have impressed the Chinese, but it was sufficient for the other Powers at this time.[33]

Although lyrically acclaimed by many as a diplomatic triumph at the time, the Washington conference of November 1921–February 1922 soon lost some of its fashionable luster. Within a decade those who had originally championed its treaties and resolutions had fallen ominously quiet, while those who had consistently opposed its tacit appeasement of Japan in the western Pacific were able to claim that their fears for the future had been proven right all along. Thereafter, as the cause of peace was progressively abandoned by the fascist dictatorships in the 1930s, the so-called Washington system became an increasingly beleaguered monument to a profoundly different era, one in which monetary restraint and military disarmament had gone hand in hand with a certain measure of diplomatic opportunism and judicial idealism.

Seventy years after the event, the Washington conference still excites much controversy among historians. Critics claim that its principal architects were prepared to sacrifice too much in the quest for a dramatic political solution to the diverse and challenging problems which beset the former Allied and Associated Powers after the war. Far from making provision for a safer world, the chief delegates at Washington stand accused of unwittingly weakening the Western democracies and ironically strengthening the militaristic tendencies of their potential rivals.[34] Admirers of the work performed at the conference by Hughes, Balfour, and Katō naturally refute these allegations. They point out that the leading delegates were neither naive nor unrealistic, but shrewd and pragmatic individuals who strove tirelessly and with great skill and tenacity for nearly three months to secure agreement on a range of very delicate issues that had previously divided the Powers for several years.[35]

Whether damned for their recklessness or praised for their boldness, the authors of the Washington system obviously created a profound impact on international relations that continued to be felt throughout the interwar period. In reexamining the record of the Washington conference, this chapter has sought to explain why neither of these popular interpretations need necessarily be considered wildly inaccurate, since aspects of these treaties may indeed be judged to be both potentially dangerous and yet courageously imaginative.

NOTES

1. Stephen W. Roskill, *Naval Policy between the Wars*, Vol. I: *The Period of Anglo-American Antagonism, 1919–1929* (London, 1968), 71.

2. Roger Dingman, *Power in the Pacific: The Origins of Naval Arms Limitation* (Chicago, 1976), 122–35, 178–95.

3. Josephus Daniels, *The Wilson Era*, Vol. I: *Years of Peace—1910–1917* (Chapel Hill, N.C., 1946), 326–29.

4. J. Kenneth McDonald, "The Washington Conference and the Naval Balance of

Power, 1921–2,'' in John B. Hattendorf and Robert S. Jordan, eds., *Maritime Strategy and the Balance of Power* (London, 1989), 189–213. For discussion of the Yap cable controversy, see Mark R. Peattie, *Nan'yo: The Rise and Fall of the Japanese in Micronesia, 1885–1945* (Honolulu, Hawaii, 1988), 55–61; and William R. Braisted, *The United States Navy in the Pacific, 1909–1922* (Austin, Tex., 1971), 527–34.

5. Ian H. Nish, *Alliance in Decline* (London, 1972), 115–367.

6. Ibid., 324–53; and Roskill, *Naval Policy*, 292–98.

7. Malcolm H. Murfett, '' 'Are We Ready?' The Development of American and British Naval Strategy, 1922–39,'' in Hattendorf and Jordan, *Maritime Strategy*, 214–42.

8. Nish, *Alliance in Decline*, 354–67.

9. Harold Sprout and Margaret Sprout, *Toward a New Order of Sea Power* (Princeton, N.J., 1940), 145–56.

10. Ibid., 110–17.

11. Braisted, *The United States Navy*, 596–617; and Roskill, *Naval Policy*, I, 300–30. From the outset of the conference, the Italian delegation, consisting of Senator Carlo Schanzer, Ambassador Vittorio Ricci, and Senator Luigi Albertini, insisted upon the ''Big Three'' recognizing its country's claims to naval equality with France. Italian policy at Washington is discussed in Muriel Currey, *Italian Foreign Policy 1918–1932* (London, 1932), 67–70.

12. Raymond L. Buell, *The Washington Conference* (New York, 1970), 152–54, 374–93.

13. Ibid.; and Dexter Perkins, *Charles Evans Hughes and American Democratic Statesmanship* (Boston, 1956), 100–01.

14. Braisted, *United States Navy*, 629–38; and Sprout and Sprout, *Sea Power*, 177–85.

15. Roskill, *Naval Policy*, 312–15.

16. Buell, *Washington Conference*, 159.

17. Braisted, *United States Navy*, 603–17.

18. In fact, the USS *West Virginia* was retained in place of USS *Washington*, which was scrapped. See Buell, *Washington Conference*, 160–63.

19. Sprout and Sprout, *Sea Power*, 173–76.

20. Roskill, *Naval Policy*, 247–48, 322.

21. Braisted, *United States Navy*, 639–47; Buell, *Washington Treaty*, 163–71; and Dingman, *Power in the Pacific*, 80–81, 188–89, 192–93, 202–4.

22. Sprout and Sprout, *Sea Power*, 239–47.

23. Buell, *Washington Conference*, 378.

24. Murfett, ''Are We Ready,'' in Hattendorf and Jordan, *Maritime Strategy*, 214–42.

25. Buell, *Washington Conference*, 172–200; and Nish, *Alliance in Decline*, 368–82.

26. Buell, *Washington Conference*, 212–16.

27. Ibid., 216–22; and Roskill, *Naval Policy*, 327–28.

28. Buell, *Washington Conference*, 223–28.

29. Sprout and Sprout, *Sea Power*, 227–32.

30. Ibid., 232–35; Buell, *Washington Conference*, 209–10, 235, 238–39; and Roskill, *Naval Policy*, 323–24.

31. Braisted, *United States Navy*, 648–54; and Buell, *Washington Conference*, 240–79.

32. Buell, *Washington Conference*, 261; and Sprout and Sprout, *Sea Power*, 248–50.

33. Buell, *Washington Treaty*, 272–76.

34. For a contemporary view of the results of the conference, see Braisted, *United States Navy*, 670–75; and Sprout and Sprout, *Sea Power*, 251–77. One of the most vehement of its subsequent critics is Correlli Barnett, *The Collapse of British Power* (London, 1972), 267–73.

35. Cf. Dingman, *Power in the Pacific*, 196–219; Norman H. Gibbs, *Grand Strategy*, Vol. I: *Rearmament Policy* (London, 1976), 22–24; and W. Roger Louis, *British Strategy in the Far East, 1919–1939* (Oxford, 1971), 79–108.

Index